S0-ARL-932

Self Processes and Development

The Minnesota Symposia on Child Psychology

Volume 23

Self Processes and Development

The Minnesota Symposia on Child Development

Volume 23

Edited by
MEGAN R. GUNNAR
L. ALAN SROUFE
University of Minnesota

LEA
LAWRENCE ERLBAUM ASSOCIATES, PUBLISHERS
1991 Hillsdale, New Jersey Hove and London

Lawrence Erlbaum Associates, Inc., Publishers
365 Broadway
Hillsdale, New Jersey 07642

Library of Congress Cataloging-in-Publication Data

Self processes and development / edited by Megan R. Gunnar, L. Alan Sroufe.
p. cm. — (The Minnesota symposia on child psychology ; v. 23)
"Contains chapters based on papers presented at the 23rd Minnesota Symposium on Child Psychology, held October 27–29, 1988, at the University of Minnesota, Minneapolis"—Pref.
Includes bibliographical references.
ISBN 0–8058–0695–4
1. Human information processing in children—Congresses. 2. Cognition in children—Congresses. 3. Personality development—Congresses. I. Gunnar, Megan R. II. Sroufe, L. Alan. III. Minnesota Symposium on Child Psychology (23rd : 1988 : University of Minnesota) IV. Series: Minnesota symposia on child psychology (Series) ; v. 23.
BF723.I63S44 1990
155.4′182—dc20 90–35249
CIP

Printed in the United States of America
10 9 8 7 6 5 4 3 2 1

Contents

Preface ix

1. **Pouring New Wine into Old Bottles: The Social Self as Internal Working Model** 1
Inge Bretherton

Introduction *1*
Theories of the Social Self *2*
Working Models of Self and Others: Insights from Theories of Representational and Social Cognitive Development *15*
Ego and Internal Working Models: Concluding Remarks *32*
References *34*

2. **Competence, Autonomy, and Relatedness: A Motivational Analysis of Self-system Processes** 43
James P. Connell and James G. Wellborn

Overview *43*
Theoretical Approaches to the Study of Self *43*
Self-System Processes of Children and Adolescents in Educational Contexts *53*
Summary of the Model *70*
Implications of the Model for Institutional Reform *70*
References *74*

3. Cognitive-experiential Self Theory: Implications for Developmental Psychology **79**
Seymour Epstein

Definition of the Self *79*
The Basic Theory *81*
The Development of Personal Theories of Reality *92*
The Maintenance of Maladaptive Schemata *96*
The Construct of Constructive Thinking *101*
Research *102*
Implications of Cognitive-Experiential Self-Theory for Developmental Psychology *119*
References *121*

4. Development of Self-regulatory and Self-evaluative Processes: Costs, Benefits, and Tradeoffs **125**
E. Tory Higgins

Tradeoffs from Intellectual Development *126*
Tradeoffs from Socialization *142*
Concluding Comments *158*
References *159*

5. Development and Perceived Control: A Dynamic Model of Action in Context **167**
Ellen A. Skinner

Introduction *167*
A Functional Model of Perceived Control *175*
A Functional Model of the Development of Perceived Control *184*
A Structural Model of the Development of Control-Related Beliefs *192*
Conclusion *207*
References *212*

6. Learning to Love: Mechanisms and Milestones **217**
Everett Waters, Kiyomi Kondo-Ikemura, German Posada, and John E. Richters

Paradigms and Perspectives *218*
From Drives to Control Systems *219*
A Revised Developmental Analysis *229*
Conclusion *253*
References *254*

Author Index **257**
Subject Index **265**

Preface

This volume contains chapters based on papers presented at the 23rd Minnesota Symposium on Child Psychology, held October 27–29, 1988, at the University of Minnesota. As has been the tradition for this annual series, the faculty of the Institute of Child Development invited internationally eminent researchers to present their work and to consider problems of mutual concern.

The theme of this volume is self processes and development. The psychological study of the self has a long history in the field of psychology. It is a study, however, which has been rediscovered in recent year as researchers attempt to grapple with views of the developing child as an active organism who plays an important role in the shaping of his or her own competencies and personality. (See Bretherton's chapter on "Pouring Old Wine into New bottles.") If the child is active, how do we describe *and* predict that activity? If the child plays a role in organizing development, what are the organizing principles? These are questions about the self. Indeed, they are questions that William James would ascribe to the self as "I" or "knower," rather than the self as "Me" or "known." Thus they are dynamic processes, emotional and cognitive, evolving out of experience and influencing experience. The goal of this volume was to assemble a group of scholars with diverse perspectives on the dynamic organizing processes of the self.

To this end, we are fortunate to have as contributors to this volume some of the most outstanding current scholars in this area. The contributors are Inge Bretherton, James Connell and James Wellborn, Seymour Epstein, E. Tory Higgins, Ellen Skinner, and Everett Waters. In addition, L. Alan Sroufe served as coeditor of this volume and co-organizer of the 1988 symposium. He also served, along with Hazel Markus, as a discussant during the symposium.

Traditionally, in each Minnesota Symposium on Child Psychology, the Institute of Child Development faculty have set the talks around issues that are on the cutting edge of the field. This 23rd symposium was no exception. As noted, the shift toward a view of the child as an active, organizing organism has lead to an emergence of interest in the self as "I" or "knower"; the self as an active organizing agent. In the first chapter of the volume, Inge Bretherton discusses early theories of the self as agent and considers how these perspectives are represented in current models of self processes, particularly those dealing with working models of the self in the tradition of attachment theory. However, as Bretherton notes, the processes of the "working model" are only vaguely specified. Given that these working models are viewed as "mental" models, Bretherton goes on to draw on cognitive theories to flesh out the self processes of the working model and to consider how developmental changes in cognition might influence them.

While Bretherton looks to cognitive theories to help flesh out self processes, Connell and Wellborn emphasize the importance of motivational approaches. They argue that these motivational approaches share a common focus on how self-understanding and emotional experiences develop in relation to organismically based priorities. The priorities that Connell and Wellborn identify as organizing self processes are those of competence, autonomy, and relatedness. Connell and Wellborn then go on to discuss how these motivations interact, their developmental course and how these self-system processes influence patterns of action, particularly in the context of school. Ellen Skinner, a comember of the Human Motivation Research Group at the University of Rochester, presents in her chapter an elegant discussion of the processes organized by the competence priority. Central among these is perceived control. However, Skinner argues that to understand how perceived control influences action one must distinguish between Control or the individual's belief that outcomes can be influenced, Means–ends beliefs or the individual's beliefs about how outcomes are influenced, and Agency beliefs or the individual's belief's about his or her capacity to perform actions. She goes on to show that these three types of belief systems can be identified empirically, and then discusses how various combinations of beliefs in these three subsystems might be linked with action and emotional outcomes.

One theme running through these chapters on self processes is the importance of emotion as an organizing aspect of the self. This is the theme of Seymour Epstein's chapter on Cognitive-Experiential Self theory. Epstein argues that the self can be divided, conceptually, into at least two major components. One is the cognitive self. This self is very rational and, according to Epstein, is less influential in guiding human action that most of us would like to believe. More influential, he argues, is the Experiential Self. The processes of this aspect of self are emotionally toned. Building first a case for the importance of the Experiential Self and its processes, Epstein then discusses the developmental implications of this view of personality.

While Higgins also emphasizes emotion, like Bretherton, in searching for the processes of the self as knower, he draws heavily on cognitive theory. Specifically, using Case's model of development, Higgins proposes a stage theory of the development of self processes. Using this model, he then goes on to make the provocative argument that the elaboration of self processes which at earlier stages of development may have many benefits for the child, at later stages of development can have serious costs. He applies this analysis to the socialization of girls versus boys in our culture, and links the self processes evolving from female socialization to vulnerability to depression after childhood.

Finally, in another highly provocative chapter, Everett Waters and his colleagues provide a critique and elaboration of attachment theory in which they attempt to identify the processes that link attachment to self-development. In their terms, they attempt to replace "magic" with mechanisms. In doing so, they note that attachment theory has a great deal to gain from detailing the roles that parent behavior and traditional learning theory mechanisms play in the development of attachment. They propose that a process they term "informal inference" plays a major role in the development of attachment and the organization of secure base behavior. They also propose eight stages in the development of attachment. These stages encompass and modify those proposed by Bowlby, and help link early attachment to adult forms of attachment.

In all, the chapters in this volume provide a highly rich discussion of the self and the processes related to the self. They, however, reflect only part of the richness of the symposium held in October of 1988. In addition, two discussants, L. Alan Sroufe and Hazel Markus, added to the array of concepts presented and analyzed during the course of the three-day meeting. A number of other scholars contributed to conversation hours held around various topics. Included were Ann Masten, Norman Garmezy, Auke Tellegen, Mark Snyder, W. Andrew Collins, and Martha Erickson. These individuals took part in and helped to lead conversation hours on: "Self Processes and Resiliency," "Social, Personality and Developmental Psychology's Perspectives on the Self," "Models of the Self: Issues of Stability and Change Throughout the Life-span," and "Parental Self Processes and Parenting Competence." We wish to thank all of these individuals, as well as our speakers, for making the 1988 symposium a great success.

Finally, thanks are also due to Lonnie Behrendt and Helen Dickison who, as support staff of the institute, saw to many of the administrative details, and to Kaye O'Geay, who helped with the copy-editing of the manuscripts.

I would also like to acknowledge financial support for the symposium from the General Mills Foundation and the National Institute of Child Health and Human Development, 2 R13 HD 21906.

Megan R. Gunnar

1 Pouring New Wine into Old Bottles: The Social Self as Internal Working Model

Inge Bretherton
University of Wisconsin–Madison

INTRODUCTION

In a lively discussion about the future of developmental psychology (Bronfenbrenner, Kessel, Kessen, & White, 1986), Sheldon White remarked that it takes no more than a few minutes in any good library to discover ideas from the 1890s that have been rediscovered within the last 10 years. Does this, he asks, mean that we are engaged in nothing more than an endless process of pouring old wine into new bottles, or reissuing old theories in the guise of new terminology? White is more optimistic. Perhaps, he reflects, it is not just that the new bottles look different from the old ones, but that the old wine tastes better after being decanted into them. It is in this spirit that I would like to use ideas derived from attachment theory to take a new look at the concept of the social self.

The notion of the social self was first put forth by James (1890), Cooley (1902), Baldwin (1895, 1906, 1911) and Mead (1934). In the first part of this chapter I review the work of these groundbreaking theorists, with special emphasis on what they had to say about the *development* of the social self. I then go on to discuss related ideas that arose independently in that branch of psychoanalysis known as object relations theory. Like the classical social psychologists, object relations theorists conceived of the self as emerging out of relations with others, but unlike the former, they laid stress on individual differences in the sense of self as it emerged out of the early mother–child relationship.

In formulating attachment theory, Bowlby (1969, 1973, 1980) followed in the footsteps of the classical social psychologists and object relations theorists, but he did more than merely pour old wine into new bottles. What sets off Bowlby's ideas regarding the social self from both of the earlier perspectives is the painstaking incorporation of research on representation, information processing, and memory. In addition, Bowlby (1969, 1973, 1980) devoted much more attention than most object relations theorists to the development of healthy, as opposed to pathological and disturbed, selves. He proposed that in the course of transactions with caregivers, infants construct "internal working models" of self and parent in the attachment relationship. The function of these working models is to interpret and forecast a partner's behavior. Bowlby's contributions to the notion of the social self are discussed in the third part of this chapter.

In the fourth section, I will build on Bowlby's concept of working model, extended beyond the attachment context, to consider the development of internal working models of the self in light of recent findings from cognitive and developmental psychology. My focus is on the growing structural complexity and level of social understanding manifested in a child's developing working models, but I also consider some issues proposed by the classical theorists that have been neglected by attachment theorists.

I conclude the chapter by reconsidering the relevance to the concept of the social self of James's distinction between the *I* (self as subject or knower), and the *Me* (the self as object or as known).

THEORIES OF THE SOCIAL SELF

The Social Self in the Classical Social Psychology Literature

The classical literature on the social origin of the self (Baldwin, 1895, 1906, 1911; Cooley, 1902; James, 1890; Mead, 1934) addresses such diverse issues as the self as object and subject (the *I* and the *Me*), the social nature of the self, the unity of the self (developmental and current), the actual versus the potential or ideal self, and the question of self-worth.

For James (1890), the self had a dual nature: the *I* or self as knower or subject and the *Me,* or self as object of thought. However, James had much more to say about the *Me* than about the *I,* and it is on the *Me* that this chapter is primarily focused. James viewed the *Me* or empirical self as a trilevel structure, with the material *Me* (including the body and material possessions) forming the lowest level, followed by the social *Me* (derived from the recognition a person receives from others), and the spiritual *Me* (derived from the capacity to think of oneself as a thinker). The social *Me* itself was not conceived as a unified structure, but a composite. Because James considered that the social *Me* originated in social relations, he speculated that an individual had to have as many social selves as there were people who carried an image of him or her in their minds and groups of people about whom he or she cared. There could be discordant splitting or harmonious integration of the different me's (or representations of self), but there was never just one social self. James also postulated that the material, social and spiritual *Me*'s each came in an actual and a potential or ideal version. The ideal *Me* is that self-image toward which an individual strives. Self-worth is determined by the discrepancy between an individual's actual and potential *Me*'s.

Mead (1934) took James's proposition about the integration of different social selves a step further. He pointed out that in order to view the self as object, individuals need to take the role of the other toward themselves, or in more current language, to construct a model of self from the perspective of a partner. This is reminiscent of Cooley's notion of the "looking glass self" (1902). However, unlike the other writers, Mead proposed that this process had two developmental stages. First, children learn to take the role of several *particular* others. This ability manifests itself in pretend play where children are continually taking the attitudes of those who control and nurture them. At this period of development the self is not unified. The second stage begins when children learn to participate in rule-governed games that require participants to take the attitude of the group (or generalized other) toward the self. When a child plays a game with others, he or she must be ready to take the attitude of all the other participants, that is, to see himself or herself from the stance of each individual player. Furthermore, he or she must also understand the relationship of all the game-related roles to each other. The effect of taking the attitude of the group or generalized other toward the self is therefore twofold: the individual (a) incorporates the rules of society and (b) integrates the multiple selves that originated in different dyadic relationships with others into a whole unified self. The representational processes whereby this is achieved are not specified, but their hypothesized outcome is an understanding of self and other in a system of relationships. Individuals at this level should hence be able to construct normative models of the role of child and parent within the family context.

It was not Mead, however, who presented the most detailed account of the origins and development of the social self, but his predecessor, James Mark Baldwin. Although some influence of Baldwin on Mead is detectable, Baldwin's ideas are much richer and more elaborated as far as early development is concerned. Baldwin contends (1894) that the self is not the isolate-and-in-one-body-alone-situated abstraction that theories of personality usually lead us to think (he does not specify which theories he is referring to). Self and other are, for Baldwin, mutually interdependent because they develop together from infancy, each reflecting on the other. In observing his own infants, Baldwin had noted that even 2-month-olds could distinguish between mother and nurse in the dark by touch. On the basis of such observations, he surmised that what the infant had learned were characteristic methods of being picked up, patted and so forth. He did not claim, however, that this ability to tell the difference between two persons implied that the young infant could attribute subjectivity to the other. Initially, infants understand others only as "projects," people known through their behavior and their effect. A major milestone is passed when the child understands others as selves through the realization that "other people's bodies . . . . have experiences *in them* such as mine has. They are also 'me's'; let them be assimilated to my me-copy" (1906, p. 14). Baldwin coined the term "ejection" to denote this process: "The child's subject sense goes out by a sort of return dialectic to illuminate the other persons. The 'project' of the earlier period is now lighted up, claimed, clothed on with the raiment of selfhood" (1906, p. 14). Ejecting the self is, in a sense, like calling the self into another.

Through "ejection," the child not only reaches a new level of understanding self and other, the process also leads to the emergence of prosocial feelings (a sense of justice and empathy). Because self and other are equated, the child now allows others what is allowed to the self. When self-interest conflicts with the interests of others, this newly fledged sense of justice is therefore violated.

Not only does the child come to understand others by attributing selfhood to them, the process also works in the reverse direction. The developing self benefits by appropriating the experiences of others through imitating their behavior. It is crucial to note, in this context, that what Baldwin understands by imitation includes much of what we would presently call representation. Imitation à la Baldwin operates in both directions. He speaks of imitation when one individual uses another individual as a copy or model for his own behavior, but also when the imitator imitates himself or herself. The first of these phenomena is termed social imitation, the second psychic imitation. For Baldwin, the process is the same whether an idea originates in the person's mind or is introduced by someone else.

Although Baldwin does not discuss the notion of the unified self directly, he seems to subscribe to James's idea of multiple social selves but with a different twist. He proposes that, through interacting with different others, such as siblings and parents, children learn to classify patterns of interactive behavior irrespective of who is performing the behavior. The patterns (or schemata) thus acquired facilitate adaptation to re-encounters with a similar interactive situations. In other words, children will respond differently, depending on how the interactive behavior of the other is classified. "So he (the child) at every stage is really in part someone else, even in his own thought of himself" (1906, p. 30).

Baldwin also reflects briefly on the origin of individual differences. In commenting on "the extraordinary variety which the same parental suggestions take on in the active interpretations by different children" (1906, p. 33), he explains that there is "always the fusion of the *old* self with the *new* elements coming in from the selves external to it" (1906, p. 33). However, despite individual differences, there must also be commonalities. Children's games depend on the "sameness of the personal thoughts" of the whole group in each situation (an idea later elaborated by Mead). Without each participant's understanding of others' thoughts, cooperative action would be impossible. The same can be said of the more general social self that is shared by family members: "But apart from the personal form in which the family suggestions are worked over by each child, we may say that the material of the social life of the family is largely common stock for all the members of the family. This means that the alter to each ego is largely common to them all" (1906, p. 35).

Baldwin also considered the differential impact of various social partners on the budding social self. Relationships with other children are primarily seen as a context for practice or assimilation. Authority relations with parents, by contrast, are said to give rise to new learning (accommodation), especially as regards the development of the ethical self. Through obeying parents—whether on the basis of punishment or suggestion—the child acquires a sense that there are limits to his or her social freedom. This experience forms the copy (representation) of the child's personal law or authority, and this in turn constitutes the construction of the ideal or ethical self. As Baldwin puts it: "His elevation to this higher plane is by absorption of 'copies,' patterns, examples from the social life about him" (1906, p. 67). This newly acquired ethical self is subsequently ejected into all the members of the family. For this reason, the child who has agreed to obey, expects other family members to abide by the same rules.

In summary, Baldwin went beyond James, Cooley, and Mead by dwelling on the child's own constructive activity in acquiring a sense of self, by imputing subjectivity to others, by expanding experience through imitation of others, and by assimilating new experiences into already available "me"-copies or what, in more modern terms, would be termed representations or self-schemata (Markus, 1977). It is only in considering the development of the ethical self that Baldwin emphasizes the active intervention of caregivers and other adults. Of the four classical theorists, Baldwin alone laid stress on reciprocal feedback between the emerging sense of self and the sense of others as selves. Only he explored mechanisms that could explain individual differences among individual selves as well the development of normative group selves. Finally, he began—much more deeply than the others—to grapple with the representational processes that underlie the sense of self. His writings thus contain, in germinal form, many of the issues that still vex us today. So much for the old wine in old bottles as far as classical social psychology is concerned.

The Social Self in Psychoanalytical Object Relations Theory

Although individual differences play some role in the classical social psychology literature about the social self, especially in Baldwin's writings the main emphasis is on general processes rather than on the effect that different relationship histories have on different selves. Psychoanalysts working in the object relations tradition, on the other hand, have made this topic, (particularly the healthy versus pathological development of the social self) their primary focus. In this context I have chosen to discuss the views of Sullivan (1953) and Winnicott (1965). Other important figures are Fairbairn (1952), Guntrip (1971), Kernberg (1976), and more recently Kohut (1982).

Sullivan was the founder of the American school of interpersonal psychiatry while Winnicott was a prominent member of the British object relations school of psychoanalysis. This difference in background notwithstanding, both theorists held remarkably congruent ideas regarding the origin of individual differences in the development of the social self. They both diverged from Freud by proposing that relatedness (not gratification) was the infant's most basic need, but both also emphasized that the development of a healthy self is dependent on the mother's sensitive responsiveness to her infant (Greenberg & Mitchell, 1982).

Sullivan. Sullivan ascribes individual differences in the development of the self to the tender as opposed to anxious caregiving provided by the "mothering one." Sensitive caregiving is experienced by the baby as "good mother," while anxious and hence anxiety-provoking caregiving is experienced as "bad mother." The infant initially organizes good and bad experiences with caregivers into two separate *personifications* (schemata of experience of self with caregivers, in more modern parlance). Sullivan (1953) describes the personification of good mother in infancy as follows:

> This personification is not the "real mother"—a particular living being considered as an entity. It is an elaborate organization of the infant's experience. . . . It is important to understand that the infant's personification of the mother is composed of, or made up of from, or organized from, or elaborated out of, what has occurred in the infant's relation to what you might call the "real" mother in satisfaction-giving integrations with her. (p. 112).

Only gradually do the separate but generic (i.e., not person-specific) good and bad personifications come to be differentiated and integrated into representations of specific caregivers who are both good and bad.

Later in the first year the infant also creates personifications of self. "Good me" organizes experience in which tender maternal caregiving was satisfying for the infant, whereas "bad me" organizes experience in which caregiving was associated with anxiety. Finally, "not me" derives from experience that is so intensely anxious that it becomes inaccessible to awareness. Note that the personifications of the mothering one and of "me" are, according to Sullivan, built up and differentiated from the same interpersonal experiences, and that they are hence complementary to each other. In the course of development, personifications of "mother" and "me" come to be subsumed by the self-system (ego). The self-system protects the person from anxiety through security-operations (or defense mechanisms) that repress past experiences of "bad me" and "not me." Unfortunately, security operations "interfere with observation and analysis, and for this reason prevent the profit one might gain from experience" (Sullivan, 1953, p. 346).

As regards development, Sullivan delineates a sequence in which needs for different forms of relatedness predominate at different periods of the life-span, first with parents, later with best friends and finally with a sexual partner. However, throughout these different relationships, maladaptive "me–you" patterns (representations or schemata of self and other) that an individual has acquired in early dysfunctional relationships are hypothesized to become the basis for a dysfunctional self in later relationships.

Winnicott. Like Sullivan, Winnicott ascribes a vital role to the quality of mother–infant interaction in the development of self. The ordinary good-enough mother is said to provide a "holding environment" within which the infant who begins life in a state of unintegration can become organized as a person. As Winnicott puts it: "An infant who has no one person to gather his bits together starts with a handicap in his self-integrating task" (1958, p. 150).

The mother's task is made easier by an initial state of "primary preoccupation" during which she is wholly focused on her baby's moods and needs. During this period the "good-enough" mother plays two important roles. First, by responding promptly and appropriately to her baby she provides him or her with a feeling of omnipotence. Second, by remaining nondemanding during periods when the baby does not need her she supports the development of a capacity for aloneness that Winnicott considers central to the development of a stable self. It is maternal attunement to *both* these tendencies that allows the baby to become attuned to his or her own bodily processes and impulses.

Inability by the mother to fulfill these two functions has grave consequences. Where Sullivan dwelt on the danger of maternal anxiety for the development of a healthy self, Winnicott drew attention to the twin threats of excessive maternal under- and overinvolvement. Each endangers the emerging self in different ways. If the infant is excessively ignored by the mother no stable self may develop at all, but if the mother intrudes or impinges inappropriately the infant develops a "false self on a compliant basis." By becoming prematurely attuned to the claims and requests of others the infant runs a risk of losing touch with his or her spontaneous needs. The true self goes into hiding, avoiding expression, leading ultimately to dissociation between cognitive and affective processes.

According to Winnicott, primary maternal preoccupation is only necessary until the infant has acquired a feeling of "omnipotence" (in more current language one would probably say a sence of efficacy and competence). Once omnipotence is firmly establish the infant must learn that his or her omnipotence is not complete. This realization occurs gradually as the mother's responsiveness wanes, and she is no longer so exquisitely attuned to her infant's signals, moods, and needs. Winnicott believes that the mother's carefully graduated failures in adaptation have two consequences. On the one hand, they play a vital and necessary role in the infant's self-differentiation, but on the other they induce experiences of anger toward the no longer perfectly responsive mother. When this occurs, the mother's most important task is to show that she is "durable" and "nonretaliatory" in the face of the baby's negative feelings. In this way she is able to demonstrate that the infant's anger cannot really harm her, that she is resilient and and can survive the destructiveness of negative affect. At the same time, Winnicott's statements about excessive maternal over- and underinvolvement still hold. Although no longer perfectly attuned, the good-enough mother must remain attuned-enough to support the development of a healthy self in her child.

The Social Self in Attachment Theory

Attachment theory has deep roots in ethology, but it has even deeper roots in psychoanalysis, especially object relations theory. It is therefore not surprising that Bowlby's views regarding the development of self in attachment relationships coincide with Sullivan's and Winnicott's in a number of respects. All three theorists stress that the infant is prepared to engage in social relations from birth, that maternal responsiveness is crucial for the developing self, that patterns of actual mother–child transactions come to be reflected in mental representations of self and mother, and that later patterns of relating are built upon earlier ones. Where Bowlby differs considerably from Sullivan and also to some extent from Winnicott is in his much greater emphasis on the development of the healthy (versus pathological) self. Where he differs from the object relations theorists as well as the classical social psychologists is in his extensive reliance on theories and findings from outside the object relations tradition and psychoanalysis in general. To return to the metaphor with which I began this chapter, Bowlby does not pour old wine into new bottles or reissue old theory in the guise of new terminology. Rather, his theoretical work and the ensuing empirical studies of attachment at the representational level are filling old bottles with new wine, that is, providing new and enriched content to old theoretical notions.

Bowlby (1969) proposed that, in the course of interacting with the physical and personal world, an individual constructs "internal working models" of important aspects of that world. The function of such working models is to aid the individual in perceiving and interpreting events, in forecasting the future, and in constructing plans. One may legitimately ask why Bowlby chose to introduce the new term "working models" instead of retaining more traditional labels such as "cognitive map" or "representations." In answer to this question, Bowlby (1969) points out that the older terms have static connotations whereas the concept of "internal working model" suggests dynamic mental structures on which an individual can operate in order to conduct small-scale experiments in the head. Bowlby derived the notion of internal working models from an insightful book by Craik on *The Nature of Explanations* (1943). Craik was a psychologist involved in the construction of intelligent rocket-guidance systems. To quote Craik:

> By a model we thus mean any physical or chemical system which has a similar relation-structure to that of the process it imitates. By "relation-structure" I do not mean some obscure nonphysical entity which attends the model, but the fact that it

> is a physical working model which works in the same way as the process it parallels. . . . If the organism carries a "small-scale model" of external reality and of its own possible actions within its head, it is able to try out various alternatives, conclude which is the best of them, react to future situations before they arise, utilize the knowledge of past events in dealing with the present and future, and in every way to react in a much fuller, safer and more competent manner to the emergencies which face it. (p. 61)

Craik stressed that, to be useful, internal working models needed neither be fully accurate, nor very detailed. To be adequate to their function of prediction and planning it was merely necessary that the relation-structure (meaning spatial, temporal, and causal relations) of working models be consistent with the reality they represented.

What Craik described is an elaborated version of what psychoanalysts had hitherto called "the internal world." Freud (1924, cited in Hartmann, 1958), for example, referred to the internal world as a copy of the external world, made up from a store of memories of earlier perceptions. He described thinking as an *experimental action* using small quantities of energy. Likewise, Hartmann contended that "in higher organisms, *trial activity* is increasingly displaced into the interior of the organism, and no longer appears in the form of motor action directed toward the external world." Along similar lines, psychoanalytical object relations theorists seem to conceptualize representations of self and other as internalized chunks of experienced relationship patterns. For example, Sullivan (1953) speaks of "personifications of mother and me" and of "me–you patterns," Fairbairn (1952) proposed the notion of internal (love) objects and associated parts of the ego, Sandler and Sandler (1978) mention "interactions between self and object representations" that make unconscious dialogues with love objects possible, and Kernberg (1976) talks of self-object-affect units (positive or negatively toned interaction schemata) that become the basis of self and object representations. It should therefore come as no surprise that Bowlby, a psychoanalyst himself, was drawn to the idea of representation as internal working models.

Bowlby (1969) hypothesized that internal working models of self and attachment figure emerge out of actual patterns of infant–caregiver transactions sometime around the end of the first year when the infant has attained object permanence (Piaget, 1954) and begins to acquire language. Because of their basis in transactional patterns, working models of self and attachment figure(s) develop in close complementarity so that, taken together, they represent the relationship. Hence a working model of self can only be fully understood in terms of the relationship(s) within which it emerged and continues to develop. For example, a child who experiences parental figures as emotionally available and supportive, will most probably construct a working model of the self as competent and loved. By contrast, a child who experiences—and hence represents—attachment figures as primarily rejecting, may form a complementary internal working model of the self as unworthy. In fact (although Bowlby does not explicitly do so) it is possible to postulate even more complex interrelationships of working models. If attachment figures cannot provide a child with sufficient emotional support, the child may form a working model of the world as a dangerous place while the self is perceived as weak (Guidano & Liotti, 1983). There is even evidence from ethnographic studies that in societies where parents are acceptant of children, adults' working model of the supernatural world is benevolent. The converse holds in societies where parents' behavior to children is relatively rejecting, (Rohner, 1975). In this chapter, however, I will restrict myself to considering the complementarity of working models of self and significant figures (especially attachment figures).

To remain adequate to their task of guiding the interpretation and planning of interpersonal transactions with the caregiver, working models of self and other in relationship cannot remain rigid once they are formed. Rather, they must be repeatedly deconstructed and reconstructed to accommodate developmental changes. As the child becomes more competent and has more highly differentiated thought processes at his or her disposal, the caregiver responds differently to the child. If all goes well, these developments come to be reflected in the complexity and content of child's (and the parents') internal working models. This does not, however, imply that the basic affective climate of the relationship must change. Internal working models of self as loved and competent, and the attachment figure as emotionally supportive and encouraging of autonomy can retain affective stability despite changes in cognitive and affective sophistication.

While developmental changes *must* occur to keep working models optimally adapted to reality, qualitative changes in a positive or negative direction *may* occur in response to changed life circumstances (such as onset or cessation of a family member's severe illness; onset or cessation of prolonged separations, and so forth). Even in these cases, however, the quality of the prior relationship (as reflected in well-adapted working models) is likely to moderate the influence of external stresses.

Notwithstanding the necessity for change, it is equally important to realize that internal working models cannot be in a state of continuous flux. Research on controlled and automatic processing shows that ways of acting and thinking that are at first under deliberate guidance tend to become less accessible to awareness as processing becomes more unreflecting and automatic (Bowlby, 1980; Shiffrin & Schneider, 1977). This frees the person to focus available attentional resources on new and unfamiliar situations. It also leads to relative stability in how a person construes the interpersonal world, albeit at the cost of oversimplification and perhaps some distortion. Individuals will feel compelled to better accommodate their working models to new circumstances only when the lack of fit between actual interchanges and the corresponding internal working models becomes so great that the old model is no longer helpful.

However, problems arise in the normal updating of working models when processes Bowlby called *defensive* exclusion come into play. It is by now a truism that humans and other organisms do not process all incoming information at the same level. Some aspects, deemed less important, are selectively excluded from processing in order to focus attention on what is most relevant to the task at hand. For example, when two incompatible messages are presented to both ears the subject normally "hears" only one of them. There is evidence, however, that the other message is being monitored outside the subject's awareness: Subjects tend to hear their name even when it is presented to the "unattending" ear. Defensive exclusion may rely on similar mechanisms as selective exclusion, but is believed to occur in response to intolerable mental pain or conflict. Clinical case material (e.g., Cain & Fast, 1972) suggests that such conflict is likely to arise when an attachment figure habitually ridicules a child's security-seeking behaviors, reinterprets rejection of the child as motivated by parental love, or otherwise disavows or denies the child's anxious, angry or loving feelings toward attachment figures (Bowlby, 1973, 1980). Under such circumstances, it is common for a child to defensively exclude from awareness the working model of the "bad" unloving parent, and retain conscious access only to the loving model ("the good parent"). Since the internal working model of an unconditionally loving and supportive parent cannot correspond to reality, such idealized models are maladaptive. Although the individual may obtain relief from mental pain, confusion, or conflict, defensive exclusion severely hampers the future accommodation of internal working models to reality. Indeed, Bowlby (1973) notes that some clinical data can best be explained by supposing that individuals sometimes operate with two or more conflicting working models of the same attachment figure and two or more conflicting models of self. In cases where multiple models of a single individual are operative they are likely to differ in regard to their origin, their dominance and the extent to which the subject is aware of them. In individuals suffering from emotional disturbance it is common to find that the model with greatest influence on behavior and feelings is one that developed early in life, and of which the person may be relatively unaware; at the same time, there may be a second, perhaps radically incompatible model, that was influenced by what the person was told, and of which the person is more fully aware (Bowlby, 1973).

Defensive exclusion in the service of temporary peace of mind may be regarded as adaptive in the immediate sense, but will tend to interfere with the adequate updating of working models and hence with optimal future coping and development. Defensive exclusion is also importantly implicated in the intergenerational transmission of relationship patterns via working models of self and attachment figures (Bowlby, 1973, p. 322). Individuals who grow up to become relatively stable and self-reliant, Bowlby postulates, normally have parents who are supportive when called upon, but who also permit and encourage autonomy. Such parents tend not only to engage in fairly frank communication of their own working models, but also indicate to the child that working models are open to questioning and revision. To quote Bowlby:

> Because in all these respects children tend unwittingly to identify with parents and therefore to adopt, when they become parents, the same patterns of behaviour towards children that they themselves have experienced during their own childhood, patterns of interaction are transmitted, more or less faithfully, from one generation to another. Thus the inheritance of mental health and of mental ill health through the medium of family microculture is certainly no less important, and may well be far more important, than is their inheritance through the medium of genes. (p. 323)

Bowlby cites longitudinal studies by Peck and Havighurst (1960), Offer (1969), and Murphey, Silber, Coelho, Hamburg, and Greenberg (1963) in support of these claims.

Empirical findings from observational studies of parent–infant or parent–toddler attachments, and from attachment-related interview and storytelling studies with preschoolers, kindergartners, and adults present a picture that is remarkably consistent with Bowlby's formulations. The observational studies conducted with infants and toddlers indicate that in relationships where the child's attachment or autonomy signals consistently go unheeded, or are consistently misread, the development of open communication between the partners becomes impeded (e.g., Ainsworth & Bell, 1969; Ainsworth, Bell & Stayton, 1974; Blehar, Lieberman, & Ainsworth, 1977; Grossmann & Grossmann, in press). Such restricted communication is presumed to lead to inadequate working models (for further discussion of this point, see Bretherton, in press).

Studies with preschoolers, kindergartners and adults, based on projective material and interviews, support the conclusions drawn from the interactional studies (Bretherton, Biringen, Ridgeway, Maslin, & Sherman, 1989; Bretherton, Ridgeway, & Cassidy, in press; Cassidy, 1988; Eichberg, 1987; Grossmann, Fremmer–Bombik, Rudolph, & Grossmann, in press; Kobak & Sceery, 1988; Main, & Goldwyn, in press; Main, Kaplan, & Cassidy, 1985). Secure children, parents, and young adults are able to communicate about attachment issues with ease, and to discuss attachment relationships coherently without necessarily insisting that they or their attachment figures are absolutely perfect. By contrast, insecure-avoidant children and adults (those dismissing of attachment) tend to defend themselves against closeness by processes that restrict the flow of ideas about attachment relationships intrapsychically and interpersonally. They tend to give an aloof and nonempathic impression. At the same time, they have a strong tendency to idealize parents or themselves when making general statements, but cannot illustrate their global judgments with autobiographical memories (the memories may be absent or contradict the generalizations). A third major pattern is characterized by ambivalence to reunion in infancy and by preoccupation with conflictual attachment issues in adulthood. The corresponding patterns for children have not been as easy to pinpoint. In a fourth group, the underlying problem in the adults seems to be unresolved mourning for a childhood attachment figure. Infants of these parents were classified as disorganized/disoriented during the Strange Situation (Main & Hesse, in press). At 6, the same children were overly controlling of the relationship—using either a caregiving or a punitive mode of interaction with the parent in the separation-reunion procedure (Main & Cassidy, in press). It is important to note, however, that disorganization in thought about attachment did show up the children's responses to projective tests at 6.

Taken as a whole, the empirical findings reviewed in this section allow us to understand more clearly the process of intergenerational transmission of attachment patterns as suggested by Bowlby in the second volume of the attachment trilogy (1973). Even before their infants are born, parents have internal working models of themselves as caregivers and of the unborn infant (Zeanah, Keener, Stewart, & Anders, 1985). On the basis of Main & Goldwyn's (in press) findings one may assume that these anticipatory working models of the infant are strongly influenced by the parents' own experiences in childhood, although later relationship experiences and other factors are also likely to play a role. When the parents encounter the real infant, these anticipatory working models are imposed on the new relationship. To be adaptive, however, they must be fine-tuned to fit the individual baby's temperament and needs. This will be relatively easy if the parents' anticipatory working models are coherent, well organized and easily accessible to awareness with a minimum of defensive exclusion. It will be much more difficult, if parents' internal working models are ill-organized and subject to much defensive exclusion. In this case the parents will not read the baby's cues sensitively, nor will they be able to take the baby's perspective, notice what the baby's goals are or respond empathically (Ainsworth et al., 1974). In a relationship in which the baby's signals are not adequately read by the parent, the baby's own budding working models are also likely to become biased, distorted, and inflexible.

Although attachment theory has provided the framework for studying the origins of individual differences in the social self and the transmission of social selves across generations, some of the issues raised by the classical social psychologists have not yet been successfully tackled by attachment theory. One of these is the problem of multiple social selves raised by James (1890) and Mead (1934). Bowlby (1973) made provision in his theory for discordant working models about the self in the *same* relationship, one defensively excluded and one accessible to awareness, but the question of different *Me*'s in different attachment relationships remains to be worked out. The issue is crucial because it has now been amply documented that the quality of an infant's relationship to mother and to father (and hence the working model of self in either relationship) can be divergent. The first such study was conducted by Lamb (1977). The second was undertaken by Main and Weston (1981), who assessed infants with father and mother at 12 and 18 months. Neither reported concordant secure and insecure patterns of attachment with respect to both parents. Similar findings were obtained by Grossmann, Grossmann, Huber, and Wartner, (1981) in Germany, and by Sagi, et al. (1985) in Israel, where the infant was assessed with father, mother, and metapelet. If a child's different relationship history with both parents (and possibly with other major caregivers, siblings, and close friends) matters for the development of self, the question arises whether the child ends up with several discordant working models of self. Or are the various models of the self developed in different relationships somehow averaged, or integrated? Or does one become dominant?

Main et al. (1985) offer some relevant insights. They found that an assessment of the child's representation of attachment at 6 years of age (in response to a family picture and to a projective test about separation) was highly predictable from the earlier attachment pattern with the mother, but not with the father. These results suggest that, in the construction of the working model of the self, one parent—most probably the principal attachment figure—may be the more influential. Ricks's intergenerational data (1985) point in the same direction. A mother's reported acceptance by her own mother (not by her father) was particularly strongly related to her infant's attachment security as evaluated in the Strange Situation at 12 months. On the other hand, some studies seem to support the "averaging hypothesis": less favorable child outcomes are found when the relationship to both parents is insecure, intermediate outcomes occur if the relationship to one parent is insecure while the other is secure, and the least favorably outcomes are observed when both relationships are insecure (Main & Weston, 1981).

A second unresolved issue concerns the construction of a potential or ideal self. Main's (1985) findings on secure-autonomous adults with insecure childhoods may be relevant here. She found that what most strongly predicted child security was the parent's attitude to attachment in general, not the security or insecurity of early relationships. Similarly, Grossmann et al. found that children were secure if the parent expressed the wish that their own parents had been more supportive.

A third issue unresolved by attachment theorists is the growing complexity of working models with age. Attachment-theoretical studies of children, young adults, and parents have stressed qualitative stability despite developmental change. Developmentally appropriate assessment tools were chosen on the basis of intuitive insight, not systematic investigation.

Finally, while the concept of working model offers advantages over the older static terms (image, internal object, object representation) it is not a fully fledged theory of representation. From some points of view it is useful and sufficient to regard representations of self and other as "inner persons" that can engage in imaginary interactions. Ultimately, however, we will not make further progress in understanding working models of self if we do not base our theorizing on the most up-to-date findings from the study of representation.

To extend our understanding of the self as working model and on the development of working models in general, we can draw on useful ideas from several other fields of study which I will discuss in the following section of this chapter. First, I will consider how theories of event representation can help us to think about the structure of working models. In the second and third subsections I will go on to review helpful insights on the development of working models to be gained from studies of social cognition, especially with respect to a growing capacity for intersubjectivity.

Like all good analogies that are taken too literally, the metaphor of pouring new wine into old bottles which I used to characterize Bowlby's contribution begins to break down here. I see the next section as adding more complexity to the bouquet of the new wine in old bottles, rather than as adding entirely new wine.

WORKING MODELS OF SELF AND OTHERS: INSIGHTS FROM THEORIES OF REPRESENTATIONAL AND SOCIAL COGNITIVE DEVELOPMENT

Event Representation and Script Theory as Related to Internal Working Models

The dynamic concept of internal working model requires a representational system that operates with dynamic event- or agent-action-object structures rather than with static images, concept hierarchies, and logical operations alone. Of the classical social psychologists, only Baldwin attempted to grapple with the question of representation by proposing a theory of internal "copies" of self in relation to others. James, Cooley, and Mead merely assumed representational processes without speculating as to their precise nature while psychoanalytical object relations theorists used metaphorical concepts ("the internal world"). Furthermore, even Craik's notion of a working model cannot be considered a theory, and may best be characterized as offering an elaborated metaphor for thinking about the self. It was certainly not a developmental theory. To account for the development of working models, Bowlby had to rely on Piaget's (1951, 1954) theory or sensorimotor development, governed by the twin processes of assimilation and accommodation. By acting on the world the world the infant was said to develop schemata into which relevant experiences could subsequently be assimilated, but which could also be refined or accommodated so as to better fit external reality.

Unfortunately, Piaget was not interested in developing a *schema theory* at the *representational* level that allowed for the construction of mental models of the everyday world. In his work beyond the sensorimotor period, Piaget decided to devote his energies primarily to clarifying the development of operative thinking guided by logicomathematical structures dealing with time, space, causality, and conservation of quantity. However, operational thought cannot in and of itself explain the human ability to simulate the external world internally. Recent theories with roots in Craik's (1943) propositions about working models, and in Bartlett's (1933) prior work on the role of schemata in memory are more useful in helping us to sharpen the concept of working models.

Quite independently of Bowlby, Johnson–Laird (1983) rediscovered Craik's (1943) writings about representational processes conceived as mental working models, and brought the term into wider circulation among cognitive scientists. Taking an evolutionary perspective, Johnson–Laird pointed out that an organism with the capacity to construct mental models is afforded considerable survival advantages because mental models permit both insightful and foresightful behavior. The more adequately mental models can simulate relevant structural–causal relationships found in the external world, the better the potential planning and responding capacity of an organism (see also G. Mandler, 1986).

The higher primates differ from other animals not only in their ability to construct more complex working models of the physical and social world. Just as crucial is their ability to create internal working models of themselves that include, at least in humans, their own and their partners' representational processes. It is this ability that underlies the development of reflective self-awareness, of perspective taking, and the capacity for intersubjectivity to which I will turn later.

Johnson–Laird (1983) hypothesized that mental models are constructed, tested out and revised in working memory from elements (representations of people or objects) and relations (spatial, temporal, causal) stored in an individual's long-term knowledge base. This implies mental models at two levels: models composed of dissociable elements that are stored in long-term memory and "temporary" mental models that are constructed afresh in short-term memory as the need arises. Such a view requires (1) a flexibly organized representational system that stores event components or part-schemata in long-term memory, (2) a mechanism whereby these components and schemata are located, and (3) a mechanism whereby they are retrieved or copied into a temporary "scratch space" where they can be manipulated and recombined in a variety of ways (Hendrix, 1979; for similar ideas see also Leslie, 1987, and Perner, 1988). Finally, we have to posit a process whereby some of the schemata constructed in working or short-term memory are fed back into the long-term representational system.

Johnson–Laird did not make these distinctions very explicit, because his research speaks primarily to the construction of working models in short-term memory. In empirical work with adults, Johnson–Laird and his colleagues asked subjects to reason about logical problems that were either embedded in familiar everyday situations or that were couched in abstract symbols without concrete content (Johnson–Laird, Legrenzi, & Legrenzi, 1972; Wason & Johnson–Laird, 1972). It turns out when a complex logical problem is embedded in a familiar context (thus permitting the construction of a mental model from prior components stored in long-term memory) individuals can solve it fairly easily. Yet, when the very same problem is presented in purely abstract terms (i.e., using contentless symbols) many individuals do much worse.

In contrast to Johnson–Laird, theorists building on Bartlett's (1933) work (Mandler, 1979, 1983; Nelson & Gruendel, 1981; Nelson & Ross, 1982; Schank, 1982; Schank & Abelson, 1977) focused most of their efforts on defining the schematic structure of *long-term memory,* without paying much heed to the construction of mental models in working memory. They proposed that the representational system consists of mental structures that summarize skeletal information about recurring similar events. These hypothetical structures, termed *event schemata* or *scripts,* were defined as sequentially organized structures with "slots" for specific agent-roles, for action sequences motivated by specific goals and emotions, for recipients of actions, and for locales. Schank suggested that appropriate scripts are "instantiated" or called up when a person re-experiences a relevant event, and that they are useful in helping the person predict what may happen next. Note that Schank is tacitly assuming that mental models in long-term memory are retrieved into working memory by proposing the notion of script "instantiation." He does not, however, thereby solve the problem of how an individual can extrapolate to new, never before encountered events.

This issue is tackled in a revised formulation of early script theory in which Schank (1982) refined his ideas regarding script instantiation. He argued that information derived from episodic or autobiographical memories is reprocessed, partitioned, cross-indexed, and summarized into a variety of different schema categories, each of which preserve some aspect of the spatiotemporal-causal structure of experiences in the external world. Only some of these schemata order mini-event representations into coordinated, longer event sequences (such as the "script" of going to a restaurant or putting a baby to bed), others summarize information from similar mini-events (all feeding situations regardless of context), and yet others generalize across different event sequences (e.g., all caregiving routines). Schank's new conceptualization deliberately blurs the distinction between episodic and semantic memory originally proposed by Tulving (1972, 1983) and substitutes instead multiply interconnected hierarchies composed of schemata that range from being very experience-near to being very general and abstract. These hierarchies are constructed and continually revised and refined on the basis of new input (for related ideas, see Nelson, 1986). They also make implicit provision for recombining elements of old information for the sake of creating new mental models.

Event Schemata and Working Models of Self and Specific Others

Until now, studies of event representation have been concerned with group data. It may therefore not be immediately obvious how these insights could apply to individual differences in internal working models of self and specific others in social relationships. This issue is easily resolved, however, when we consider that nothing in these theories precludes the idea that individuals develop schemata of interaction with specific partners, and that these interaction schemata can be organized into a schema hierarchy as envisaged by Schank (1982).

In this connection, I have found Epstein's (1973, 1980, this volume) notion of the self-concept especially useful. Epstein, following in Kelley's (1955) footsteps, contends that the self-concept (internal working model of the self) is best understood as part of an individual's theory of reality. A self-theory, according to Epstein, consists of several hierarchically organized postulate-systems into which new experiences are assimilated. Epstein's formulation is strikingly close to Bowlby's notion of complementary working models of self and attachment figure (see Ricks, 1985, for elaborations on this point). A person with high self-esteem "in effect carries within him a loving parent, one who is proud of his successes and acceptant of his failures," whereas the person with low self-esteem "carries within him a disapproving parent who is harshly critical of his failures" (Epstein, 1980, p. 106). By translating Epstein into the language of event representation, we can now conceptualize working models of self and significant others as schema hierarchies derived from actual transactions (see also Markus, 1977). On the lowest level would be interactional schemata that are very experience-near ("When I hurt myself, my mommy always comes to comfort and help me"). Above this level would be more general schemata ("My mommy is usually there for me when I need her") that subsume a variety of lower-level schemata of need-fulfilling events with mother. Somewhere near the top of the hierarchy would be both "My mother is a loving person" and "I am loved," in turn subsuming a variety of general schemata. Note that I am not advocating a trilevel system, but one with multiple levels of unknown number. I *am* proposing that we go beyond a notion of working models as composed of a two-level system based on autobiographical (episodic) and general (semantic) memory as suggested by Bowlby (1980). To think of internal working models of self and attachment figure as multiple-level schema-hierarchies (instead of an internalized person) will, I think make the concept more amenable to detailed study.

Summary. Taken together, the ideas proposed by Schank (1982) Johnson–Laird (1983), Perner (1988) and Leslie (1987) can help us understand how an individual might extrapolate from a working model of self and other (stored in long-term memory) to new or hypothetical interpersonal situations. Schank's work is primarily relevant to the organization of working models in long-term memory, whereas Johnson–Laird's (1983) speaks to the construction of mental models in working memory with the aid of components retrieved from long-term memory. Johnson–Laird further points out that, through verbal communication, individuals can co-construct new realities with others for which they do *not* have a prior *shared* script. It is only necessary that partners possess enough shared representational building blocks.

Other puzzle-pieces also fall into place. Schank's (1982) notion of schema abstraction and schema partitioning helps us conceptualize how schemata representing experiences with specific others (e.g., attachment figures), when subsumed into other more general schemata, can contribute to what I have called normative working models of a social role (e.g., the role of child or parent). Observation of other parents and other children would also feed into this general model, but one's own personal experience may be especially potent even in the creation of generalized models.

Finally, although Schank was not specifically concerned with biased or incomplete processing, I propose that his revised theory of event representation can also shed new light on defensive phenomena. If parts of autobiographical memories enter into cross-referenced schemata at many hierarchical levels, it is possible to see how material that has been defensively excluded from recall as an autobiographical memory might still influence schema formation at other levels. Moreover, once the lines of communication within an individual's representational system are broken, biased or incomplete processing is bound to follow because existing incomplete schemata now guide the processing of new experience (Erdelyi, 1985).

The Development of Event Representation

Early studies on event representation and scripts were restricted to adult subjects, raising the question as to whether these theories could be extended downward to children, perhaps even to infants. Evidence shows that this is feasible. Recent studies of infant memory have documented that cued recall of motor acts is possible as early as 3 months (e.g., Rovee–Collier & Fagan, 1981; Rovee–Collier & Lipsitt, 1981). Based on these results, Stern (1985) postulated that infants may register routine interaction sequences with a caregiver as generalized episodes that store *small coherent chunks of lived experience including not only actions, but sensations, goals and affects of self and other in a temporal-physical-causal relationship*. Stern called these generalized memory structures RIGs, (Representations of Interactions that have been Generalized) in analogy to Nelson's concept of GERs (Generalized Event Representations; see Nelson & Gruendel, 1981). To avoid conceptual confusion, however, it should be noted at this point that Stern's use of the term representation in this context is nontraditional, and implies recognition but not recall memory.

RIGs storing and guiding the processing of experiences would be interactive events such as being held and molding to a comfortable warm body or being tossed in the air and caught. Stern hypothesizes that RIGs are accessed whenever a familiar self-with-other episode recurs, suggesting that RIGs might be the sensorimotor basis for the construction of representational interaction schemata that can be imaged or verbalized independently of action. The notion of RIGs is supported by studies showing that older infants can anticipate another person's behavior in context. For example, Izard (1978) reported that by 8 months infants cringe in fear while their arm is being prepared for an injection and subsequently refuse to interact with the nurse responsible for the unpleasant experience. At this age infants also display anticipatory smiles during peekaboo games *before* a playmate reappears from behind a cloth (Sroufe & Wunsch, 1972) and anticipatory distress when an attachment figures prepares for departure (Piaget, 1954).

With the onset of representation in the traditional sense, toddlers demonstrate in their pretend play and language that information about everyday events is available to them in schema form. In pretense, they reenact events from everyday life, beginning with single acts such as sleeping or eating performed on themselves and progressing to complex sequenced acts that include others (people or dolls) as actors and recipients (see Bretherton, 1984, for a review). The ability to encode simple events in language develops concurrently (e.g., Shore, O'Connell, & Bates, 1984; Greenfield & Smith, 1976).

By age 3, the development of event schemata can be investigated more formally because children of this age can be asked to give verbal descriptions of routine events such a having dinner or attending a birthday party. In this connection, Nelson and Gruendel (1981) found that the 3-year-olds they interviewed had a remarkably good grasp of the order in which the action sequences of routine events take place. This was especially true when event sequences were causally related (e.g., the candles on the birthday cake must be blown out, and it must be cut before it can be eaten). Interestingly, autobiographical memories of a specific everyday event—such as eating dinner *last night*—could not easily be elicited. Three-year-olds tended to produce dinner scripts instead of talking about a particular dinner episode. At this early age, an event had to be truly extraordinary (going to the circus for the first time) to be recalled as an episodic or autobiographical memory. Moreover, young children did not seem to require a large number of exposures to an event in order to construct a schema of it (Fivush, 1984; Price & Goodman, 1985). Indeed, when children expect an event to be repeated (such as going to school), they seem to use the impersonal "you" and the timeless present tense usually reserved for scripts even to describe the first day at school (". . . and then you do reading or something"; Fivush, 1984). The major difference between older and younger children was that the older ones invariably described more actions. In addition their statements tended to be more probabilistic (they reported what might, but need not happen; Fivush & Slackman, 1986). Older children were also better at correcting script-based stories with out-of-order action sequences. Four-your-olds merely tended to leave out the misordered actions on retelling the stories while the 5-year-olds reinserted them in the appropriate place or transformed them to make better sense (Hudson & Nelson, 1983).

Although studies of event representation attest to the growing elaboration of the internal world, there remains the more specific question how these working models may increase in psychological complexity. I will turn to these issues in the next two subsections.

Evidence for the Hierarchical Structure of Working Models

Empirical evidence about the hierarchical organization of working models of self and others (implicit in Schank, 1982, and explicit in Epstein, 1973) can be gleaned from a number of social cognitive studies in which children were asked to give verbal or written descriptions of themselves and others. In these studies, younger children's descriptions of self were composed of concrete statements about behavior, appearance, and possessions. By adolescence they had evolved into abstract, well-organized narratives about personality traits and interpersonal relationships. For example, in questioning children about differences between themselves and others, Bannister and Agnew (1977) discovered that 5-year-olds restricted themselves to comments about physical features or activities, while 9-year-olds mentioned traits such as "I'm not quiet," "I have different thoughts." Likewise, in Guardo and Bohan's (1971) study of self-identity in 6- to 9-year-olds, 6-year-olds recognized themselves as distinct individuals in terms of behavior and appearance, whereas 9-year-olds realized that their identity rested on feelings and attitudes as well.

In line with Baldwin's claim that the sense of self develops in close interdependence with the sense of other, Livesley and Bromley (1973) discovered similar developmental changes in studies where children were asked to describe specific others whom they either liked or disliked. Seven-year-olds tended to talk about other individuals in terms of their behavior, possessions, and physical appearance, rather than in terms of abstract psychological traits. Those psychological or evaluative terms that were used were extremely general (such as "he is very nice"). By 8, however, children began to mention differentiated traits and dispositions (instead of merely "nice," others are now said to be "considerate" or "helpful"). In spite of this progress, their statements still tended to be strung together in list-like fashion without conveying a coherent personality description ("He does silly things and is very stupid. He has brown hair and cruel eyes"). It was only after age 13 that young people attempted to integrate the available information, even when it appeared contradictory on the surface, into coherent descriptions reflecting an individual's uniqueness: "She is always very sensible and willing to help people. Sometimes she gets a bit cross but that doesn't last long and soon she is her normal self. . . ." (p. 222).

Damon's (1977) study of friendship also documented a developmental progression from action-based to trait-based descriptions. In interviews, children up to about 7 tended to characterize best friends in terms of behavior or very simple traits: "Someone who plays with me" or as "someone who gives me toys," "someone who is nice (or fun)." Children over 7, on the other hand, incorporated more abstract concepts, such as helping and trusting one another, as well as favorable personality traits, into their statements about best friends. Finally, adolescents described best friends as individuals who understand one another, who share their innermost thoughts and feelings and secrets, and who help one another with psychological problems (see also Selman, 1980). Finally, Rosenberg (1979) discovered that the trait labels used by preadolescents tend to focus on character traits (honest, brave) or temperament (lose my temper). By mid-adolescence, individuals incorporate interpersonal traits (friendly, shy) into their descriptions. Eighteen-year-olds, on the other hand, describe an inner world of attitudes, emotions, wishes, and secrets.

As children's descriptions of self and other become more mentalistic, they also demonstrate a growing ability to integrate seemingly incompatible trait descriptions, irrespective of whether they are requested to talk about themselves or another individual. Harter (1982) reports, for example, that preschoolers did not understand that a person could have two contradictory traits at the same time, that is, be smart in some respects and dumb in others. Livesley and Bromley (1973) recognized the same tendency for one-sided descriptions in 7-year-olds. The self as well as others were either all good or all bad. By 8, however, children mentioned opposing traits, but merely juxtaposed them without integration ("sometimes he is good, and sometimes he is bad"). Only adolescents wove contradictory information into one coherent picture ("she is very reserved, but once you get to know her she is exactly the opposite"). Selman (1980) and Hand (1981; see also Harter, 1983) corroborate Harter's findings. According to Hand, young children could not comprehend that the same person can be both nice and mean, but adolescents were able to create a plausible integration of both traits.

In summary, the interview studies do suggest that, with respect to information that is directly accessible to conscious recall *out of context,* working models of self and other develop from very simple structures during the preschool period into considerably more complex, multilayered, differentiated, multiply connected hierarchies at adolescence. Hence working models of self and others should become more difficult to reorganize and reconstruct after adolescence, an issue that needs to be resolved by research (Bowlby, 1973; see also Sroufe, in press).

Although these findings indicate a growing differentiation and hierarchical integration in working models of self, they consistently suggest that young children use only concrete behavioral categories in representations of self and others. As I will show in the following section, children who are observed in everyday settings, or who are asked to reflect on simple interpersonal situations (as opposed to describing personalities or solving dilemmas) show a considerably more sophisticated level in understanding their own and others' thoughts and feelings, even at an early age.

Understanding Self and Other (Developing a Theory of Mind)

It has become a truism that the human infant is prepared from birth to engage in social interaction with a caregiver. It is only more recently, however, that investigators have returned to Baldwin's interest in the infant's *inner experience* of self and other. A host of studies in infant perception, social cognition and language acquisition now permit us to develop empirically grounded working hypotheses about the young infant's psychological understanding (Stern, 1985). These are complementary to the research on event representation which has tended to focus more on action sequences than on mental processes, even though intentionality, desires, foresight, and goal-directedness are now seen as playing an important role how humans understand events.

It turns out that, given the right conditions, children understand mental processes in self and other much earlier than the work on self- and other-descriptions would suggest. Stern's (1985) extensive review of recent research has led him to advance a theory about the development of the sense of self and of interpersonal relatedness that begins at birth. He cites empirical findings that support the view that even newborn infants can begin to extract self-invariance and other-invariance from the stream of experience, invalidating the traditional notion (e.g., Mahler, Pine, & Bergman, 1975; Piaget, 1952) that there is ever a period during postnatal life when self and external world are completely confused. I will not review Stern's careful account of infants' sense of *core self, core other,* and *core relatedness* during the early months (see also Emde, 1983). Instead, I will concentrate on the latter part of the first year when psychological understanding of self and other seems to take a giant leap.

Interfacing of Minds (Preverbal Stage, 9–14 Months). The acquisition of object permanence (Piaget, 1954) indexes a transition from exclusive reliance on sensorimotor interaction schemata (Stern's RIGs) to representational schemata or working models. At the same time (around 9 months) evidence suggests that infants realize, at some rudimentary level, that inner experiences, attention, intentions, and affective states can be shared with another person (e.g., Bretherton, MacNew, & Beegly–Smith, 1981; Feinman, 1982; Klinnert, Campos, Sorce, Emde, & Sveijda, 1983; Trevarthen & Hubley, 1979). Representational working models, in other words, have a psychological component from the beginning.

For example, 9-month-olds reliably and easily follow their mothers' line of regard (Scaife & Bruner, 1975). Prior to 9 months such shared reference is only sporadically observed. Also at around 9 months, infants begin to follow mother's pointing gestures, an ability that becomes more sophisticated in the ensuing months (Murphy & Messer, 1977). A related change occurs in the function of emotion signaling. From 6 to 9 months infants respond to an adult's negative facial-vocal displays with frowning, crying, or sobering that looks like emotional resonance (Charlesworth & Kreutzer, 1973). After about 9 months, however, infants seem to understand that a partner's emotional expressions can convey information about a third event. A 10-month-old is therefore much less likely to approach a remote-controlled robot if the mother frowns when the the infant looks up to reference her face than if she smiles (see Campos & Stenberg, 1981;

Feinman, 1982). This newfound ability to understand communications about a joint topic has also been observed in studies of mother–infant play. Nine-month-olds, but not younger infants, are able to understand some simple maternal instructions. When mother demonstrates how a peg is to be inserted into a bottle by repeatedly lifting it in and out of the bottle's mouth, the infant rather than copying this motion literally tries to drop the peg into the bottle (Trevarthen & Hubley, 1979). During the same period of development, Bates, Camaioni, and Volterra (1975) observed the infant's active attempts to set up joint interaction through intentional communication (see also Bates, Benigni, Bretherton, Camaioni, & Volterra, 1979). In 9 to 12 months such intent is inferred from a variety of behaviors, such as looking back and forth from a pointed-at object to a person (as if making sure that the partner is attending to the signal), substitution of one gesture for another if the first gesture does not work (known as repair of failed messages), and ritualization of previously instrumental gestures (using a noninstrumental brushing-aside motion to indicate an object is not wanted). Along similar lines, Ross and Kay (1980) found that, in turn-taking games with an unfamiliar adult companion, 12-month-olds resorted to a variety of strategies for reviving reciprocal games. In the Ross and Kay paradigm the adult "stopped playing the game" for 10 seconds after smooth turn-taking had been established. Infants responded to this interruption by looking back and forth from adult to toy, by partially or fully retaking their own turn and then waiting, or by holding up their hands to invite a turn from the adult (in object exchange games). These signals occurred almost exclusively during game interruptions. The infants also watched the adult playmate's face more during interruptions, whereas they looked more at her hands and at game-related objects during the normal phases of the game. Inspection of the data provided by Ross (1980) revealed that all infants had several strategies at their disposal. In view of the variety of behaviors infants used to reinstitute interrupted games it makes sense to assume that they expected the partner to understand their signals.

In sum, infants' affective, vocal, and gestural communications seem intended to attract and direct the addressee's attention to topics of mutual interest. At the same time infants begin to understand others' communications to them as messages. Bretherton and Bates (1979) suggest that the most parsimonious explanation for these phenomena is to assume that, by the end of the first year, infants have acquired a rudimentary "theory of mind" or ability to impute mental states to self and other (see Premack & Woodruff, 1978) and further, that they implicitly understand that one mind can be interfaced with another through conventional or mutually comprehensible signals.

The phenomenon of maternal affect attunement which emerges concurrently with intentional intersubjectivity is interpreted by Stern (1985) as the caregiver's response to these changes in the baby's psychological understanding. Prior to 9 months, mothers tend to imitate their babies' behavior literally. After 9 months, mothers match the affective information carried in the temporal beat, the intensity contours, the duration and/or spatial shape of the baby's behavior, but they often do so in a different modality than the infant. For example, a mother may attune to her baby's fast, energetic, joyful, up-and-down arm-movements by recreating the same affect through fast, undulating, energetic, and joyful vocalizations (see Stern, 1985, for further details). Stern suggests that such cross-modal reverberations focus the infant's attention on psychological as opposed to behavioral sharing. Individual differences in affect attunement are important factors in the development individual differences in the working model of self. Some mothers consistently "underattune" or "overattune" to certain infant behaviors, falling short of or exaggerating the infant's affect in their attunement to it. If done consistently, this may undermine the infant's ability to pay attention to his or her own inner states. Indeed, overattunement (exaggerated "overdone" attunement to infant behavior) can, as Stern sees it, become a form of emotional theft, where mother is modeling for the infant how and how intensely he or she *ought* to feel, as opposed to affirming how the infant *does* feel. In contrast, maternal failure to attune to particular states at all may mean that these states will remain isolated from the interpersonal context and will be experienced as something that cannot be shared. For Stern, maternal attunement thus plays an important role in the infant's developing ability to engage in open emotional communication, and while his remarks are largely speculative, the Grossmanns' findings on parent–infant communication in secure and insecure attachment relationships offer corroboration (Escher–Graeub & Grossmann, 1983; Grossmann & Grossmann, 1984; Grossmann, Grossmann, & Schwan, 1986). The overstimulating mothers described by Grossmann and Grossmann (1984) are, in Stern's terminology, engaged in overattunement while the mother's of insecure-avoidant infants described by Escher–Graueb and Grossmann seem to be engaging in nonattunement to stressful signals. Furthermore, Stern's arguments need not be restricted to affect attunement, but can easily be extrapolated to other forms of communication between mother and infant.

Interfacing Minds Through Language (The Early Verbal Stage). Although the intentional attention-getting and directing signals from the preverbal stage continue to play a crucial role in communication between parent and infant, the insertion of single words into gestural message structures can lead to more precision in the interfacing of minds (for a review, see Bretherton, 1988). Infants' capacity for intentional intersubjectivity becomes even more striking once they have acquired some object names and some relational words (i.e., all-gone, more, and uh-oh). Greenfield and Smith (1976) found that toddlers tended to use these two types of words differentially. If mother and child had already established a focus of joint attention, the children commented on the action component of the situation with a relational word. On the other hand, if a joint topic of attention had not yet been established, the infants labeled the object first (see also Scollon, 1979). This culminates around the middle of the second year in the ability to engage in simple conversations about absent objects and people in which one partner supplies the topic while the other comments on it (Bloom, 1973; Scollon, 1979).

In light of the level of psychological understanding implied in toddlers' management of communicative situations, it is perhaps not surprising that by 18 months some begin to label internal states in appropriate contexts. The earliest explicit references are to hunger, pain, disgust, ability, volition, and moral approval (Bretherton et al., 1981). This ability, along with the acquisition of the perspective-shifting pronouns (you and I), burgeons rapidly during the third year (Bretherton & Beeghly, 1982; Dunn, Bretherton, & Munn, 1987; Kagan, 1981). Concurrent developments are the capacity to express empathy toward distressed others (e.g., Zahn–Waxler, Radke–Yarrow, & King, 1979; for a review see Thompson, 1987), to use dolls as active partners in symbolic play (Bretherton, O'Connell, Shore, & Bates, 1984; Wolf, Rygh, & Altshuler, 1984), and to recognize the self in a mirror (Lewis & Brooks–Gunn, 1979). Bretherton and Beeghly (1982) have attributed this shift to a gradual transition from an implicit to a more explicit theory of mind. Although this transition makes more complex relations with others possible, the acquisition of verbal labels for inner experiences also has its dangers. Stern (1985) points out that some experiences of preverbal, sensorimotor relatedness cannot easily be recreated on the verbal level. What is more, some parents may offer a verbal child "sanitized" explanations of events that are completely at variance with the child's own interpretation of the experience (Bowlby, 1973), resulting in intrapsychic contradictions between verbal working models that are accessible to conscious reflection and nonverbal working models that may become defensively excluded from awareness.

Interfacing Minds Through Language (Transition to Early Childhood). The proposition that children in the second year begin to entertain a more explicit theory of mind was initially based on findings obtained through mothers who were trained to record their children's utterances about internal states in everyday contexts (Bretherton & Beeghly, 1982; Ridgeway, Waters, & Kuczaj, 1985). These results were subsequently corroborated through direct observation of family conversations in the home (Dunn et al., 1987).

Bretherton and Beeghly (1982) found that, by 28 months, a majority of their sample of 30 children used a fairly rich vocabulary to discuss internal states. Almost all talked about perceptions, sensations, physiological states, and volition/ability, and about two thirds of the sample labeled at least some emotions. Only a few children used terms referring to moral judgment (except for the ubiquitous good/bad distinction) and utterances about cognitive processes were even rarer, although these become more common after 30 months (Shatz, Wellman, & Silber, 1983). There was a tendency for the 28-month-olds to attribute internal states to themselves before they imputed them to others, but the lag was very slight. In addition, many of the children were able to converse about past or anticipated states experienced by self and other.

Perhaps most intriguing in terms of internal working models was the finding that toddlers made many causal statements about internal states. The word "causal" in this context does not mean that the utterances invariably contained causal connectives like "so," "because," or "if," but that they referred to internal states in causally related sequences ("Grandma mad [because] I wrote on wall"). Hood and Bloom (1979) provide detailed justification for interpreting such utterances as causal. Three types of causal statements about internal states occurred in the Bretherton and Beeghly (1982) data: (1) Utterances about the events or actions that precede or cause a particular state, (2) Utterances about negative states as motivators or causes of subsequent behavior and (3) Utterances explaining an emotion in terms of a related mental state or in terms of behavioral/expressive correlates (e.g., "Katie not happy face, Katie sad"). The underlying causal notion in the latter type of utterance is the logical inference "Katie looks unhappy. This makes me think she must be sad." Data from a project by Radke–Yarrow and Zahn–Waxler (1973) corroborate and extend the earlier findings (see Bretherton, Fritz, Zahn–Waxler, & Ridgeway, 1986, for a review). Finally there is evidence that 2- to 3-year-olds are able to impute emotions and intentions to themselves, dolls and playmates in make-believe play, as well as to manipulate parents' and siblings' feeling states (Dunn et al., 1986; Wolf, Rygh, & Altshuler, 1984; reviewed in Bretherton et al, 1986).

Although some investigators (e.g., Shatz, 1983) have questioned the advisability of using the term "theory of mind" to describe toddler's talk about internal states, Wellman (1988) concurs that such a case can be made for 2½-year-olds. Not satisfied with Premack and Woodruff's (1978) simpler definition, Wellman proposed that three criteria must be met in order to grant that an individual has an explicit theory of mind. First, the individual must have basic constructs or categories for defining reality. Second, these basic constructs or categories must be organized into a coherent system of interrelationships, and third, the individual must have developed a causal-attributional framework of human behavior. Do young children have a theory of mind in this sense?

At least some of the 28-months-olds in the Bretherton and Beeghly (1982) study meet Wellman's criteria. For example, a few of the children explicitly distinguished real from nonreal ("Is that monster real?"; "It's only pretend"), or defined one mental state in terms of another (looking unhappy = sadness), and many talked about causes and consequences of emotions (sad, happy, scared, mad) and of physiological states (e.g., hunger, thirst, and disgust). Furthermore, in a study of mental verb acquisition, Shatz et al., (1983) were able to show that utterances distinguishing between reality and internal states become quite frequent during the second half of the third year.

Understanding Mind: The Preschool Years and Beyond. More formal questioning techniques can be attempted by the time children reach 3, yielding even more persuasive data. Wellman (1988) found that 3-year-olds could explicitly distinguish between concrete objects and thought objects. They explained that a real cookie could be touched, whereas a thought-cookie could not (or could only be touched with "with my dream-hands"). When asked about absent objects as opposed to "pictures in your head" (Estes, Wellman, & Wooley, 1988), children aged 3, 4 and 5, gave different reasons for not being able to touch a real, absent object ("because it's not there") as contrasted with a thought-object ("it's not real"). These findings demonstrate that young children have categories for distinguishing mental from nonmental phenomena, thus satisfying Wellman's first criterion for a theory of mind. In addition, Wellman's 3-year-olds defined mental states by recourse to other mental states ("It's like dreaming"; "People can't see my imagination"), satisfying his second criterion. With respect to the third criterion, a causal explanatory framework, Wellman directs our attention to social cognitive studies of emotional understanding (see Bretherton et al., 1986 for a review). For example, Trabasso, Stein, and Johnson (1981) have shown that children as young as 3 can produce plausible causes and consequences for a variety of positive and negative emotions (see also Farber & Moely, 1979). Studies of intentionality (Shultz, 1980) have extended our knowledge of psychological causality beyond the emotional realm. For example, Schultz found that 3-year-olds are quite expert at distinguishing deliberate acts from mistakes, reflexes, and passive movements. What is more, these children seemed to think of intentions as causes of behavior. Based on this and similar evidence, Wellman (1988) reasons that 3-year-olds seem to be engaged in the same interpretive enterprise as older children and adults in the sense that they do not seem to hold a stimulus response or mechanistic theory of human behavior. On the other hand, 3-year-olds' theory of mind is more limited than that of older children or adults in a number of important respects.

Further progress in children's psychological understanding is dependent on changes in their conception of mind (Chandler & Boyes, 1982; Wellman, 1988). The younger child seems to have a theory of mind as a container that holds information. However, by 4 much of children's reasoning about cognitions and feelings is more consonant with an implicit theory of mind as processor that construes and interprets information (Perner, 1988). The differences between 3-year-olds' and 4- to 5-year-olds' conceptions of mind are clearly evident in their responses to false belief tasks. Four-year-olds who have been allowed to glance inside a matchbox filled with candy will correctly predict that another child, not initiated into the secret, would wrongly guess that the matchbox contained matches. Most 3-year-olds, by contrast, are incapable of imputing such false beliefs. They say that the other child will guess correctly. Along similar lines, 4- to 5-year-olds can impute knowledge to others that they do not themselves possess. When they watch a child look into a cardboard box whose contents they themselves are not permitted to see, they correctly impute knowledge to the other child (Wimmer, Hofgrefe, & Perner, in press). This is not the case for 3-year-olds. In other words, only the older preschoolers are able to grasp that their truth is not necessarily another child's truth. In addition, only 4- to 5-year-olds are able to discuss changes in their representations (what they used to think, and what they now think; Gopnik & Astington, 1988) and can give explicit explanations of the appearance-reality distinction. A sponge painted to simulate a rock is now described as "really and truly a sponge" that "looks like a rock to my eyes" (Flavell, Flavell, & Green, 1983). Three-year-olds cannot make this double description. In the domain of emotional understanding parallel changes occur (see Bretherton et al., 1986, for a review). Four- to 5-year-olds understand that two children who receive the same gift can feel differently about it (Gove & Keating, 1979). They are also able to reconcile two conflicting emotional cues, such as a child's unhappy expression during a birthday party (Gnepp, 1983).

Perner (1988) took over the concept of mental models proposed by Johnson–Laird (1983, following Craik, 1943) to explain these developments. Young infants, he suggested, have mental models but cannot yet manipulate them out of context. This is the level of *presentation.* Toddlers, by contrast, can rearrange components of mental models (elements and relations holding between them) to create alternative realities as in pretense, or to predict the future as in anticipation. They have reached the level of *representation.* Perner draws attention to the fact that, at this level toddlers must be able to do something analogous to copying models and parts of models stored in long-term memory into a working space where they can be manipulated on a trial basis without permanently altering the representational system itself (see Hendrix, 1979, cited in Johnson–Laird, 1983; see also Leslie, 1987, for similar ideas). By about 4 an additional ability, *metarepresentation,* comes into play. Older preschoolers do not just manipulate alternative models of events, they construct mental models of belief states *about* events, that is, they manipulate mental models of mental models.

After about 7 years of age, the capacity for metarepresentation (i.e., complex forms of conceptual perspective taking) develops further. Children are now able to think not only about what others believe or think, but what others may be thinking about them (Miller, Kessel, & Flavell, 1970). This requires an ability to create and manipulate a mental model of two individuals' belief states about each other. This capacity to construct mental models of mental models also seems to underlie children's insight into other's deceptive intentions in hiding-guessing games (Shultz, 1980), their ability to understand second-order false beliefs (Perner & Wimmer, 1985) and the realization that others as well as the self can be deliberately fooled about what the self feels (Selman, 1981). The same holds for 7- to 9-year-olds' understanding that negative feelings can spill over into subsequent interactions with blameless individuals (Harris, Olthof, & Terwogt, 1981; see also Harris, 1983), and that similar outcomes (success or failure) will be evaluated quite differently, depending on the psychological causes assigned to them (Weiner, Graham, Stern & Larson, 1982).

Individual Differences in Working Models of Self in Light of Social Cognitive Development

The developmental progression in the differentiation and integration of the self reported in the literature on the development of psychological understanding is congruent with what attachment researchers (e.g., Main, 1985) have discovered about *secure* individuals at corresponding developmental stages. Is is also consonant with the communication perspective on attachment pursued by Bretherton (1987), as well as Grossmann and Grossmann (in press). In secure relationships, signals are mutually acknowledged, allowing for an open flow of emotional information between the partners. As long as this continues, internal working models of self and other in relationship can develop more adequately because they are more easily updated. At the same time, they become more hierarchically organized and mentalistic as reported in the studies on self-description.

Whereas there is congruency between research on the development of social-cognitive or psychological understanding and attachment theorists' descriptions of internal working models of self in secure attachment relationships, attachment research has, so far, not directly profited from the new insights, nor have social cognitive studies been influenced by attachment theory; that is, social cognitive researchers have not looked at the functional implications of their findings on self-awareness and self-identity. For the most part, they have been content to show *what changes with development*. Nevertheless, it does not take a giant conceptual leap to see that new levels of psychological understanding (i.e., more complex working models of self and other) have functional implications for the way relationships are conducted. Attachment researchers and others interested in internal working models of self need now to employ these tools explicitly instead of relying on intuitive knowledge of children's social understanding in assessing working models of self as related to actual relationships.

The literature on social cognitive development is much less helpful when it comes to conceptualizing internal working models of self in *insecure* attachment relationships. Empirical findings suggest that infants whose signals are consistently ignored or misunderstood do not simply construct an increasingly complex and integrated working model of self and other in a mutually unsatisfying relationship. Two processes seem to prevent this. First, there is reason to believe that the caregiver in such a relationship does not provide sufficient meaningful feedback to the child's signals (possibly on the basis of his or her own inadequate working models). Second, defensive processes prevent the child from adequately representing parental insensitivity (it is too painful). According to this line of reasoning, internal working models of self in insecure attachments (and by inference other nonsatisfying family relationships) are not only less coherently organized from the beginning, but are also less likely to become well integrated *even as metarepresentational processes emerge* in development. Because new information is always processed in terms of already existing schemata, it is a much more difficult feat to revise and update inadequate working models of the self than it is to revise well-organized, adequate models. Moreover, if the arguments just presented are correct, reconstruction of working models cannot be achieved by "lifting repressions" or removing barriers which allow well-encoded, but hitherto inaccessible, information to come into conscious awareness. Something much more akin to complete reorganization and reinterpretation will be necessary. But is this possible?

Research on the intergenerational transmission of attachment patterns by Main et al. (1985), Morris (1980), and Ricks (1985) has shown that some adults with very painful childhood experiences have secure-autonomous working models of self with respect to attachment. These adults have children that are securely attached to them (and by inference are developing well-organized working models of self). Let us assume, in line with theory, that these adults grew up with ill-organized working models of self. If true, then the studies by Main, Morris, and Ricks can be taken as evidence that reconstruction of inadequate working models of self is possible.

Furthermore, changes in quality of attachment, and by inference in internal working models of self and caregiver, have also been documented during earlier and later childhood. All short-term longitudinal studies of attachment during the period from 12 months to 6 years have found that, over time, some secure relationships became insecure and vice versa, with the proportion of changed attachments small when family circumstances remain fairly constant (Main & Weston, 1981; Main et al., 1985; Wartner & Grossmann, 1987; Waters, 1978) and greater when family life is disrupted by stressful events (Thompson, Lamb, & Estes, 1982; Vaughn, Egeland, Sroufe, & Waters, 1979). More specifically, positive changes have been noted in cases where a mother who has had little social support acquires a stable partner (Sroufe, 1988).

What is still lacking, however, is an explanation of the processes that mediate positive changes in relationship quality and in internal working models of self (see also Waters, this volume). Because subjects in longitudinal studies are not normally seen often enough, investigators can only resort to intelligent guesswork in their attempts to explain observed changes in internal working models. Clinicians, on the other hand, have made it their business to understand the processes that bring about change in their patients' internal world. Admittedly, clinical data are generally not sufficiently systematic to qualify as empirical studies. Nevertheless, some of the insights derived from clinical work may be helpful in designing studies that will allow us to understand how working models of self are reconstructed.

Different schools of therapy use their own terminology, but an overall consensus has developed (Gustafson, 1986). A trusting empathic relationship with a therapist who respects the patient is the first prerequisite for risking the reconstruction of internal working models. In the language of attachment theory, an empathic therapist provides the secure base from which the patient can explore his or her internal world, and thus go on to create revisions of old working models of self (Bowlby, 1985). Where theorists of therapeutic change differ is in their view of how actively the therapist should intervene in order to help the patient accomplish this goal. Some (e.g., Bowlby, 1985) recommend that the therapist's stance be primarily supportive and responsive, others (e.g., Sullivan, 1953) advocate that the analyst challenge the patient's maladaptive interpersonal patterns somewhat more directly.

It is of course not only in therapeutic situations that an individual may encounter a partner's empathic understanding (sensitive responsiveness), coupled with exploration of and cognitive or experiential challenge to his or her working models of self. Such processes can and do occur spontaneously in close friendships or marital relationships, especially during normal psychosocial transitions (courtship, transition to parenthood) or stressful life events. They may even occur in ongoing attachment relationships between parent and child, if a highly stressed parent begins to receive more adequate social support. Whether severely inadequate, rigid and outdated working models of attachment figures and self can be restructured *only* within a close trusting relationship, as the clinical evidence would suggest, is an important topic for future research.

We also need developmental studies of defensive processes in children. A major contribution of attachment theory to the future study of the self could derive from the hypothesis that insecure relationship patterns are associated with ill-organized working models of self. Much remains to be discovered about selective (Bowlby, 1980) and biased (Erdelyi, 1985) processing.

EGO AND INTERNAL WORKING MODELS: CONCLUDING REMARKS

Until now I have refrained from considering the interdependence between the *I* as knower and the *Me* as representation or working model of the self (James, 1890). James was not the only theorist to differentiate between these two aspects of the self. Mead's writings also addressed the topic (1934). In addition, a number of psychoanalytical theorists have made a comparable distinction between the executive ego and self-representations (e.g., Hartmann, 1958; Jacobson, 1964), but none have treated this issue extensively. The dual nature of the self was not fully addressed by Sullivan, Winnicott, Stern, and Bowlby or by investigators of social cognitive development.

Recent ideas presented by Johnson–Laird (1983) have persuaded me that the relationship between the *I* as executive or operating system and the *Me* as representation or internal working model of self deserves both further thought and further study. Johnson–Laird suggests that consciousness is the experience we have of our own executive system. He assumes that our executive or operating system (the *I*) is a serial processor, capable of monitoring and processing input from from a large number of lower-level processors, but only in sequential fashion. The lower-level processors, by contrast, are presumed to operate in parallel. The operating system has access to the output of these parallel systems, but not to their inner workings. Similarly, the operating system gives only general, high-level commands to the lower-level processors which are then responsible for translating them into specific actions. Commands to pursue a specific goal, for example, are passed to the lower-level processors in the form of higher-order instructions. It is the lower-level processors that convert the high-level commands into instructions for specific movement patterns.

The executive system or *I*, then, is more than a knower. It can more properly be understood as a metasystem that sets priorities among inputs from various lower-level processors which may at times send it conflicting commands. An especially interesting aspect of the operating system (or *I*) as envisaged by Johnson–Laird is that it does not have complete control over the lower-level processors which are hypothesized to retain some autonomy. The notion of relative willpower, says Johnson–Laird, derives from the degree to which the operating system (or *I*) can enforce its decisions. Under certain circumstances, executive plans may be interrupted or disrupted by motivational systems that regulate survival-promoting behavior (such as escape behavior, aggressive behavior or attachment behavior). If this were not so, individuals might fail to attend and respond to emergency signals from these systems. An ability by lower-level systems to override the operating system can hence serve an adaptive function. Maladaptive behavior may result, however, when the operating system is either completely overwhelmed by lower-level processors (undercontrol) or when it overcontrols lower-level systems concerned with survival functions. In both cases incoming information will not be optimally processed.

How is the optimal development of the executive *I* related to the development of a well-integrated *Me?* In the course of processing information from the external world and deciding on desirable courses of action, the executive system constantly consults internal working models of the world and especially of the self. If these working models are inadequate (distorted) or if parts of working models are dissociated from one another (as postulated by Bowlby, 1973) the *I* cannot properly do its work of forecasting, interpreting and guiding action. This line of reasoning suggests that, in addition to studying working models, we would do well to examine the interrelation between *I* and *Me* in secure and insecure relationships.

Extrapolating from attachment theory and research, it appears that the development of a coherent, well-organized *Me* (as described in the social cognitive literature) must always be understood in terms of the concurrent development of a coherent, integrated, well-functioning executive system. If an infant feels secure in attachment relationships, the *I* and *Me* will function well in relation to one another, but if the infant feels insecure the optimal integration of I and Me will be disturbed, a disturbance that will be difficult, but not impossible, to correct later.

The same argument holds for the hypothesized transmission of working models from parent to infant. It now appears that this process is more complex than I at first presented it. In infancy, when the executive operating system is still primitive and not well coordinated, and when internal working models exist only at a sensorimotor level, infants must rely on an auxiliary ego (Spitz, 1965) or external regulatory system in order to develop. The persons who fulfill the role of auxiliary ego are those to whom the baby is attached. For the developing organization of the baby's *I* and *Me,* it is therefore important how well the caregivers' *I* and *Me* are integrated.

To conclude with another version of the wine-making metaphor with which I began: If we build on the insights already available to gain a deeper understanding of the *interrelationship* of *I* and *Me* throughout *development,* we could indeed be said to have set off a new phase of ideational fermentation regarding the ever-developing concept of the social self.

REFERENCES

Ainsworth, M. D. S., & Bell, S. M. (1969). Some contemporary patterns in the feeding situation. In A. Ambrose (Ed.), *Stimulation in early infancy* (pp. 133–170). London: Academic Press.

Ainsworth, M. D. S., Bell, S. M., & Stayton, D. (1974). Infant–mother attachment and social development. In M. P. Richards (Ed.), *The introduction of the child into a social world* (pp. 99–135). London: Cambridge University Press.

Baldwin, J. M. (1895). *Mental development of the child and the race: Methods and processes.* New York: Macmillan.

Baldwin, J. M. (1906). *Social and ethical interpretations in mental development* (4th ed.). London: Macmillan.

Baldwin, J. M. (1911). *The individual and society.* Boston: Goreham.

Bannister, D., & Agnew, J. (1977). The child's construing of self. In J. Cole (Ed.), *Nebraska Symposium on Motivation* (pp. 99–125). Lincoln, NE: University of Nebraska Press.

Bartlett, F. C. (1933). *Remembering: A study in experimental and social psychology.* London: Cambridge University Press.

Bates, E., Benigni, L., Bretherton, I., Camaioni, L., & Volterra, V. (1979). *The emergence of symbols.* New York: Academic Press.

Bates, E., Camaioni, L., & Volterra, V. (1975). The acquisition of performatives prior to speech. *Merrill–Palmer Quarterly, 21,* 205–226.

Blehar, M. C., Lieberman, A. F., & Ainsworth, M. D. S. (1977). Early face-to-face interaction and its relation to later infant–mother attachment. *Child Development, 48,* 182–194.

Bloom, L. (1973). *One word at a time.* The Hague: Mouton.

Bowlby, J. (1969). *Attachment and loss. Vol. 1: Attachment.* New York: Basic Books (2nd rev. ed., 1982).

Bowlby, J. (1973). *Attachment and loss. Vol. 2: Separation.* New York: Basic Books.

Bowlby, J. (1980). *Attachment and loss, Vol. 3: Loss, sadness and depression.* New York: Basic Books.

Bowlby, J. (1985). The role of childhood experience in cognitive disturbance. In M. J. Mahoney & A. Freeman (Eds.), *Cognition and psychotherapy* (pp. 181–200). New York: Plenum Press.

Bretherton, I. (1984). Representing the social world in symbolic play: Reality and fantasy. In Bretherton I. (Ed.), *Symbolic play: the development of social understanding* (pp. 3–41). New York: Academic Press.

Bretherton, I. (1985). Attachment theory: Retrospect and prospect. In I. Bretherton & E. Waters (Eds.), Growing points of attachment theory and research. *Monographs of the Society for Research in Child Development, 50*(Serial No. 209, 1–2), 3–35.

Bretherton, I. (1987). New perspectives on attachment relations: Security, communication, and internal working models. In J. Osofsky (Ed.), *Handbook of infant development* (pp. 1061–1100). New York: Wiley.

Bretherton, I. (1988). How to do things with one word: The ontogenesis of intentional message making in infancy. In M. Smith & J. Lock (Eds.), *The emergent lexicon* (pp. 225–260). New York: Academic Press.

Bretherton, I. (in press). Open communication and internal working models: Their role in the development of attachment relationships. In R. A. Thompson (Ed.), *Nebraska symposium on motivation: Socio-emotional development.* Lincoln, NE: University of Nebraska Press.

Bretherton, I., & Bates, E. (1979). The emergence of intentional communication. In I. Uzgiris (Ed.), *New Directions for Child Development, 4,* 81–100.

Bretherton, I., & Beeghly, M. (1982). Talking about internal states: The acquisition of an explicit theory of mind. *Developmental Psychology, 18,* 906–921.

Bretherton, I., Biringen, Z., Ridgeway, D, Maslin, C., & Sherman, M. (1989), Attachment: The parental perspective. *Infant Mental Health Journal, 10,* 203–221.

Bretherton, I., Fritz, J., Zahn–Waxler, C., & Ridgeway, D. (1986). Learning to talk about emotion: A functionalist perspective. *Child Development, 57,* 529–548.

Bretherton, I., McNew, S., & Beeghly–Smith, M. (1981). Early person knowledge as expressed in verbal and gestural communication: When do infants acquire a "theory of mind"? In M. E. Lamb & L. R. Sherrod (Eds.), *Infant social cognition* (pp. 333–373). Hillsdale, NJ: Lawrence Erlbaum Associates.

Bretherton, I., O'Connell, B., Shore, C., & Bates, E. (1984). The effect of contextual variation on symbolic play development from 20 to 28 months. In I. Bretherton (Ed.), *Symbolic play* (pp. 271–296). New York: Academic Press.

Bretherton, I., Ridgeway, D., & Cassidy, J. (in press). The role of internal working models in the attachment relationship as assessed in a story completion task for 3-year-olds. In M. Greenberg, D. Cicchetti, & E. M. Cummings (Eds.). *Attachment during the preschool years.* Chicago: University of Chicago Press.

Bronfenbrenner, U., Kessel, F., Kessen, W., & White, S. (1986). Toward a critical social history of developmental psychology: A propaedeutic discussion. *American Psychologist, 41,* 1218–1230.

Cain, A. C., & Fast, I. (1972). Children's disturbed reactions to parent suicide. In A. C. Cain (Ed.), *Survivors of suicide* (pp. 93–111). Springfield, IL: C. C. Thomas.

Campos, J. J., & Stenberg, C. R. (1981). Perception, appraisal and emotion: the onset of social referencing. In M. E. Lamb & L. R. Sherrod (Eds.), *Infant social cognition* (pp. 273–314). Hillsdale, NJ: Lawrence Erlbaum Associates.

Cassidy, J. (1988). The self as related to child–mother attachment at six. *Child Development, 59,* 121–134.

Chandler, M. J., & Boyes, (1982). Social cognitive development. In B. Wolman (Ed.), *Handbook of developmental psychology* (pp. 387–451). Englewood Cliffs, NJ: Prentice–Hall.

Charlesworth, W. R., & Kreutzer, M. A. (1973). An ethological approach to research on facial expressions. In P. Ekman (Ed.), *Darwin and facial expressions* (pp. 317–334). New York: Academic Press.

Cooley, C. H. (1902). *Human nature and the social order.* New York: Scribner's.

Craik, K. (1943). *The nature of explanation.* Cambridge, England: Cambridge University Press.

Damon, W. (1977). *The social world of the child.* San Francisco: Jossey–Bass.

Dunn, J., Bretherton, I., & Munn, P. (1987). Conversations about feeling states between mothers and their young children. *Developmental Psychology, 23,* 132–139.

Eichberg, D. (1987, April). *Quality of infant–parent attachment: Related to mother's representation of her own relationship history.* Paper presented in the symposium on Working Models of Attachment in Adolescence and Adulthood (M. Main, chair) at a meeting of the Society for Research in Child Development, Baltimore.

Emde, R. N. (1983). The pre-representational self and its affective core. *Psychoanalytic Study of the Child, 38,* 165–192.

Epstein, S. (1973). The self-concept revisited or a theory of a theory. *American Psychologist, 28,* 404–416.

Epstein, S. (1980). A review and the proposal of an integrated theory of personality. In E. Staub (Ed.), *Personality: Basic aspects and current research* (pp. 82–131). Englewood Cliffs, NJ: Prentice–Hall.

Erdelyi, H. M. (1985). *Psychoanalysis: Freud's cognitive psychology.* San Francisco: W. H. Freeman.

Escher–Graeub, D., & Grossmann, K. E. (1983). *Bindungssicherheit im zweiten Lebensjahr-die Regensburger Querschnittuntersuchung* [attachment security in the second year of life: the Regensburg cross-sectional study]. Research Report, University of Regensburg.

Estes, D., Wellman, H. M., & Wooley, J. D. (1988). Children's understanding of mental phenomena. In H. Reese (Ed.), *Advances in child development and behavior.* New York: Academic Press.

Fairbairn, W. R. D. (1952). *Psychoanalytic studies of the personality.* London: Tavistock.

Farber, E. A., & Moely, B. F. (1979, March). *Inferring others' affective states: The use of interpersonal, vocal and facial cues by children of three age levels.* Paper presented at a meeting of the Society for Research in Child Development, San Francisco.

Feinman, S. (1982). Social referencing in infancy. *Merrill–Palmer Quarterly, 28,* 445–470.

Fivush, R. (1984). Learning about school: The development of kindergartners' school scripts. *Child Development, 55,* 1697–1709.

Fivush, R., & Slackman, E. (1986). The acquisition and development of scripts. In K. Nelson, *Event knowledge: Structure and function in development* (pp. 71–96). Hillsdale, NJ: Lawrence Erlbaum Associates.

Flavell, J., Flavell, E. R., & Green, F. L. (1983). Development of the appearance–reality distinction. *Cognitive Psychology, 15,* 95–120.

Gnepp, J. (1983). Children's social sensitivity: Inferring emotions from conflicting cues. *Developmental Psychology, 19,* 805–814.

Gopnik, A., & Astington, J. W. (1988). Children's understanding of representational change and its relation to the understanding of false belief and the appearance–reality distinction. *Child Development, 59,* 26–37.

Gove, F. L., & Keating, D. (1979). Empathic role-taking precursors. *Developmental Psychology, 15,* 594–600.

Greenberg, J. R., & Mitchell, S. A. (1982). *Object relations in psychoanalytic theory.* Cambridge, MA: Harvard University Press.

Greenfield, P. M., & Smith, J. H. (1976). *The structure of communication in early development.* New York: Academic Press.

Grossmann, K., Fremmer–Bombik, E., Rudolph, J., & Grossmann, K. E. (in press.) Maternal attachment representations as related to patterns of infant–mother attachment and maternal care during the first year. In R. A. Hinde & J. Stevenson–Hinde (Eds.), *Relationships within families.* Oxford, England: Oxford University Press.

Grossmann, K. E., & Grossmann, K. (in press). The wider concept of attachment in cross-cultural research. *Human Development.*

Grossmann, K. E., & Grossmann, K. (1984, September). *The development of conversational styles in the first year of life and its relationship to maternal sensitivity and attachment quality between mother and child.* Paper presented at the Congress of the German Society for Psychology, Vienna.

Grossmann, K. E., Grossmann, K., Huber, F., & Wartner, U. (1981). German children's behavior toward their mothers at 12 months and their fathers at 18 months in Ainsworth's Strange Situation. *International Journal of Behavioral Development, 4,* 157–181.

Grossmann, K. E., Grossmann, K., & Schwan, A. (1986). Capturing the wider view of attachment: A reanalysis of Ainsworth's Strange Situation. In C. E. Izard & P. B. Read (Eds.), *Measuring emotions in infants and children* (Vol. 2, pp. 124–171). New York: Cambridge University Press.

Guardo, C. J., & Bohan, J. B. (1971). Development of a sense of identity in children. *Child Development, 42,* 1909–1921.

Guidano, V. F., & Liotti, G. (1983). *Cognitive processes and emotional disorders.* New York: Guilford Press.

Guntrip, J. S. (1971). *Psychoanalytic theory, therapy, and the self.* New York: Basic Books.

Gustafson, J. P. (1986). *The complex secrets of brief psychotherapy.* New York: Norton.

Hand, H. (1981). *The development of concepts of social interaction: Children's understanding of nice and mean.* Unpublished doctoral dissertation, University of Denver.

Harris, P. L. (1983). Children's understanding of the link between situation and emotion. *Journal of Experimental Child Psychology, 36,* 490–509.

Harris, P. L., Olthof, T., & Terwogt, M. M. (1981). Children's knowledge of emotion. *Journal of Child Psychiatry and Psychology, 22,* 247–261.

Harter, S. (1982). Children's understanding of multiple emotions: A cognitive-developmental approach. In W. F. Overton (Ed.), *The relationship between cognitive and social development.* Hillsdale, NJ: Lawrence Erlbaum Associates.

Harter, S. (1983). Developmental perspectives on the self-system. In E. M. Hetherington (Ed.), *Handbook of child psychology, Vol. 4: Socialization, personality and social development* (pp. 275–385). New York: Wiley.

Hartmann, H. (1958). *Ego psychology and the problem of adaptation.* New York: International Universities Press.

Hendrix (1979). Encoding knowledge in partitioned networks. In N. V. Findler (Ed.), *Associative networks: Representation and use of knowledge by computers* (pp. 51–92). New York: Academic Press.

Hood, L., & Bloom, L. (1979). What, when, and how about why: A longitudinal study of early expressions in causality. *Monographs of the Society for Research in Child Development, 44,*(2), Serial No. 181.

Hudson, J., & Nelson, K. (1983). Effects of script structure on children's story recall. *Developmental Psychology, 19,* 625–635.

Izard, C. E. (1978). Emotions as motivations: An evolutionary-developmental perspective. In R. A. Dienstbier (Eds.), *Nebraska symposium on motivation* (pp. 163–200). Lincoln, NE: University of Nebraska Press.

Jacobson, E. (1964). *The self and the object world.* New York: International Universities Press.

James, W. (1890). *The principles of psychology* (Vol. 1). New York: Henry Holt.

Johnson–Laird, P. N. (1983). *Mental models.* Cambridge, MA: Harvard University Press.

Johnson–Laird, P. N., Legrenzi, P., & Legrenzi, M. S. (1972). Reasoning and a sense of reality. *British Journal of Psychology, 63,* 395–400.

Kelley, G. A. (1955). *The psychology of personal constructs.* New York: Norton.

Kernberg, O. (1976). *Object relations theory and clinical psychoanalysis.* New York: Aronson.

Klinnert, M. D., Campos, J. J., Sorce, J. F., Emde, R. N., & Svejda, M. (1983). Emotions as behavior regulators: social referencing in infancy. In R. Plutchik & H. Kellerman (Eds.), *The emotions, Vol. 2: Emotions in early development* (pp. 57–86). New York: Academic Press.

Kobak, R. R., & Sceery, A. (1988). Attachment in late adolescence: Working models, affect regulation, and perceptions of self and others. *Child Development, 59,* 135–146.

Kohut, O. (1982). Introspection, empathy, and the semi-circle of mental health. *International Journal of Psycho-Analysis, 63,* 395–407.

Lamb, M. E. (1977). Father-infant and mother–infant interaction in the first year of life. *Child Development, 48.*

Leslie, A. M. (1987). Pretense and representation: The origins of "theory of mind." *Psychological Review, 94,* 412–426.

Lewis, M., & Brooks–Gunn, J. (1979). *Social cognition and the acquisition of self.* New York: Plenum Press.

Livesley, W. J., & Bromley, D. B. (1973). *Person perception in childhood and adolescence.* London: Wiley.

Mahler, M. S., Pine, F., & Bergman, A. (1975). *The psychological birth of the human infant.* New York: Basic Books.

Main, M., & Goldwyn, R. (in press). Interview-based adult attachment classification: Related to mother-infant and father-infant attachment. *Developmental Psychology.*

Main, M., & Cassidy, J. (in press). Categories of responses to reunion with the parent at age 6: Predictable from infancy and stable over a one-month period. *Developmental Psychology.*

Main, M., & Hesse, E. (in press). The insecure disorganized/disoriented attachment pattern in infancy: Precursors & sequelae. In M. Greenberg, D. Cicchetti, and E. M. Cummings (Eds.), *Attachment during the preschool years: Theory, research, and intervention.* Chicago, University of Chicago Press.

Main, M., Kaplan, K., & Cassidy, J. (1985). Security in infancy, childhood and adulthood: A move to the level of representation. In I. Bretherton & E. Waters (Eds.), Growing points of attachment theory and research, *Monographs of the Society for Research in Child Development, 50,* Serial No. 209 (1–2), 66–104.

Main, M., & Weston, D. (1981). The quality of the toddler's relationship to mother and father: Related to conflict behavior and the readiness to establish new relationships. *Child Development, 52,* 834–840.

Mandler, G. (1986). *Cognitive psychology.* Hillsdale, NJ: Lawrence Erlbaum Associates.

Mandler, J. H. (1979). Categorical and schematic organization in memory. In C. R. Puff (Ed.), *Memory organization and structure* (pp. 259–299). New York: Academic Press.

Mandler, J. H. (1983). Representation. In J. H. Flavell & E. M. Markman (Eds.), *Handbook of child psychology, Vol. 3: cognitive development* (pp. 420–494). New York: Wiley.

Markus, H. (1977). Self-schemas and processing information about the self. *Journal of Personality and Social Psychology, 35,* 63–78.

Matas, L., Arend, R. A., & Sroufe, L. A. (1978). Continuity and adaptation in the second year: The relationship between quality of attachment and later competence. *Child Development, 49,* 547–556.

Mead, G. H. (1934). *Mind, self and society.* Chicago: University of Chicago Press.

Miller, P. H., Kessel, F. S., & Flavell, J. H. (1970). Thinking about people thinking about people thinking about . . . : A study of social cognitive development. *Child Development, 41,* 613–623.

Morris, D. (1980). *Infant attachment and problem solving in the toddler: relations to mother's family history.* Unpublished doctoral dissertation, University Of Minnesota.

Murphey, E. B., Silber, E., Coelho, G. V., Hamburg, D. A., & Greenberg, I. (1963). The development of autonomy and parent–child interaction in late adolescence. *American Journal of Orthopsychiatry, 33* 643–652.

Murphy, D. J., & Messer, D. J. (1977). Mothers and infants pointing: A study of gesture. In R. H. Schaffer (Ed.), *Studies in mother–infant interaction* (pp. 323–354). New York: Academic Press.

Nelson, K. (1986). *Event knowledge: Structure and function in development.* Hillsdale, NJ: Lawrence Erlbaum Associates.

Nelson, K., & Gruendel. J. (1981). Generalized event representations: Basic building blocks of cognitive development. In M. E. Lamb & A. Brown (Eds.), *Advances in developmental psychology* (Vol. 1, pp. 131–158). Hillsdale, NJ: Lawrence Erlbaum Associates.

Nelson, K., & Ross, G. (1982). The general and specifics of long-term memory in infants and young children. In M. Perlmutter (Ed.), *Naturalistic approaches to memory* (pp. 87–101). San Francisco: Jossey–Bass.

Offer, D. (1969). *The psychological world of the teenager: A study of normal adolescent boys.* New York: Basic Books.

Peck, R. F., & Havighurst, R. J. (1960). *The psychology of character development.* New York: Wiley.

Perner, J. (1988). Developing semantics for theories of mind: From propositional attitudes to mental representation. In J. W. Astington, P. L. Harris, & D. R. Olson (Eds.), *Developing theories of mind* (pp. 141–172). New York: Cambridge University Press.

Perner, J., & Wimmer, H. (1985). "John thinks that Mary thinks that . . . : Attribution of second-order beliefs by 5- to 10-year-old children. *Journal of Experimental and Child Psychology, 39,* 437–471.

Piaget, J. (1951). *The origin of intelligence in children.* New York: International Universities Press.

Piaget, J. (1954). *The construction of reality in the child.* New York: Basic Books.

Premack, D., & Woodruff, G. (1978). Does the chimpanzee have a "theory of mind"? *Brain and Behavioural Sciences, 1,* 515–526.

Price, D., & Goodman, G. S. (1985, April). *Preschool children's comprehension of a recurring episode.* Paper presented at a meeting of the Society for Research in Child Development, Toronto.

Radke–Yarrow, M., & Zahn–Waxler, C. (1973). *Developmental studies of altruism.* NIMH Protocol, Clinical Project No. 73–M–02, J00.111.

Ricks, M. H. (1985). The social transmission of parenting: Attachment across generations. In I. Bretherton & E. Waters (Eds.), Growing points of attachment theory and research, *Monographs of the Society for Research in Child Development, 50,* Serial No. 209 (1–2), 211–227.

Ridgeway, D., Waters, E., & Kuczaj, S. A. (1985). The acquisition of emotion descriptive language: receptive and productive vocabulary norms for 18 months to 6 years. *Developmental Psychology, 21,* 901–908.

Rohner, R. P. (1975). *They love me, they love me not.* New Haven, CT: Human Area Relations Files.

Rosenberg, M. (1979). *Conceiving the self.* New York: Basic Books.

Ross, H. S. (1980, April). *Infants' use of turn-alternation signals in games.* Paper presented at the International Conference on Infant Studies, New Haven, CT.

Ross, H. S., & Kay, D. A. (1980). The origins of social games. In K. Rubin (Ed.), *Children's play* (pp. 17–32). San Francisco: Jossey–Bass.

Rovee–Collier, C. K., & Fagan, C. W. (1981). The retrieval of memory in early infancy. In L. P. Lipsitt (Ed.), *Advances in infancy research.* (Vol. 1, pp. 225–254). Norwood, NJ: Ablex.

Rovee–Collier, C. K., & Lipsitt, L. P. (1981). Learning, adaptation, and memory. In P. M. Stratton (Ed.), *Psychobiology of the human newborn* (pp. 147–190). New York: Wiley.

Sagi, A., Lamb, M. E., Lewkowicz, K. S., Shoham, R., Dvir, R., & Estes, D. (1985). Security of infant–mother, –father, and –metapelet among kibbutz reared Israeli children. In I. Bretherton & E. Waters (Eds.), Growing points of attachment theory and research, *Monographs of the Society for Research in Child Development.* Serial No. 209 (1–2), 257–275.

Sandler, J., & Sandler, A. (1978). The development of object relationships and affects. *Journal of Psycho-Analysis, 59,* 285–296.

Scaife, M., & Bruner, J. S. (1975). The capacity for joint visual attention in the infant. *Nature, 253,* 265–266.

Schank, R. C. (1982). *Dynamic memory: A theory of reminding and learning in computers and people.* Cambridge, England: Cambridge University Press.

Schank, R. C., & Abelson, R. P. (1977). *Scripts, plans, goals and under standing*. Hillsdale, NJ: Lawrence Erlbaum Associates.

Scollon, R. (1979). An unzippered condensation of a dissertation on child language. In E. Ochs & B. B. Schieffelin (Eds.), *Developmental pragmatics* (pp. 215–227). New York: Academic Press.

Selman, R. L. (1981). What children understand of the intrapsychic processes. In E. K. Shapiro & E. Weber (Eds.), *Cognitive and affective growth* (pp. 187–215). Hillsdale, NJ: Lawrence Erlbaum Associates.

Selman, R. F. (1980). *The growth of interpersonal understanding*. New York: Academic Press.

Shatz, M. (1983). Communication. In J. H. Flavell & E. M. Markman (Eds.), *Handbook of child psychology. Vol. 3: Cognitive development* (pp. 841–889). New York: Wiley.

Shatz, M., Wellman, H. M., & Silber, S. (1983). The acquisition of mental verbs: A systematic investigation of the first reference to mental state. *Cognition, 14,* 301–321.

Shiffrin, R. M., & Schneider, W. (1977). Controlled and automatic human information processing: 2. Perceptual learning, automatic attending, and a general theory. *Psychological Review, 84,* 127–190.

Shore, C., O'Connell, B., & Bates, E. (1984). First sentences in language and symbolic play. *Developmental Psychology, 20,* 872–880.

Shultz, T. R. (1980). Development of the concept of intention. In W. A. Collins (Ed.), *Minnesota symposia on child psychology* (pp. 131–164). Hillsdale, NJ: Lawrence Erlbaum Associates.

Spitz, R. (1965). *The first year of life* New York: International Universities Press.

Sroufe, L. A. (in press). Relationships, self, and individual adaptation. In A. J. Sameroff & R. N. Emde (Eds.), *Relationshipships and disturbances in early childhood: A developmental approach.* New York: Basic Books.

Sroufe, L. A. (1988). The role of infant–caregiver attachment in development. In J. Belsky & T. Nezworksi (Eds.), *Clinical implications of attachment* (pp. 18–38). Hillsdale, NJ: Lawrence Erlbaum Associates.

Sroufe, L. A., & Wunsch, J. P. (1972). The development of laughter in the first year of life. *Child Development, 43,* 1326–1344.

Stern, D. N. (1985). *The interpersonal world of the infant*. New York: Basic Books.

Sullivan, H. S. (1953). *The interpersonal theory of psychiatry*. New York: Norton.

Thompson, R. A. (1987). Empathy and emotional understanding: the early development of empathy. In N. Eisenberg & J. Strayer (Eds.), *Empathy and its development*. Cambridge, England: Cambridge University Press.

Thompson, R. A., Lamb, M. E., & Estes, D. (1982). Stability of infant–mother attachment and its relationship to changing life circumstances in an unselected middle-class sample. *Child Development, 53,* 144–148.

Trabasso, T., Stein, N. L., & Johnson, L. R. (1981). Children's knowledge of events: A causal analysis of knowledge structure. *The psychology of learning and motivation* (Vol. 15, pp. 237–282). New York: Academic Press.

Trevarthen, C., & Hubley, P. (1979). Secondary intersubjectivity: Confidence, confiding, and acts of meaning in the first year. In A. Lock (Ed.), *Action, gesture and symbol* (pp. 183–229). New York: Academic Press.

Tulving, E. (1972). Episodic and semantic memory. In E. Tulving & W. Donaldson (Eds.), *Organization of memory* (pp. 382–403). New York: Academic Press.

Tulving, E. (1983). *Elements of episodic memory*. New York: Oxford University Press.

Vaughn, B., Egeland, B., Sroufe, L. A., & Waters, E. (1979). Individual differences in infant–mother attachment at twelve and eighteen months: Stability and change in families under stress. *Child Development, 50,* 971–975.

Wartner, U. G., & Grossmann, K. (1987). *Stability of attachment patterns and their disorganizations from infancy to age six in South Germany*. Unpublished manuscript, University of Virginia.

Wason, P. C., & Johnson–Laird, P. N. (1972). *Psychology of reasoning: Structure and content*. Cambridge, MA: Harvard University Press.

Waters, E. (1978). The reliability and stability of individual differences in infant–mother attachment. *Child Development, 49,* 483–494.

Weiner, B., Graham, S., Stern, P., & Larson, M. E. (1982). Using affective cues to infer causal thoughts. *Developmental Psychology, 18,* 278–286.

Wellman, H. M. (1988). First steps in the child's theorizing about the mind. In J. Astington, P. Harris, & D. Olson (Eds.), *Developing theories of mind* (pp. 64–92). New York: Cambridge University Press.

Wimmer, H., & Hofgrefe, J., & Perner, J. (in press). Understanding of informational access as source of knowledge. *Child Development.*

Winnicott, D. W. (1958). *From paediatrics to psycho-analysis.* London: Hogarth Press.

Winnicott, D. W. (1965). *The maturational processes and the facilitating environment.* New York: International Universities Press.

Wolf, D. P., Rygh, J., & Altshuler, J. (1984). Agency and experience: actions and states in play narratives. In I. Bretherton (Eds.), *Symbolic play: the development of social understanding* (pp. 195–217). New York: Academic Press.

Zahn–Waxler, C., Radke–Yarrow, M., & King, R. (1979). Childrearing and children's prosocial initiations towards victims of distress. *Child Development, 50,* 319–330.

Zeanah, C. H., Keener, M. A., Stewart, L., & Anders, T. F. (1985). Prenatal perception of infant personality: A preliminary investigation. *Journal of the American Academy of Child Psychiatry, 24,* 204–210.

2 Competence, Autonomy, and Relatedness: A Motivational Analysis of Self-system Processes

James P. Connell
James G. Wellborn
University of Rochester

OVERVIEW

The purpose of this chapter is to present a theoretical model of self-system processes across the life-span. This model is based on a motivational analysis of self-system functioning that features three fundamental psychological needs: competence, autonomy, and relatedness. After evaluating selected theoretical approaches to the study of self, the defining features of the new model will be presented. An application of the model within the enterprise of school will be discussed, including data from studies of self-system processes in children and adolescents. The chapter concludes with a discussion of the model's implications for institutional reform.

THEORETICAL APPROACHES TO THE STUDY OF SELF

The psychological study of self has been shaped by a broad range of theoretical perspectives. Since the turn of the century writings by William James (1890), James Baldwin (1897), George Herbert Mead (1934) and Charles H. Cooley (1902), most major strands of modern psychological and sociological thought have been represented in theoretical and empirical studies of self. For example, cognitive theories of self reflect the two major branches of cognitive psychology, structural and information processing approaches. Modern learning theorists such as Julian Rotter (1954), Albert Bandura (1977), Martin E. P. Seligman (e.g., Abramson, Seligman, & Teasdale, 1978) have all made important contributions to the elaboration of self-related phenomena. Psychodynamic and psychosocial theories such as those of Sigmund Freud, Anna Freud and Erik Erikson have had important influences on the study of self, as have other clinically based theorists such as Carl Rogers. Object relations and ego psychological theories have also investigated the emergence and unfolding of the self. Finally, sociologists within the symbolic interactionist tradition have continued to show theoretical and empirical interest in the self and its social rudiments (e.g., Gergen, 1984; and Brim, 1976). Developmental treatments of self draw on this eclectic set of theoretical influences. Our colleagues participating in this symposium reflect the diversity of contemporary views on this central developmental issue of "how we come to be who we are." Attempting to classify such a rich and diverse set of theoretical approaches to the study of self is a daunting task, one easily given to oversimplification. Nonetheless, an attempt will be made to address the strengths and weaknesses of a number of approaches to understanding the self within the traditions of *cognitive, social, and motivational* psychology.

Cognitive Approaches to the Study of Self

Cognitive approaches to the study of self share an emphasis on the cognitive underpinnings of our sense of "who we are." The key terms in these approaches—knowledge, beliefs, theories, schema—suggest that a developing sense of self involves what is *known* about one's self. What develops then is the acquisition and organization of this knowledge. Structural approaches investigate developmental changes in the way self-knowledge is organized. For example, Damon and his colleagues (e.g., Damon & Hart, 1982) rely on theoretical methods drawn from Piagetian theory to describe the developmental progression of children's moral understanding. McGuire and his colleagues (e.g., McGuire, 1981) examine organizational changes in the *content* of childrens' and adolescents' responses to the question "Who Am I?" and point to shifts in the thematic content of these responses. Epstein's (1973) explication of self-theory is linked to cognitive models of scientific thought while Carver and Scheier (1981) employ computational metaphors in their research on processing of self-relevant information. Markus (1977), in her work on *self-schema,* examines how self develops drawing on research in social psychology and language development.

Another cognitive approach to the development of self is that of "action theory." While considerable diversity exists within this theoretical network, researchers using this approach (see, for example, Sabini & Frese, 1985) emphasize interrelations among individual goals, beliefs about strategies for achieving these goals, actions driven by these beliefs, and the consequences of these actions. One fundamental aspect of an action theoretical conceptualization is that goal-directed behavior is regulated by an internal model of the action that will result in goal attainment (Frese & Stewart, 1984).

These cognitive approaches vary primarily in their metaphors for the development of self-knowledge. Structural theorists depict age-graded change in the thematic content and complexity of self-knowledge. Information-processing theorists, on the other hand, employ computational metaphors to describe the way information regarding self is processed.

Social Approaches to the Study of Self

Approaches to studying the self within the tradition of social psychology and sociology share an emphasis on the social context as the matrix within which the self develops. However, these conceptualizations disagree on the social interactive *mechanisms* of development. Cooley's (1902) metaphor of the "looking glass self" formed the foundation of the symbolic interactionist view of self in which the sense of self develops out of the reflected appraisals of significant others in the social surround. Early behaviorists such as Watson (1919) and, later, B. F. Skinner (1953), while maintaining an emphasis on social factors (i.e., reinforcement) had no use for the notion of self. Unlike the symbolic interactionists and the early behaviorists who gave little credence to intrapsychic processes in their formulations, later social learning theorists began to include beliefs about the self as important concepts within their theoretical models. Bandura's self-efficacy expectations (1977) and Rotter's (1966) concept of locus of control placed *self-perceptions* within their respective theoretical frameworks. Nevertheless, these social theorists identify the *source* of these self-perceptions as the patterning of socially administered rewards and punishments.

Object relations theorists such as Winnicott (1965) and Mahler (Mahler, Pine, & Bergman, 1975) and self theorists such as Kohut (1977) also locate the genesis of self in social interactions. These theorists specify *internalization* of self-relevant information as a central developmental process. In these descriptions, these theorists draw a much more abstract and developmentally variegated picture both of the kinds of information communicated by significant others (e.g., affective, behavioral, cognitive) and the mechanisms of change in self development (e.g., mirroring, individuation) than do the social learning theorists who tend to focus exclusively on behavior as the content of change and on either direct or vicarious reinforcement processes as the mechanisms of change.

Attachment theorists such as Bowlby (1969), Ainsworth (Ainsworth, Blehar, Waters, & Wall, 1978) and, more recently, Bretherton (1985) and Main and her colleagues (Main, Kaplan, & Cassidy, 1985) have linked the emergence and quality of working models of self to early and ongoing experiences with the caretaking environment. In their formulations, the sensitivity and responsivity of the social surround are the primary social interactive processes responsible for the individual's developing sense of self in relation to significant others.

Motivational Approaches to the Study of Self

A third category of self theorists are those who have proposed motivationally based conceptualizations of self. These motivational approaches share a common focus on how self-related cognition and affect develop in relation to *organismically based priorities*. These priorities vary among motivational theorists, sometimes dramatically.

Building on James's (1890) early discussions of self-esteem, theorists such as Coopersmith (1967), Covington (1984), and Harter (1983a) have emphasized the developmental significance of global and domain specific beliefs regarding self-worth. These theorists, along with Rogers (1951), implicate self-worth or self-esteem as an *organizational construct* (Sroufe & Waters, 1977). As such, self-worth is hypothesized to be related to variables such as perceived competence and attributions for success and failure. According to Harter (1983a), self-worth is also an important mediator of emotional experience in multiple domains.

Psychodynamic theorists trace the roots of self-development to the complex interplay among fundamental *biological* drives and identification processes. Freud (1927) proposed that one's sense of self (i.e., ego) arises out of the dynamic relationship between the press of instinctual needs and the constraints of the external world. Psychosocial theorists such as Erikson (1950), while retaining much of Freud's basic formulation, *co*-emphasize psychodynamic processes and the sociocultural structuring of the life course.

Motivational theories such as those of Maslow (1970), McClelland (1985), White (1959), and Deci (1980) link the development of self to *psychological* needs. Maslow's (1970) conceptualization was based on a hierarchical organization of biological drives and psychological needs. Deci (1980) incorporates a sense of self within his conceptualization of self-determination. McClelland (1985) treats needs for power, achievement, and affiliation as distinct, theoretical entities of relevance to the development of self.

Evaluation of Theoretical Approaches

Many of the theoretical positions within the cognitive, social, and motivational approaches to the study of self have not been tested empirically, nor were they designed to be. Nevertheless, it is possible to review these positions critically by posing a common set of questions for each to address. These questions were thought to be particularly relevant to developmentalists interested in the empirical and theoretical study of the self. First, what is each approach's view of the developing person? Second, what role is ascribed to the social context in the development of self? Third, according to each perspective, what difference does the "self" make in what people actually do in their everyday lives?

Views of the Developing Person. Cognitive approaches clearly view the developing person as a *knower* of self, as a constructor and processor of information about the self. In her comprehensive review of developmental literature on self-system processes, Harter (1983b) revived the philosophical distinction discussed earlier by James (1890) between the *I* and the *me*. The *me* represents the objective self, the *I* the subjective; the me, what is to be known, the I, the knower.

Ironically, theorists within a cognitive tradition concentrate on what can be objectively *known* about the self rather than on the subjective "*knower*." These theorists clearly emphasize the *content* of self; on how what is known about the self develops, is progressively organized, and is differentiated. For example, both information-processing approaches and action theoretical approaches use "goals" as a central variable in their general models. Goals are clearly a central feature of the *knower*. But, there is little or no discussion of what these goals are or where these goals come from. Instead, the focus of information processing and action theory approaches is on how goals translate into cognitive strategies and are calibrated by behavioral and cognitive outcomes. Without a discussion of the nature and origin of goals the knower remains shapeless, a mystery.

Social approaches, while clearly distinct from cognitive approaches in their terminology and emphasis, also view the organism as relatively shapeless, *until* it is woven into the social fabric. The most radical exemplar of this perspective is Watson's (1919) oft-cited "give me a dozen babies" challenge to proponents of nativist perspectives. By exercising specific control over the physical and social environment, Watson asserted that specific types of children could be produced regardless of their heritage. Other, more moderate theorists within the social tradition do attribute delimiting and facilitating parameters to the developing person. Indeed, in some social approaches, the organism becomes a *negotiator* with the social surround by early in the third year of life (e.g., Bowlby's, 1969, notion of a goal-directed partnership). Typically, however, these social theorists do not provide a clear specification of what the person *brings* to the negotiating table other than a history of social interaction. Even in the most dialectical treatments of social influences on the development of self (e.g., Gergen, 1984; Reigle, 1973), the analysis of how the self develops still proceeds from the social unit (dyad, family, society) to the individual's sense of self.

According to motivational theorists, emotional processes and psychological needs play a central role in shaping the development of self. Maslow (1970), White (1959), and Deci (1980) hold a *teleological* view of the developing person, with superordinate and, to some extent, distal organismic goals (e.g., Maslow's self-actualization; Deci's self-determination; and White's competence) driving the organism's proximal development. Psychodynamic theorists (Freud, 1927), on the other hand, present a more *ballistic* view in which the frustration of early instinctual drives sets a firm trajectory for the future development of self.

Role of the Social Context. As with their views of the developing person, theorists vary greatly on both *what* and *how much* they have to say about the role of the social context in the development of self. Cognitive approaches tend not to address social contextual influences in the construction of self-knowledge. Indeed, there has been a historical tendency within the cognitive psychology tradition to downplay social influences on cognitive development. Notable exceptions to this include the seminal work of Vygotsky (1962) on the social bases of language and thought, applications of Fischer's (1980) skill theory to the development of self, and an emerging literature on autobiographical memory and the social construction of self (Barclay & Hodges, 1988).

By definition, social approaches to the study of self have a great deal to say about the role of the social context. Social theorists nevertheless vary greatly in their views of *how* the social context shapes the course of self-development. For example, there is disagreement on the degree to which the individual shapes or is shaped by their social interactions. Social learning theorists tend to characterize the relationship between the individual and their social context in the form of a unidirectional model from social context to self. On the other hand, modern attachment theories (e.g., Bretherton, 1985; Connell & Thompson, 1986) and life-span developmental views (e.g., Baltes, 1987; Dannefer, 1984; Lerner & Busch–Rossnagel, 1981) place the person in a more active, initiating role with respect to the social context.

Unlike most social learning views of self, attachment and object relations theorists highlight certain periods of development and particular significant others as crucial in the development of self. Within objects relations and self psychology traditions (e.g., Kohut, 1977; Winnicott, 1965), mothers are viewed as singularly important both in the genesis of the self and its subsequent developmental progression. Social learning theorists, however, tend to be less concerned with developmental issues and relatively undifferentiated in their a priori emphasis on one or another social partner.

Social approaches also vary in the *level* of analysis employed in exploring the development of self and in the mechanisms or processes used to link social experience with the construction and revision of self. Investigations of social influences on the self range from the microanalysis of mother-child interaction represented by the work of Stern (1977) to macroanalyses of sociocultural influences on self-development by Smith (1985) and Elder (1984). Mechanisms being explored at a microanalytical level include patterns of emotional sensitivity or contingent responsiveness (e.g., Ainsworth et al., 1978; Gewirtz, 1972). At the macrolevel, investigators are examining how cultural icons and symbols, abstract ideologies, and rhetoric shape and transform individual and collective views of self.

Motivational approaches tend to view the social context as a facilitating or inhibitory milieu in which the sense of self develops. Facilitating aspects of this milieu include notions of unconditional, positive regard (Rogers, 1951), support of autonomy (Deci & Ryan, 1985), and the channeling of motivational energies toward culturally acceptable enterprises (Freud, 1927). Conversely, inhibitory or conflict-producing aspects of the social context would include withholding emotional support from the individual, seeking to control organismic initiations, and noncontingent responses to the person's initiations toward culturally approved ends.

Self and Action Linkages. What difference does the self make in what people do in their everyday lives? Many self theorists do not even consider this question. Those that do often do not specify *how*, by what process, our sense of self relates to our behavior. Within the cognitive tradition, most structural approaches do not elaborate how structural differentiation of self-knowledge affects action. This critique should not be taken to imply that self-knowledge doesn't affect broader patterns of action in everyday life, it's just that many of these cognitive/structural approaches do not typically address these issues. Information processing approaches such as those of Carver and Scheier (1981) and certain action theoretical approaches (e.g., Kuhl, 1984) include action/behavior in their microanalytical models. However, due to the level of these cognitive analyses, the behaviors studied tend to be covert cognitions within small problem-solving loops. Other cognitive theorists concerned with the development of self-schemata (e.g., Markus, 1977) do examine how these schemata affect memory processes both in laboratory experiments and in everyday life. Finally, self-related beliefs have also been implicated in the constructions of autobiographical histories (e.g., Barclay & Hodges, 1988).

Early social approaches to the study of self (e.g., Cooley, 1902), emphasized the social *construction* of self but not the social *implications* of the self. Modern social learning research has addressed behavioral correlates of self-related beliefs in laboratory and survey studies but have yet to specify fully the processes underlying these empirical linkages. Object relations and attachment theories of self-development argue that the working models of self develop out of the primary attachment relationship and have direct implications for subsequent extrafamilial relationships, including peer and intimate adult relationships. *How* these working models regulate action in everyday life is less clearly delineated. An emerging clinical literature on childhood psychopathology is beginning to demonstrate the negative effects of psychopathological symptoms on social support and subsequent decrements in self-functioning (Cicchetti, 1989). In these studies, behavioral symptoms of deficient self-functioning are thought to elicit withdrawal of social support which in turn exacerbates the difficulties of self-functioning.

Motivational approaches to the study of self vary in their portrayals of how self-functioning affects behavior. Psychodynamic and psychosocial theories point to idiographic symptoms such as regressive and neurotic behavior as evidence of deficits in self-development, but little attention is given by these theorists to the behavioral consequences of *optimal* self-development (Freud, 1927; Sullivan, 1953). Motivational theories such as those of Seligman, Abramson, and their colleagues (Abramson, et al., 1978; Seligman, 1975; Seligman, Peterson, Kaslow, Tanenbaum, Alloy, & Abramson, 1984) point to the negative emotional and behavioral outcomes of learned helplessness and attributional styles associated with learned helplessness. However, the action consequences of *adaptive* self-related beliefs are less fully explicated. The principal organization of these lines of research is a deficit model in which frustrated or undernourished psychological needs/drives lead to maladaptive behavior, self-related cognitions, and affect.

Other motivational theorists, such as Deci and Ryan (1985), do examine conditions for *optimization* of behavior. For example, these theorists assert that the experience of *autonomy support* facilitates persistence at a task when no external support is present. Clearly, a motivational approach to the study of self that can explain how self-functioning is related to optimal *and* maladaptive patterns of behavior provides a broader view of the development of self than a strictly deficit model.

Summary of Theoretical Review

According to Harter (1983b), the theoretical literature on the self is a microcosm of developmental psychology and, to some extent, of all psychology. It reveals and exemplifies the field's historical roots, its paradigmatic upheavals, and its current *Zeitgeists*. The goal of this brief review, as summarized in Fig. 2.1, was to focus on three issues that are seen as central to evaluating any comprehensive model of self. Specifically, "What is the view of the developing person?"; "What role does the social context play in the development of self?"; and, "How does the sense of self affect action?" In the next section, a new theoretical model of self-system processes will be presented in light of these same three issues.

SELECTED ISSUES FOR THEORETICAL VIEWS OF SELF

	COGNITIVE	SOCIAL	MOTIVATIONAL
VIEW OF THE DEVELOPING PERSON	-Emphasis on objective aspects of self -Person is a "knower" or "processor" of information about objective aspects of self	-Emphasis on social or relational bases of self -Person "internalizes" social communications about self	-Emphasis on emotional processes and/or organismic priorities in the development of self -Person seeks to fulfill psychological needs
ROLE OF SOCIAL CONTEXT	-Role of social context is downplayed (exceptions in Vygotsky and Fischer)	-Social surround crucial for development of self -Mechanisms/processes and levels of analyses vary	-Social context provides "nourishment" for the developing sense of self
SELF AND ACTION CONNECTIONS	-Knowledge of self regulates memory processes -Feedback from actions calibrates goals and expectancies	-Relational basis of self have implications for subsequent relationships	-Frustrated needs lead to maladaptive patterns of action -Psychological needs shape the direction of action

FIG. 2.1. Selected issues in cognitive, social, and motivational approaches to the study of the self.

Context, Self, and Action

In a recent paper (Connell, in press), a theoretical model of self-system processes was presented. The four defining features of this model are: 1) that people have fundamental psychological needs for competence, autonomy and relatedness; 2) that self-system processes develop out of the interaction of psychological needs and social context within particular cultural enterprises; 3) that the aspects of the social context most relevant to the meeting of these needs, and thus to the development of self-system processes, are the provision of structure, autonomy support, and involvement; and, 4) that inter- and intra-individual variation in self-system processes produce variability in patterns of action within cultural enterprises. (See Fig. 2.2). This model will now be examined in light of the three issues used to discuss the cognitive, social, and motivational approaches to the study of self.

In this model, *the developing person* is viewed as an active partner in the construction of the self-system from the first moments of life. The self-system is viewed as a set of appraisal processes whereby the individual evaluates his or her status within particular contexts with respect to three fundamental psychological needs: competence, autonomy and relatedness. These three needs are then the organismic priorities around which the self-system is organized. Thus the new model embraces a motivational perspective in its view of the developing person.

The need for *competence* (e.g., White, 1959; Deci & Ryan, 1985) has been defined as "the need to experience oneself as capable of producing desired outcomes and avoiding negative outcomes". The need for *autonomy* is defined as "the experience of choice in the initiation, maintenance and regulation of activity and the experience of connectedness between one's actions and personal goals and values". The need for *relatedness* "encompasses the need to feel securely connected to the social surround and the need to experience oneself as worthy

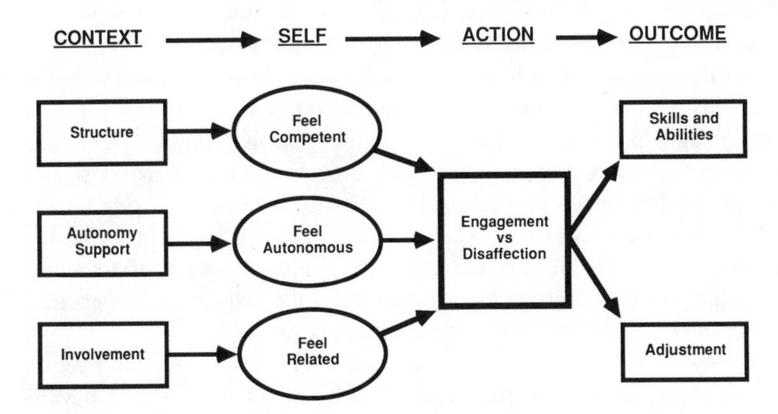

FIG. 2.2. A simple process model of the relations between context, self, action, and outcomes. (adapted from Connell, in press).

and capable of love and respect". (All definitions from Connell, in press.) The person's role in the development of the self-system is manifested throughout development as he/she seeks out experiences that fulfill the needs for competence, autonomy, and relatedness. Thus, it is the subjective self, the *knower,* that orients action, thought and emotion with reference to these psychological needs. According to this model, the objective self is the individual's appraisals of how competent, autonomous and related he or she feels within and across particular contexts. These appraisal processes are referred to as self-system processes.

One of the defining features of this model is that self-system processes develop out of interactions between people within particular sociocultural and historical contexts. This assumption is consistent with the views of socially oriented self-theorists in that intra- and interindividual variability in self-system processes are thought to be primarily a function of social interchanges. However, unlike sociological or social psychological approaches to the study of self, the theoretical analysis of the role of context proceeds not from the social to the individual, but from the individual to the social. In asking "what about social interaction contributes to the development of self-system processes?", this analysis looks directly to the three psychological needs described herein and deduces that social interactions that either enhance or inhibit the experience of competence, autonomy, and relatedness are the aspects of the social context of most relevance to the development of self.

Finally, the model addresses the *connection between self and action* through the constructs of engagement and disaffection. Patterns of action are evidenced both in the "flow" of ongoing activity within a particular enterprise, as well as in reactions to challenge (Wellborn & Connell, in preparation). When psychological needs are being met within particular cultural enterprises such as family, school or work, engagement will occur and be manifested in affect, behavior, and cognition. Conversely, when psychological needs are not being met, disaffection will result along with its adverse effects on these same action components.

According to the model (shown in Fig. 2.2), self-system processes associated with the three needs also affect the skills and abilities and personal adjustment of individuals within a particular enterprise. However, the self-to-action-to-outcome linkages proposed in this model differ from that guiding most studies of self-perceptions and performance where **direct** relations between self-perceptions and performance or adjustment are usually investigated. (See for example Findley and Cooper's [1983] meta-analysis of research on children's locus of control and school achievement.) In the new model, patterns of action *mediate* the relation between self-system processes and the acquisition of specific skills and personal adjustment within these enterprises.

Over the past 7 years, this general model of context, self, and action, and pieces thereof, have been used to study self-system processes in a variety of cultural enterprises including family systems (Chapin, 1989), work organizations (Deci, Connell, & Ryan, 1989) and, infant-parent relationships (Connell, in press; Connell, Bridges, & Grolnick, 1989). In the next section of the chapter, operationalizations of the various constructs in the general model within the enterprise of schooling will be presented. Data addressing linkages hypothesized in the model shown in Fig. 2.2 are discussed.

SELF-SYSTEM PROCESSES OF CHILDREN AND ADOLESCENTS IN EDUCATIONAL CONTEXTS

Schooling is clearly a central cultural enterprise in the lives of children and adolescents in many societies. The general theoretical model shown in Fig. 2.3 has been developed and refined based in large part on data collected in educational settings. Initial efforts were directed at conceptualizing and operationalizing specific self-system processes associated with psychological needs for competence, autonomy, and relatedness within the domain of school (Connell, 1985; Skinner, Wellborn, & Connell, 1990; Connell and Ryan, 1987; Connell, Wellborn, & Lynch, 1988). Next, assessments of the social context were developed (Wellborn and Connell, 1987). Recent work has focused on operationalizing dimensions and prototypes of engagement and disaffection (Wellborn & Connell, in preparation). A multimethod assessment of these variables—*The Rochester Assessment Package for Schools* (RAPS; Wellborn & Connell, 1987)—has been developed using student, teacher, and parent reports. The specific operationalizations of the variables in the model will be presented briefly. (These operationalizations are described in greater detail in Connell, in press, and in Wellborn & Connell, 1987.) Results will then be presented from studies using the RAPS instruments to assess the constructs in the general model.

Operationalization of Constructs

Perceived Strategies and Capacities for School-related Competence. In order to experience a sense of competence in school, two component self-system process are proposed: (1) knowledge about how to do well in school, i.e., perceived strategies for achieving outcomes; and (2) beliefs that one can execute those strategies, i.e., perceived capacities. For perceived strategies, items are included that ask students about five possible strategies for doing well in school and for avoiding poor performance in school. These strategies are unknown ("I don't know how to do well/avoid failure in school"); powerful others ("I have to get teachers to like me to do well/avoid failure in school"); luck ("I have to be lucky to do well/avoid failure in school"); effort ("Working hard is the best way for me to do well/avoid failure in school"); and ability ("I have to be smart to do well/avoid failure in school").

Perceived capacity statements were derived directly from the strategy statements. Children are asked to endorse the degree to which they believe they have

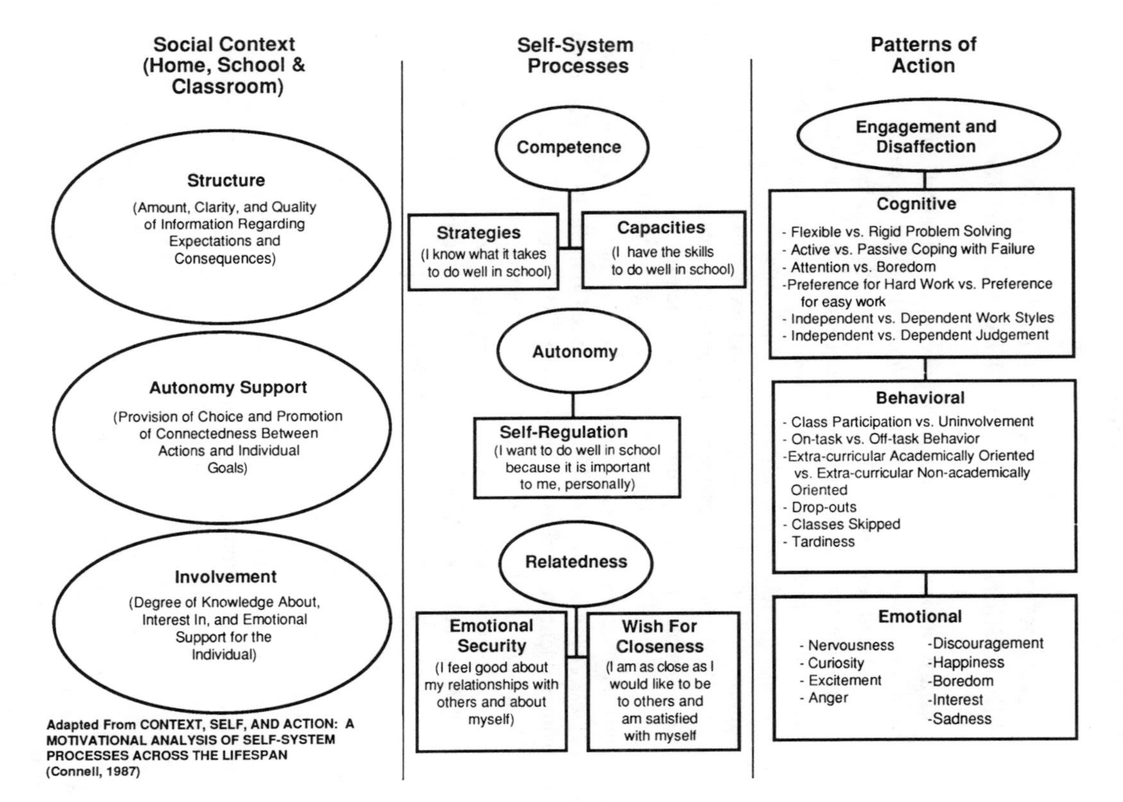

FIG. 2.3. A motivational model of context, self, and action (Connell, in press).

or do not have the capacity for executing effort, ability, powerful others, and luck strategies.[1] For example, "I can (cannot) get the teacher to like me" is a capacity statement tied to the powerful others strategy statement.

Perceived Autonomy: Self-regulatory Styles. The operationalization of the self-system processes associated with the need for autonomy involves assessments of students' self-regulatory styles (Connell & Ryan, 1984, 1987; Ryan & Connell, 1989; Chandler, 1981; Ryan, Connell & Deci, 1985). This measure assesses student's self-regulation with regard to activities in school. *Intrinsically self-regulated* students are those who engaged in school-related tasks because they enjoy the activity. These students work on hard problems, try to answer hard questions, and do their homework "because it is fun." Students who have not internalized the value of school and, therefore, have the least experience of autonomy in the classroom are *externally self-regulated.* These students complete their homework or work on hard problems "because I will get in trouble if I don't." Students who have begun to regulate their own behavior but link their self-esteem to the outcomes of their behavior (grades, test scores) are manifesting an *introjected self-regulatory style.* These students do schoolwork and homework "because I will feel bad about myself it doesn't get done." Finally, the most autonomous form of self-regulation in tasks that are not intrinsically interesting is *identified self-regulation.* Students who evidence identified self-regulation complete school-related work because "it is important for my future goals."

Perceived Relatedness. The measure of students' quality of relatedness to social partners is derived from two sets of items. *Perceived emotional security* is measured through self-reports of the emotional quality of a student's relationships with important social partners. These items are emotional descriptors following the statement "When I'm with my parent, teacher, friend, etc., I feel." Descriptors include happy, sad, angry, bored, unimportant, unhappy, and ignored. These items are positively and negatively weighted to form a single composite reflecting high or low emotional security with that particular social partner.

To assess *perceived need for a closer relationship,* students are asked to endorse statements such as "I wish I was closer to my father," "I wish my father spent more time with me," and "I wish my father knew me better." Items for each social partner are combined into a single composite reflecting the degree to which students want to have a closer relationship with that person.

---

[1]The absence of a strategy precludes the execution of that strategy. Consequently, no capacity statements regarding "unknown strategies are presented."

Social Context Variables: Structure, Autonomy Support, and Involvement. The RAPS-S contains statements that reflect the three dimensions of the social context thought to be relevant to the psychological needs for competence, autonomy, and relatedness.

Positive *structure* items on the RAPS student report are behavioral descriptions of parents communicating clear expectations for performance (e.g., "My parents let me know what the rules are about homework"); consistent consequences (e.g., "My parents always do what they say they're going to do"); optimal challenge ("My parents don't expect me to do things I can't do."); and positive competence feedback ("My parents tell me their proud of what I've done."). Items designed to tap provision of structure by teachers refer to similar communications (e.g., "I know what my teacher(s) expect of me"; "My teacher(s) do what they say they're going to do.").

Lack of structure in the home and school context refers to students' experience of confusion about adult expectations, and unpredictable consequences. For example, in the home, "I never know what my parents expect of me in school." Lack of structure in the school context is tapped by items such as "My teacher(s) don't make it clear what they expect on school assignments; When I don't do well on a test, I never know how my teacher(s) will act."

Autonomy support refers to the amount of choice provided by teachers and parents and to helping children connect their behavior to their own personal goals and values. For example, items related to provision of choice include: "My teacher lets me do my schoolwork according to my own schedule" and "My teacher lets me make a lot of my own decisions when it comes to schoolwork." Items that assess the connection between activity and personal goals include "My parents discuss important decisions with me."

The *involvement* dimension refers to the dedication of psychological resources (e.g., time, interest) in the context of positive affect. (Grolnick & Ryan, 1987, 1989; Wellborn & Connell, 1987) The RAPS assesses each of these components with items such as: "My parents/teachers . . . know a lot about what happens to me in school; spend time helping me do better in school; seem to enjoy being with me."

Ongoing Engagement versus Disaffection and Student Prototypes of Engagement and Disaffection. Ongoing engagement versus disaffection is measured by asking students or teachers to rate students' typical emotion, cognition and behavior evidenced within the course of the schoolday. The emotion component is measured by emotional descriptors following the statement "When I'm (this student is) in class, I feel (this student appears) . . . The descriptors include bored, interested, discouraged, happy, and angry. Items assessing ongoing student cognition and behavior include ratings of class participation, attention, on-task behavior, flexible problem solving, and extracurricular academics.

Engagement and disaffection in the face of challenge is assessed using a measure of student's coping with perceived failure in school (e.g., not doing well on a test, not being able to answer a question in class). Tero and Connell (1984) identified four coping styles that are included in the RAPS assessments: *positive coping,* where the student actively seeks information and persists following the perceived failure; *projection,* where the student gets angry and blames others; *denial,* where the student denies the importance of the activity and seeks to avoid facing the negative event; and, *anxiety amplification,* where the student self-denigrates and becomes anxious about others' negative evaluations. Children's coping scores on each of these four dimensions are obtained from each of the three reporters (student, teacher and parent) on the RAPS measure.

STUDENT PROTOTYPES OF ENGAGEMENT AND DISAFFECTION

INNOVATIVE

This student is engaged in his schoolwork for the most part. However, he seems to march to the beat of his own drummer, achieving many of the same ends as other students but doing so in his own way. This student sometimes shows a lack of attention when material isn't of particular interest to him. He is creative and really seems to enjoy the process of learning when he is interested in the material.

ENMESHED

This student is very involved in doing schoolwork. You sometimes wonder whether she is taking school too seriously. Her self-concept is too tied up with her academic performance. Although she works very hard, she does it in a very anxious way.

CONFORMIST

This student is the prototypic, well-behaved student. He works up to his ability, follows directions, seems to know exactly how you want the assignment to be done, participates in class, and generally does everything that you expect of him. He seems quite content to follow the rules and regulations in class.

REBELLIOUS

This student acts out in class and refuses to do anything. She doesn't do her work except when forced to and resists attempts to structure her. She seems to operate under her own set of rules that are different from those of the school and the classroom.

RITUALISTIC

This student simply goes through the motions in class. He doesn't cause any serious problems. He simply does schoolwork in order to get it done, without any interest or enjoyment.

WITHDRAWN

Many times, this student appears to have given up and withdraws from class activities. She never seems to get excited about what's going on in class and only participates when you make her do so.

FIG. 2.4. Paragraph descriptions used to identify student prototypes of engagement and disaffection.

Another measure of student patterns of action in school assesses specific student prototypes within the classroom (Wellborn & Connell, in preparation). Three engaged student prototypes and three disaffected student prototypes were identified using paragraph descriptors of each student prototype (Fig. 2.4). The three engaged student prototypes are enmeshed, conformist, and innovative. The enmeshed student prototype represents students who "take school too seriously." Conformist student prototypes represent the prototypically good student who "does everything (the teacher) expects of him/her." The third engaged student prototype is labeled innovative. The innovative student prototype values school but shows inconsistency in engagement across subjects because he/she attends to activities based primarily on his or her own interest.

The three disaffected student prototypes are labeled withdrawn, ritualistic, and rebellious. Withdrawn student prototypes have "given up." The ritualistic student prototype does not seem to value school learning, although he or she will "go through the motions." The third disaffected student prototype, rebellious, represents students who are disruptive, angry, and seem to take little responsibility for their own learning in school. (For a more elaborate discussion of this general concept, see Wellborn & Connell, in preparation).

Empirical Studies of Self-System Processes in Educational Contexts

The data to be presented are taken from ongoing studies in school settings being conducted by our research group. The first set of studies examines the relations between the self-system variables, measures of student engagement and disaffection in school, and indices of student performance. Results from three samples will be reported. The first sample consists of all third through sixth grade students (n = 245), their teachers, and parents in a rural/suburban community participating in a longitudinal research project in which all three forms of the RAPS, student, parent, and teacher forms are administered. The second sample is 542 4th through 6th grade students from a predominantly working class, suburban school district where all three forms of the RAPS measure are administered. Finally, RAPS student-report data were collected in an urban sample (60% minority) of approximately 700 7th through 10th grade students.

This series of studies examined students' self-system processes in relation to multiple measures of engagement and disaffection in school. These assessments include teacher and student reports of engagement versus disaffection collected in the rural/suburban sample as well as teacher ratings of student prototypes of engaged and disaffected patterns of action collected in the predominantly working-class sample. A third index of engagement and disaffection was used in the urban school district (Crichlow & Vito, 1989). This index identifies students at risk for academic failure based on the presence of five behavioral indicators (Fig. 2.5). Students with three or more of these five "flags" are classified as "at-risk."

Students who are characterized by three or more of the following criteria are considered to be "at-risk" for academic failure.

1. **Standardized Achievement Test Scores.** Total reading score at or below 36 percentile and total math score at or below 37 percentile or either score below the 15 percentile.

2. **Core Academic Subject Failure.** Failure of two or more of the following core subjects: English, math, social studies, science.

3. **Long- or Short-Term Suspension.** Two or more instructional days lost due to suspension.

4. **Age Relative to Grade in School.** One or more years over-age for grade level.

5. **Average Daily Attendance.** Absent 19 percent or more days during the academic year.

(from Crichlow & Vito, 1989)

FIG. 2.5. Criteria for classifying students as "at-risk." (Crichlow & Vito, 1989).

Relations between these indicators of engagement and disaffection in school and the set of self-system processes associated with the needs for competence, autonomy, and relatedness will now be presented.

Perceived Competence

The most extensive investigation of relations between self and action has been in the area of perceived competence. As predicted by the model and by previous research on this and related constructs (see Skinner, this volume), consistent relations have been demonstrated between beliefs about perceived competence and patterns of action in school. As part of a recent study (Skinner, et al., 1990), theoretically derived combinations of these competence-related beliefs were shown to be particularly relevant for undermining or promoting engagement in school.

Path analyses revealed direct relations between positive and negative aspects of perceived competence and student engagement (Fig. 2.6). Support was also obtained for a direct relation between teacher reports of student engaged versus disaffected patterns of action in school and important school outcomes such as academic achievement and grades. In addition, low but significant direct relations between perceived control and grades and achievement were obtained with engagement partialled out of the outcome variables. These residual relations between self and academic outcomes may be due to reciprocal effects of actual school performance on children's beliefs about their own competence. For example, children may calibrate their perceived competence based directly on performance feedback such as grades and test scores. A longitudinal investigation of

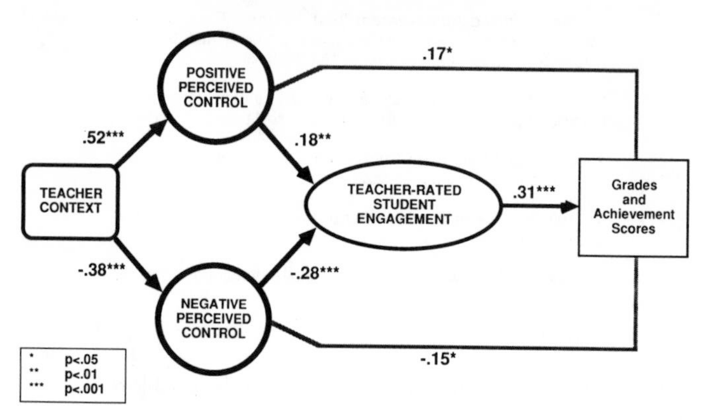

FIG. 2.6. Path analysis of the antecedents and consequences of perceived competence for a rural/suburban elementary school sample (grades 3–6, $n = 220$). Positive perceived competence is a combination of control-related beliefs hypothesized to promote engagement. Negative perceived competence is a combination of beliefs hypothesized to undermine engagement. Teacher context is children's perceptions of teacher contingency and involvement combined. (from Skinner, et al., 1990)

these feedback effects is currently under way (Skinner, 1990; Connell & Wellborn, in preparation).

The second set of results includes relations between students' perceived strategies and capacities and teacher reports of student engagement and disaffection in the suburban, working class sample. For these analyses, students were rated by their teacher as either *good* or *poor* exemplars of each prototypic pattern of engagement and disaffection using the RAPS teacher report form shown in Fig. 2.4. Good and poor exemplars of each prototype were then compared on their perceived strategies and capacities for doing well in school. Only data on the three disaffected prototypes will be reported here.

As can be seen in Fig. 2.7, each of the three disaffected prototypes has a distinctive profile of perceived strategies and capacities. The rebellious and ritualistic prototypes share the beliefs that they cannot put out effort in school and that pleasing powerful others (teachers) is the way to do well in school. These prototypes diverge in that the ritualistic prototype is marked by reports of not knowing what it takes to do well or avoid failure in school and by low perceived ability. The withdrawn prototype shows a completely distinctive profile on these self-system variables reporting that luck is what counts in school and that they

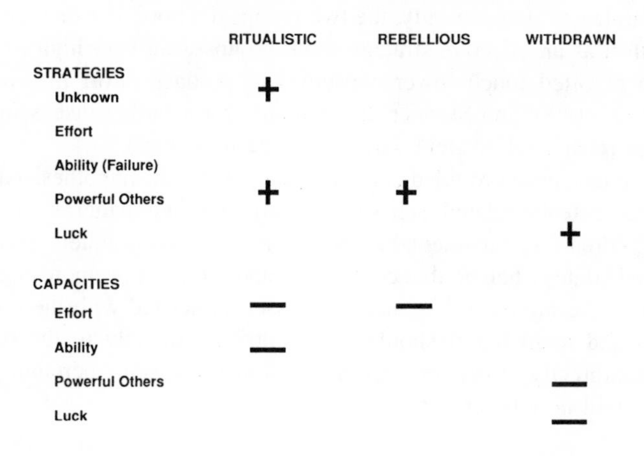

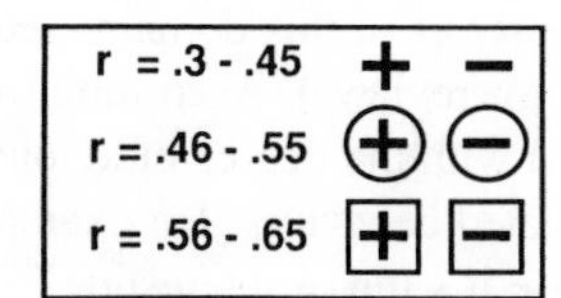

FIG. 2.7. Comparisons of students rated by their teachers as good exemplars of each prototype with those rated as poor exemplars of each prototype on the self-system processes associated with perceived competence.

are unlucky. These withdrawn students also report not being able to get the teacher to like them. These data encourage us to continue using this more idiographic approach to the study of engaged and disaffected patterns of action.

A third set of studies in the urban sample examined linkages between perceived competence and the five behavioral indicators of disaffected patterns of action. In the urban district, students were classified as either "at risk" or "nonlabeled" based on the "5-Flag" at-risk classification system described earlier (Crichlow & Vito, 1989). Mean level differences between these two groups were then examined to determine whether the perceived strategy and perceived capacity variables would significantly discriminate between the engaged and disaffected groups of students. The profile differences were clear. Junior and senior high school students labelled *at risk* reported significantly higher levels of unknown, powerful others, ability, and luck strategies for achieving success and avoiding failure in school than did their nonlabeled classmates. These at-risk students also reported significantly lower capacities to execute these more highly endorsed strategies. Interestingly, the two groups did not differ on their endorsement of effort as an effective strategy (both groups were very high), but the at-risk group reported much lower capacities to produce effort in school. (See Skinner et al., 1990; and Skinner, this volume, for a further discussion of how competence-related self-system variables relate to action.)

Studies to date have provided consistent support for the hypothesized relations between competence-related self-system variables and patterns of action in school. Children's engagement has been shown to be uniquely predicted by capacity and strategy beliefs that combine to undermine or promote engagement. According to the model, self-system processes associated with the other needs (autonomy and relatedness) should also contribute directly to the patterns of action and indirectly to performance in this domain. Results pertaining to these hypotheses will now be presented.

Perceived Autonomy

Relations obtained between perceived autonomy and patterns of action in school have confirmed the importance of this construct in this domain (see Connell & Ryan, 1987; and Ryan & Connell, 1989, for reviews). According to the model, engagement in school should be associated with the degree of autonomy experienced in the regulation of achievement-related behaviors. For example, children who report doing their homework "because it's fun or interesting" should show different patterns of cognition, behavior and emotion than children who are doing their homework "because they'll get in trouble if they don't". In order to examine these hypothesized relations, correlations were obtained between perceived autonomy (Relative Autonomy Index), teacher reports of student engagement, and a composite index of school performance.[2]

In the rural/suburban elementary sample, the correlations between the Relative Autonomy Index and the engagement and performance measures were $rs =$ .24 ($p < .001$) and .12, ($p < .10$) respectively. Path analyses were then conducted to test for the hypothesized direct and indirect effects of perceived autonomy on engagement and performance. The results of the path analysis shown in Fig. 2.8 support the hypothesized relations. Children who report higher levels of

[2]Perceived autonomy is assessed using a composite of the self-regulatory styles ordered along a continuum, from external regulation to introjected regulation to identified regulation to intrinsic regulation (Connell and Ryan, 1987; Ryan, Connell, and Grolnick, in press). The teacher report of ongoing engagement versus disaffection is composed of 14 items that tap emotion and behavior in the class. Finally, academic performance is assessed by a composite score of grade point average and achievement test scores as described in the Skinner et al. study. 1990

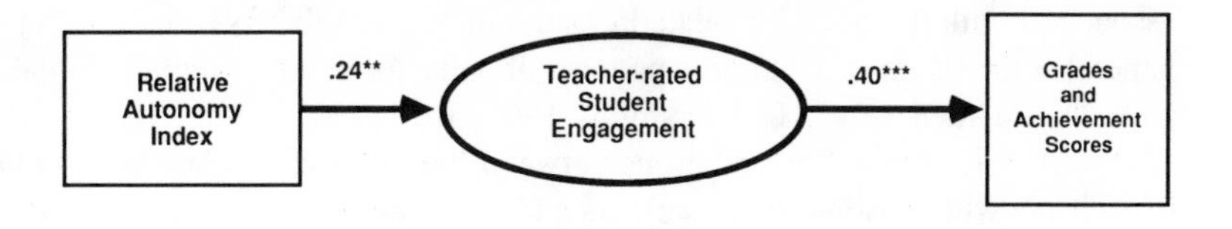

FIG. 2.8. Path analysis of relations between self-system processes associated with autonomy, teacher-rated student engagement versus disaffection in school, and academic performance for a rural/suburban elementary-school sample (grades 3 to 6, $n = 220$).

perceived autonomy are reported by their teachers to be more engaged in class and show higher levels of school performance. In the suburban working-class district, a significant correlation ($r = .31, p < .001$) was also obtained between the relative autonomy index and teacher reports of student engagement and disaffection.

Differences in perceived autonomy between at-risk and nonlabeled students in the urban sample were also examined. At-risk students ($M = 7.39$, SD = 3.2) were significantly lower than the nonlabeled students ($M = 7.96$, SD = 3.3) on the Relative Autonomy Index ($t = 2.24, p < .05$). In the working-class suburban sample, autonomy differences were also evident between the elementary student prototypes of engaged and disaffected patterns of action as rated by teachers. For example, innovative student prototypes report significantly higher levels of intrinsic self-regulation than enmeshed student prototypes although both prototypes are considered to be engaged in their school work. It appears that enmeshed students, while clearly working hard and doing well in school, are doing so for less intrinsic reasons than are students who are seen as more creative and innovative in their patterns of action in school. In contrast, withdrawn students show significantly lower levels of intrinsic regulation than either of the two engaged prototypes just described.

Like perceived competence, perceived autonomy shows consistent empirical relations to students' patterns of action in school in diverse student populations. Support for the hypothesized direct and indirect relations between self, action, and performance outcomes was also obtained in the suburban/rural elementary sample. Children and adolescents who experience themselves as regulating their *own* behavior in school are more engaged in this domain and these engaged patterns of action are associated with higher levels of academic accomplishment.

Perceived Relatedness

The final set of self-system processes included in the theoretical model are those associated with the need for relatedness to others and self. Associations between general self-esteem and adaptive patterns of behavior in the academic domain are well-documented (e.g., Coopersmith, 1967; Rosenberg, 1965; Harter, 1982). Less well-documented are relations between the quality of relatedness children *experience* with various social partners and their motivation in the school setting. Considerably more attention has been paid to the behavior and attitudes of parents (e.g., Baumrind, 1971; Grolnick & Ryan, 1989) and teachers (e.g., Deci, Schwartz, Scheinman, & Ryan, 1981; Brophy, 1986; Dweck & Elliot, 1983) as predictors of student behavior and performance. In the results reported below, correlations were obtained between a) the degree of emotional security experienced by children in their interactions with parents, teachers, and classmates; b) the engagement shown by the students in class as reported by the children's teachers; and, c) an academic performance composite of grades and achievement test scores. As shown in Fig. 2.9, emotional security with all three sets of social partners is significantly associated with teacher ratings of engagement in school. Interestingly, *none* of the relatedness variables is significantly correlated with the academic performance composite.

Next, path analyses were conducted to test for two indirect effect of relatedness on academic performance: one from relatedness with teachers and peers through engagement; and one from relatedness with parents through relatedness with teachers and peers and *then* through student engagement to student performance. The hypothesis was that children's experience of emotional security with their parents may affect their engagement in school indirectly through the quality of the relationships with others more proximally situated in a particular enterprise (in this case teachers and classmates). The results of the path analysis shown in Fig. 2.10 provided preliminary support for both of these hypotheses.

	Teacher-reported Engagement vs. Disaffection	Academic Performance
Emotional Security With Parents	.13*	.08
Emotional Security With Teacher	.23***	.004
Emotional Security With Peers	.21***	.09

FIG. 2.9. Correlations of self-system processes associated with relatedness to others with teacher-rated student engagement and academic performance.

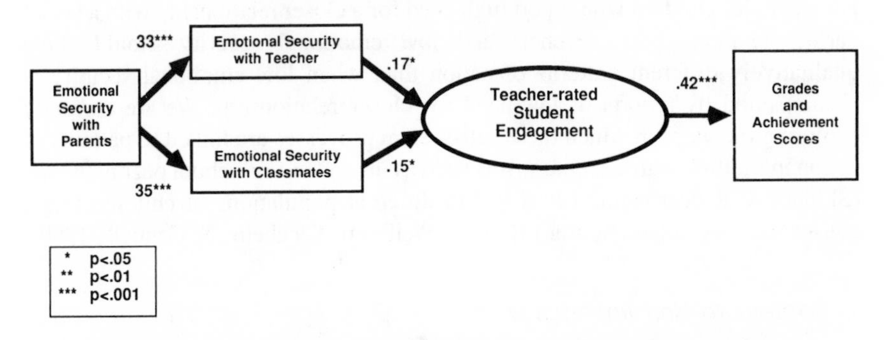

FIG. 2.10. Path analysis of relations among relatedness variables and teacher ratings of student engagement in a rural/suburban elementary-school sample (grades 3 to 6, $n = 220$).

This absence of a direct relation between self-system processes (in this case emotional security with others) and domain-specific performance (in this case school achievement) highlights the importance of the engagement construct in the general model. Without it, the inference from correlational data would be that children's feelings of emotional security with others in school are unrelated to their school accomplishments. As the results of the path analysis show, emotional security with classmates and teachers uniquely predict engaged patterns of action which *in turn* predict school performance. By postulating engagement and disaffection as qualities of action that directly affect performance and are affected by self-system functioning, a more detailed empirical picture emerges of the process whereby beliefs about self affect culturally defined performance outcomes.

These findings also suggest that one way in which children's relationships with their parents influence school engagement is through the influence that parent-child relations have on the quality of students' relationships with significant others in school; in this case, classmates and teachers. This "relational" path of influence has not been as fully examined as have the influences of parent behavior (e.g., helping behavior, monitoring school progress) and parent attitudes and aspirations regarding school achievement. Evidence from research on infant– and toddler–parent relationships also suggests that the emotional quality of these relationships predicts the emotional quality of the child's relationships with other adults and peers in different interactive contexts (Bridges, Connell, & Belsky, 1988; Lynch & Wellborn, 1989). These studies also reveal that the quality of these relationships with other social partners has important consequences for the child's engagement in these situations.

Future work with the relatedness constructs will explore *configural* approaches to relations between emotional security and need for closeness to others as two dimensions of relatedness (Connell, Wellborn, & Lynch, in preparation). For example, children who report high need for a closer relationship with a social partner (parent, peer, teacher) and low emotional security should show qualitatively different patterns of action than when low emotional security is accompanied by reports of *low* need for closer relationship. We are currently exploring the ways in which these self-system processes are linked to patterns of action in multiple cultural enterprises such as in- and out-of-school peer networks (Skinner & Kindermann, 1989) and in different populations of children (e.g., abused and neglected children) (Lynch, Wellborn, Cicchetti, & Connell, 1989).

Context to Self-linkages

As discussed earlier, three dimensions of the social context are hypothesized to directly influence the development of self-system processes: *autonomy support, structure, and involvement.* According to the model, it is children's *experience* of these motivationally relevant aspects of the social environment that contributes to the development of their self-system. Thus, studies of the contextual aspect of this model focused on children's *perceptions* of the social context and specifically the degree of autonomy support, structure, and involvement experienced at home and in school (Connell & Ryan, 1987; Ryan & Grolnick, 1986; Skinner et al., 1990).

In these studies, student perceptions of the structure, autonomy support, and involvement have consistently shown the predicted pattern of correlations with the self-system processes associated with each of the needs (e.g., Fig. 2.6). For example, elementary school children's experience of structure in their homes and classrooms is consistently negatively associated with their reports of not knowing strategies for achieving success and avoiding failure in school; and, significantly, but less strongly, with their reports that being lucky and getting powerful others to like them are the ways to get ahead in school. These findings suggest that children who experience clear expectations regarding their schoolwork, are optimally challenged, and receive consistent, competence-related feedback will better understand what it takes to do well in school. Conversely, the experience of labile or overly stringent expectations and inconsistent consequences may result in the child's not knowing how to go about doing well in school and/or lead to the beliefs that success and failure are due to the whims of others or to fate.

Both maternal and paternal *involvement* as reported by students has been found to correlate positively with children's perceived capacities for effort and ability and with their reported emotional security with their parents. The dedication of time and effort by parents in the context of positive affect may be the matrix in which children can safely test their developing competencies. Then, by repeatedly observing the successful application of these efforts, children can develop adaptive beliefs about their own capacities to produce effort and eventually about their ability to do well in school.

Grolnick and Ryan (1989) used clinical interview techniques with parents to derive a rating of the degree of structure and involvement present in the home context. They also administered Connell's (1985) measure of children's perceptions of control (a forerunner of the RAPS student report assessment of perceived strategies and capacities). Consistent with the model predictions, these researchers found that children who had home contexts rated as *low in structure* reported *high levels of unknown control* on the Connell measure. Grolnick and Ryan also report significant positive relations between the clinical ratings of parental *involvement* and children's *perceived cognitive competence* (a measure conceptually akin to the measure of perceived effort and ability capacities from the RAPS). This study, using ratings of clinical interview material, lends further support to the hypothesized linkage between the contextual variables of structure and involvement and the two sets of self-system processes associated with the need for competence.

In a third set of related studies, questionnaire assessments were obtained from parents and teachers of the suburban working-class sample asking how much *structure* autonomy support, and *involvement* they provide their children in relation to schoolwork. In addition, teachers were asked to report for themselves *and* give their best estimate of the parents' degree of involvement and provision of structure, and vice versa. Two groups of junior high school students were then compared on these parent and teacher reports: one group had been labeled "at risk" using criteria similar to those described in Fig. 2.5; the other group of children were selected randomly from the same classrooms.

Both sets of adults reported that they were less involved and more controlling with the "at risk" group but that they provide similar levels of structure to both groups. However, when the cross-reports of the parents and teachers were examined (teachers reporting on parents and parents reporting on teachers), a very different pattern of findings emerged: teachers and parents report each other showing similar levels of involvement and autonomy support but providing less structure to the "at risk" group than the random group.

These findings, while not directly addressing the linkages between contextual and self-system variables, do suggest that, in this sample, both parents and teachers report providing disaffected students with *less* involvement and autonomy support than do parents of non-labeled students. However, according to the model, these at-risk students need *more* involvement and autonomy support if the self-system processes associated with engagement are to be enhanced. The cross-report findings, suggesting that teachers and parents see each other but not themselves as providing less structure to the "at risk" students, may tell us more about *adult* self-system processes than the children's motivation. These results also reveal a negative vortex for these disaffected youth, their families, and their teachers such that disaffected patterns of behavior by the children are being met by the adults with less involvement and more controlling behavior. According to the model, this withdrawal of autonomy support and involvement will further erode the motivational foundation for adaptive self-system functioning and future engagement.

Summary of Findings

Results from a program of school-based research provide evidence for the validity of the model within this domain. At this point, almost all findings are based on cross-sectional data. Thus, these results can only be interpreted as suggestive of the proposed causal influences specified in the model. What is encouraging about these cross-sectional findings is that: (a) The operationalizations of these constructs appear to work as expected theoretically; (b) Initial support for the selected linkages in the model has been obtained; and, (c) Multiple reporters' perspectives on these variables (children, teachers, and parents) help provide access to some of the transactional processes at the core of this conceptualization.

Interactive and Dynamic Relations Among Competence, Autonomy, and Relatedness Needs in Educational Settings

Data presented here and elsewhere suggests that self-system processes emerging from children's social interactions with parents, teachers, and peers affect the degree and pattern of children's engagement and disaffection in school. In this chapter, research findings were presented separately according to which of the three psychological needs was being discussed. However, an important principle underlying the model is that the experience of these three needs is simultaneous; at times complementary, at times competitive, but always as part of a single, dynamic system. In this section, consideration will be given to the interactive and dynamic interrelations of the three needs as they are manifested within the educational enterprise. Empirical investigation of these interrelations is just beginning; a brief discussion of these issues will serve to highlight current directions for these studies.

Interactive Relations. Interactive relations among the psychological needs would hold if the effects of competence-related self-system processes were moderated by autonomy-related self-system processes. For example, a child's not knowing why he or she succeeds or fails at a particular task (unknown strategy) could increase engagement in that task if the child is doing the task just for the enjoyment of doing it (intrinsic regulation). However, the same unknown strategy could produce disaffection if the child was doing the task because "I'd be ashamed if I didn't do it" (introjected regulation) or because "I get yelled at if I don't do it" (eternal regulation). In this case, the effects of self-system processes associated with the need for competence are interacting with autonomy-related self-system processes in their impact on patterns of action (Skinner & Connell, 1986).

Teacher-child relatedness may also interact with competence-related beliefs in their effects on children's engagement. Children who report they are having difficulty trying hard in school (low effort capacity) but who say they have a good relationship with their teacher may experience less disaffection than children with similarly problematic, competence-related beliefs and a poor relationship with their teacher. For the first set of children, relatedness may buffer the effects of the problematic competence-related beliefs and allow these children to continue engaging in achievement-related behaviors. This continued engagement could then eventuate in progressively more positive beliefs about the capacity to try hard in school.

Dynamic Relations. Dynamic relations among the psychological needs exist when the needs come into conflict or tension (competitive dynamics), or when the needs are aligned in a synergistic configuration (complementary dynamics). While conceptual and statistical models exist for describing and evaluating interactive effects among sets of variables, developing conceptual models and empirical tests for dynamic relations among the three sets of self-system processes present a formidable challenge. Recent work by Ryan (in press) and Ryan and Lynch (1989) has pointed to the possibilities both of competitive and complementary dynamics between autonomy and relatedness during adolescence and young adulthood. Emde and Buchsbaum (in press) have also discussed the dynamic interrelations between these two needs over the first years of life as have Mahler and her colleagues in their object relations framework (Mahler et al., 1975).

Given that the ostensible mission of schools is to promote academic and intellectual competence, we might expect competitive and complementary motivational dynamics between competence and the other needs to be present. Indeed, if institutional structures exist that are not sensitive to teachers' and students' needs for autonomy and relatedness, competitive dynamics between the institutional goals for competent performance and individual needs for autonomy and relatedness may occur. The result would be increased disaffection of the participants. For example, many school systems have adopted what are called "teacher-" and "child-proof" curricula. The intent of these curricula is to improve teaching and learning and to enhance students' and teachers' sense of competence in the process. Most teachers report a firm understanding of how to go about executing these teaching methods and a belief in their own capacity to execute them. But, teachers also report feeling controlled and pressured by these curricula. In this case, the low autonomy afforded by these curricula undermines the potential benefits of clearly defined expectations and teaching/learning strategies. These competitive dynamics between competence and autonomy have resulted in more "ritualistic" patterns of disaffection both in children and teachers rather than the increased engagement that was expected. Synergistic or complementary dynamics between the three needs within the enterprise of schooling are more difficult to identify. While the paths to disaffection are clearly marked, for many children the path to optimal engagement is difficult to find. Ideally, when the child is being optimally challenged (perceived competence) on a task that is meaningful and/or fun (perceived autonomy) and when others involved in the activity are experienced as emotionally supportive (perceived relatedness), synergy will occur resulting in optimal engagement. One important step toward these ideal conditions may be to expand the priorities of schools to include *engagement* in learning as a central institutional goal along with meeting certain performance standards. How the new motivational model can be used to inform such reform efforts will be discussed in the final section of the chapter.

SUMMARY OF THE MODEL

The model of self-system processes presented in this chapter draws on the rich and varied tradition of motivational, social, and cognitive/action perspectives on the development of self. What is *distinctive* about the model is also directly related to these historical influences. The *motivational* analysis of the three psychological needs for competence, autonomy, and relatedness guided the selection of the self-system processes to be included in the model. *Social* perspectives informed the conceptualization of the three aspects of the social context most relevant to the meeting of the three needs. And, concerns about how self-related attitudes, values, and beliefs are connected to action, so central to *cognitive/action* formulations, led to the inclusion of patterns of engagement in the model.

In this chapter, theoretical relations between this new model of self-system processes and other perspectives on the development of self have been described. Applications of the model to the enterprise of schooling, and specifically to *students'* self-system processes, have also been presented. In the concluding discussion, speculations will be offered as to how this model may be useful in designing social contexts that facilitate engagement in cultural enterprises such as school.

IMPLICATIONS OF THE MODEL FOR INSTITUTIONAL REFORM

The discussion that follows is based on our ongoing collaborative efforts with colleagues in educational settings to enhance student and teacher motivation through institutional reform (Connell, Wellborn, and Pierson, 1989). These efforts are just beginning, but two concepts are emerging as central. The first is that the theoretical constructs in the model can be and must be applied to the multiple constituencies involved in the educational enterprise including students, parents, teachers, etc.. Studying the self-system processes of students alone does not provide an adequate knowledge base to guide effective institutional reform. The second concept is that motivationally relevant information is drawn from a set of embedded contexts that include and also emanate beyond immediate social interactions. In this concluding section, these two concepts will be briefly elaborated using examples from our collaborative research efforts with school-based colleagues.

Self-system Processes in Teachers

Theory and experience in working with school systems suggest that efforts to improve the motivational quality of children's lives in school are significantly enhanced by recognizing that teachers, as providers of motivational nutriments to children, are themselves embedded in a social context above and beyond that of the classroom. The degree to which these social contexts facilitate or inhibit teachers' own needs for competence, autonomy, and relatedness affects teachers' engagement in their professional activities. By extending the model to issues of teacher self-system processes, multiple constituencies within the educational enterprise are explicitly recognized as having common motivational needs and as contributing to each others' fulfillment of these needs. When we recognize that the same motivational issues are shared by teachers and students and then examine transactional processes affecting students' *and* teachers' engagement, our

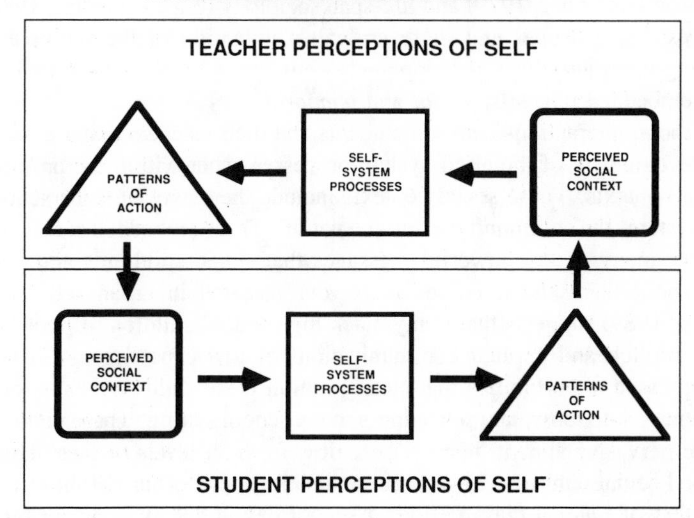

FIG. 2.11. The transactional context of teacher-student relationships.

efforts to improve the quality of these interactions have been enhanced considerably.

Current investigations of *teachers'* self-system processes focus on how teachers' experiences of competence, autonomy and relatedness are influenced by *teachers'* perceptions of the degree of autonomy support, structure, and involvement provided in their work context. Following these initial studies, two additional hypotheses regarding transactional processes between students and teachers will be explored: first, that teachers' engagement and disaffection will influence the provision of autonomy support, structure and involvement to their students; and, second, that students' patterns of action and resulting educational outcomes will be aspects of the *teachers'* social context that influence their self-system processes and patterns of engagement and disaffection in the classroom (see Figure 2.11).

Embedded Contexts

The notion of *embedded contexts* is the second concept that links the model to issues of institutional reform. Embedded contexts refer to the various sets of social and historical influences that impinge upon individuals' appraisals of self within particular enterprises. Again, our theory and experience suggest that attempts to promote meaningful institutional change will have to recognize that all participants in the educational enterprise are embedded in multiple social and temporal contexts and that these embedded contexts each, and in combination, impact these participants' experience of competence, autonomy and relatedness in their everyday lives (See Figure 2.12). The growing awareness of this concept within such traditions as life-span psychology (e.g., Lerner & Busch-Rossnagel, 1981; Bronfenbrenner, 1979) and life-span sociology (e.g., Dannefer, 1984) will make possible a deeper and more critical examination of the multiple forces impinging upon individual development. Thus far, we have conceptualized two sets of embedded contexts: *social* and *temporal.*

The social interactions between students and their teachers that are so critical to the development of their self-system processes occur within a broadening set of *social* contexts. These social contexts include the classroom, the school, the school system, the community; even, the nation. These embedded social contexts also carry many of the powerful messages that shape children's and teacher's beliefs about themselves. For example, our research in urban settings (e.g., Crichlow, 1989) suggests that many black high school children of poor families receive implicit and explicit communications of low expectations, disinterest, and suppressed opportunities that clearly inhibit these children's experiences of competence, autonomy, and relatedness in the school setting. These communications are pervasive and, in many cases, flow from all levels of these children's embedded social contexts. These communications also occur within a telescoping context of *time:* a class period, a school day, a school year, an historical period. Again, studies of these issues in urban settings reveal that children's

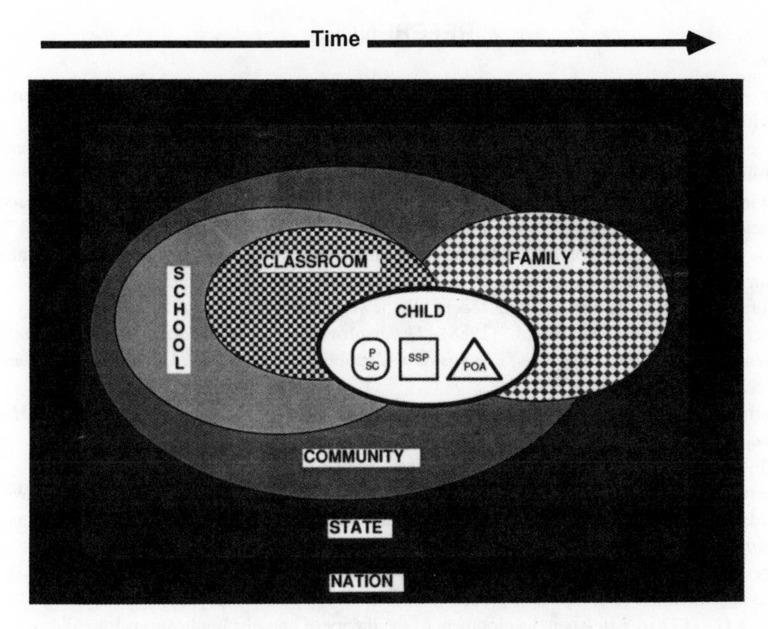

FIG. 2.12. The embedded contexts of student motivation.

beliefs about themselves are shaped not only by communications from the contemporary social contexts of the classroom, the school, and the family but also by the history of these communications in the child's own life and that of his peers, siblings, and parents.

In sum, we proceed from the assumption that the needs for competence, autonomy, and relatedness are universal psychological needs that are experienced in and influenced by multi-leveled socio-historical contexts. More specifically, we and our school-based colleagues have undertaken a critical examination of institutional practices and structures in light of these motivational issues. We will then attempt to use this motivational analysis to develop and test in practice new models for social interactions in the context of the children's everyday lives.

ACKNOWLEDGMENTS

The ideas presented in this chapter are due in large part to the collaborative efforts of members of the Human Motivation Research Group at the University of Rochester. Substantial contributions have been made by (in alphabetical order) Edward L. Deci, Wendy S. Grolnick, Richard M. Ryan, and Ellen A. Skinner. The authors wish to thank the W. T. Grant Foundation for their support of this research.

REFERENCES

Abramson, L. Y., Seligman, M. E. P., & Teasdale, J. D. (1978). Learned helplessness in humans: Critique and reformulation. *Journal of Abnormal Psychology, 87,* 49–74.

Ainsworth, M. D. S., Blehar, M. C., Waters, E., & Wall, S. (1978). *Patterns of attachment.* Hillsdale, NJ: Lawrence Erlbaum Associates.

Baldwin, J. M. (1897). The self-conscious person. In C. Gordon & K. Gergen (Eds.), *The self in social interaction* (pp. 161–169). New York: Wiley.

Baltes, P. B. (1987). Theoretical propositions of life-span developmental psychology: On the dynamics between growth and decline. *Developmental Psychology, 23* 611–626.

Bandura, A. (1977). *Social learning theory.* Englewood Cliffs, NJ: Prentice-Hall.

Barclay, C. R., & Hodges, R. M. (1988). *The improvisational self: Narrative truth in the momentary meanings of instant self composition.* Unpublished manuscript, University of Rochester, Rochester, NY.

Baumrind, D. (1971). Current patterns of parental authority. *Developmental Psychology Monographs, 4,* 1–102.

Bowlby, J. (1969). *Attachment.* New York: Basic Books.

Bretherton, I. (1985). Attachment theory: Retrospect and prospect. In I. Bretherton & E. Waters (Eds.), Growing points of attachment theory and research. *Monographs of the Society for Research in Child Development, 50*(1–2, Serial No. 209), 3–35.

Bridges, L., Connell, J. P., & Belsky, J. (1988). Infant–mother and infant–father interaction in the strange situation: A component process analysis. *Developmental Psychology, 24,* 92–100.

Brim, O. G. (1976). Life-span development of the theory of oneself: Implications for child development. In H. W. Reese & L. P. Lipsitt (Eds.), *Advances in child development and behavior,* Vol. 2. New York: Academic Press.

Bronfenbrenner, U. (1979). *The ecology of human development.* Cambridge, MA: Harvard University Press.

Brophy, J. (1986). Teacher influences on student motivation. *American Psychologist, 41,* 1069–1071.

Carver, C. S., & Scheier, M. F. (1981). *Attention and self-regulation: A control theory approach to human behavior.* New York: Springer-Verlag.

Chandler, C. (1981). *The effects of parenting techniques on the development of motivational orientations in children.* Unpublished doctoral dissertation, University of Denver.

Chapin, S. L. (1989). *Family interaction style and self-system processes in children: A theoretical model and empirical investigation.* Unpublished doctoral dissertation, University of Rochester, Rochester, NY.

Cicchetti, D. (1989). The organization and coherence of socio-emotional, cognitive and representational development: Illustrations through a developmental psychopathology perspective on Down Syndrome and child maltreatment. In R. Thompson (Ed.), *Nebraska Symposium on Motivation* (Vol. 36). Lincoln, NE: University of Nebraska Press.

Connell, J. P. (1985). A new multidimensional measure of children's perceptions of control. *Child Development, 56,* 1018–1041.

Connell, J. P. (in press). Context, self and action: A motivational analysis of self-system processes across the life-span. In D. Cicchetti (Ed.), *The self in transition: From infancy to childhood.* Chicago: University of Chicago Press.

Connell, J. P., Bridges, L., & Grolnick, W. S. (1989). *The development of emotional self-regulation.* Grant submitted to National Institute of Child Health and Development.

Connell, J. P. & Thompson, R. (1986). Emotion and social interaction in the strange situation: Consistencies and asymmetric influences in the second year. *Child Development, 57,* 733–745.

Connell, J. P., & Ryan, R. M. (1984). *Motivation and internalization in the academic domain: The development of self-regulation.* Paper presented at the meeting of the American Education Research Association, New Orleans.

Connell, J. P., & Ryan, R. M. (1987). *Autonomy in the classroom: A theory and assessment of children's self-regulatory styles in the academic domain.* Unpublished manuscript, University of Rochester, Rochester, NY.

Connell, J. P., Wellborn, J., & Lynch, M. L. (in preparation). *Relatedness to others in middle childhood and adolescence.* Manuscript in preparation, University of Rochester, Rochester, NY.

Connell, J. P., Wellborn, J. G., & Pierson, L. H. (1989). Students at-risk for academic failure and personal maladjustment: A theory based approach to intervention and prevention. Grant submitted to W. T. Grant Foundation.

Cooley, C. (1902). *Human nature and the social order.* New York: Scribner.

Coopersmith, S. (1967). *The antecedents of self-esteem.* San Francisco: W. H. Freeman.

Covington, M. V. (1984). The motive for self-worth. In R. Ames & C. Ames (Eds.), *Research on motivation in education.* New York: Academic Press.

Crichlow, W. E. (1989). A social analysis of black youth commitment and disaffection in an urban high school. Dissertation proposal. University of Rochester, Rochester, New York.

Crichlow, W., & Vito, R. C. (1989). *Evaluation of intervention projects for at-risk students: comparative results of the Rochester Assessment Package for Schools administered in five at-risk project schools.* Unpublished manuscript, University of Rochester, Rochester, NY.

Damon, W., & Hart, D. (1982). The development of self-understanding from infancy through adolescence. *Child Development, 53,* 831–857.

Dannefer, D. (1984). Adult development and social theory: A paradigmatic reappraisal. *American Sociological Review, 49,* 100–116.

Deci, E. L. (1980). *The psychology of self-determination.* Lexington, MA: D. C. Heath.

Deci, E. L., Connell, J. P., & Ryan, R. M. (1989). Self-determination in a work organization. *Journal of Applied Psychology, 74,* 580–590.

Deci, E. L., & Ryan, R. M. (1985). *Intrinsic motivation and self-determination in human behavior.* New York: Plenum Press.

Deci, E. L., Schwartz, A. J., Sheinman, L., & Ryan, R. M. (1981). An instrument to assess adults' orientation toward control versus autonomy with children: Reflection on intrinsic motivation and perceived competence. *Journal of Education and Psychology, 73,* 642–650.

Dweck, C. S. & Elliot, E. S. (1983). Achievement motivation. In P. H. Mussen (Ed.), *Handbook of Child Psychology* (4th ed., Vol. 4, pp. 643–691). New York: Wiley.

Elder, G. H., Jr. (1984). Families, kin, and the life course: A sociological perspective. In R. D. Parke, R. N. Emde, H. P. McAdoo, & G. P. Sackett (Eds.), *Review of Child Development. Vol. 7: The Family* (pp. 80–136). Chicago: University of Chicago Press.

Emde, R. M., & Buchsbaum, H. K. (in press). "Didn't you hear me mommy?" Autonomy with connectedness in moral self emergence. In D. Cicchetti (Ed.), *The self in transition: Infancy to childhood.* Chicago: University of Chicago Press.

Epstein, S. (1973). The self-concept revisited: Or a theory of a theory. *American Psychologist, 28,* 404–416.

Erikson, E. (1950). *Childhood and society.* New York: Norton.

Findley, M. J., & Cooper, H. M. (1983). Locus of control and academic achievement: A literature review. *Journal of personality and social psychology, 44,* 419–427.

Fischer, K. W. (1980). A theory of cognitive development: The control and construction of hierarchies of skills. *Psychological Review, 87,* 477–531.

Frese, M., & Stewart, J. (1984). Skill learning as a concept in life-span developmental psychology: An action-theoretical analysis. *Human Development, 27,* 145–162.

Freud, S. (1927). *The ego and the id.* London: Hogarth.

Gergen, K. J. (1984). Theory of the self: Impasse and evolution. In L. Bekowitz (Ed.), *Advances in experimental social psychology* (Vol. 17, pp. 49–115). New York: Academic Press.

Gewirtz, J. (1972). Attachment, dependence, and a distinction in terms of stimulus control. In J. Gewirtz (Ed.), *Attachment and dependency*. Washington, DC: Winston.

Grolnick, W. S., & Ryan, R. M. (1987). Autonomy support in education: Creating the facilitating environment. In N. Hastings & J. Schwieso (Eds.), *New directions in educational psychology, Vol. 2: Behaviour and motivation*. London: Falmer Press.

Grolnick, W. S., & Ryan, R. M. (1989). Parent-styles associated with children's self-regulation and competence in school. *Educational Psychology, 81,* 143–154.

Harter, S. (1982). The perceived competence scale for children. *Child Development, 53,* 87–97.

Harter, S. (1983a). Competence as a dimension of self-evaluation: Toward a comprehensive model of self-worth. In R. Leahy (Ed.), *The development of self* (pp. 55–121). New York: Academic Press.

Harter, S. (1983b). Developmental perspectives on the self-system. In E. M. Hetherington (Ed.), *Handbook of child psychology. Vol. 4: Socialization, personality and social development* (4th ed., pp. 275–386). New York: Wiley.

James, W. (1890). *The principles of psychology*. New York: Holt.

Kohut, H. (1977). *The restoration of the self.* New York: International Universities Press.

Kuhl, J. (1984). Volitional aspects of achievement motivation and learned helplessness: Toward a comprehensive theory of action control. In B. A. Maher (Ed.), *Progress in experimental personality research* (Vol. 13). New York: Academic Press.

Lerner, R. M., & Busch-Rossnagel, N. A. (Eds.). (1981). *Individuals as producers of their development: A life-span perspective*. New York: Academic Press.

Lynch, M. D., & Wellborn, J. G. (1989). *Patterns of relatedness in maltreated and matched-control children: A look at mother–child relationships beyond infancy*. Paper presented at a meeting of the Society for Research in Child Development. Kansas City, MO.

Lynch, M. D., Wellborn, J. G., Cicchetti, D., & Connell, J. P. (1989). *Patterns of relatedness in maltreated and matched-control children across childhoods*. Manuscript in preparation. University of Rochester, Rochester, NY.

Mahler, M. S., Pine, F., & Bergman, A. (1975). *The psychological birth of the human infant*. New York: Basic Books.

Main, M., Kaplan, N., & Cassidy, J. (1985). Security in infancy, childhood, and adulthood: A move to the level of representation. In I. Bretherton & E. Waters (Eds.), Growing points of attachment theory and research. *Monographs for the Society for Research in Child Development, 50*(1–2, Serial No. 209), 66–104.

Markus, H. (1977). Self-schemata and the processing of information about the self. *Journal of Personality and Social Psychology, 35,* 63–78.

Maslow, A. H. (1970). *Motivation and personality* (2nd ed.). New York: Harper & Row.

McClelland, D. C. (1985). *Human motivation*. Dallas: Scott, Foresman.

McGuire, W. (1981). The spontaneous self-concept as affected by personal distinctiveness. In A. A. Norem-Hebersen & M. Lynch (Eds.), *Self-concept*. Cambridge, MA: Ballinger.

Mead, G. H. (1934). Self. In A. Strauss (Ed.), *George Herbert Mead on social psychology* (pp. 199–246). Chicago: Phoenix.

Reigle, K. F. (1973). An epitaph for a paradigm. *Human Development, 16,* 1–7.

Rogers, C. (1951). *Client centered therapy*. Boston: Houghton Mifflin.

Rosenberg, M. *Society and adolescent self-image*. Princeton, NJ: Princeton University Press, 1965.

Rotter, J. B. (1966). Generalized expectancies for internal versus external control of reinforcement. *Psychological Monographs, 80,* (1, Whole No. 609). pp. 1–28.

Ryan, R. M. (in press). The nature of the self in autonomy and relatedness. In A. Goethals and J. Straun (Eds.), *Multidisciplinary perspectives on the self.* New York: Springer-Verlag.

Ryan, R. M., & Connell, J. P. (1989). *Perceived locus of causality and internalization: Examining reasons for acting in two domains. Journal of Personality and Social Psychology, 57,* 749–761.

Ryan, R. M., Connell, J. P., & Deci, E. L. (1985). A motivational analysis of self-determination and self-regulation in education. In C. Ames & R. E. Ames (Eds.), *Research on motivation in education: The classroom milieu* (pp. 13–51). New York: Academic Press.

Ryan, R. M., & Grolnick, W. S. (1986). Origins and pawns in the classroom: Self-report and projective assessments of individual differences in children's perception. *Journal of Personality and Social Psychology, 50,* 550–558.

Ryan, R. M., & Lynch, J. H. (1989). Emotional autonomy versus detachment: Revisiting the vicissitudes of adolescence and young adulthood. *Child Development, 60,* 340–356.

Sabini, J., & Frese, M. (1985). Action theory: An introduction. In M. Frese & J. Sabini (Eds.), *Goal directed behavior: The concept of action in psychology.* Hillsdale, NJ: Lawrence Erlbaum Associates.

Seligman, M. E. P. (1975). *Helplessness: On depression, development, and death.* San Francisco: Freeman.

Seligman, M. E. P., Peterson, C., Kaslow, N. J., Tanenbaum, R. L., Alloy, C. B., & Abramson, L. Y. (1984). Attributional style and depressive symptoms among children. *Journal of Abnormal Psychology, 93,* 235–238.

Skinner, B. F. (1953). *Science and human behavior.* New York: Macmillan.

Skinner, E. A. (this volume). Development and perceived control: A dynamic model of action in context. In M. Gunnar & L. A. Sroufe (Eds.), *Minnesota Symposium on Child Psychology,* Vol. XXIII. Hillsdale: Lawrence Erlbaum Associates.

Skinner, E., & Connell, J. P. (1986). Control understanding: Suggestions for a developmental framework. In M. M. Baltes & P. B. Baltes (Eds.), *Aging and the psychology of control* (pp. 35–61). Hillsdale, NJ: Lawrence Erlbaum Associates.

Skinner, E. A., Connell, J. P., & Wellborn, J. G. (in preparation). *A longitudinal study of children's beliefs about strategies and capacities: A model of context, self, and action.* University of Rochester, Rochester, New York.

Skinner, E. A., & Kindermann, T. A. (1989). *Motivation in school: Impact of teachers and peer groups.* Grant submitted to National Institute of Child Health and Human Development.

Skinner, E. A., Wellborn, J. G., & Connell, J. P. (1990). *What it takes to do well in school and whether I've got it: The role of perceived control in children's engagement and school achievement. Journal of Educational Psychology, 82.*

Smith, M. B. (1985). The metaphorical basis of selfhood. In A. J. Marsella, G. DeVos, & F. C. K. Hsu (Eds.), *Culture and self: Asian and western perspectives* (pp. 57–88). New York: Tavistock.

Sroufe, & Waters, (1977). Attachment as an organizational construct. *Child Development, 48,* 1184–1199.

Stern, D. (1977). *The first relationship: Mother and infant.* Cambridge, MA: Harvard University Press.

Sullivan, H. S. (1953). *The interpersonal theory of psychiatry.* New York: Norton.

Tero, P. F., & Connell, J. P. (1983, April). *Children's academic coping inventory: A new self-report measure.* Paper presented at the meeting of the American Education Research Association, Montreal.

Vygotsky, L. S. (1962). *Thought and language.* New York: Wiley.

Watson, J. B. (1919). *Psychology from the standpoint of a behaviorist.* Philadelphia: J. P. Lippincott.

Wellborn, J. G., & Connell, J. P. (1987). *Manual for the Rochester Assessment Package for Schools.* Unpublished manuscript, University of Rochester, Rochester, NY.

Wellborn, J. G., & Connell, J. P. (in preparation). *Engagement versus disaffection: Motivated patterns of action in the academic domain.* University of Rochester, Rochester, NY.

White, R. W. (1959). Motivation reconsidered: The concept of competence. *Psychological Review, 66,* 297–333.

Winnicott, D. W. (1965). *The maturational process and the facilitating environment.* New York: International Universities Press.

3 Cognitive-experiential Self Theory: Implications for Developmental Psychology

Seymour Epstein
University of Massachusetts

The purpose of this presentation is to provide a review of *Cognitive-experiential Self-theory* (CEST) with an emphasis on recent theoretical developments and research that are particularly relevant to developmental psychology. A thorough review of CEST is beyond the scope of this chapter. The interested reader can find additional information in a number of publications, most of which provide an overview of the theory plus a detailed elaboration of selected aspects (Epstein, 1973, 1976, 1980, 1981, 1983, 1985, 1987, in press; Epstein & Erskine, 1983). For present purposes, a brief review that highlights the most fundamental assumptions and incorporates new developments will suffice.

DEFINITION OF THE SELF

Before proceeding further, it will be helpful to identify what the self is and to distinguish the self as agent, "knower," or the "I," from the self as the object of knowledge, or the "me." Ever since William James (1910) presented his influential analysis of the self, the concept of self has been a sourse of controversy among personality psychologists. According to some, there is no more important concept in psychology, and any personality theory that does not accord it a central role is, at best, superficial, and, at worst, misguided. According to others, not only is the self dispensable, but it is a source of confusion and complication, for everything that has been attributed to the self can be explained as well without it.

The argument about the importance of the concept of self cannot be resolved without addressing the distinction between the self as object and the self as agent. There has never been any disagreement about the value of the former, as everyone recognizes that people have views about themselves that have an important influence on their feelings and behavior. Moreover, the self as object readily lends itself to research, as it is possible to measure people's views about themselves with self-report procedures that can be treated like objective data. The situation is different for the self as agent, which cannot be measured, but is simply a theoretical construct that has been disparagingly referred to as "the ghost in the machine" and as a homunculus residing in the head. Those who criticize the self as agent point out that there can be no advantage to such a concept because it simply displaces the task of explaining the behavior of a real person to the task of explaining the behavior of the homunculus that controls the real person. The concept of self as agent, it is concluded, is unscientific and reminiscent of a time when people believed that the essence of human beings was their souls. James (1910), who adhered to this view, concluded that the self as "knower" was a topic best banished to the realm of philosophy. Allport, who initially believed there was some value in the concept of self as agent (Allport, 1955), ultimately agreed with James that it was a scientifically useless concept (Allport, 1961). Although the arguments against an agentic self seem compelling, as will be seen shortly, the concept of an agentic self is scientifically viable.

The self as object can be defined as all of the beliefs that individuals hold about themselves. However, this must be qualified in CEST, by the consideration that there are two conceptual systems that contain selves as objects, a rational system and an experiential one. The self as object in the rational system consists of the views a person holds about himself or herself that can readily be reported. It is the self that is measured by direct self-report in personality inventories and interviews. The self as object in the experiential system, on the other hand, consists primarily of cognitions derived from emotionally significant experiences of which the person may or may not be aware.

As an illustration of the difference between the self as object in the two systems, consider the case of a person with high self-esteem in the rational system and low self-esteem in the experiential system. In an interview or in response to a self-report inventory, such a person would report that he or she is highly self-accepting and confident. Yet direct observation of the person's behavior would suggest the opposite by a number of objective indicators. For example, the person might stutter or stammer, avoid eye contact, exhibit false bravado, take offense readily, and be aggressively defensive, all of which, on theoretical grounds, are suggestive of low self-esteem. Since most researchers are interested in the implications of their measures for behavior, self-esteem at the experiential level is the most relevant concern for them. Yet, they usually measure self-esteem at the rational level because it is easy to obtain and they are unaware of the distinction. They are able to get by, within limits, with such a procedure because, for most people, there is considerable overlap between the two systems. Nevertheless, a failure to make explicit the distinction between the two systems can result in conceptual confusion, reduced accuracy of prediction, and an absence of research on the discrepancy between the systems, an important source of maladjustment.

The self as agent corresponds to (can be defined as) an individual's self theory (Epstein, 1973), which, in addition to containing descriptive beliefs, contains motivational beliefs, or beliefs about the relations of self-initiated actions to outcomes. Thus, the self as agent differs from the self as object in two important ways: It is hierarchically organized into a theory and it contains propositions about means–end relations. The organization of the self into a theory with means–end propositions identifies a system that is able to interact selectively with the environment in a manner that promotes assimilation and accommodation, thereby producing an increasingly differentiated and integrated model of reality. All theories have agentic properties in the sense that they selectively influence the pursuit, organization, and retrieval, of information, and self theories are no exception. All that needs to be added to have a viable organism that is capable of adaptive action is a reason for acting, which is provided initially by sensations and emotions (e.g., candy tastes good and horseradish does not) and later by more complex motivational cognitions (e.g., awareness that good behavior results in approval, which is desirable, and bad behavior results in disapproval, which is undesirable). In this respect, it is important to recognize that a personal theory of reality is assumed not to develop for its own sake, but as a conceptual tool for facilitating living in an emotionally satisfying way. That is, a personal self theory is conceived of, in CEST, as emotionally driven. This follows from the assumptions that that organisms prefer to feel good than to feel bad and that the schemata in a personal theory of reality are primarily derived from emotionally significant experiences.

Just as there are rational and experiential selves as objects, there are rational and experiential selves as agents. The rational agentic self organizes experience and directs behavior according to a self theory that is based on conscious, presumably rational beliefs. The experiential agentic self, on the other hand, organizes experiences and directs behavior according to a self theory based on experientially derived schemata. As the two agentic selves can direct the individual to different ends, conflict between the two can occur. Such conflicts, commonly identified as conflicts between the heart and the mind, often occur as minor sources of stress in everyday life, but can also be the source of major distress.

THE BASIC THEORY

The Fundamental Need to Construct a Theory of Reality

Like it or not, everyone constructs a theory of reality. A person does not set about to do so consciously and deliberately. Rather, the theory develops spontaneously in the course of everyday living. Given its capacity to represent experience, the brain automatically goes about its business of building a model of emotionally significant events. A person's theory of reality includes two major subtheories, a self theory and a world theory, and propositions connecting them. As a personal theory of reality exists at a preconscious level of awareness, people cannot necessarily describe its contents if asked to do so any more than they can describe how they automatically maintain size constancy or ignore the double vision of stimuli that are out of focus. To be sure, people hold conscious views about what they and the world are like and what they have to do to get along in it, but such conscious, intellective views are not those of primary concern to CEST. Rather, CEST is mainly concerned with experientially derived schemata, including basic postulates, lower-order beliefs, values, motives, plans, and scripts, all of which are organized into an overall conceptual system.

The tendency to construct a model of the world is so fundamental that it can be observed in subhuman as well as human animals. It is, of course, not surprising that such a tendency developed in the course of evolution as it is difficult to imagine how higher-order animals that rely on learning instead of instinct could survive without it.

The fundamental nature of the need to develop and maintain a model of the world is demonstrated in a famous experiment by Pavlov in which he produced serious disturbance in a dog by requiring it to discriminate between a circle and an ellipse. One of the stimuli had been associated with the delivery of food and the other with its absence. So long as the animal could make the discrimination, as indicated by an appropriate salivary response, all was well. However, when the appearance of the ellipse was made to approach that of the circle, a dramatic change occurred in the animal's behavior when it could no longer discriminate. It became excited, howled, and tore at its halter. This was followed by a widespread breakdown in adaptive behavior, which Pavlov called an animal neurosis, but which might more accurately be referred to as an animal psychosis because it involved a complete disorganization of the animal's conceptual system. Pavlov's experiment dramatically illustrates how important it is to higher-order animals to maintain a model of the world.

The 4 Basic Functions of Personal Theories of Reality

As previously noted, it is assumed that a personal theory of reality is not developed for its own sake, but is a conceptual tool for coping with life's problems. So far I have discussed two basic functions of a self theory, to maximize pleasure and minimize pain and to develop and maintain a model of reality. According to CEST, a personal theory of reality has two additional basic functions. The four basic functions are: to enhance the pleasure–pain ratio over the foreseeable future, to assimilate the data of reality (which subsumes the need to maintain the conceptual system), to maintain relatedness to others, and to enhance self-esteem. It is noteworthy that other personality theories emphasize one or another of these functions, but none accords a central role to all. According to learning theory and psychoanalysis, the one most important motive in human behavior is seeking pleasure and avoiding pain. This is referred to as the pleasure principle in psychoanalysis and the reinforcement principle in learning theory. The assimilation of the data of reality and, relatedly, the maintenance of the stability of the system that does the assimilating, are emphasized in phenomenological self theories (e.g., Lecky, 1945/1961; Snygg & Combs, 1949; Rogers, 1951) and in Kelly's (1955) theory of constructive alternativism. The importance of relationships with others is emphasized in Bowlby's (1973) theory and in object relations theory (Cashdan, 1988). The need to enhance self-esteem is regarded as a primary motive by Allport (1961) and by Rogers (1951). According to CEST, these motives are all of central importance, and any one of them can dominate the others.

Behavior is considered to be the outcome of a compromise among the four basic motives. Accordingly, the basic motives provide a set of checks and balances against each other. Thus, the need to enhance the self does not normally result in delusions of grandeur because it is constrained by the needs to assimilate realistically the data of reality and to maintain relatedness with others. As the result of a compromise among these motives, it is not surprising that it has been repeatedly found that most people exhibit a modest self-enhancing bias (see review in Taylor & Brown, 1988). Contrary to some interpretations, these findings do not indicate that reality-awareness is an unimportant criterion of mental health, but only that it is not the only criterion.

A breakdown in the balance among the four functions is characteristic of maladaptive behavior. Such an imbalance can be produced by a threat to any of the functions. Thus, a serious threat to self-esteem can produce overcompensation to the point that the need to enhance the self overwhelms the other functions, resulting in delusions of grandeur. Different disorders are associated with the dominance of different basic needs (Epstein, 1980). In schizophrenia, the need to assimilate realistically the data of reality is sacrificed in order to enhance self-esteem or reduce misery. In depression, the need to assimilate realistically the data of reality is satisfied at the cost of an unfavorable pleasure–pain balance and a low level of self-esteem.

4 Basic Beliefs Associated with the 4 Basic Functions

In order for the experiential system to guide behavior in a manner that maximizes the fulfillment of the four basic functions, it is necessary for there to be an assessment of the degree to which each of the functions is being fulfilled. It follows that there are four basic dimensions of belief associated with the four basic functions. Every person within his or her personal theory of reality has an intuitive assessment corresponding to the degree to which (1) The world is considered to be a source of pleasure versus misery, (2) The world is considered to be meaningful (including predictable, controllable, and just) versus capricious, chaotic, and uncontrollable, (3) People are viewed as desirable to relate to and as a source of support and affection versus threatening and a source of disappointment and hostility, and (4) The self is viewed as worthy, including competent, moral, and lovable, versus unworthy, including incompetent, bad, and unlovable.

3 Conceptual Systems

Social-cognitive psychologists typically assume there is a single conceptual system. Although they sometimes speak of hot and cold cognitions, they view emotions as modifiers of parameters in a single system. Emotions, for example, are regarded as amplifiers of response tendencies. *Cognitive-experiential Self-theory,* on the other hand, assumes the existence of three conceptual systems, a rational system that operates primarily at the conscious level, an experiential system that operates primarily at the preconscious level, and an associationistic system that operates primarily at the unconscious level. In this respect, CEST has more in common with psychonalytic theory, which assumes at least two separate systems, a conscious and an unconscious one. Although psychoanalytic theory recognizes the existence of a preconscious level of functioning, it does not view the preconscious as constituting a separate system with its own rules of operation. Rather, it is regarded as a way station between the conscious and unconscious systems, and is assumed to operate by the same rules as the conscious system. Cognitive-experiential Self-theory, on the other hand, accords a central role to the preconscious level of awareness, for it is at this level that the experiential system, the system that automatically interprets reality and directs behavior in everyday life, primarily operates.

The rational conceptual system operates predominantly at the conscious level, where it functions within constraints imposed by socially prescribed rules of inference. Cognitive-experiential Self-theory has nothing new to say about this system. The experiential and associationistic systems each have their own rules of operation. Since the experiential system is the system of greatest concern to CEST, it will be described in detail shortly. The associationistic system corresponds to a state of altered consciousness and is viewed as similar to Freud's unconscious system, which operates according to the rules of primary process thinking. However, although the associationistic system is assumed to operate according to primary process thinking, it also includes elements of the unconscious as described by Jung. That is, it is regarded as a source of creativity, as making inferences about the future as well as the past, and, in general, as a more sophisticated system than the Freudian unconscious. This is not the place for a detailed discussion of the associationistic system. Further discussion of the rational and associationistic systems, including their topographical representation, can be found in a previous article (Epstein, 1983). Let us now turn to the experiential system.

The Experiential Conceptual System

The experiential system is the system most responsible for everyday behavior. People falsely believe their behavior is primarily directed by their rational thinking. This is because they are aware of their conscious thinking and can usually rationalize their behavior. It is important to recognize that the experiential system is a highly adaptive system that has evolved in human-like ancestors for more than 7 million years. Although it is the same system that directs the behavior of nonhuman higher-order animals, it can be assumed to be more complex in humans, who have a more highly developed cerebral cortex and can use language. In comparison, the rational conceptual system, with its use of socially established signs, symbols, rules of inference, and consideration of evidence, is relatively new. The use of written symbols, signs, and numbers is estimated to be less than 5,000 years old. The first alphabet by the Greeks and pure mathematics are no more than 2,500 years old. The modern scientific method is less than 500 years old. The point is that the experiential system is a highly efficient tried and true system for organizing experience and directing behavior, and it does so automatically, without conscious effort. It would be wondrous, indeed, if nature were willing to abandon completely the gains of 7 million years of evolution in favor of a system that has hardly had time to be tested and whose future, at this point, appears highly questionable.

Evidence for an Independent Experiential System. There is abundant evidence in everyday experience of the existence of an experiential system that operates by different rules from the rational system. First, there are the ubiquitous conflicts between the heart and the mind. Obviously the heart cannot have desires, it can only beat. The conflict must reside in different construals in the brain. When one says, "My reason told me to buy the Volkswagen, but my heart told me to buy the Stingray," one is describing a conflict between competing cognitions about a desirable course of action arrived at through different operations. When a student says, "I did not feel like studying, but I made myself do so," who is the I who thought it best to study, and who is the myself who had to be made to? According to CEST, the self that operated by reason resides in the rational system and the one that operated by emotion resides in the experiential system. Parenthetically, it is noteworthy that people tend to view the rational system as a task-master that forces the experiential part of oneself, regarded as the more natural, authentic self, to do unpleasant tasks and forgo immediate pleasure.

Socrates, in Plato's Republic, intuitively recognized the two systems when he discussed a conflict between desire and reason. Desire, he said, is linked with pleasure and reason with forbearance. Desire bids a man drink; reason forbids it. He concluded that peace of mind can be achieved only through reason. Here he parts ways with CEST, which considers the experiential mind as no less wise and adaptive than the rational mind, but in a different way.

Irrational fears provide additional evidence of a system that operates independently from the rational system. There are many people who, despite knowing that the statistical evidence indicates that it is far safer to travel by air than to drive an automobile, feel safer in their cars, and elect to drive long distances rather than fly. This is an example of the two systems arriving at opposite conclusions. A further example of the difference between the two systems is provided by a comparison of insight and intellective knowledge. Therapists have long known there is an important difference between the two. They have found that it is often worse than useless to provide a client with intellectual information about his or her difficulties. On the other hand, having the patient learn about himself or herself through emotionally significant experience, such as a transference relationship, can produce significant behavior change. Apparently, there is knowledge and knowledge, and experiential knowledge has different consequences with respect to feelings and behavior from intellectual knowledge.

Cigarette advertisements provide an interesting example of the existence of the two systems. It is a matter of wonderment that advertisers are willing to spend millions of dollars to spread the message that their product can kill. Apparently, they intuitively recognize that a picture in which their product is associated with any of a variety of pleasant events, including nature scenes, liberated woman who have come a long way, and ruggedly handsome men who desire to have their Luckys lit, can readily override a straightforward written appeal to reason. This makes perfect sense if it is assumed that there are two conceptual systems, one more responsive to images and emotions and the other to words and reason, and it is the former that often has the more powerful influence on behavior.

Evidence of two conceptual systems that should be particularly convincing to developmental psychologists is provided by Piaget (1973). He describes an informal experiment in which young children were asked to hit a target with a tether ball by releasing the string while spinning around. With some practice they were able to accomplish the feat. When asked to explain how, they said they released the ball when it was pointing at the target. If they did, it would, of course, have hit the wrong wall. Older children, on the other hand, correctly reported that they released the ball when it was at a right angle to the target. Piaget's point is that unless the child has an appropriate conscious schema for assimilating the information, he or she is unable to report the nonverbal knowledge that was acquired. For present purposes, the example well illustrates that there is a difference between knowing in the experiential system and knowing in the rational system.

Attributes of the Experiential System. Unlike the rational system, which guides behavior by direct assessment of stimuli, the direction of behavior by the experiential system is mediated by feelings, or "vibes," which can be either vague, unidentified feelings or full-blown emotions. The experiential system is assumed to operate in the following manner. When an individual is confronted with a new situation, the mind automatically scans its memory banks for schemata derived from emotionally significant similar past experiences. If such experiences are detected, the person experiences "vibes" consonant with the previous experiences. The vibes arouse action tendencies to do something to maintain or enhance the state if the vibes are pleasant and to curtail the state if they are unpleasant. The whole process occurs extremely rapidly, so that to all appearances the behavior that is instigated is a direct, immediate reaction to the eliciting stimulus. In the case of humans, the vibes not only produce tendencies to act in certain ways, but also to think in certain ways.

If the experiential system is a distinct system, it must have its own rules of operation that differ from that of the rational system. Table 3.1 contrasts the rules of operation of the two systems. The list is a tentative one that was derived from an analysis of people's thinking during highly charged emotional situations in comparison with their thinking when discussing more impersonal issues. It was also influenced by analysis of the appeals made in advertising and in politics and by findings with the *Constructive Thinking Inventory* (CTI), to be discussed later.

According to the first item in Table 3.1, the experiential system is holistic in

TABLE 3.1
A Comparison of the Attributes of the Experiential and Rational Systems

Experiential System	*Rational System*
1. Holistic	1. Analytical
2. Emotional: Pleasure–pain oriented (What feels good)	2. Logical: Reason-oriented (What is sensible)
3. Behavior mediated by "vibes" from past experiences	3. Behavior mediated by conscious appraisal of events
4. Encodes reality in concrete images and metaphors	4. Encodes reality in abstract symbols: Words and numbers
5. Rapid processing: Oriented toward immediate action	5. Slower processing: Oriented toward delayed action
6. Slow to change: Changes with repetitive experience, direct or vicarious	6. Changes rapidly: Changes with speed of thought
7. Learns directly from experience	7. Learns from symbolic representations of experience
8. Crudely differentiated and integrated: Associationistic, categorical, and organized into emotional complexes	8. More highly differentiated and integrated
9. Experienced passively and preconsciously: We are seized by our emotions	9. Experienced actively and consciously: We are in control of our thoughts
10. Self-evidently valid: "Experiencing is believing"	10. Requires justification via logic and evidence

contrast to the rational system, which is analytical. Each of these modes of operation has its advantages and disadvantages. Holistic appraisal, since it is based on perception of the entire stimulus as a whole, is more rapid than analytical appraisal. In that it is less differentiated, holistic appraisal is a cruder form of thinking. Yet, analytical analysis, by breaking the whole into its components, runs the risk of losing the forest for the trees. Holistic appraisal, in that it involves spontaneous, immediate reaction to the environment, can be expected to be more closely associated with emotions than analytical thinking, which tends to dampen emotional reactivity. Whether analytical or holistic thinking is preferable depends on the circumstances. If one wishes to react spontaneously and experience emotions fully, then holistic thinking is necessary. Of course, one does not have to choose between the two; one can use both. If one wishes to delay behavior until alternatives have been weighed, then clearly analytical thinking is necessary. If one wishes to get in touch with one's feelings in order to learn from, or discipline them, then it is necessary to employ both processes in conjunction with each other.

The second comparison in Table 3.1 is between emotions and reason. The experiential conceptual system could just as well have been called the emotional conceptual system. However, it is important to realize that, although emotions are intimately associated with the experiential system, the experiential system is a cognitive structure, one that influences emotions, exerts its influence on thought and behavior through emotions, and is influenced by emotions, but is conceptually distinct from emotions. That is, cognitions affect feelings and feelings affect cognitions, but cognitions are not feelings, nor is the reverse true.

The third comparison is between a system that directs behavior directly and one whose influence on behavior is mediated by vibes. This distinction has already been discussed. A particularly important implication of mediation through vibes is that people's conscious thinking is apt to be unconsciously influenced for reasons other than repression.

The fourth comparison refers to the differences in encoding information by the experiential and rational systems. The former relies primarily on visual images and metaphors, and the latter on words and numbers. I do not mean to imply there is no overlap between the systems. The rational system employs metaphors and images, and the experiential system employs words. In fact, it is their overlap into each other's domains that permits communication between the two systems and that provides particularly rich experiences, as in poetry, classical music, and insight, where both systems are simultaneously involved. Words, of course, can be used to paint word pictures and pictures can be used to present analytical material, as in pictures of anatomy in medical textbooks.

The fifth comparison is between rapid and delayed processing of information. The experiential system evolved in a manner that makes it ideally suited for reacting to emergencies by facilitating rapid processing of information and rapid action. The rational system, on the other hand, is particularly suited for delayed action, for planning, and for anticipating long-term consequences.

The sixth comparison is between susceptibility to change in the two systems. Learning in the experiential system is determined by the intensity and frequency of relevant experiences and by the centrality of the schemata subjected to change. The more central a schema, the more resistant it is to change. Unless events are of overwhelming emotional intensity, most experiential learning requires considerable repetition. Learning within the rational system is less dependent on intensity and repetition. Simply being exposed to written information can produce immediate learning in the rational system.

The seventh comparison is between learning directly from experience and learning from symbolic representations of experience. Symbolic learning in the form of words and numbers can, of course, be far more complex than learning directly from experience. The experiential system does not lend itself to the invention of calculus or an atomic chart, nor is it suitable for transmitting complex learning from one generation to the next. On the other hand, learning in the rational system is of very limited value for acquiring certain kinds of skills, such as playing a piano and interpersonal skills.

The eighth comparison is between crude and refined discrimination. As a more primitive system, the experiential system is less differentiated and integrated than the rational system. It has a broader generalization gradient and, relatedly, is more categorical. Another way in which the experiential system is less integrated than the rational system is that a change in emotions initiates a cognitive gestalt switch. That is, when a certain emotion occurs, it is associated with a particular set of cognitions becoming dominant, such as, in the case of anger, that someone is bad and deserves to be punished. When such a shift in the dominance of cognitions takes place, the entire phenomenological field rearranges itself. Emotions can be regarded as cognitive-affective structures that bias the interpretation of reality and the tendency to react in certain ways, such as attacking, withdrawing, and expressing affection. When a person is experiencing a particular emotion, he or she, in effect, undergoes a change in personality. To a certain extent, then, emotions are like multiple personalities. They consist of multiple realities with different implications for action.

The ninth comparison is between feeling that one is in control of a process versus feeling that one is controlled by it. As the experiential system operates automatically at the preconscious level of awareness, people do not normally feel in control of it. Rather, they passively experience their emotions as if they are independent from their cognitions. This is partly because people tend to equate all of their cognitions with their conscious cognitions. Accordingly, they experience being "seized" by their emotions, and their thoughts seem to have nothing to do with the process. We fail to realize that in the vast majority of circumstances, our emotional reactions are mediated by our interpretations of events. The situation is, of course, very different for the conscious thoughts within our rational conceptual system. We are not seized by such thoughts, but believe we will them into existence. We believe we can think as we wish no less than we can act as we wish. It is ironic, in this respect, that unidentified vibes in the experiential system can influence our conscious thoughts without our awareness. It follows that the control that we phenomenologically experience over our rational processes is often illusory. Given the influence of vibes on conscious thinking, one way people can gain conscious control of their thoughts is by identifying the vibes that automatically influence their thinking, and then taking the influence into account in their decision making.

The tenth comparison concerns the nature of validity in the two systems. Experiences within the experiential system are inherently convincing, that is, they are self-evidently valid by virtue of having been experienced. There is no more direct route to believing something than to experience it directly. Conclusions arrived at via the rational system, on the other hand, are not intrinsically convincing. Their level of conviction is determined by inferences based on logic and evidence. Thus, beliefs in the rational system can readily be invalidated by contrary information. What appears to be a correct mathematical solution one moment, may quickly be recognized as incorrect the next. Such is clearly not the case with a conviction derived from a strong emotional experience, such as being rejected by a loved one.

Resistance to Awareness of the Experiential Conceptual System. If the experiential system is as important as I have claimed it is, how is it possible that it has been overlooked for so long? There are several reasons for this. One is that the experiential system is in the background of mental activity, whereas conscious thinking is in the foreground. As Carlysle noted, if a fish had an inquiring mind, the last thing it would discover is water. People look out onto reality and not reflexively back onto their structuring of it. Reality is experienced as objectively out there and not as a subjective organization or interpretation of otherwise unorganized impersonal data.

A second reason why people are readily able to avoid awareness of the experiential system is that, no matter what its cause, they usually can explain their behavior rationally, that is, they can "rationalize" it.

A third reason is that people resist awareness of their experiential system because awareness is burdensome. One is reminded of the centipede who, when asked to describe the order in which it moved its many feet became so confused that it forgot how to walk. Yet, something more is often involved in resistance to awareness of the experiential system than simply the effort that is required. Becoming aware of preconscious thoughts that structure emotions confronts people with the role they play in producing their emotions, which has implications for responsibility and disciplining one's mind. Many prefer to believe they are passive victims of their emotions rather than to assume responsibility.

A final reason for resistance to a preconscious system that operates below the threshold of awareness is that Freud got there first. Since there are already well-established theories that emphasize unconscious processes, most psychologists are satisfied with their explanations of irrational behavior. As Kuhn (1970) has reminded us, old paradigms die hard.

Emotions and Moods

Emotions and moods are of particular interest to CEST for two reasons. First, most schemata in the experiential system have been inductively derived from emotionally significant experiences. Second, emotions provide a royal road to a person's preconscious schemata. That is, emotions are indicators, par excellence, of the cognitions in the experiential system. The greater the emotional reaction a person has to a stimulus, the more it can be assumed that a significant belief in the person's theory of reality has been implicated. Thus, if one wishes to map the important schemata in a personal theory of reality, a useful way to proceed is to note the situations that cause the person to react emotionally. Of particular interest, in this respect, emotional responses often belie conscious statements, so emotions provide a way of acquiring information about schemata in the experiential system that are distinguishable from beliefs in the rational system.

Let us examine the manner in which cognitions influence emotions. If someone preconsciously interprets an injury as undeserved and believes the perpetrator should be punished, the person will feel anger. If the same person regards the same event as an example of humankind's destructive nature that will ultimately have dire consequences about which nothing can be done, the emotion will most likely be sadness. The person could even feel sympathy if he or she considered the perpetrator as an unfortunate soul who, because of an unbearable degree of frustration, behaved unreasonably, and deserved to be helped, not punished.

The recognition that preconscious thoughts are normally the effective stimuli that elicit emotions has important implications for the control of emotions, for it follows that by altering one's preconscious cognitions it is possible to change one's emotions. That this relation has important implications for behavior change has not been lost on cognitive therapists, such as Beck (1976) and Ellis (1962). What has been said of emotions is also true of moods, but on a grander scale. As was previously noted, emotions are cognitive-affective structures, somewhat like multiple personalities. The same is true of moods. They differ in that emotions are episodic reactions that occur in response to specific stimuli, whereas moods are more enduring states that often occur in the absence of identifiable stimuli. Thus, emotions may be superimposed on moods. A person in a sad mood may experience an emotion of joy when given some pleasant news, only to have it recede and the feeling return to baseline. In time, of course, moods do shift, but they do not shift as readily as emotions. It has been said, in this respect, that emotions are to moods as the waves are to the tides.

From the perspective of CEST, a basic difference between moods and emotions is that emotions are produced by preconscious appraisals of the momentary implications of a particular stimulus, whereas moods are produced by preconscious appraisals on a much larger scale, namely, where one currently stands in life and how one considers one's future prospects. This is not to deny that moods can also be influenced by other factors, including biological ones. Nor is it to deny that the influence between cognitions and feeling states goes in both directions. A depressed person is apt to interpret a particular stimulus in a different manner from the way he or she would in a happier frame of mind. Thus, it is obvious that feeling states can influence cognitions as well as the other way around.

THE DEVELOPMENT OF PERSONAL THEORIES OF REALITY

How is a personal theory of reality constructed over time? In order to answer this question, it is first necessary to consider what it is that has to be constructed.

As noted previously, a personal theory of reality consists of a self theory, a world theory, and propositions connecting the two. The overall theory of reality as well as its subtheories consist of hierchically organized schemata and networks of schemata. The most basic schemata in a personal theory of reality are referred to as postulates. Among the most important postulates are the four derived from the basic functions of a personal theory of reality. As the basic postulates represent the highest constructs in the hierarchy of a personal theory of reality, to invalidate any of them would have a profound destabilizing effect on the entire personality structure. As one descends down the hierarchy, schemata become narrower and more closely related to direct experience. The very lowest-order schemata are situation-specific cognitions, which are not very informative about a person's personality structure in the absence of knowledge about their connections to higher-order constructs. Relatedly, lower-order constructs can readily change without affecting higher-order ones. The result is that the overall hierarchical organization of the system is remarkably adaptive because it allows stability to be maintained at the upper organization level, while accommodating change at lower levels. In sum, the system is simultaneously stable and flexible.

Basic beliefs can be divided into two kinds: descriptive and motivational schemata. Descriptive schemata include beliefs about what the self and the world are like, as in the four basic postulates. Motivational schemata are beliefs about what one has to do to obtain what one desires and avoid what one dislikes. Motivational schemata, like other cognitions in the experiential system, are derived primarily from emotionally significant experiences, and are thus emotionally charged, that is, they are hot, not cold, cognitions about how to act in the world. Consider the case of a child with a rejecting mother. Such a child is likely to develop the descriptive postulates that the world is malevolent and untrustworthy and the motivational postulates that the only way to get by is to take what one wants and avoid attachments. (Unless stated otherwise, it should be understood that I am referring to beliefs in the experiential system, which may be quite different from a person's conscious beliefs.) Motivational schemata, like descriptive schemata, exist at various levels of generality and complexity, and include constructs such as values, goals, and plans.

Personal theories of reality, in common with scientific theories, serve the purpose of organizing the data of experience and directing behavior. In the case of scientific theories, the data that are organized are the subject matter of the science, and the behavior that is directed is the scientist's pursuit of understanding for its own sake. In the case of personal theories of reality, the data that are organized are the experiences of everyday living, and the behavior that is directed is how the individual goes about living his or her daily life. Whereas the scientist is presumably motivated only to understand the phenomena he or she studies, the person in everyday life is motivated to live in an emotionally satisfying way. In this respect, CEST can be contrasted with Kelly's (1955) theory of *Constructive Alternativism*. Kelly assumes that the only purpose of a personal conceptual system is to understand the world for its own sake, whereas in CEST the function of the cognitive system is to make life as emotionally satisfying under the perceived circumstances as possible, which is not to say that it necessarily succeeds in this endeavor.

One source of growth in personality is a basic biological drive for stimulation within homeostatic limits. It follows that individuals who are not already overstimulated will seek new experiences. Another is that the assimilation of new information and the resolution of inconsistencies produces pleasant feelings (the "aha" reaction of insight or discovery), whereas a failure to assimilate emotionally significant experiences is a source of anxiety. When viewed from this perspective, there is nothing magical or even strange about the assumption of humanistic psychologists, such as Adler, Rogers, and Maslow, that there is a "growth principle" that provides an inherent source of improvement (increased differentiation and integration of personal theories of reality) that is the therapist's best ally.

Having identified the developmental task that is to be accomplished as the construction of a hierarchical conceptual system that can be used to make life as emotionally satisfying as possible, and having described two intrinsic sources of growth, we are now in a position to consider how the child goes about the task of developing a theory of reality (see also Epstein & Erskine, 1983).

Precursors to the Development of a Personal Theory of Reality

The neonate does not have a theory of reality, but is programmed to acquire one rapidly. Several processes stand it in good stead for this endeavor, including its need for stimulation, its pleasure and pain centers, and the external conditions that promote habituation and conditioning. The infant has innate alerting reactions that cause it to attend to stimuli that are salient because of their energetic component, which includes figure–ground contrasts. Through repeated exposure, habituation occurs. During the process of habituation, an object is repeatedly experienced over a wide range of arousal levels, which include optimal levels for encoding the stimulus. Thereafter, other stimuli that resemble the original one are able to draw the infant's attention by virtue of their cue component, and the infant is able to respond to the recognition of similarity with pleasure (the "aha" of recognition). Through this process, a schema for a class of objects that share one or more properties is formed. Conditioning also contributes to rudimentary concept formation by relating objects to responses and their emotional consequences. The rudimentary concepts formed by habituation and conditioning are building blocks that contribute to the development of a more complex model of the world that ultimately includes human figures, psychological processes, and emotions.

Of particular importance is the classification of objects and relationships in the emerging theory of reality as good or bad according to their affective consequences. The classification of objects as good (desirable) and bad (undesirable) is very likely the single most important classification in a personal theory of reality.

Precursors to two of the basic beliefs, the goodness or benignity, of the world and the meaningfulness of the world are present early in life. Precursors to the basic belief about the benignity of the world are the pleasant and unpleasant sensations received from the external world. The precursors to the basic belief about the meaningfulness of the world are experiences that provide information about the predictability and controllability of the environment. Such experiences include the consistency with which the mothering person is able to anticipate the needs of the infant and the consistency with which the infant, by its own efforts, such as crying or cooing, is able to influence the mothering one's behavior. Both are the outcome of an interactive process between the two.

Further Development

Rudimentary cognitions about the benignity, predictability, and controllability of the world develop following object identification when the child is able to associate particular objects and actions with pleasure and pain. [Precursors to the basic belief about the goodness of people are the pleasant and unpleasant sensations received in conjunction with those who care for the infant's needs.] With the advent of object identification, cognitions are formed about aspects of the mother that are desirable and undesirable, such as her warmth, her smell, and her way of holding and engaging the child.

As object discrimination and integration advance with maturation and experience, the child learns to identify its mother and, later, other people. Its emotions develop from rudimentary affective responses to more differentiated and elaborated cognitive-affective complexes. That is, more differentiated versions of anger, fear, affection, and sadness replace more primitive versions. When the child responds emotionally to recognition of its mother, this paves the way for more complex interactions, which, in turn, facilitate more complex cognitions about human behavior, including what can be done to influence other people.

A particularly important development takes place when the child is able to identify itself as a human-like creature that is similar to other humans, yet distinctive. With the emergence of self-recognition and awareness of intentional behavior, the infant is propelled into a much more complex mode of existence (Piaget, 1981). The stage is set for the development of self-esteem, or the overall favorability of self-evaluation, the fourth basic postulate, and, associated with it, the development of conscience.

It is often assumed that a child would not develop a self-concept in the absence of relationships with significant others. Presumably, the self is formed exclusively from the internalization of reflected appraisals (e.g., Cooley, 1902; Mead, 1934). Whereas reflected appraisals are extremely important for forming a normal social self, a more rudimentary self can be formed without them. All that is required is a crude level of inference, such as recognizing that if one has a head, feet, and body that are more similar to those of humans than to other animals, then one is probably one of the former kind of creature. That the level of conceptualization required for developing such a rudimentary self is neither very great nor contingent on reflected appraisals of others is indicated by evidence that chimpanzees can recognize themselves in a mirror (Gallup, 1968). The same inferential process that allows the child to recognize that it is similar to others in external appearance, allows it to arrive at a similar conclusion with respect to inner processes, including thoughts, emotions, and volition. That is, it takes no great inferential leap to recognize that if one is like others in external ways, one is probably like them in internal ways, and therefore, if one has thoughts, feelings, and intentions, so probably do others.

Where reflected appraisals are of particular importance is in the internalization of values about the self and others, and therefore in the development of self-esteem and conscience. The main source of the child's valuation of itself is its perception of how lovable it is in the eyes of the parents. However, there is another significant early source of self-esteem, and that is the child's mastery of its environment, such as when it learns to stand, crawl, and speak (White, 1959).

Once the rudiments of the four basic postulates have been established, they will develop further according to the emotionally significant experiences that the individual encounters, becoming more differentiated and integrated in the process. Self-esteem, for example, while retaining its status as a general, higher-order construct, will also exist at the level of more differentiated midlevel constructs, including implicit self-assessments of lovability, competence, likeability, moral self-approval, and body image (O'Brien & Epstein, 1988). It will also exist at the level of much narrower schemata within situation- and response-specific domains. As with the overall personal theory of reality, change will occur more readily at the periphery of the conceptual system, so that overall self-esteem will remain relatively stable. Although it is true that temporary shifts can readily be induced in global self-esteem, barring extreme experiences, it will quickly return to baseline.

Emotions as Cognitive-affective Nuclei

Basic emotions, such as anger, fear, sadness, and affection, can be viewed as inherent ways of reacting to the world with a bias toward certain broad classes of adaptive intregrative behavior, such as attacking, withdrawing, and expressing affection. Thus, basic emotions are able to function as nuclei for the development of more complex cognitive-affective networks that organize perception, memory, and behavior into adaptive systems. Such cognitive-affective systems can readily develop into major subsystems in personal theories of reality. It is noteworthy that Horney (1945) identifies the following three ways of relating to the world as basic dimensions of personality: moving toward others, moving away from others, and moving against others. All of these are action tendencies associated with basic emotions.

In normal development, a flexible balance is achieved among the different cognitive-emotional systems. The result is that the individual is able to shift adaptively from one system to another according to situational requirements. When development occurs under conditions of extreme stress, however, there is a tendency for the individual to rely predominantly on a single mode of reacting. Given a high degree of stress, the child turns to whatever response system has worked for it in the past. Having some mode of response is anxiety reducing and staves off disorganization. With repeated use, such a cognitive-affective subsystem it apt to assimilate an ever-widening range of situations, thereby becoming a central organizing complex in the person's personality. To the extent to which it lacks flexibility and becomes the only system that is used, it is maladaptive. As will be seen shortly, it is relevant to the construct of "sensitivities and compulsions," which has widespread implications for maladaptive behaviors.

THE MAINTENANCE OF MALADAPTIVE SCHEMATA

As noted previously, the schemata in a personal theory of reality are derived primarily from emotionally significant experiences. If an individual has experienced the world as malevolent and unpredictable, it is understandable that the individual will develop a schema of the world in which it is represented as malevolent and unpredictable. On the face of it, encoding emotionally significant experiences veridically would seem to be highly adaptive, and in most circumstances, it is. However, a problem arises when individuals develop beliefs that accurately describe the world of their early experience, but that are inaccurate with respect to the broader world and, relatedly, with later experience. This raises an extremely important question, namely, why do people not accommodate their maladaptive schemata when presented with new evidence? There are at least four reasons why maladaptive beliefs are maintained despite conditions that would seem to favor their modification or abandonment: repression, insulation of higher order schemata from the data of experience, the need to maintain the stability of personal theories of reality, and the development of sensitivities and compulsions. We turn to a consideration of each of these next.

Repression

In Freudian theory, the concept of repression carries the entire burden of explaining why maladaptive reactions acquired in childhood are maintained in adulthood despite an absence of supporting conditions. As a result of repression, unacceptable memories and impulses become unavailable for correction by conscious reappraisal and learning. There is nothing magical about repression. All that is required is that individuals divert their thinking away from a course that, if pursued, would lead to the repressed material. The diversion is mediated by twinges of anxiety, referred to as signal anxiety, that are instigated when thoughts approach the area of repression. *Cognitive-experiential Self-theory* accepts the psychoanalytic concepts of unconscious conflict and repression, but believes their range of application has been overextended and that there are other equally important explanatory concepts that psychoanalysis has overlooked.

Insulation of Higher-order Schemata from Experience

As noted at the beginning of this chapter, higher-order schemata are insulated from the direct influence of experience. Given a hierarchically organized conceptual system in which lower-order schemata are situation-specific and higher-order constructs are broad generalizations that subsume many levels of lower-order constructs and a wide range of situation-specific experiences, it follows that specific events, unless of overwhelming significance, as in the case of trauma, are apt to have little effect on higher-order beliefs. As beliefs acquired early in life are apt to become higher-order postulates, it can be expected that they will be resistant to modification. This is not to say that they cannot be changed, but that, to the extent that they have become higher-order constructs they will be difficult to change.

Maintenance of the Stability of the Conceptual System

People have a vested interest in maintaining the stability of their personal theories of reality for they are the only systems they have for making sense of the world and guiding their behavior. As threats to the stability of their conceptual system mount, they experience increasing anxiety and a tendency of their conceptual systems to disorganize. As disorganization becomes imminent, the anxiety becomes overwhelming, and people will do whatever they can to reduce its intensity and prevent disorganization (for a more detailed discussion of anxiety and disorganization and their relation to schizophrenia, see Epstein, 1976, 1979).

There are several strategies that can be used to maintain the integrity of basic beliefs despite disconfirming evidence. Three basic ones are framing the beliefs in a nontestable manner, selectively perceiving and interpreting events to support current beliefs, and selectively seeking out experiences and shaping events so that they confirm extant beliefs (Epstein & Erskine, 1983; Swann, 1983). It is important to realize that the need to maintain basic beliefs applies as well to maladaptive as to adaptive beliefs. The decision to maintain a maladaptive belief is not made consciously, but occurs at the preconscious level, where it is mediated by anxiety signals that arise whenever the stability of the conceptual system is threatened. A woman who was battered as a child, and who later falls in love with a man who batters her, does not make a deliberate choice to do so. Rather the choice is made for her by her preconscious cognitions and the emotions to which they give rise.

Sensitivities and Compulsions

Sensitivities refer to experientially derived generalizations that certain kinds of people, situations, or events are dangerous. Compulsions refer to experientially derived generalizations that certain kinds of behavior are effective ways of reducing threat. The former correspond to preconscious descriptive schemata and the latter to preconscious motivational schemata. Sensitivities and compulsions as used in CEST differ from their diagnostic use in clinical psychology in one very important respect. When used to describe abnormal behaviors, they refer to narrowly defined classes of stimuli and behavior. Thus, individuals are diagnosed as having a hand-washing compulsion or a compulsion to engage in private rituals. In CEST the meaning of the terms is expanded to refer to more complex, broad patterns of behavior that, although maladaptive, are generally not considered abnormal in the usual sense of the term.

The hallmark of a sensitivity is that whenever certain stimuli or situations arise, the individual becomes excessively distressed. Sensitivities can be identified by situations that "get to people," that "bug them," that their friends recognize they must avoid if they wish to maintain peace. The hallmarks of a compulsion are as follows: (1) The person acts in a rigid way across a variety of situations, such as always having to be dominant or always having to be ingratiating, (2) The person experiences distress when he or she is unable to behave in a manner consistent with the compulsion, (3) The compulsion becomes exaggerated when the person is threatened, particularly when the threat involves a sensitivity. It is assumed that sensitivities were learned under conditions of high threat and that compulsions were learned as ways of coping with sensitivities. In order to understand the fundamental nature of sensitivities and compulsions it will be helpful to consider the nature of anxiety.

Anxiety became established as part of their inherited repertoire in higher-order species because of its adaptive properties. When an animal, such as a rabbit, has a threatening experience, such as being attacked by a hawk, it experiences anxiety. From that point on, whenever a stimulus that is reminiscent of the original threatening stimulus appears, the anxiety alarm sounds and the animal automatically responds with whatever actions it previously made that were followed by a reduction in anxiety. Normally, the anxiety and the responses to it are adaptive as they provide the animal with an automatic warning signal and an automatic response for escaping from the danger. In time, if similar stimuli are experienced in the absence of danger, the anxiety gradually subsides, which, of course, is also adaptive. The greater the initial anxiety, the broader the gradient of generalization and the more resistant the responses that reduced the anxiety to extinction. The classes of stimuli that evoke anxiety as a result of being associated with the original stressor are sensitivities. The automatic responses that are produced to these stimuli as a way of reducing anxiety are compulsions.

Sensitivities and compulsions provide an important key to understanding human personality. They are a common source of maladaptive behavior that can be widely observed in otherwise normal individuals as well as in people who are more seriously disturbed. From the viewpoint of CEST, sensitivities and compulsions, not unconscious conflict and repression, are the most fundamental sources of maladjustment. Unconscious conflict and repression are complications that make the sources and sometimes the nature of sensitivities and compulsions unavailable to awareness. Accordingly, in many cases, removing repression, that is, making the unconscious conscious, is not enough to correct maladaptive behavior, as the initial sensitivities and compulsions remain. All that may be accomplished is transforming a neurotic without insight into one with insight.

As already noted, sensitivities correspond to descriptive schemata about sources of danger. Compulsions correspond to motivational schemata about how to avoid or escape from danger. The maladaptiveness of these schemata depends on how general (undifferentiated, rigid, inflexible) they are and how resistant they are to modification. The earlier such cognitions are acquired and the greater the intensity and repetition of the emotional experiences on which they are based, the more likely they are to be incorporated as central postulates in a personal theory of reality and therefore to be self-maintaining.

The acquisition of sensitivities and compulsions can account for many of the phenomena that psychoanalysts attribute to unconscious conflict. There is thus the danger that behavior will be diagnosed and treated as if unconscious conflict were present, when, in fact, it is not. To state this is not to deny the importance of unconscious conflict, but to suggest that it is less general than psychoanalysts assume, and to draw attention to another kind of unconscious behavior with which it is often confused. To make the distinction clear, it will be helpful to provide an example.

Some time ago, a young woman graduate student made repeated negative remarks or snickered whenever I spoke up in public. (Details in the story that follows have been altered to preserve anonymity.) I called her to my office after one such incident, and asked her what about my behavior distressed her so. She looked astonished, and said that she was not aware of reacting negatively to me, and that, in fact, she liked and admired me.

How is one to explain such a gross lack of awareness? A psychoanalyst would most likely say she had unconscious hostile feelings toward someone, perhaps a parent or other authority figure, that she was displacing on me. I suggested a little experiment to her. I asked her if she would be willing to monitor her "vibes" whenever I spoke in public. The idea of an experiment appealed to her, and she agreed to do so. Two weeks later she came to my office with the results. After some practice, she had learned to detect her vibes, and it became apparent to her that they were not very good when she heard me speak. They made her want to defend her autonomy by putting me down. She recognized that they were the same feelings she had toward her father, toward whom she was consciously hostile. Since the hostility toward her father was conscious, the case for displacement of unconscious conflict is not tenable. The behavior can more simply be explained by assuming that the young woman had become sensitized to her father's voice and the sensitivity had generalized to my voice. As the generalization occurred at a preconscious level in the experiential system, there was no reason for her to be consciously aware of her reaction. In fact, since the negative reaction to me was inconsistent with her conscious thinking about me, there was reason for her not consciously to recognize her aggressive behavior, as it made no sense. As a further indication that unconscious conflict was not present, she experienced no resistance when she detected the vibes. All that was necessary for her to become aware of the vibes and the thoughts with which they were associated was an act of attention. This case well illustrates the manner in which vibes control thought and behavior in the absence of awareness, which is the way, according to CEST, that most behavior is controlled in everyday life.

Such behavior can be a source of serious problems in living, as indicated by the following thought experiment. Imagine that I embarrassed the graduate student in public by responding in kind to her negative comments. This would have provided her with an objective reason for being hostile to me, which could have easily escalated into an ongoing conflict between us. Such conflicts regularly occur between spouses, parents and children, friends, and in the workplace, where they can have devastating consequences. It follows that unconscious conflict is not the sine qua non of maladaptive behavior as psychoanalysts maintain.

THE CONSTRUCT OF CONSTRUCTIVE THINKING

Up to this point, maladaptive behavior has been discussed in terms of how such behavior is acquired and how it is then maintained through the use of a variety of cognitive strategies. I wish to now introduce another, more general, contribution that CEST has to make to an understanding of maladaptive behavior, one that is based on a recently introduced concept of "constructive thinking."

The logic behind constructive thinking is as follows. If emotions and, to a large extent, behavior, are determined automatically by the functioning of the experiential conceptual system, as CEST maintains, then the effectiveness with which the experiential system operates should play an important role in determining a person's success in everyday living. This raises an interesting question. Is it possible that one could obtain a measure of the overall effectiveness of the experiential system in a manner analogous to the use of intelligence tests to measure the effectiveness of the rational system? If so, what is it that would have to be measured? The answer is that one would have to sample a person's typical automatic thinking.

There are two aspects of automatic thinking that need to be sampled: content and process. Content refers to the specific beliefs in a personal theory of reality, such as whether the world is considered to be benign or malevolent or whether people are considered to be trustworthy or not. Process refers to the manner of functioning of the system. It includes concepts such as overgeneralization, categorical thinking, and magical thinking. To illustrate these two concept, let us consider some specific examples. The item, "When I fail a test, I feel like a total failure and that I will never amount to anything," illustrates poor functioning with respect to both content and process. At the content level, it is unduly pessimistic; at the process level, it is characterized by gross overgeneralization. Contrast this item to the following: "When I do very well on an important test, I feel that I am a total success and will succeed in whatever I undertake." Here the content is positive, but the process is again indicative of gross overgeneralization. Now consider an item describing a constructive response: "When I fail a test, I realize it is only a single test, and learn what I can from the experience without getting very upset." Parenthetically, it is noteworthy that people who think destructively may have high IQs and even recognize that their thinking is maladaptive, but this does not mean they can control it. Thus, it is clear that intellective intelligence and constructive thinking refer to very different problem-solving abilities.

The assumption is made that there are individual differences in the ability to solve everyday problems in living at a minimal cost in stress. This ability is referred to as constructive thinking. The level of constructive thinking on this dimension is determined largely by the intelligence of the experiential system. High constructive thinking consists of thinking that facilitates coping with problems in living in a manner that maximizes the likelihood of an effective solution at a minimal cost in stress. Low constructive thinking (or high destructive thinking) consists of thinking that results in a relatively high cost in stress relative to the adequacy of the solutions achieved.

It is assumed that constructive thinking is more influenced by nurture and less by nature than rational intelligence. It is further assumed that early experiences in childhood, particularly those that evoke strong emotions, initiate automatic coping reactions that tend, over time, to become strong habits. Consequently, although constructive thinking is, in all likelihood, more susceptible to change than rational intelligence, it is nevertheless not easy to change, and it is more responsive to direct or indirect experience than to logical argument.

Having provided some background on constructive thinking, we are now ready to consider the research that has been done on the construct, which is discussed in the next section.

RESEARCH

Research on Constructive Thinking

The CTI was developed by sampling thousands of constructive and destructive thoughts in everyday life. An example of a constructive thought is, "When I do poorly on a test, I try to learn from the experience so that I can do better next time." An example of a destructive thought is, "When I fail a test, I think that I am totally inadequate and that I will never amount to anything." When the items in the CTI were factor-analyzed, a global factor of constructive thinking emerged plus the following six group factors: *Emotional Coping, Behavioral Coping, Categorical Thinking, Superstitious Thinking, Naïve Optimism,* and *Negative Thinking*. These factors were converted to scales by selecting the items with the highest loadings and winnowing them further according to the magnitude of their item–scale correlations. (For a more detailed description of the construction of the CTI, see Epstein & Meier, 1989.)

The Nature of the CTI Scales. Important insights into the nature of constructive thinking can be obtained by examining the composition of the scales in the (CTI). The CTI contains, in addition to a Global scale, six subscales: Emotional Coping, Behavioral Coping, Categorical Thinking, Superstitious Thinking, Negative Thinking, and Naïve Optimism.

The *Global* scale is a composite of all the other scales except Naïve Optimism. It was obtained from a single-factor extraction in a factor analysis. Nearly all the items in the CTI, except those in the Naïve Optimism scale were found to have loadings greater than .30 on this factor. The finding of a global factor is of considerable theoretical interest with respect to the nature of constructive thinking.

The scales of *Emotional Coping* and *Behavioral Coping* account for more than half the total variance of all six factors, thereby indicating that the domain of coping can be largely divided into coping with the inner world of emotions and thoughts and the outer world of events. This division is similar to one that has been referred to by Folkman and Lazarus (1980; Lazarus & Folkman, 1984) as "emotion-focused coping" versus "problem-focused coping."

The items in the *Naïve Optimism* scale refer to stereotyped, simplistic thinking (e.g., "I believe that people can accomplish anything they want to if they have enough willpower.") and to broad generalizations following the occurrence of positive events. Unlike optimistic items in the Behavioral Coping scale, the optimistic items in the Naïve Optimism scale are grossly unrealistic and have a pollyannish quality about them. An example of an item is, "If I were accepted at an important job interview, I would feel very good and think that I would always be able to get a good job." Naïve Optimism is the only scale that is neither significantly correlated with the global scale nor with any of the other scales.

The scale *Negative Thinking* is, in a way, the counterpart of Naïve Optimism. Whereas the naïve optimist unrealistically overemphasizes the positive, the negative thinker equally unrealistically overemphasizes the negative. If the phrase were not awkward, the scale might be called, Naïve Pessimism. Negative Thinking is conceptually related to Emotional Coping. The main difference between them is that the negative items in the Emotional Coping scale refer to taking things personally and worrying about what others think, whereas the negative items in the Negative Thinking scale refer to a pervasive doom-and-gloom orientation, suspiciousness of others, and emotions that interfere with performance. Negative Thinking is more strongly associated with depression than with anxiety, whereas the reverse is true of Emotional Coping.

Categorical Thinking and Superstitious Thinking are of special interest because they refer to two fundamental thought processes, one involving degree of differentiation in thinking and the other reality orientation. They also provide an interesting pair for comparison. Accordingly, I shall discuss them in greater detail than I have discussed the other scales. (For more information on all of the scales, see Epstein & Meier, 1989.)

Categorical Thinking, in that it involves broad, undifferentiated categorization, is also present in overgeneralization and overreactivity, as these are characterized by undifferentiated, or unmodulated thinking. It is instructive to examine the items in the Categorical Thinking scale. Most of them are direct examples of categorical thinking, as in the items "There are basically two kinds of people in this world, good and bad," and "I tend to classify people as either for me or against me." However, there are also other kinds of items that were retained in the scale because of their high correlations with the rest of the scale, indicating that they were contributing to the same overall construct. Included are items that refer to intolerance, to being judgmental of others, and to overgeneralizing and overreacting following a single incident of failure or rejection, for example,

"When someone I know is rejected by a person they love, I feel they are inadequate and will never be able to accomplish anything." Given the conceptual relatedness of categorical thinking to overgeneralization and overreactivity, it is understandable why such items were psychometrically qualified for inclusion in the scale. It is less obvious why intolerance and being judgmental should be included in the scale. One possibility is that they are related to conditions in upbringing that foster categorical thinking. As the overall constellation of attributes has much in common with the description of the authoritarian personality by Adorno, Frenkel–Brunswik, Levinson, and Sanford (1950), the hypothesis is suggested that categorical thinking is fostered by raising children in an environment that is authoritarian and repressive as well as by authoritarian parents directly modeling such thinking.

When the CTI is correlated with the *Primary Emotions and Traits Scales* (PETS), an adjective checklist that contains bipolar scales of the basic emotions plus scales derived from higher-order factors, a number of informative correlations between the PETS and Categorical Thinking emerge (see Table 3.2). Categorical Thinking is most strongly associated (above .25) with high neuroticism, low ego strength, high negative relative to positive affect, high anxiety, high anger, and high emotional arousal. When correlated with the Mother-Father-Peer (MFP) scale, Categorical Thinking is found to be more strongly negatively associated with independence-encouragement by parents than with their acceptance.

TABLE 3.2
Categorical Thinking and Superstitious Thinking Correlated with Primary Emotions and Traits Scales (PETS) (N = 246)

PETS Scales	*Categorical Thinking*	*Superstitious Thinking*
Consistency	−.18*	−.23*
Pos–Neg State	−.30*	−.33*
Extroversion–introversion	−.13	−.13
Nonneuroticism	−.32*	−.27*
Ego strength	−.29*	−.34*
Happy–depressed	−.20*	−.29*
Calm–anxious	−.32*	−.22*
Agreeable–angry	−.37*	−.09
Caring–uncaring	−.19*	.06
Vigor–fatigue	.02	−.09
Self-esteem	−.16*	−.20*
Integration	−.08	−.18*
Emotional arousal	.28*	.17

Note: *Significant at the .01 level.
Adjectives are scored with high scores in the direction of the first term.

TABLE 3.3
Correlations of CTI Scales with Mother-Father-Peer Inventory
(N = 257)

	CTI Scales						
MFP Scales	*Const. Th.*	*Emot. Cpg.*	*Behav. Cpg.*	*Categ. Th.*	*Supst. Th.*	*Naive Opt.*	*Neg. Th.*
Mother Encouraged Independence vs. Overprotective	.30*	.23*	.25*	−.22*	−.10	.02	−.31*
Mother Accepting vs. Rejecting	.05	.02	−.01	−.12	.00	.09	−.17*
Father Encouraged Independence vs. Overprotective	.29*	.20*	.26*	−.16*	−.22*	.04	−.28*
Father Accepting vs. Rejecting	.12	.10	.03	−.05	−.07	.11	−.12
Peers Accepting vs. Rejecting	.26*	.19*	.18*	−.22*	−.22*	.12	−.23*

*Significant at the .01 level.

Turning to *Superstitious Thinking,* the items in this scale include formal superstitions (e.g., black cats are bad luck), private superstitions, and beliefs in esoteric and questionable phenomena, such as astrology and the existence of ghosts. Most of the items are private superstitions, which refer to the unrealistic mental games that people play in their heads. Examples are, "I sometimes think that if I want something to happen too badly, it will keep it from happening" and, "When something good happens to me, I believe it will be balanced by something bad." It is noteworthy that the items in Superstitious Thinking as in Categorical Thinking are focused on distressing events. Superstitious Thinking produces its strongest correlations [(at least .20) with high negative relative to positive affect, high neuroticism, high depression, low ego strength and low self-esteem (see Table 3.2)]. Like Categorical Thinking, it is more strongly negatively associated with the PETS scale of parental Independence-encouragement than with the PETS scale of Acceptance. Although there is considerable overlap between the correlations that Superstitious Thinking and Categorical Thinking establish with other variables, there are also important differences. Categorical Thinking is more strongly associated with anger, anxiety, and arousal than Superstitious Thinking, whereas Superstitious Thinking is more strongly associated with Depression and low Ego strength.

How is one to understand personal superstitious thinking? Why should people prevent themselves from enjoying good experiences by convincing themselves they will be followed by equally bad ones, or that they should not express their hopes, as doing so will keep them from materializing? A clue is provided by a consideration of superstitious thinking in primitive societies. Societies resort to superstitious thinking and rituals when they feel helpless in dealing with critical life events. Believing in superstitions and engaging in rituals are comforting because they provide an illusion of understanding and control. To the extent that the same is true for personal superstitious thinking, it suggests that those who engage in such thinking were raised under conditions that fostered feelings of helplessness. It is noteworthy, in this respect, that superstitious thinking is correlated with feelings of depression.

Construct Validity of the CTI. To test the hypothesis that constructive thinking is a broad measure of coping ability independent of intellective intelligence, a group of college students was given the CTI, two tests designed to measure coping style, a test of social support, and an intelligence test. The nonintellective tests included the Seligman Attribution Style Questionnaire (ASQ), the Sarason Social Support Questionnaire (SSQ) and the Rotter Internal-external Scale (IE). The results of a factor analysis of the two best scales from each of the tests (with the exception of the IE, which has only one scale) are presented in Table 3.4. In support of hypothesis, all the nonintellective measures loaded exclusively on the first factor, whereas the two IQ measures, Abstract Thinking and Vocabulary, loaded exclusively on the second factor. It is noteworthy that the highest loadings on the first factor were obtained by the two CTI scales.

To examine the relation of the various tests to a variety of indexes of success in living, a study was conducted (Epstein & Meier, in press) in which the criteria of success consisted of success in the workplace, social relationships, love relationships, academic achievement, mental health, and physical health. Subjects were 181 undergraduates who volunteered to participate for extra credit in their courses. The indexes of success were composites of objective and subjective items. For example, success in work was measured by a scale of four items that included hours of work during the past year, rate of pay during the last job, total earnings during the past year, and estimation of employer satisfaction as indi-

TABLE 3.4
Factor Analysis of 2 Most General Scales per Test
(N = 119)

Variable	*Factor 1*	*Factor 2*
CTI emotional coping	.66	−.11
CTI behavioral coping	.72	−.06
A S Q negative composite	−.41	−.03
A S Q positive composite	.41	.05
I–E scale[a]	−.50	−.18
S S Q satisfaction with support	.35	−.09
S S Q quantity of support	.31	−.05
Vocabulary IQ	.04	.46
Abstract IQ	.03	.70

[a]Scored in the direction of externality.

TABLE 3.5
Correlations Between Major Scales and Criteria of Success in Living

Scale	*Work*	*Love*	*Social Relationships*	*Academic Achievement*	*Psychological Symptoms*	*Physical Symptoms*	*Self-Discipline Problems*	*Alcohol & Drug Problems*
CTI								
CTI Global Scale	.19*	.26***	.36***	.14	−.39***	−.22**	−.25***	−.22**
CTI Emotional Coping	.15*	.26***	.30***	.01	−.46***	−.28***	−.11	−.23**
CTI Behavioral Coping	.26***	.25***	.27***	.11	−.31***	−.18*	−.25***	−.15
I–E scale[a]	−.05	−.04	−.22**	−.04	.21**	.17*	.15	.09
ASQ								
ASQ Overall Composite	−.01	.16*	.34***	.16*	−.05	−.02	−.13	−.06
ASQ Negative Composite	.09	−.21**	−.25**	−.09	.16*	.13	−.12	.15
ASQ Positive Composite	.06	.04	.23**	.14	.07	.09	−.07	.05
SSQ								
SSQ Overall Support	.07	.32***	.62***	−.06	−.09	.01	.00	−.14
SSQ Satisfaction with Support	.00	.31***	.43***	−.07	.03	.17*	−.04	−.18*
SSQ Quantity of Support	.10	.16*	.49***	.04	−.04	−.02	−.01	−.15
IQ								
Total IQ	.11	−.04	−.10	.43***	.17*	−.04	−.14	−.02
Vocabulary IQ	.10	−.07	−.15	.30***	.14	−.08	−.22**	−.02
Abstract Thinking IQ	.07	−.02	−.05	.39***	.11	−.01	−.02	−.03

Note. CTI = Constructive Thinking Inventory; I–E scale = Internal–External Locus of Control Scale; ASQ = Attributional Style Questionnaire; SSQ = Social Support Questionnaire.

[a]Scored in the direction of externality.

$^{*}p < .05$. $^{**}p < .01$. $^{***}p < .001$.

cated by invitations to return, bonuses, promotions, being fired, salary increases, and estimated favorableness of the letter of recommendation the employer would write if asked to do so. Items were included in a scale if they contributed to an increase in the internal-consistency reliability (coefficient alpha) of the scale.

Table 3.5 presents the correlations of the best scales from the various tests of coping style with the criterion measures. It can be seen that the CTI scales correlate significantly with all criteria other than academic achievement. The measures of IQ, on the other hand, correlate most strongly with academic achievement and with little else. The other inventory scales correlate with some of the criteria, but, overall, less widely and less strongly than the CTI scales. It was further found that the various scales of the CTI produced different patterns of relations among the different criteria, thereby indicating that constructive thinking, like intellective intelligence, is a global variable with specific components.

In other research (Green, 1988) it was found that the CTI scales are significantly correlated with job satisfaction and mental and physical health in middle-aged public school administrators. Other research has demonstrated that the scales of the CTI are differentially associated with emotions and with scales in other personality inventories in a coherent manner (Epstein, 1988).

It may be concluded that the CTI is a promising measure of a broad, nonintellective factor with specific components that has important implications for coping with stress and success in everyday living.

Research on Basic Beliefs

How is one to study the variables that influence the basic beliefs in a personal theory of reality? According to CEST, basic beliefs are higher-order schemata that are derived from emotionally significant experiences. Because they are higher-order constructs, they are not readily affected by specific experiences. In order to change such beliefs in the laboratory in a significant way, it would be necessary to create situations of such great emotional impact that they would be unethical to use. Fortunately, at least for research purposes, nature provides its own experiments that produce significant changes in basic beliefs. These natural experiments consist of traumatic events, such as criminal assaults, natural disasters, warfare, and incapacitating illness.

According to CEST, the essence of the traumatic neurosis is the invalidation of the basic postulates in a personal theory of reality, which results in the destabilization of the personality structure (Epstein, 1976, 1990). This is followed by attempts to establish a new integration, which can be accomplished by either finding new ways to assimilate the traumatic experience into the old structure (which is usually not possible), by modifying the old structure, or by establishing a radically new structure. Although a great deal of interesting research has been done on the influence of traumatic events from the perspective of theories that are concerned with social attributions (e.g., Bulman & Wortman,

1977; Wortman, 1976), social comparisons (e.g., Taylor, Wood, & Lichtman, 1983) and interpersonal interactions (e.g., Wortman & Dunkel–Schetter, 1979), with rare exception, this work has not focused on the concept of basic beliefs. An exception is the research of Janoff–Bulman, who, using concepts influenced by CEST, has examined the relation of extreme life events to changes in basic beliefs.

Based on a review of the literature on traumatic events, Janoff–Bulman (in press) concluded that following such events there is a widespread change in feelings of vulnerability. People, at the experiential level, recognize, for the first time, how vulnerable they actually are. Accompanying the change in perceptions of vulnerability are the following changes in basic assumptions about the self and the world: The world is perceived as less benevolent and less meaningful (including predictable, controllable, and just), and the self is perceived as less worthy than before the event. It is noteworthy that these three basic beliefs correspond to three of the four basic beliefs in CEST. The fourth belief in CEST concerns relatedness. Interestingly, Janoff–Bulman includes this belief as a subcategory of the belief in the benevolence of the world because it appears in the same factor when a factor analysis is done of the beliefs. However, she notes that it should not simply be merged with the belief in the impersonal world as benevolent because it produces distinct correlations with other variables. In sum, then, a review of the research on trauma provides striking confirmation of the four basic beliefs postulated by CEST.

The Janoff–Bulman Study of Current Beliefs as Related to Reports of Childhood Trauma. In a study expressly designed to examine the influence of traumatic events on basic beliefs, Janoff–Bulman (1989) had 338 undergraduates indicate whether they had experienced any of the following events: death of a parent, death of a sibling, incest, rape, fire that destroyed their home, and an accident that resulted in a serious disability. As the subjects who filled out the reports were in late adolescence, it can be assumed that most of the events they reported occurred at various periods during childhood. Subjects also filled out a brief self-report inventory that provided information on current basic beliefs. The individual events were of low frequency and tended to produce similar results, so they were combined into an overall score. The main finding was that victims had significantly more negative views than nonvictims with respect to benevolence of the impersonal world, self-worth, and belief in the random occurrence of significant events. The strongest findings were with self-worth.

It should be considered that the failure to find significant differences in beliefs about the benevolence of people could be a result of the kinds of trauma that were investigated or the kinds of items in the scale, which were statements of abstract beliefs about the benevolence of people, rather than statements about emotionally charged personal beliefs. The same factors could also account for a failure to find that specific events are differentially associated with different beliefs.

In summary, the Janoff–Bulman study provides evidence that reports of childhood trauma are related to the favorability of basic beliefs that people report they hold about themselves and the world many years later. It fails to find evidence for distinctive relations between certain kinds of events and certain kinds of beliefs.

The Catlin and Epstein Study of the Relation of Significant Life Events to Current Basic Beliefs. Catlin and Epstein (1988), in an elaboration of the Janoff–Bulman study, examined current beliefs as a function of emotionally significant events, the age at which the events occurred, and the quality of the subjects' childhood relationships with their parents. We were particularly interested in determining whether specific relations could be demonstrated between specific events and specific beliefs. We were also interested in determining the relative influence of extreme life events on basic beliefs compared with the influence of early relationships with parents, and whether the quality of parental relationships moderated the influence of life events on beliefs. Of further interest to us was the effect of positive events relative to negative events on basic beliefs, and how the influence of both changes over time.

Subjects were 305 undergraduates who filled out a *Major Life Events Schedule* in which they reported whether they had experienced any of the following events, and, if so, at what age: an emotionally significant move to another environment, death of a loved one, a major success, such as winning a prize in an athletic contest, a significant rejection, a significant love relationship outside of the family, parental divorce, a significant immoral act, an accident that was one's own fault, an accident that was someone else's fault, sexual abuse, a violent crime, a nonviolent crime, or a natural disaster, such as a fire or a hurricane. Subjects also rated the immediate and long-term influence of each of the events on their self-esteem and on their attitude toward others. In addition, they took the Mother-Father-Peer Inventory (MFP) and the Basic Beliefs Test. The MFP is a self-report inventory that contains highly reliable scales of acceptance versus rejection and independence-encouragement versus overprotection by mother and father figures during childhood and a scale of acceptance versus rejection by childhood peers. The Basic Beliefs Test provides scales on the following current beliefs: Benign World (e.g., "By and large, I feel that my personal world is a reasonably safe and secure place."), Meaningful World (e.g., My life is lacking in purpose and meaning."), Predictable-Controllable World ("I feel that I have little control over the important events in my life."), Just World ("I feel I get a raw deal out of life."), Valuation of Relationships (e.g., "I like people and believe in giving them the benefit of the doubt."), Global Self-esteem ("I nearly always have a highly positive opinion of myself."), Competence ("I am often lacking in self-confidence."), and Lovability (e.g., "There are times when I have doubts about my capacity for maintaining a close love relationship.").

The *Basic Beliefs Test* differs from the Janoff–Bulman version in two important respects: It is a longer test that has higher reliability, and, consistent with the emphasis in CEST on experiential learning, its items refer to personal, experiential beliefs rather than abstract statements. Preliminary research indicated that reports of personal reactions produced stronger relations with other variables than reports of abstract beliefs. It is noteworthy, in this respect, that the strongest relations in the Janoff–Bulman study were with the self-esteem scale, which was the only scale in which the items predominantly referred to personal reactions.

The results confirmed the findings of Janoff–Bulman that those who reported experiencing traumatic events had less favorable current beliefs about themselves and the world than those who did not. However, there was no evidence that self-esteem was more strongly associated with significant life events than other basic beliefs. Moreover, unlike the findings in the Janoff–Bulman study, there was reliable evidence that the occurrence of specific events was differentially associated with specific beliefs. This was indicated in a series of MANOVAs in which the eight beliefs were the dependent variables and the events, taken one at a time, with subjects divided according to whether they had or had not experienced an event, were the independent variables. The multivariate analyses were followed by univariate analyses. The results indicated that significantly different patterns of beliefs were associated with different events. For example, positive and negative events did not produce equal but opposite effects, but were significantly associated with different belief-dimensions. The two positive events, Significant Love Relationship and Major Success, were the only events significantly associated with the beliefs Meaningful World and Competence. In contrast, significant differences in Just World were found only for the four negative events. Subjects apparently did not believe there was anything unjust in outcomes that favored them, but believed the world was lacking in justice when events occurred that were to their disadvantage, and this was true even following an unfortunate event for which they acknowledged responsibility. It may come as no surprise that people's views about justice are influenced by a self-serving bias. Apparently people do not simply generalize directly from experience, but they employ cognitive strategies that bias the meanings that situations have for them.

Among the negative events, rejection and sexual abuse had the most widespread associations with basic beliefs. Rejection was significantly associated with reduced favorability ratings on the basic beliefs of Benign World, Just World, Predictable-Controllable World, and Global Self-esteem. Sexual abuse was significantly associated with reduced favorability ratings on the same current beliefs plus two others, Valuation of Relationships, and Love-worthiness. Surprisingly, Death of a Loved One and Divorce were not significantly associated with any belief. This may be because death of a loved one and divorce can include a wide range of experiences, including events that were acceptable, such as the death of a grandparent following a long period of suffering, and the removal from the household of a parent who had made life insufferable. In the case of both kinds of events, there need not have been any disruption of bonds with a primary caretaker, and, in fact, relationships with a primary caretaker could even have improved following the event. A further consideration for death of a loved one, as will be seen later, is that it can have long-term positive consequences, such as fostering the development of independence.

Further evidence of specific relations between events and beliefs was provided by analysis of the ratings of the immediate and long-term effects of each of the events on self-esteem and attitudes toward others. When the initial effects on self-esteem relative to the effects on attitudes toward others were compared for each of the events (see Table 3.6), the following events were found to be significantly more strongly associated with self-esteem: Death of a Loved One, Major Success, Rejection, Significant Love Relationship, Immoral Act, and Accident that was One's Own Fault. In contrast, only the following two events were found to be more strongly associated with attitudes toward others: Victim of a Violent Crime and Victim of a Nonviolent Crime. The following five events did not exhibit a significantly different impact on self-esteem and attitudes toward others: Move, Divorce, Sexual Abuse, an Accident that was Another's Responsibility, and a Natural Disaster. All of these, except the last, which had a very low frequency of occurrence, had a significant initial effect on both attitudes toward self and others.

Turning to the enduring effect of events on beliefs, it can be seen in Table 3.6 that the relative effect of some events on attitudes toward self and others changed over time. Thus, Divorce and Sexual Abuse, which produced similar initial negative effects on acceptance of self and others, produced significantly greater lasting negative effects on acceptance of others than on acceptance of self. Apparently, the allocation of blame for these events shifted increasingly from self to others over time.

Overall, the results indicate that, in addition to widespread general effects on all beliefs following significant life events, there are also specific associations between certain events and certain beliefs. It should not be surprising that there are, to a considerable extent, common effects across beliefs in view of the moderately high correlations among the different beliefs, mainly between .40 and .60. The results are consistent with the conclusion that following an extreme negative event, all basic beliefs tend to change in an unfavorable direction, but that, depending on the event, some beliefs change more than others. Moreover, assimilation of the meaning of significant events is an ongoing process, and is characterized by a tendency for the events, in general, to become less significant over time and for some events that were initially viewed as negative to be reassessed as positive.

Of particular interest, the effect of significant life events on beliefs was not determined solely by the operation of a veridical generalization process. Rather, it was determined by the manner in which the event was cognitively processed. There appear to be at least three kinds of variables that influence how significant life events are cognitively processed: the cognitive ability of the individual, the use of self-serving strategies, such as ones that enhance self-esteem and facilitate

TABLE 3.6
Comparison of Initial and Lasting Effects of Major Life Events on Self- and Other-acceptance ($N = 305$)

		Mean Initial Effect			Mean Lasting Effect		
Event	No. of Occurrences	Self-Acceptance	Other-Acceptance	*t*	Self-Acceptance	Other-Acceptance	*t*
Move	153	−.17*	−.04	1.96	.59***	.25**	5.16***
Death	202	−.50***	−.11*	7.15***	.07	.06	.32
Major success	241	1.45***	.60***	15.71***	1.00***	.38***	13.61***
Rejection	148	−1.38***	−.85***	8.22***	−.22***	−.30***	1.21
Love	222	1.43***	1.07***	7.81***	1.08***	.77***	5.67***
Immoral act	140	−1.13***	−.43***	9.40***	−.34***	−.20***	2.33*
Divorce	67	−.54***	−.62***	.87	.14	−.22**	5.07***
Accident (own responsibility)	44	−1.04***	−.24*	5.64***	−.24*	.02	3.08***
Accident (other's responsibility)	56	−.34***	−.37***	.70	−.02	−.09	.85
Sexual abuse	45	−1.24***	−1.24***	0	−.57***	−.76***	2.28*
Victim of violent crime	25	−.46**	−1.17***	2.13*	−.04	−.54**	3.61**
Victim of non-violent crime	88	−.93***	−1.27***	7.57***	−.09	−.44***	9.05***
Natural disaster	18	−.21	−.11	1.00	.10	.05	1.00

Note: A positive score signifies a favorable reaction and a negative score an unfavorable reaction.

Asterisks next to means indicate significance of mean compared with no effect of event. Asterisks next to *t* indicate significance of difference between effect on self-acceptance and other-acceptance.

*$p < .05$.
**$p < .01$.
***$p < .001$.

the maintenance of an optimistic orientation, and the use of experientially derived automatic rules for interpreting events. An example of the influence of cognitive ability was the change that occurred over time in the way individuals evaluated the effect of divorce on attitudes toward self and others. Subjects reported that at a younger age they reacted to their parents' divorce by becoming more negative to themselves than to others, whereas at an older age the balance between negative attitudes toward self and others shifted in the opposite direction. Although other interpretations are possible, one reasonable interpretation is that the young child is less able to assess accurately his or her role in a divorce than the older child, and thus is more apt to assume that he or she was responsible. Evidence for the operation of self-serving biases in construing and assimilating critical life events over time was provided by the different kinds of effects on basic beliefs following the occurrence of favorable in comparison with unfavorable life events. One example is the belief that the world is more just after having experienced a favorable event than after having experienced an unfavorable event. Another is in the increasingly favorable reassessment of certain events over time.

The influence of automatic rules for interpreting events was illustrated by reports that the death of a loved one and the rejection by a loved one instigated more negative beliefs about the self than about others. On a logical basis, it is no more reasonable to be negative toward the self than to others following such events. Moreover, blaming others would conform with a self-serving bias, and therefore be more rewarding. Why, then, should people cognitively process these events in a self-denigrating manner?

Under normal conditions of child-rearing, it can be expected that a close association develops between receiving love from others and self-love, or heightened self-esteem and between withdrawal of love and feelings of unworthiness and lowered self-esteem (Epstein, 1973). When a mother withdraws affection from a child in response to unacceptable behavior, the child is much more likely to believe that he or she, not the mother, was bad. Self-blame, under the circumstances, is adaptive as the child is dependent on the mother, and the self-blame motivates one to alter behavior to please her. Through such experiences, the identification of being loved with being a good and worthy person becomes established in the experiential system as an automatic rule for interpreting loss of love as an indication that one is bad or unworthy. The strength of this belief can be expected to vary with the perception of withdrawal of love in childhood, which would, of course, be influenced by the child's cognitive capacity. The result is that there is a widespread tendency for people to experience automatically a diminution in self-esteem following the loss of a relationship with a significant other, notwithstanding any conscious rational views they may later have that this is foolish. It is important to remember, in this respect, that the automatic rules of interpretation, having been experientially derived, operate in the experiential, not the rational system.

Other findings of interest can be summarized as follows.

1. There were highly significant positive relations between favorable childhood relationships with parents and the favorability of all basic beliefs.
2. Parental acceptance and independence-encouragement were associated much more strongly than single life events with current beliefs. However, a composite score of overall favorability of multiple life events was as strongly associated with current beliefs as was relationships with parents.
3. Reported relationships with parents in childhood moderated the relation between events and beliefs. For subjects who reported a high level of acceptance by their parents, there was a highly significant positive relation between a composite score of favorability of multiple life events and current beliefs with respect to Meaningful World and Predictable-Controllable World, whereas for a group who reported low parental acceptance, the relation was nonsignificant. Fig. 3.1 presents the results for Meaningful World. The results for Predictable-Controllable World were highly similar. One interpretation of these findings is that for those with low parental acceptance, parental acceptance is the dominant influence on their view of the world as meaningless, unpredictable and uncontrollable, and specific events, therefore, have relatively little influence. It is assumed that negative views are apt to be more fixated than positive ones.

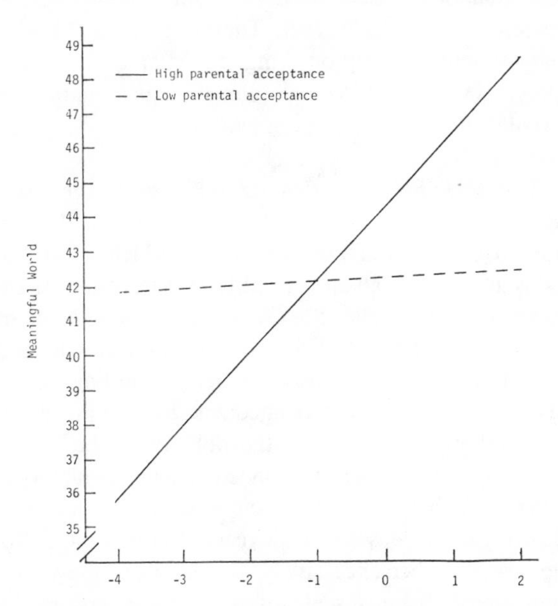

FIG. 3.1. Perception of the world as meaningful as a function of the favorableness of major life events for subjects reporting high and low levels of parental acceptance.

> The opposite beliefs for people who reported high parental acceptance, on the other hand, are sensitive to environmental influence. If the world provides experiences that are consonant with positive relationships with the parents, this strongly confirms the belief that the word is meaningful, predictable, and controllable. Should the world, however, provide experiences that are contrary to the positive experiences in the family, a contrast effect results, and the world is viewed as particularly meaningless, unpredictable, and uncontrollable. It is noteworthy that these results run counter to the psychoanalytical view that a positive relationship with parents fosters the development of ego strength, thereby contributing to the ability to cope emotionally with the vicissitudes of life. The results of this study suggest that such a view needs to be qualified by considering that experiences in or out of the family establish expectancies, and when these expectancies are violated, the world is viewed as more capricious and uncontrollable than it would have been if there were less favorable expectancies to begin with.

It may be concluded that the overall findings from the Catlin and Epstein study are consistent with the assumption in CEST that basic beliefs in the experiential system are generalizations from emotionally significant experiences. However, the generalizations are not always direct simple ones that can be predicted from the nature of the situation by itself. Rather the generalizations are mediated by the cognitive processes of the individual. There are at least three kinds of person variables that influence such processing: the cognitive maturity of the individual, the employment of self-serving coping strategies, and the operation of experientially derived rules for interpreting events.

The Fletcher Study of Basic Beliefs as Related to Posttraumatic Stress Disorder in Vietnam Veterans. In a doctoral dissertation that examined the influence of posttraumatic stress disorder (PTSD) on basic beliefs, Fletcher (1988) gave a battery of specially designed questionnaires to 214 veterans of the Vietnam war. Information was obtained on the veteran's experiences in Vietnam, including amount and kind of combat experienced. Tests included scales for measuring symptoms of PTSD and for measuring various beliefs, including the four basic beliefs in CEST and beliefs specifically associated with the war in Vietnam, such as beliefs about war, authority figures, and the policies of the United States government. Most items on beliefs were responded to with respect to four time periods: before Vietnam, during Vietnam, 6 months after discharge, and the current period, which, for most, was about 15 years after discharge. To control for biased ratings that were either excessively favorable or unfavorable at the different time periods, items from a scale of defensiveness were embedded among the other items for each time period. Defensiveness scores were then partialed out of the relations between basic beliefs at a particular period and other variables.

In addition to the relation of basic beliefs to general and specific traumatic events, the study was concerned with changes in beliefs over time and with corresponding changes in symptoms of PTSD. According to CEST, the primary cause of traumatic neurosis is the invalidation of the basic beliefs in a personal theory of reality (Epstein, in press). It was therefore hypothesized that basic beliefs change in a negative direction following exposure to combat, and that the change is greater and more enduring in those suffering from PTSD than in others. Interest also was in whether the effect of traumatic events would be general across all basic beliefs or whether certain beliefs would change more than others, depending on the kind of combat experiences a veteran had.

The data were statistically evaluated in two ways: First, correlations within each of the four periods were computed for the total group between basic beliefs and symptoms of PTSD. Second, in order to examine changes over time, the veterans were divided into three groups, a noncombat control group, a combat control group without PTSD, and a combat group with PTSD. The noncombat control group consisted of 70 veterans who had been stationed in Vietnam, but had been exposed to no or very little combat and were symptom-free. Four veterans who had symptoms of PTSD despite having been exposed to little combat were not included in this part of the study. The remaining 140 combat veterans were divided at the median into two groups of 70 each according to their scores on the scale of PTSD symptoms. All in the low PTSD group had scores below the threshold of a diagnosis of PTSD according to DSM–III. The high PTSD group consisted of 49 veterans who were enrolled in a Veterans Administration treatment program that accepted only the most extreme cases of PTSD among a large number of applicants plus 21 others who had scores on the PTSD scale above the median for all combat veterans.

In support of hypothesis, there were highly reliable differences among the groups in their scores on the four basic beliefs following, but not preceding, Vietnam. Since the results to a large degree were similar across the four basic beliefs, and the four basic beliefs were highly intercorrelated, an overall score of favorableness of beliefs was obtained by combining the four beliefs. There were no significant group differences for the period before Vietnam, when the ratings tended to be highly favorable. All the groups reported that, before Vietnam, they viewed the world as benign, meaningful, controllable, just, and predictable, the self as worthy, and other people as a source of comfort and worth relating to. In Fig. 3.2, the data are plotted as deviations from the pre-Vietnam ratings. It can be seen that, although favorability of beliefs decreases for all groups during Vietnam, the decrease is greatest for the PTSD group. Interestingly, the decline in favorability continues for all groups up to the period 6 months after discharge. However, the decline is greatest for the PTSD group. The other groups then exhibit a rebound effect that continues to the present period, although they never reach their prewar level of favorability. Youthful innocence has apparently been replaced by a sadder but wiser vision of what the individual and the world are like. The PTSD group, on the other hand, continues its decline to the current period.

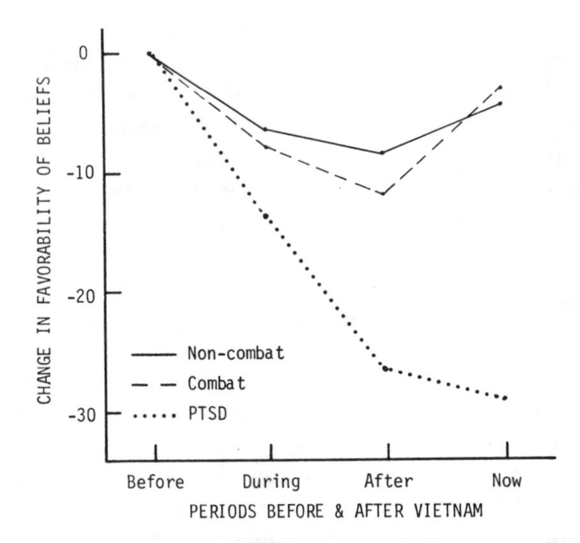

FIG. 3.2. Change in overall favorability of basic beliefs from prewar baseline at three periods for the following groups of veterans: a non-combat control group, a combat control group, a combat group with symptoms of PTSD.

There was marginal evidence that specific kinds of combat experiences were more strongly associated with some basic beliefs than with others. (All of the relations that follow are with defensiveness partialed out.) There was a tendency for amount of exposure to combat to be most strongly negatively associated with Benignity of the World and least strongly negatively associated with Valuation of Relationships. Exposure to Discomfort, on the other hand, was significantly negatively associated with Predictable-controllable World and Self-worth and was neither significantly associated with Benignity of the World nor with Valuation of Relationships. Exposure to uncertainty in combat was most strongly associated negatively with Predictable-Controllable World and Valuation of Relationships and least strongly associated with Self-worth and Benignity of the World. The relation with Valuation of Relationships can probably be attributed to the observation that officers and other authority figures were frequently blamed by the men for exposing them to poorly defined dangerous conditions. Relatedly, Poor Leadership was most strongly associated with Controllable-predictable World and Valuation of Relationships and least strongly associated with Self-worth.

There was stronger evidence of specific relations between events and beliefs for the lower-order beliefs. For example, amount of exposure to combat was significantly correlated with hardened beliefs about war and the enemy but not with attitudes toward authority, nor toward the United States government. On the other hand, exposure to poor leadership was most strongly associated with attitudes toward authority and the United States government, but was not significantly associated with hardened beliefs about war and the enemy.

In summary, the findings indicate that traumatic events of the magnitude of sustained combat have pervasive effects on basic beliefs. The result is that differential relations between certain kinds of events and beliefs tend to be overshadowed by the more general effect. Nevertheless, some beliefs tend to be more associated than others with certain kinds of events, and this is particularly true for lower-order beliefs.

A finding of particular interest was the continuous downward spiral in veterans with symptoms of PTSD in contrast to the rebound effect exhibited by other veterans. This raises the question of why, when combat was over for a veteran who had been exposed to a great amount of combat and other adverse conditions, and he was removed to more favorable surroundings, did he not develop more favorable views about himself and the world? Despite attempts to find evidence of initial personality differences between the PTSD group and the combat control group, no such evidence was forthcoming, which is consistent with previous studies of Vietnam veterans. The only variables that differentiated the groups were ones relating to environmental conditions, such as amount and kind of combat to which the veterans had been exposed, poor leadership, and conditions of uncertainty.

A possible explanation for the downward spiral is that following prolonged exposure to a traumatic situation, a new personality structure, or theory of reality, becomes stabilized, one that is more consonant with the traumatic environment than with the normal one. Once consolidated, the new theory of reality increasingly assimilates new experiences, including those in the nontraumatic environment, according to its basic postulates. In order to sustain the new belief system and prevent re-experiencing the threat of personality disorganization and the overwhelming anxiety associated with it, the individual increasingly seeks out and interprets experiences in a manner that is concordant with the new, traumatic view of the world. Despite its manifest maladaptive consequences, there are adaptive advantages to such an approach, for it ensures that the individual will never be surprised and overwhelmed again in the way he or she was by the traumatic event. It is beyond the scope of this presentation to pursue this issue further. The interested reader can find further discussion in Fletcher's (1988) dissertation and in an article by Epstein (1990) on the traumatic neurosis and its treatment.

IMPLICATIONS OF COGNITIVE-EXPERIENTIAL SELF-THEORY FOR DEVELOPMENTAL PSYCHOLOGY

What are the most important implications of CEST for developmental psychology? None has more far reaching consequences than the assumption that there are separate experiential and rational systems. If there are two such systems, as proposed, then the usual practice of referring to the development of *the* conceptual system is misguided. The fact that the two overlap is, very likely, a major reason why the distinction has been overlooked. Given sufficient overlap, one can get by, within limits, by measuring either system and ignoring the other. The price for doing so, however, is conceptual confusion and a loss of precision.

It might be argued that there is nothing new in the concept of separate experiential and conceptual systems, as Piaget included a similar differentiation in his distinction between sensorimotor intelligence and concrete operations, on the one hand, and formal operations, on the other. However, Piaget's conceptualization is very different from that of CEST, for Piaget conceived of a sequential development of cognitive abilities, with each stage laying the groundwork for the next, which then replaced it. According to CEST, the experiential and rational systems operate alongside each other, with the former frequently influencing the latter. Thus, even when behavior appears to be completely governed by intellective thought, the conscious thoughts are often influenced by the experiential system. Clearly the view of everyday mental functioning in adults, as proposed by CEST, is based on a model of the mind that is much less rational than in Piaget's conceptualization. It follows, if one is to take the viewpoint of CEST seriously, that it is important to do research on the differences between the two systems and the interactions between them.

A second implication of CEST is that the course of development of constructive thinking over the life-span warrants investigation. Very likely, its trajectory will be found to be different from that of intellective intelligence. It would be particularly interesting to determine what the contribution of each is to that elusive form of functioning referred to as wisdom, which, like constructive thinking, appears to require a certain amount of experience in living. Although experience is necessary for wisdom and constructive thinking, it is obviously not sufficient.

A third important implication of CEST is that the Freudian conception of the unconscious is highly limited, and should be replaced by a more inclusive model. A theory of the unconscious is required in which the need for maintaining coherence and stability of the experiential system is recognized as exerting a more widespread influence on human behavior than the need to fend off taboo thoughts and impulses. This is not to deny the existence of repression, but to suggest that it can be incorporated into a broader model that recognizes that the dissociation of unacceptable mental content is but a subset of the methods that individuals employ to preserve the coherence of their conceptual systems.

A fourth implication is that it is important to study the influences on the different kinds of content and processes in the experiential conceptual system. Important questions are as follows: What are the factors that determine a person's beliefs with respect to the four basic postulates? What influences on basic beliefs are there in addition to the direct impact of emotionally significant events? What are the factors that influence basic processes within the experiential system, including overgeneralization, overreactivity, categorical thinking and superstitious thinking? What are the influences of different kinds of child-rearing practices and of different kinds of experiences outside of the family on the development of adaptive and maladaptive beliefs and thought processes?

A fifth important implication concerns remedial procedures for improving constructive thinking. It follows from the nature of the experiential system that, in addition to emotionally relevant experience, imagery should be an important vehicle for reaching the experiential system. It thus becomes important to conduct research on the use of imagery to change maladaptive beliefs and thought processes in the experiential system. Research should also be conducted on the influence of different kinds of didactic procedures for changing maladaptive beliefs and thought processes in the experiential system.

A final implication of CEST is that it is just as important to educate the experiential mind as to educate the rational mind. Assuming that the experiential system is at least as important as the rational system for success in everyday living, and, moreover, that the functioning of the rational mind is influenced by the experiential mind, it is ironic, indeed, that society demands 12 years of education for the rational mind and none for the experiential mind. A particularly important challenge for the future is to develop training procedures for the experiential mind that can be implemented in the school system.

ACKNOWLEDGMENT

Preparation of this manuscript and the research reported in it were supported by NIMH Research Grant MH01293 and NIMH Research Scientist Award MH00363.

REFERENCES

Adorno, T. W., Frenkel–Brunswik, E., Levinson, D. J., & Sanford, R. N. (1950). *The authoritarian personality*. New York: Harper.

Allport, G. W. (1955). *Becoming*. New Haven, CT: Yale University Press.

Allport, G. W. (1961). *Pattern and growth in personality*. New York: Harcourt, Brace, & World.

Beck, A. T. (1976). *Cognitive therapy and the emotional disorders*. New York: International Universities Press.

Bowlby, J. (1973). *Attachment and loss. Vol. 2: Separation anxiety and anger*. New York: Basic Books.

Bulman, R. J., & Wortman, C. B. (1977). Attributions of blame and coping in the "real world": Severe accident victims react to their lot. *Journal of Personality and Social Psychology, 35*, 351–363.

Cashdan, S. (1988). *Object relations therapy: Using the relationship*. New York: Norton.

Catlin, G., & Epstein, S. (1988). *The relation of basic beliefs to extreme life events and childhood relationships with parents.* Unpublished paper.

Cooley, C. H. (1902). *Human nature and the social order.* New York: Scribner's.

Ellis, A. (1962). *Reason and emotion in psychotherapy.* New York: Lyle Stewart.

Epstein, S. (1973). The self-concept revisited, or a theory of a theory. *American Psychologist, 28,* 404–416.

Epstein, S. (1976). Anxiety, arousal, and the self-concept. In I. G. Sarason & C. D. Spielberger (Eds.), *Stress and anxiety.* (Vol. 3). Washington, DC: Hemisphere Publishing Corp.

Epstein, S. (1980). The self-concept: A review and the proposal of an integrated theory of personality. In E. Staub (Ed.), *Personality: Basic issues and current research.* Englewood Cliffs, NJ: Prentice–Hall.

Epstein, S. (1981). The unity principle versus the reality and pleasure principles, or the tale of the scorpion and the frog. In M. D. Lynch, A. A. Norem–Hebeisen, & K. J. Gergen (Eds.), *Self-concept, advances in theory and research.* Cambridge, MA: Ballinger.

Epstein, S. (1983). The unconscious, the preconscious and the self-concept. In J. Suls & A. Greenwald (Eds.), *Psychological perspectives on the self* (Vol. 2). Hillsdale, NJ: Lawrence Erlbaum Associates.

Epstein, S. (1985). The implications of Cognitive-experiential Self-theory for research in social psychology and personality. *Journal for the Theory of Social Behavior, 15,* 283–309.

Epstein, S. (1987). Implications of cognitive self-theory for psychopathology and psychotherapy. In N. Cheshire & H. Thomas (Eds.), *Self-esteem and psychotherapy.* New York: Wiley.

Epstein, S. (1988). *The measurement of drive and conflict in humans.* NIMH Progress Report.

Epstein, S. (1990). The self-concept, the traumatic neurosis, and the structure of personality. In D. Ozer, J. M. Healy, Jr., & A. J. Stewart (Eds.), *Perspectives on personality* (Vol. 3), Greenwich, CT: JAI Press.

Epstein, S., & Erskine, N. (1983). The development of personal theories of reality. In D. Magnusson & V. L. Allen (Eds.), *Human development: An interactional perspective.* New York: Academic Press.

Epstein, S., & Meier, P. (1989). Constructive thinking: A broad coping variable with specific components. *Journal of Personality and Social Psychology, 57,* 332–350.

Fletcher, K. E. (1988). *Belief systems, exposure to stress, and post-traumatic stress disorder in Vietnam veterans.* Unpublished doctoral dissertation, University of Massachusetts at Amherst.

Folkman, S., & Lazarus, R. S. (1980). An analysis of coping in a middle-aged community sample. *Journal of Health and Social Behavior, 21,* 219–239.

Gallup, G. G. (1968). Mirror-image stimulation. *Psychological Bulletin, 70,* 782–793.

Green, M. A. (1988). *Occupational stress: A study of public school administrators in southeast Massachusetts.* Unpublished doctoral dissertation, University of Massachusetts at Amherst.

Horney, K. (1945). *Our inner conflicts.* New York: Norton.

James, W. (1910). *Psychology: The briefer course.* New York: Holt.

Janoff–Bulman, R. (1989). Assumptive worlds and the stress of traumatic events: Applications of the schema construct. *Social Cognition, 7,* 113–136.

Kelly, G. A. (1955). *The psychology of personal constructs.* New York: Norton.

Kuhn, T. S. (1970). *The structure of scientific revolutions.* Chicago: University of Chicago Press.

Lazarus, R. S., & Folkman, S. (1984). *Stress, appraisal, and coping.* New York: Springer Publishing.

Lecky, P. (1961). *Self-consistency: A theory of personality.* Garden City, NY: Anchor Books.

Mead, G. H. (1934). *Mind, self, and society.* Chicago: University of Chicago Press.

O'Brien, E. J., & Epstein, S. (1988). *Multidimensional Self-Esteem Inventory.* Odessa, FL: Psychological Assessment Resources, Inc.

Piaget, J. (1973). The affective unconscious and the cognitive unconscious. *Journal of the American Psychoanalytic Association, 21,* 249–261.

Piaget, J. (1981). Intelligence and affectivity: Their relationship during childhood development. *Annual Reviews Monograph.*

Rogers, C. R. (1951). *Client-centered therapy.* New York: Houghton Mifflin.

Snygg, D., & Combs, A. W. (1949). *Individual behavior.* New York: Harper & Row.

Swann, W. B., Jr. (1983). Self-verification: Bringing social reality into harmony with the self. In J. Suls & A. G. Greenwald (Eds.), *Social psychological perspectives on the self* (Vol 2, pp. 33–66). Hillsdale, NJ: Lawrence Erlbaum Associates.

Taylor, S. E., & Brown, J. D. (1988). Illusion and well-being: A social psychological perspective on mental health. *Psychological Bulletin, 103,* 193–210.

Taylor, S. E., Wood, J. V., & Lichtman, R. R. (1983). It could be worse: Selective evaluation as a response to victimization. *Journal of Social Issues, 39* (2), 19–40.

White, R. W. (1959). *Motivation reconsidered: The concept of competence. 66,* 297–333.

Wortman, C. B. (1976). Causal attributions and personal control. In J. H. Harvey, W. J. Ickes, & R. F. Kidd (Eds.), *New directions in attributions research* (Vol. 1). Hillsdale, NJ: Lawrence Erlbaum Associates.

Wortman, C. B., & Dunkel–Schetter, C. (1979). Interpersonal relationship and cancer: A theoretical analysis. *Journal of Social Issues, 3* (5), 120–155.

4 Development of Self-regulatory and Self-evaluative Processes: Costs, Benefits, and Tradeoffs

E. Tory Higgins
Columbia University

It is natural for parents, especially in the "land of opportunity," to want their child to have the best of everything, to "have it all." Most parents would like to socialize their child in such a way that all the person features they value are maximized in their child. For many parents these valued features include prosocial behavior, an absence of antisocial behavior, happiness and security, high performance standards and accomplishments, and an ability to enjoy challenging tasks. What sort of socialization might fulfill this goal? In seeking an answer to this question, one approach would be to search for distinct groups of children that differ in the extent to which this goal is fulfilled and then identify the distinctive socializing methods associated with the more successful group.

Recent reviews of the literature on children's social behavior, psychopathology, and achievement (e.g., American Psychiatric Association, DSM–III, 1980; Dweck, 1986; Huston, 1983; Maccoby & Martin, 1983; Nolen–Hoeksema, Seligman, & Girgus, in press; Parke & Slaby, 1983; Radke–Yarrow, Zahn-Waxler, & Chapman, 1983; Rutter & Garmezy, 1983), suggest that there are two such groups generally differing in the extent to which this maximization goal has been fulfilled: girls and boys. A comparison of girls and boys in the early elementary schoolyears reveals that girls are more prosocial and less antisocial than boys (e.g., more polite and well-mannered, less disruptive and destructive). Girls have less conduct disturbances, depression, and anxiety. And girls obtain higher grades than boys.

All this suggests that the secret to fulfilling the maximization goal might be to determine what socialization methods, if any, are used differentially for girls and boys, and then use these methods to socialize all children—girls *and* boys. Unfortunately, there is a fly in the ointment. When one reviews the adolescent and adult literature, the sex differences just described are no longer as evident. Sex differences in school grades disappear or even reverse for some subjects (e.g., mathematics). Perhaps most important, females are more likely to suffer from severe emotional problems than males. Thus, to the extent that socialization methods cause these sex differences, then those methods associated with benefits to females at an early age are associated with costs to females at a later age. Using these methods to socialize all children, therefore, will not fulfill the maximization goal. In fact, maximization may be an impossible goal because all socialization involves both costs and benefits with respect to children acquiring those features valued by parents and society. Socioemotional development is a story of tradeoffs. The purpose of this chapter is to use self-discrepancy theory (Higgins, 1987, 1989a) as a framework to provide a preliminary account of this story.

The chapter begins with a description of developmental changes in children's self-concepts, self-regulatory processes, and self-evaluative processes—the self system—that are associated with developmental shifts in their mental representational capacity. Both costs and benefits of these developmental changes are considered. The next section identifies different modes of caretaker–child interaction that involve different kinds of psychological experiences for the child. These different modes are distinguished in terms of the likelihood that the child will acquire strong standards or self-guides. It is proposed that possessing strong self-guides has both costs and benefits, and that these costs and benefits change as children move from elementary school to high school. Sex differences in socioemotional development are then reconsidered as an example of such tradeoffs.

TRADEOFFS FROM INTELLECTUAL DEVELOPMENT

The influence on socioemotional development of changes in children's mental representational capacity has received increasing attention in recent years (e.g., Case, Hayward, Lewis, & Hurst, 1987; Fischer & Watson, 1981; Harter, 1983, 1986; Higgins, 1989b; Pascual–Leone, 1983). A key aspect of this development involves changes in the self system that impact on children's self-regulatory and self-evaluative processes. The purpose of this section is to use self-discrepancy theory (Higgins, 1987, 1989a) to consider some tradeoffs in this development. To begin with, the basic parameters and assumptions of self-discrepancy theory will be described.

Self-discrepancy Theory

Self-discrepancy theory provides a general framework for considering the relation between self and affect. A basic assumption of the theory is that psychologically significant patterns formed by distinct interrelations among self-state representations serve as the basis of people's vulnerabilities. The theory proposes that interrelations among different types of self-beliefs form different patterns and each pattern as a whole has a particular psychological significance. When a self-belief element in a pattern is activated, the pattern as a whole is activated and a person experiences the psychological significance represented by the pattern. The psychological significance represented by the pattern in turn induces a particular emotional/motivational state (see Higgins, 1989a).

To distinguish among different types of self-state representations or self-beliefs, self-discrepancy theory proposes two psychological parameters: *domains of the self* and *standpoints on the self.* In Higgins (1987), three types of self-domains were identified: (1) the *Actual* self, which is your representation of the attributes that someone (yourself or another) believes you actually possess; (2) the *Ideal* self, which is your representation of the attributes that someone (yourself or another) would like you, ideally, to possess (i.e., a representation of someone's hopes, wishes or aspirations for you); and (3) the *Ought* self, which is your representation of the attributes that someone (yourself or another) believes you should or ought to possess (i.e., a representation of someone's sense of your duty, obligation, or responsibilities). Two types of standpoints on the self were also identified: (1) your *own* personal standpoint; and (2) the standpoint of some significant *other* (e.g. mother, father, spouse, closest friend).

Different types of self-state representations were identified by combining each of the different types of self-domains with each of the different types of standpoints on the self, as follows: actual/own, actual/other, ideal/own, ideal/other, ought/own, and ought/other. People's *self-concept* involves a representation of the attributes that they believe they actually possess—the Actual self from their own standpoint. Other combinations of self-domains and standpoints define valued self-states or self-directive standards that people are motivated to meet—*self guides*. Ideal/other self-guides, for example, involve people's representation of a significant other's hopes, wishes, or aspirations for them, and ought/other self-guides involve people's representation of a significant other's beliefs about their duty, obligations, or responsibilities.

Consistent with several previous perspectives (e.g., Carver & Scheier, 1981; Duval & Wicklund, 1972; James, 1948), self-discrepancy theory assumes that people use self-guides for both self-regulatory and self-evaluative purposes. People use self-guides both to self-regulate their actual-self features (e.g., their actions and appearance) and to evaluate or monitor their progress in such self-regulation ("How am I doing?"). The self-evaluative process contributes to the self-regulatory process by providing feedback concerning the extent to which self-regulation has successfully reduced any discrepancy between the actual state and the self-guide.

Self-discrepancy assumes that relations among different types of self-state representations themselves represent *different types of psychological situations*. It is hypothesized that these different types of psychological situations, in turn, are associated with distinct emotional/motivational states. For example, a discrepancy between the self-concept and an ideal self-guide represents *the absence of positive outcomes* (i.e., nonobtainment of hopes and wishes) whereas a discrepancy between the self-concept and an ought self-guide represents *the presence of negative outcomes* (i.e., expectation of punishment from violation of duties and obligations). Because of the relations between these different types of psychological situations and different kinds of emotional/motivational states, self-discrepancy theory predicts that actual–ideal discrepancies would be associated with dejection-related problems (e.g., feeling dissatisfied, disappointed, discouraged, sad), while actual–ought discrepancies would be associated with agitation-related problems (e.g., feeling worried, threatened, on edge). These predictions have been supported in various studies (see Higgins, 1987, 1989a).

Self-discrepancy theory also assumes that self-discrepancies function like *available knowledge structures*. The theory predicts that, as such, priming or activating self-discrepancies should produce emotional/motivational episodes (see Higgins, 1989a). These is considerable support for this prediction as well (see Higgins, Bond, Klein, & Strauman, 1986; Strauman & Higgins, 1987; Strauman, in press).

Thus, discrepancies between self-concepts and self-guides have been shown to be a vulnerability factor. But where do such discrepancies come from? What are the developmental underpinnings of self-guides and their relations to self-concepts? One critical factor involves changes in children's mental representational capacity. How does intellectual development influence the development of the self-system, and what are the costs and benefits of this self-system development? To facilitate exposition, the self-system changes associated with intellectual development will be described in terms of five major developmental shifts (see Higgins, 1989b). The general shifts described are consistent with various models of intellectual development (e.g., Damon & Hart, 1986; Fischer, 1980; Piaget, 1970; Selman, 1980) but rely most heavily on Case's (1985) model.

Level 1: Early Sensorimotor Development

By the end of the first year of life children are capable of representing the relation between two events, such as the relation between a response produced by them and their mothers' response to them. This ability permits children to produce and interpret communicative signals and to experience emotions that involve anticipating the occurrence of some event. Even at this early stage, then, children are capable of the preliminary form of role taking described by Mead (1934), the ability to anticipate the responses of a significant other with whom one is interacting. This represents a major step toward the acquisition of the self-other contingency knowledge that will underlie both self-regulatory and self-evaluative processes.

Another major development during this first stage involves children's ability to experience both the two major positive and the two major negative types of actual and anticipated psychological situations:

1. The *presence of positive outcomes,* as when children feel their mother's nipple between their lips or anticipate their mother's face when playing peekaboo, which is associated with feeling satisfaction and joy (e.g., Case, 1988; Sroufe, 1984).
2. The *absence of negative outcomes,* as when a mother removes noxious stimulation from a child or removes a child from a situation that the child finds threatening, which is associated with the child's feeling calm, secure, and reassured (e.g., Case, 1988; Sroufe, 1984).
3. *The absence of positive outcomes,* as when a child's mother changes from affectionate face-to-face play to withholding communication from the child or when a child's sought after (but not visible) toy cannot be found, which is associated with the feeling of sadness, disappointment, and frustration/anger (e.g., Campos & Barrett, 1984; Kagan, 1984; Sroufe, 1984; Trevarthen, 1984).
4. *The presence of negative outcomes,* as when a child suffers from noxious stimulation or is confronted by an unexpected and potentially harmful person or situation, which is associated with the feeling of distress and fear (Emde, 1984; Kagan, 1984).

Level 2: Late Sensorimotor and Early Interrelational Development

Between 18 months and 2 years of age there is a dramatic shift in children's ability to represent events (e.g., Bruner, 1964; Case, 1985; Fischer, 1980; Piaget, 1951; Werner & Kaplan, 1963), a shift that has traditionally been associated with the emergence of symbolic representation (see Huttenlocher & Higgins, 1978). As described by Case (1985), children become generally capable of recognizing the higher-order relation that exists between two other relations, of using a scheme representing the relation between two objects as a *means* to obtaining a represented and specified goal pertaining to two other objects.

Children can now consider the bidirectional relationship between themselves and another person, such as their mother, as an interrelation between self-as-object and other-as-object (see Bertenthal & Fischer, 1978; Harter, 1983; Lewis & Brooks–Gunn, 1979). At this stage, children can represent *the relation between two relations:* (1) The relation between a particular kind of self-feature (e.g., action, response, appearance, mood) and a particular kind of response by another person, such as the relation between the child making a fuss or a mess at mealtime and mother frowning, yelling, or leaving; and (2) The relation between a particular kind of response by another person and a particular kind of psychological situation they will experience, such as the relation between mother's frowning, yelling, or leaving and the child experiencing a negative psychological situation. The shift between children's ability at Level 1 to represent relation (1) and their ability at Level 2 to represent the higher-order relationship between relation (1) and relation (2) is illustrated in Fig. 4.1.

As shown in Fig. 4.1, children can now represent *self-other contingencies,* as follows:

My displaying Feature X is associated with Person A displaying Feature Y, and Person A displaying Feature Y is associated with my experiencing Psychological Situation Z.

At Level 2, then, children can represent how significant others in their life

LEVEL 5: LATE VECTORIAL DEVELOPMENT

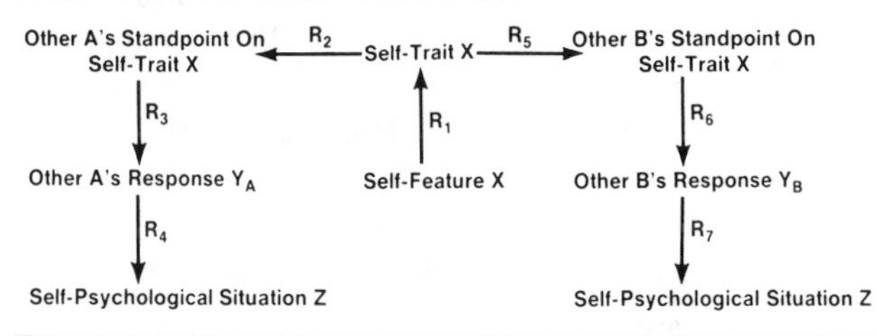

LEVEL 4: LATE DIMENSIONAL AND EARLY VECTORIAL DEVELOPMENT

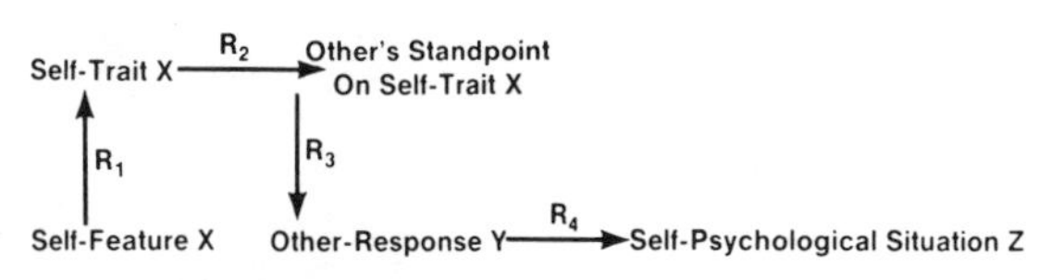

LEVEL 3: LATE INTERRELATIONAL AND EARLY DIMENSIONAL DEVELOPMENT

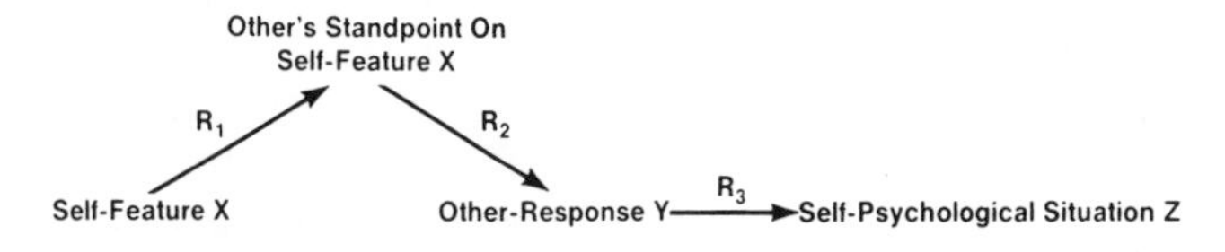

LEVEL 2: LATE SENSORIMOTOR AND EARLY INTERRELATIONAL DEVELOPMENT

Self-Feature X —R_1→ Other-Response Y —R_2→ Self-Psychological Situation Z

LEVEL 1: EARLY SENSORIMOTOR DEVELOPMENT

Self-Feature X —R_1→ Other-Response Y

FIG. 4.1. Illustration of developmental changes in children's ability to represent self-other contingencies.

respond to their features, which in turn places them in particular psychological situations. Thus, the significant others link a child to the larger society by providing the child with the social meanings of the child's features.

Although such self-other contingency representations are still only representations of relations between sensorimotor relations, they can be used by children in a means–end fashion to control their features, to plan their actions, responses, or appearance so as to approach positive psychological situations and avoid negative psychological situations. Children's mental representational capacity at Level 2, then, introduces a major benefit for them—the ability to self-regulate for the purpose of controlling outcomes.

By being able to represent the social and personal significance of their actions and retrieve this significance prior to responding, children at this stage are better able to delay gratification, to control their momentary impulses, and to free themselves from the demands and forces of the immediate situation (see Miller & Green, 1985; Mischel & Patterson, 1978). As suggested by Anna Freud (1937), children at this stage are capable of interiorizing a representative of the outside world and anticipating suffering that may be inflicted by outside agents.

This new capacity for *interiorized compliance* allows children to deal more successfully with social demands, which introduces feelings of pride and joy. On the other hand, the possibility of failure to comply introduces feelings of abandonment and rejection by others (see Campos & Barrett, 1984; Case, 1988; Kagan, 1984; Sroufe, 1984). Moreover, children can now suffer unnecessarily (e.g., feeling sad or afraid) by thinking about the negative psychological situations that would occur if they behaved in certain ways even though they have not recently behaved in that manner.

Level 3: Late Interrelational and Early Dimensional Development

Between 4 and 6 another dramatic shift in children's mental representational capacity occurs (see Case, 1985; Feffer, 1970; Fischer, 1980; Flavell, Botkin, Fry, Wright, & Jarvis, 1968; Piaget, 1965; Selman & Byrne, 1974; Werner, 1957), the classic shift from the absence to the presence of perspective-taking ability (see Higgins, 1981; Shantz, 1983). Perspective- or role-taking ability involves the ability to evaluate a target person (self or other) from a perspective or viewpoint other than one's own when one's own current viewpoint is both accessible and different. It requires both the ability to prevent one's own immediate reactions to the target from intruding on one's judgment and the ability to coordinate simultaneously two distinct factors (Higgins, 1981).

More generally, children at this stage possess an executive control structure that permits the coordination of two systems of interrelations that are qualitatively distinct (Case, 1985). They are able to infer a mediating relation between two other relations. For example, they are able to understand that the relation between current situation and an alternative preferred situation can mediate the relation between the current situation and someone's response to the situation (e.g., "Bill is unhappy because he got less marbles than he wanted."). Thus, children can now infer the thoughts, expectations, motives, and intentions of others (see Shantz, 1983). This new inferential ability has important consequences when it is applied to the case of self-other contingency knowledge. Children at this stage can monitor, plan, and evaluate their features in terms of their relation to the types or categories of features that they infer are valued, preferred, or expected by another person. They have the ability to acquire internalized standards or self-guides (see Fischer & Watson, 1981; Gesell & Ilg, 1946). Thus, children can now self-regulate and self-evaluate in terms of *a standard or self-guide for their features involving a representation of another person's viewpoint on them*. This major shift in self-other contingency knowledge is illustrated in Fig. 4.1.

As depicted in Fig. 4.1, children can now represent another person's viewpoint or standpoint on their features, which are those features of the child that the other person values or prefers (as inferred by the child). Now the relation between self-feature X and other-response Y is understood to be mediated by the relation between self-feature X and the other's standpoint on self-feature X. Children, for example, are now capable of understanding that what makes them feel bad is the discrepancy between a behavior they produced and the behavior preferred by their mother that is associated with their mother's response.

Children for the first time can evaluate themselves by comparing their perceived current features with an alternative valued or preferred state, and they are motivated to do so in order to facilitate self-regulation. Thus, children's representations of other's standpoint on them can be used as a standard for self-evaluation (e.g., "How am I doing in relation to what mother wants or expects of me?").

Children at this stage are capable of understanding that other people have different attitudes about different types of responses. They prefer some types of responses over other types. Children are now capable of reasoning that by performing the types of responses preferred by others, other people will like them and respond positively to them. Children are, therefore, motivated to learn which types of response are preferred by significant others. Although children can learn about a significant other's preferences from his or her reactions to them personally, they can also learn by observing how the significant other reacts to the responses of another person. For example, children can observe how their mother reacts to their brother's or sister's responses and thereby infer which types of responses their mother prefers. Such observational learning should enhance children's self-regulatory skills.

This shift in understanding increases children's subjective control over others' responses and thus their control over emotional experiences. Indeed, to the extent that others' responses to children *are* based on their expectations and preferences for them, then children's new ability to infer these expectations and preferences increases the likelihood of their approaching positive psychological situations and avoiding negative ones.

This shift in understanding also forms the basis for a self-regulatory shift from compliance to *identification*. Identification involves social influence based on a motivation to establish or maintain a positive relationship with a significant other (see Kelman, 1958). It typically involves imitation of a significant other serving as model (see A. Freud, 1937; Hoffman & Saltzstein, 1967; Mowrer, 1960). As Anna Freud (1936) suggested, children's self-control no longer depends on the anticipation of suffering that may be inflicted by outside agents. A permanent institution has now been set up that embodies others' wishes and requirements. In addition, conforming with others' standards can now itself produce positive emotions because evaluating a self-feature as a match to a significant other's standpoint represents a positive psychological situation.

Such standards are not as dependent on others' actual responses for their self-regulatory and self-evaluative power. This has the benefit of increasing the range of circumstances under which children can assert self-control, which in turn can increase the occasions for "self-feature—other's standpoint" matches and positive emotions. On the other hand, children's new capacity to appraise themselves in relation to another's standpoint on them could contribute to the appearance of new emotional vulnerabilities. Appraised discrepancies between self-features and others' standards for them could be associated with children believing that they have disappointed others or that others disapprove of them. Thus, children's new capacity also produces a vulnerability to shame and an early form of guilt/fear (e.g., Campos & Barrett, 1984).

Level 4: Late Dimensional and Early Vectorial Development

Between 9 and 11 children become capable of coordinating values along two distinct dimensions (see Case, 1985; Fischer, 1980; Higgins, 1981; Piaget, 1970). Children, for example, can now compare their performance with that of another child by considering simultaneously the difference in intent or effort and the difference in outcome. This makes possible for the first time inferences of comparative or relative ability, in the sense of enduring and general attributes, rather than just relative performance (see Ruble, 1983). Children can compare a target's relative standing on some attribute dimension in one circumstance to the target's relative standing on the dimension in a different circumstance, which makes dispositional or trait judgments of self and others possible for the first time. It is during this period that children first begin to represent their attributes as being both temporally stable and cross-situationally consistent (see Rholes & Ruble, 1984). At this stage, then, *children can possess a dispositional self-concept*.

Indeed, there is a shift at this stage from conceptualizing self and others in terms of physical features and stable behaviors to conceptualizing self and others in terms of dispositional abilities and traits (see Harter, 1983; Rosenberg, 1979; Ruble & Rholes, 1981; Shantz, 1983). Only at Level 4 can children conceptualize repeated success as reflecting an ability to meet others' expectations across time and space, which produces a new kind of feeling of self-confidence. On the other hand, children at this stage can also conceptualize repeated failure as representing a lack of ability, which results in their becoming vulnerable to a new kind of feeling of helplessness (see Dweck & Elliott, 1983; Rholes, Blackwell, Jordan, & Walters, 1980; Ruble & Rholes, 1981).

With their new capacity for mental representation, children can also consider and integrate multiple alternative causal factors. This makes attributions of responsibility to self and others possible for the first time. This new capacity is again a mixed blessing. On the one hand, children can attribute their successes to ability and their failures to task difficulty or bad luck, which maintains self-esteem, effort, and persistence (see Dweck & Elliott, 1983; Lepper, in press; Snyder, Stephan, & Rosenfield, 1978). On the other hand, they can attribute their failures to lack of ability and their successes to luck, which can produce feelings of helplessness and depression (see Abramson & Martin, 1981; Ickes & Layden, 1978).

As illustrated in Fig. 4.1, children at Level 4 can represent the interrelations between their self-traits and another person's standpoint on those traits. They can also relate this general trait dimension to the general dimension of features and responses. Children's capacity at this level to interrelate conceptual elements within and between these two distinct dimensions means that psychologically significant *self-concept–self-guide structures* can be formed. Children can not only evaluate a particular feature that they possess by considering another person's standpoint on that feature (e.g., "I brush my teeth in the morning and Mom likes that."), but they can now evaluate the traits that they believe they generally possess in relation to a self-guide for their general traits. Now children can appraise the particular *type of person* that they are (e.g., "Am I the 'good girl' that Mom wants me to be?").

At this stage, children are capable of understanding that is not just that other people value particular types of appearance or behavior and prefer those people who display them, but that others want or require him or her, in particular, to be a specific type of person. At Level 4, then, children are capable of evaluating the type of person that they generally are and can attribute responsibility to themselves for their condition. A shift in self-regulation has occurred from identification to *internalization*. With internalization, children are motivated to have their self-concept attributes match their self-guide attributes not in order to display self-features that others' will like or admire but in order to be *the right kind of person, a "good" person* (see Grusec, 1983; Kohlberg, 1976). At this stage, children can be motivated to perform a particular act because it matches their belief about what it means to be a "good" person even if the act has not previously been reinforced. Grusec (1983), for example, reports that manipulating Level 4 children's self-attributions of being a "nice" person increases their helping in new situations, but no such generalization occurs for Level 3 children.

An emotional benefit of this development is that behaviors that match self-guides can now produce positive feelings even when they are not responded to positively as long as they fulfill an internal standard for being a particular kind of person (see Kelman, 1958). An emotional cost is that mismatches between behaviors and self-guides can now produce negative feelings even when they are not responded to negatively. From a self-regulatory standpoint, however, the ability to make self-attributions of responsibility and respond negatively to one's actions independent of others' responses to them is the essence of what has been meant by children's new capacity for "internal" control. Indeed, Anna Freud (1937) suggests that only now can true morality begin, only now can children have a true conscience (see also Hoffman, 1983; Loevinger, 1976).

One consequence of these developmental changes is that the breadth of applicability of standards is greatly increased because the standard refers to types of traits and not just types of behaviors. It has been noted that internalization increases the range of situations involving self-regulation (e.g., Grusec, 1983; Kelman, 1958; Lepper, 1983). In addition, by representing the valued end-state in terms of general traits rather than specific behaviors, children can now produce or avoid producing novel behaviors to which no one has previously responded but that match or mismatch, respectively, self-guide traits. Thus, these developmental changes have the benefit of extending children's self-regulatory control to a greater range of situations and to situations pressing for novel behaviors.

There are also potential costs of these developmental changes. For example, self-regulation is more difficult now for at least a couple of reasons. First, it is less clear which behaviors would meet the standard when the standard is defined in terms of general traits rather than particular behaviors. Second, self-guide traits require multiple behaviors (across time and situations) to be met fully.

Another self-regulatory consequence of the developmental changes beginning at Level 3 and culminating at Level 4 is that children can use their self-guides as a basis for making decisions about how to behave rather than having to retrieve prior episodes and base their decisions on past outcomes of alternative courses of action. A potential benefit of this is that self-guide matches and mismatches would provide an efficient, relatively effortless heuristic for making decisions. A potential cost is that a mismatch could inhibit action that has not been associated with negative outcomes in the past and would, in fact, be adaptive now.

A self-evaluative consequence of these developmental changes is that children can not only emotionally appraise a particular feature that they possess by considering another person's likely response to or feelings about the feature, but they can also use a self-guide to appraise their self-concept as a whole. Thus, children at this stage can evaluate themselves in more global, overall terms. On the one hand, this means that children can now enjoy feelings of general self-worth. On the other hand, this means that children are now vulnerable to making global negative self-attributions and to feeling generally unworthy (see Bemporad, 1978; Digdon & Gotlib, 1985; McConville, Boag, & Purohit, 1973).

Level 5: Late Vectorial Development

Between 13 and 16 children become capable of interrelating different perspectives on the same object, including the self as an object (Fischer, 1980; Inhelder & Piaget, 1958; Selman & Byrne, 1974). They become capable of interrelating different systems of distinct dimensions (Case 1985) and of constructing abstract mappings in which two abstractions are related to each other (Fischer & Lamborn, in press). Given this new ability, adolescents can integrate information about distinct traits into higher-order abstractions (Case, 1985; Fischer, 1980), thus allowing their self-concepts and self-guides to contain multiple personality types and identities (Case, 1985; Harter, 1983).

One consequence of this development is to increase further children's differentiation of the self into distinct regions or "spheres of comfort." A potential benefit of this development is that these distinct regions can function as a buffer against being overwhelmed by stress arising in any one sphere of life (see Linville, 1987; Simmons & Blyth, 1987). A potential cost, however, is an increase in the structural interconnectedness among problematical, mismatching self-attributes (see Higgins, Van Hook, & Dorfman, 1988). This in turn can increase the adolescent's vulnerability to more global negative psychological situations, e.g., the "overgeneralizations" and "global negative self-attributions" described in the depression literature (see Beck, 1967; Seligman, Abramson, Semmel, & Von Baeyer, 1979).

Adolescents' new ability to interrelate distinct dimensional systems has a further consequence of major significance. In prior stages children could experience conflict between alternative courses of action, but at this stage adolescents can represent a conflict between alternative self-guide systems. The appearance of new types of inner conflicts during this period has been noted in the literature (e.g., Harter, 1986; Loevinger, 1976). For the first time two distinct self-guide systems, such as one actual self–self-guide system involving a parental standpoint and one actual self–self-guide system involving a peer standpoint, can themselves be interrelated. As illustrated in Fig. 4.1, at Level 4 the relation between self-feature X and other-response Y could be part of a higher-level system relating self-trait X and the standpoint of a particular other on self-trait X, but now at level 5 this higher-level system can itself be related to another system relating self-trait X and another person's standpoint on self-trait X.

This new ability to represent the relation between two self-systems has the potential benefit of motivating adolescents to resolve possible conflicts in their lives, such as a conflict between their friends' wishes for them and their parents' beliefs about their responsibilities. When there are such real-world conflicts, the ability to represent them is a critical first step in resolving them. Older adolescents are capable of finding solutions to or reconciling conflicting demands (see Fischer & Lamborn, in press; Loevinger, 1976). And by searching for solutions adolescents are more likely to construct or choose principles to which they can be personally committed (see Kohlberg, 1976; Loevinger, 1976). Each adolescent can now construct his or her "own" standpoint that can function as the integrated, coordinated solution to the complex array of alternative self-guides that he or she possesses.

On the other hand, many adolescents, especially younger adolescents, may be unable to reconcile conflicting demands. In such cases, adolescents' new ability to represent conflicting self-guides introduces a new vulnerability, the ability to experience self-guide–self-guide discrepancies. A self-guide–self-guide discrepancy reflects a double approach–avoidance conflict where a person is motivated to approach both self-guides and to avoid increasing any discrepancy from either self-guide (see Van Hook & Higgins, 1988). With respect to self-regulatory processes, such a discrepancy makes planning and goal-directed action difficult. Thus, this type of discrepancy should be associated with feelings of uncertainty and confusion. For example, an adolescent girl's parents may believe that it is her responsibility to place schoolwork and household duties above all other activities (to be "responsible"), whereas her peer group may want her to spend most of her time with them (to be "sociable"). In order for one system to be at least temporarily dominant to guide action and decision making, such discrepancies are also likely to be associated with rebelliousness in relation to one or the other self-guide. With respect to self-evaluative processes, a discrepancy between two self-guide systems means that the same self-feature X could be interpreted or appraised differently at different times depending on which self-guide was used as the standard for evaluation. This could produce confusion concerning one's identity and self-worth (see Van Hook & Higgins, 1988).

There is evidence suggesting that adolescence can, indeed, be a period of uncertainty, identity confusion, and rebelliousness (see Blos, 1961; Erikson, 1963; Fischer & Lamborn, in press). Harter (1986) reports that at adolescence there is a sharp rise in children perceiving attributes within the self as opposites, which in turn is associated with their feeling confused and mixed up. Van Hook and Higgins (1988) directly tested whether uncertainty and confusion-related problems are associated with adolescents' possession of self-guide–self-guide discrepancies. They found that undergraduates who possessed this type of self-discrepancy were significantly more likely than undergraduates without this discrepancy to suffer chronically from indecision, muddledness, identity confusion, distractibility, and rebelliousness.

Another important consequence of adolescents' ability to interrelate distinct systems of dimensions is that now they can compare the current state of their actual self–self-guide relations with past or future states. Thus, the self-evaluative process can now include an assessment of change in the self-system. For example, comparing a past state represented as a self-discrepancy with a current state represented as a self-congruency might make them feel both satisfied and grateful. A potential benefit, then, of this *temporal perspective* (see Erikson, 1963; Lewin, 1935; Werner, 1957) is that adolescents can feel more positive than they would simply on the basis of their current state. On the other hand, a potential cost of this temporal perspective is that adolescents can become more vulnerable to feeling discouraged or hopeless by comparing their current state with some past or future state (see Bemporad, 1978).

Thus far, this section has described qualitative shifts from birth to adolescence in children's mental representational capacity that impact on their self-system—on their self-concepts and self-other contingency knowledge, and on their self-evaluative and self-regulatory processes. Potential costs and benefits of these changes in the self-system have been discussed. One critical aspect of socioemotional adaptation has been considered: How children learn to approach positive psychological situations and avoid negative psychological situations by acquiring self-other contingency knowledge and self-guides. Another critical aspect of socioemotional adaptation is learning how to handle the emotional/motivational states produced by self-evaluative feedback, especially the distress produced by negative feedback. The nature of such coping and its relation to intellectual development is considered next.

Coping with Distress Produced by Self-evaluative Feedback

The self-evaluative process was described earlier as functioning in the service of self-regulation, providing feedback concerning the matching of self-guides. A self-evaluative judgment that there is a discrepancy between a current state and a valued end-state (e.g., a self-guide) produces a negative emotional state (e.g., disappointment, worry) that the person is motivated to change. There are two general ways of coping with this unpleasant condition. First, the discrepancy itself can be dealt with. When this leads to the reduction of the magnitude of the discrepancy, then the self-evaluative process benefits self-regulation and the control process is running smoothly. Second, just the emotional/motivational state produced by the self-evaluative process can be managed without dealing with the discrepancy itself. In this case, the self-evaluative process does not directly benefit self-regulation and may even interfere with it. Let us consider each of these possibilities more fully.

One general way that people can deal with the distress produced by a self-discrepancy is *to manage the discrepancy itself*. Following the logic of self-discrepancy theory, there are three basic ways to manage a self-discrepancy (see Higgins, 1987): (1) Change the current state or actual self to be less discrepant from the valued end-state; (2) Change the valued end-state to be less discrepant from the current state; and (3) Reduce the accessibility of the discrepancy. What methods might be used to carry out each of these management modes? How might these methods vary as function of children's intellectual capacity? What are their potential costs and benefits? These are fundamental questions that can only be addressed in a preliminary manner here.

Changing the Current State to be Less Discrepant from the Valued End-state. To change the current state to be less discrepant from the valued end-state, children can change their actual behavior or their interpretation of their behavior. The former method is within the capability of even the youngest children (e.g., infants shifting their heads when feeding to make contact with their mothers' nipple) and remains a common method for coping with discrepancies throughout life. It has the advantage of being direct and concrete. Changing behavior, however, can sometimes be very difficult or even impossible. In such cases it may be easier to change one's perception of one's current state rather than to change one's behavior. One method for doing this is available even to young children—denial. Children can simply deny the existence of their current condition. This method has the obvious disadvantage of being contradicted by reality.

An alternative method is to change one's interpretation of one's current state rather than to deny it. A major benefit of intellectual development is that children become able to use reinterpretation to deal with their discrepancies (see Band & Weisz, 1988). Children at level 4, for example, can attribute a low performance to low effort or compare their low performance with the generally low performance of others on the task, thereby judging their ability more positively and reducing the discrepancy (see Dweck & Elliot, 1983; Ruble, 1983). There is also a potential cost of this development, however. Even when children are capable of changing their behavior and thereby directly reducing the discrepancy, they may expend their energy formulating excuses instead. They may justify their discrepant actions by using pseudologic or by distorting and misusing facts—*rationalization* (see Cameron, 1963). In extreme cases, they may create bizarre interpretations of their condition that increase their anxiety and reduce their motivation to deal further with the discrepancy.

Changing the Valued End-state to be Less Discrepant from the Current State. To change the valued end-state to be less discrepant from the current state, children can shift their attention to an alternative end-state or modify the end-state. Even young children are capable of shifting their attention away from an end-state producing discomfort to an alternative end-state (e.g., leaving a toy that has stopped working to play with an alternative toy). This method is used adaptatively throughout life to shift resources from nonobtainable to obtainable goals. When a goal or end-state has a motivational history that makes it highly important, however, it can be difficult to shift attention to an alternative end-state even when it would be more productive to do so. In such cases, it may be necessary to modify the end-state itself.

When children understand that intentions and motives underlie actions (i.e., by Level 3), they become capable of reducing the importance of an end-state causing distress. This has the benefit of facilitating a shift to a more productive end-state. On the other hand, the process of readjusting the importance of an end-state can be self-delusional, as when children reject an end-state by denying that they are motivated to meet the end-state (e.g., "I don't want it anymore!"; "I don't have to do it anymore!").

With further intellectual development, children become capable of modifying their end-states by considering its appropriateness or utility in relation to other standards. Adolescents at Level 5, for example, are capable of understanding that an end-state is unreasonable or irrational. They can understand that an end-state will have more costs than benefits in the long run or is in conflict with other valued end-states. This understanding has the benefit of introducing new reasons to change a maladaptive end-state. It also has the potential risk of leading some adolescents to question all end-states, which could produce *apathy or anomie*.

Adolescents can also understand that an end-state is socially unacceptable and can redirect themselves toward some alternative end-state that is more acceptable—*sublimation* (see Case, Hayward, Lewis, & Hurst, 1987). This requires the ability to compare different end-states in relation to both their social acceptability and their ability to satisfy basic needs (i.e., Level 5). In the psychodynamic literature, sublimation has traditionally been considered the most complete and successful of all the defenses, a nonneurotic channeling of drives (see Cameron, 1963; A. Freud, 1937). From this perspective, it is a benefit of intellectual development that this mechanism becomes available for dealing with discrepancies.

Reducing the Accessibility of the Discrepancy. The third way to manage a self-discrepancy is to reduce the accessibility of the discrepancy. This can be accomplished passively by the passage of time or actively by inhibition. Simply ignoring a discrepancy by becoming involved in other activities should reduce the accessibility of a discrepancy as a result of temporal decay (see Higgins, Bargh, & Lombardi, 1985). Even young children are capable of reducing distress through behavioral distraction, and behavioral distraction is a common coping strategy at every age level (see Altshuler & Ruble, 1988). Older children are also capable of cognitive distraction strategies, such as thinking about something else (see Altshuler & Ruble, 1988; Harris, Olthof, & Terwogt, 1981; Miller & Green, 1985; Mischel, 1973). Cognitive distraction strategies have the benefit of being applicable across a greater range of circumstances.

If a discrepancy is chronically accessible, it could take a long time for the accessibility to be reduced simply through the passage of time. Thus distraction per se is not always the optimal strategy. The accessibility of a discrepancy could be reduced more quickly by actively focusing on some idea that is incompatible with the discrepancy, thereby preventing the discrepancy from being activated (see Higgins, King, & Mavin, 1982). Daydreams, fantasies, and other forms of "positive thinking" have the benefit of quickly inhibiting the accessibility of discrepancies. Such strategies have also been found to increase with intellectual development (see Altshuler & Ruble, 1988). They are made possible by the development of symbolic representation (Level 2) plus the awareness of emotionally significant mental states and the possibility of manipulating them (Level 3). These strategies, however, also have the potential cost of children becoming lost in fantasy rather than dealing with the real-world source of their problems. Moreover, extreme forms of this strategy can contribute to later pathology, as exemplified in the defense mechanism of *reaction formation*—assuming attitudes that are diametrically opposed to discrepant thoughts (Cameron, 1963; A. Freud, 1937).

There is an important difference between the first two ways of coping with discrepancies and the third way. Changing the current state to be less discrepant from the valued end-state or changing the valued end-state to be less discrepant from the current state both change the availability of the discrepancy—the original discrepancy no longer exists in memory. With the accessibility reduction methods, however, the discrepancy still exists. The original discrepancy is still available in memory and thus could be reactivated. Thus, although this way of coping with the emotional/motivational condition produced by the self-evaluative process does change the condition, it does not reduce the source of the condition. Unlike the alternative ways of coping, it does not change the current state–valued end-state discrepancy itself. In this case, then, the self-evaluative feedback has produced discomfort without contributing to self-regulatory reduction of the discrepancy.

There are other cases where coping with self-evaluative feedback does not contribute to discrepancy reduction. When self-evaluative feedback produces an intense emotional response the coping system may become directed solely to *just dealing with the distress* rather than reducing the discrepancy that was responsible for producing it. Such coping responses can be necessary, however, because it is not always possible to deal adequately with a discrepancy (see Case et al., 1987).

One benefit of intellectual development is that new procedures or mechanisms for coping with emotional distress become available (see Case et al., 1987; Kernberg, 1976; Vaillant, 1977). For example, Case et al. (1987) suggest that children toward the end of the interrelational stage become capable of using projection to control their emotions and that children toward the end of the dimensional stage become capable of using rationalization to control their emotions. Projection requires the ability to infer others' intentions, attitudes, beliefs, and so on, and thus would be expected to appear around Level 3. Rationalization requires the ability to choose among or create alternative causal attributions and thus would be expected to appear around Level 4.

Mechanisms such as projection and rationalization have the benefit of reducing emotional distress. But they have the cost of distorting reality. By explaining away one's emotional states, they discount one's true feelings, which can be dehumanizing. Indeed, mechanisms that deal only with the distress produced by self-evaluative feedback rather than the underlying discrepancy can create rather than resolve problems. For example, a person might take drugs to feel better rather than take action to better meet their standards. In extreme cases a person might commit suicide to escape the distress altogether. In such cases the self-evaluative feedback is no longer supporting the self-regulatory system to reduce discrepancies. Instead, the methods of coping with the feedback-induced distress have themselves become a serious problem. Psychodynamic theories also suggest that the defense mechanisms for dealing with distress are themselves a major source of neurotic symptoms (see Cameron, 1963; A. Freud, 1937; Vaillant, 1977).

This section has considered two critical aspects of the relation between self-system development and socioemotional development: (1) The acquisition of self-other contingency knowledge and actual self–self-guide relations used in self-regulation and self-evaluation; and (2) The acquisition of procedural strategies or coping mechanisms for resolving the emotional/motivational condition produced by self-evaluative feedback concerning self-discrepancies. Developmental changes in children's mental representational capacity were described that produce developmental shifts in children's acquisition of both of these types of knowledge. Potential costs and benefits from these developmental changes were also discussed.

Intellectual development is not the only source of variation in children's self-regulatory and self-evaluative processes. Intellectual development pertains to the self-regulatory and self-evaluative processes that children at different levels *can* perform. But children at the same level of intellectual development may nevertheless use different self-regulatory and self-evaluatory processes, depending on socialization factors (see Higgins & Wells, 1986). The next section considers such factors.

TRADEOFFS FROM SOCIALIZATION

The development of children's self-regulatory and self-evaluative processes as described in the previous section begins with the acquisition of self-other contingency knowledge and proceeds to the development of self-guides and actual self–self-guide relations. This development is based on children's early social interactions with significant others and the emotional significance of these interactions (i.e., the psychological situations experienced by children in these interactions). To understand how children's social interactions with significant others influence the development of their self-regulatory and self-evaluative processes, one must first consider what it would mean for a child to acquire strong self-guides and which general features of child–caretaker interaction would be expected to produce them (see Higgins, 1989a; Moretti & Higgins, 1989).

Characteristics of Strong Self-guides

The "strength" of self-other contingency knowledge and self-guides is defined in terms of the following characteristics:

1. Availability/accessibility—Refers to whether the self-other contingency knowledge is stored at all in long-term memory (i.e., is it available as stored knowledge to be retrieved), and, given that it is available, how likely is it to be activated and utilized (i.e., how accessible is it?). The concern in this case is not so much with momentary accessibility as with chronic accessibility (see Higgins, King, & Mavin, 1982).
2. Coherence—Refers to the extent to which the procedural force of the self-other contingency knowledge has a uniform direction (i.e., the knowledge concerning what to approach and what to avoid is pushing and pulling in the same direction toward the same end-point).
3. Commitment—Refers to the extent to which the child is motivated to use the self-other contingency knowledge in his or her self-regulatory and self-evaluative processes (i.e., the magnitude of the procedural force of the self-other contingency knowledge).

Socialization Features Producing Strong Self-guides

If one assumes that the acquisition of self-other contingency knowledge is a function of the same basic factors that determine knowledge acquisition in general, then the following features of children's interactions with their significant others would be expected to influence children's acquisition of self-guides:

1. *Frequency* of exposure to social interactions that instantiate self-other contingencies. The more frequently a child is exposed to instances of a particular type of contingency, the more likely it is that the child will acquire knowledge of the contingency.
2. *Consistency* of each self-other contingency across its instantiations. The more consistently self-feature X and other-response Y are associated and the more consistently other-response Y and self-psychological situation Z are associated, the more likely it is that a child will acquire the contingency.
3. *Clarity* of presentation of the self-other contingency instantiations. A contingency is more likely to be acquired if the instantiations present the contingent information clearly. Contingency information is clearer when it

is salient (e.g., it is prominent or distinctive) and comprehensible (e.g., it occurs without background noise, distractions, or disruptions).

4. *Significance* of the self-other contingency event. A self-other contingency is more likely to be acquired if the "other" involved in the contingency is "significant," in the sense that "other-response Y" is meaningful and produces a motivationally important "self-psychological situation Z." More generally, the more emotionally and motivationally significant is the psychological situation associated with Other-Response Y, the more likely it is that a child will acquire the contingency.

All four of these features, but especially "frequency," are likely to influence the availability and accessibility of self-other contingency knowledge. The "consistency" and "clarity" features, in particular, are likely to influence the coherence of the self-other contingency knowledge. The "frequency" feature and, especially, the "significance" feature are likely to influence the commitment to the self-other contingency knowledge.

Self-guide Acquisition Strength as a Function of Socialization Mode

By making some reasonable assumptions concerning the relation between particular socialization modes and each of the socialization features hypothesized to produce strong self-guides, it is possible to consider which socialization modes are more or less likely to lead children to acquire strong self-other contingency knowledge and self-guides (see Higgins, 1989b).

Modes more likely to produce strong self-guides—Children whose caretakers are *responsive* (i.e., who respond differentially to desired and undesired behaviors of the child) and *sensitive* (i.e., who closely monitor the attentional state of the child and adapt their demands to the child's state) are more likely to acquire strong self-guides because high responsitivity and sensitivity would increase both the frequency and the consistency of contingent interactions. Children whose caretakers are "democratic" (see Baldwin, 1955; Lewin, Lippitt, & White, 1939) or use *induction techniques* (see Hoffman, 1970), which refer to parents who communicate explicitly their rules, attitudes, and reasons for responding as they do to the child, are also more likely to acquire strong self-guides because such techniques enhance the clarity of children's experience of contingencies. Induction should be especially effective in promoting strong self-guides when it is accompanied by strong expressions of affect because both the clarity (i.e., salience and distinctiveness) and the significance of the contingencies would be increased.

Modes less likely to produce strong self-guides—Children whose caretakers are *uninvolved* (i.e., who ignore or neglect the child or are psychologically unavailable) are less likely to acquire strong self-guides because low involvement would decrease the frequency of the self-other contingent interactions. Children whose parents are either *highly permissive* (i.e., who take a tolerant, accepting attitude toward the child's impulses, make few demands, avoid enforcing rules or imposing restrictions) or *overprotective* (i.e., who supervise, restrict, and control every behavior of the child) are also less likely to acquire strong self-guides because these noncontingent responses to the child do not discriminate among the child's behaviors and are thus low in clarity. High permissiveness can also be associated with low frequency of contingent interactions. *Interparent and intra-parent inconsistency* also reduces the likelihood that children will acquire strong self-guides.

These hypothesized relations between mode of socialization and the likelihood that children will acquire strong self-guides have not been tested directly in the literature. Given that strong self-guides are associated with strong self-regulatory processes, however, one would predict that children whose parents are responsive, sensitive, and use induction should be higher in prosocial behavior and lower in antisocial behavior than children whose parents are uninvolved and highly permissive or overprotective (see Higgins, 1989a). The current evidence in the socialization literature strongly supports this prediction (see Maccoby & Martin, 1983; Olweus, 1980; Parke & Slaby, 1983; Radke–Yarrow et al., 1983).

Socialization Mode and the Child's Psychological Situation

Caretaker–child interactions vary not only in the frequency, consistency, and clarity of the self-other contingency information they provide. They also vary in the psychological situation or emotional experience they produce in the child; that is, in the self-psychological situation Z component of the self-other contingencies shown in Fig. 4.1. This psychological situation of the child is also reflected in the "significance" feature of self-other contingency events.

When a *match* occurs between a child's features and those child features valued by the caretaker, the caretaker is likely to respond to the child in a manner that places the child in a *positive psychological situation* (e.g., hugging, holding, reassuring). When a *mismatch* occurs, the caretaker is likely to respond to the child in a manner that places the child in a *negative psychological situation* (e.g., punishing, criticizing, withholding). Socialization modes vary in the extent to which they involve management sequences (i.e., engineering and planning the child's environment to bring out valued attributes in the child) versus disciplinary sequences, with the former sequences involving matches and the latter sequences involving mismatches.

Socialization modes also vary in terms of the *type of outcome orientation* that underlies the child's psychological situation:

1. *Presence and absence of positive outcomes*—In this mode, the caretaker responds to the child in such a way that the child experiences either the presence of positive outcomes (a positive psychological situation) or the absence of positive outcomes (a negative psychological situation). For example, a child smiles at the mother, the mother picks up and hugs the child, and the child feels happy (presence of positive outcomes); a child spills some food, the mother stops feeding the child and stops smiling at the child, and the child feels sad (absence of positive outcomes).
2. *Presence and absence of negative outcomes*—In this mode, the caretaker responds to the child in such a way that the child experiences either the presence of negative outcomes (a negative psychological situation) or the absence of negative outcomes (a positive psychological situation). For example, a child looks away, the mother plays roughly with the child to get his or her attention, and the child feels scared (presence of negative outcomes); a child cries out in distress, the mother removes the source of distress and reassures the child, and the child now feels safe and secure (the absence of negative outcomes).

Self-discrepancy theory postulates that caretakers who chronically appraise a child in terms of *how they would ideally like the child to be,* in terms of their hopes and aspirations for the child, are likely to respond to the child in a way that the child experiences the presence or absence of positive outcomes. For example, if a child's behavior fails to fulfill (mismatches) a mother's hopes for the child, the mother is likely to feel disappointed and dissatisfied in the child and withdraw love and attention from the child, which would cause the child to experience the absence of positive outcomes. In contrast, caretakers who chronically appraise a child in terms of *how they believe the child ought to be,* in terms of their beliefs about the child's duty and obligations, are likely to respond to the child in a way that the child experiences the presence or absence of negative outcomes. For example, if a child's behavior violates (mismatches) what a mother's believes the child ought to do, the mother is likely to criticize or punish the child, which would cause the child to experience the presence of negative outcomes.

A Classification Scheme for Modes of Caretaker-child Interaction

By organizing different patterns of socialization in terms of the strength of self-other contingency knowledge or self-guides that a child is likely to acquire, the type of "self-psychological situation Z" that a child is likely to experience, and the type of outcome orientation that a child is likely to experience, eight different modes of caretaker–child interaction can be distinguished (see Table 4.1).

TABLE 4.1
A Classification Scheme for Modes of Caretaker–child Interaction

	Child's Psychological Situation			
	Positive Types		*Negative Types*	
Acquisition strength of self-other contingency knowledge	Presence of positive outcomes	Absence of negative outcomes	Absence of positive outcomes	Presence of negative outcomes
Strong	Managing Modes		Disciplining Modes	
	Bolstering	Prudent	Love Withdrawing	Punitive/Critical
Weak	Smothering Modes		Rejecting Modes	
	Spoiling	Overprotective	Neglectful	Abusive

Note. This table represents a classification of four basic modes of caretaker-child interaction in terms of both the strength of the self-other contingency knowledge (strong or weak) that a child is likely to acquire and the type of psychological situation (positive or negative) that a child is likely to experience. Each of the four interaction modes defined by these two criteria is further divided into two subtypes depending on whether the child's psychological situation involves the presence or absence of outcomes. The entry in each of the eight cells provides a label for a specific mode of caretaker-child interaction that is defined by all these classification criteria.

Both the psychological parameters and the modes of caretaker–child interaction identified by this classificatory scheme are related to traditional socialization typologies (see, for example, Becker, 1964; Bohrnstedt & Fisher, 1986; Maccoby & Martin, 1983; Schaefer, 1959). But the present scheme differs from previous schemes by distinguishing among modes of caretaker–child interaction in terms of their *psychological impact on the child* rather than the traditional concern with parental orientations to the child (see Higgins, 1989b).

A major advantage of the proposed scheme is that it is framed in terms of the parameters of self-discrepancy theory. Thus, the different modes of caretaker–child interaction can be related directly to self-regulatory processes, self-evaluative processes, and emotional predispositions. The two "disciplinary" modes, for example, are the only caretaker–child modes that are expected to both contribute to the acquisition of strong self-guides and produce negative psychological situations in the child. The model, therefore, predicts that these modes are especially likely to be associated with vulnerability to self-system-related emotional problems in later development. Indeed, the combination of the traditional parenting variables of "strict/demanding" and "cold," which in the present model reflects the combination of "acquisition of strong self-other contingency knowledge" and "negative psychological situation," has been found to be especially predictive of undergraduates' current level of depression (see Bornstedt & Fisher, 1986). Certainly other modes, such as the "abusive" mode, can be associated with emotional problems, but these problems would be related more to suffering from real-world stress than to suffering produced by the self-system.

Tradeoffs from Stronger Self-guides

The foregoing review of the socialization literature suggests that there can be both benefits and costs of children acquiring strong self-guides. The kinds of socialization expected to produce strong self-guides have been found to be associated with children who are obedient, nonaggressive, socially responsible, and high in prosocial behavior. On the other hand, there is evidence suggesting that such socialization is also predictive of later depression. Similarly, the kinds of socialization expected to produce weak self-guides have been found to be associated with children who are disobedient, aggressive, lacking in social responsibility, and low in prosocial behavior. On the other hand, some aggressive children do not have a negative attitude about themselves and experience relatively little guilt, such as the bullys described by Olweus (1984).

These findings suggest that there can be a *tradeoff* from acquiring stronger self-guides—stronger self-guides can increase both self-regulatory processes that have positive consequences and self-evaluative processes that have negative consequences. How might this happen? Self-guides are the valued end-states in the self-system. The self-regulatory system functions to minimize the discrepancy between a person's current state and these self-guides. Self-evaluation is an aspect of the self-regulatory system that monitors the relation between the current state and the self-guides and provides feedback about the current level of discrepancy. Increasing the strength of a self-guide should increase both the self-regulatory motivation to minimize current self–self-guide discrepancies and the emotional intensity of the self-evaluative feedback.

Motivation is not the only determinant of behavior or outcome, but it can be a significant factor. People are not always experiencing current self–self-guide discrepancies, but they are common in everyone's life. When high motivation is likely to yield a valued outcome and people are experiencing discrepancies, then increasing the strength of a self-guide would be expected both to produce matches with valued end-states and increase positive self-evaluative emotions. For most people the presence of prosocial behaviors and the absence of antisocial behaviors are valued end-states and high motivation will yield matches with these end-states. Thus, these kinds of behaviors and positive feelings about oneself in relation to them should increase as the strength of self-guides increase.

When high motivation is not sufficient to yield a valued outcome, however, and people are experiencing discrepancies, then increasing the strength of a self-guide would not produce matches with valued end-states but would increase negative self-evaluative emotions. In Western culture at least, as children move through their various social-life phases (e.g., preschoolers, juveniles, preadolescents, adolescents) there is a shift in the self-attributes that they value (see

Higgins & Eccles–Parsons, 1983). For example, from the juvenile period through to adolescence there is a shift to new self-attributes associated with peer relationships, such as "popularity" and "sexual attractiveness," that reflects in part the increasing importance of peers in their lives (see Hartup, 1983; Floyd & Smith, 1972; Simmons & Blyth, 1987). Moreover, many valued self-attributes are defined relative to others, such as "smart" meaning higher grades than most other students (see Dweck & Elliot, 1983; Ruble, 1983; Veroff, 1969), in contrast to the more absolute meaning of "polite," "tidy," "nondestructive," and so on. When the identification of one's current state is based on social comparison, it is much more difficult for children to meet the standard. In these later periods, then, increased motivation from stronger self-guides often would be insufficient to produce matches with valued end-states. But the stronger self-guides would produce greater intensity of self-evaluative feedback, which in this case is likely to be negative because the discrepancy is likely to remain.

This analysis suggests that the benefits and costs of stronger self-guides vary as a function of whether high motivation is likely to produce matches between children's current state and their valued end-states. Self-attributes vary in whether high motivation is likely to produce matches, and there are developmental differences in which kinds of self-attributes are valued. When the valued self-attributes are the kind for which high motivation is likely to produce matches, then strong self-guides have both a performance and emotional health advantage. But when the valued self-attributes are the kind for which high motivation is not enough to produce matches, then strong self-guides have only a small performance advantage and a large emotional disadvantage.

In the preschool and juvenile periods, the valued self-attributes are the kind for which high motivation is likely to produce matches (see Higgins & Eccles–Parsons, 1983; Minuchin & Shapiro, 1983). In these periods, then, high self-guides should lead to both better conduct and better emotional health. As discussed earlier, in the preadolescent period and, especially, in the adolescent period, the valued self-attributes are the kind for which high motivation is not enough to produce matches. In these periods, then, high self-guides should lead to somewhat better conduct but worse emotional health.

This analysis suggests that, in general, as children move from the preschool and juvenile periods to the preadolescent and adolescent periods, their self-evaluations should become more negative. Consistent with this expectation, there is considerable evidence that children's perceived self-competence begins to decrease between the early juvenile and preadolescent periods and there is a further decline with entry into adolescence (see Aboud & Ruble, 1987; Harter, 1983; Rosenberg, 1979; Ruble & Frey, 1987; Simmons & Blyth, 1987). This analysis also explains the pattern of findings described earlier—how stronger self-guides could be associated with more prosocial behavior and less antisocial behavior in earlier periods and yet be predictive of more self-evaluative emotional problems in later periods.

Thus far, potential tradeoffs from acquiring stronger self-guides have been discussed only with respect to conduct and emotional health. But stronger self-guides may also yield tradeoffs with respect to achievement motivation and performance. As the strength of self-guides increases, the motivation to perform so as to match self-guides should increase. In achievement areas, this increased motivation should be revealed in high standards for achievement. This in turn would be associated with either a high motive to succeed (especially for Ideal-oriented individuals) or a high fear of failure (especially for Ought-oriented individuals) (see Higgins, Klein, & Strauman, 1986). In achievement areas for which high motivation is likely to produce matches with self-guides (i.e., success on the task), stronger self-guides should produce better performance and positive self-evaluative emotions (e.g., pride). But in achievement areas for which high motivation is unlikely to produce matches, stronger self-guides will increase motivation, but this increase will not necessarily improve performance. Indeed, the negative self-evaluative emotions (e.g., shame, fear) produced by a failure to match self-guides could actually impair performance.

Stronger self-guides, then, could improve or impair performance, depending on whether the achievement area is or is not the kind in which high motivation is likely to produce matches with self-guides. As children move through elementary school into high school, courses become progressively more difficult (see Dweck, 1986) and the likelihood that high motivation will yield success decreases. According to this analysis, then, stronger self-guides are more likely to enhance course performance and produce positive self-evaluative emotions in elementary school than in high school. In high school, the more a course depends on ability rather than motivation, the more likely it is that stronger self-guides will actually impair performance and produce negative self-evaluative emotions.

There are other potential tradeoffs of stronger self-guides with respect to achievement. Even for achievement areas in which high motivation is likely to produce matches, stronger self-guides may have costs as well as benefits. To the extent that a person is motivated to achieve *in order to* produce matches with his or her self-guides, he or she is extrinsically rather than intrinsically motivated (see Deci & Ryan, 1985; Kruglanski, 1975). Indeed, such extrinsic motivation will undermine intrinsic motivation. As controlling, extrinsic forces, strong self-guides may produce discomfort and even reduce creativity given that controlling extrinsic conditions have been found to produce pressure and tension and undermine task enjoyment and creativity (see Amabile, 1983; Deci & Ryan, 1985; Kruglanski, Friedman, & Zeevi, 1971).

In sum, stronger self-guides can have both benefits and costs with respect to conduct, emotional health, achievement performance, and achievement-related feelings. Moreover, the tradeoffs associated with stronger self-guides are not necessarily evident at any particular period or on any particular activity. Rather, the same underlying processes associated with stronger self-guides that produce benefits at one social-life phase or in one activity may produce costs at a later social-life phase or in another activity. As an illustration of such tradeoff patterns, let us return now to the sex differences discussed at the outset.

Sex Differences as an Illustration of Tradeoff Patterns

In the beginning of this chapter, an intriguing pattern of sex differences was described. Girls apparently have an advantage over boys with respect to conduct, emotional health, and school performance in early elementary school, but this advantage disappears or even reverses after high school. Before describing this pattern in more detail, let us consider how the developmental model of self-regulatory and self-evaluative processes proposed herein might account for such a pattern. I should first emphasize, however, that my proposed explanation for this pattern of sex differences does not rule out other factors, such as sex differences in maturation or in social roles. As for any complex pattern of findings, this pattern could be multiply determined. Moreover, I am aware that the empirical literature that I am surveying is controversial and correlational and that its reliability and validity is insufficient to permit strong conclusions. My only purpose here is to illustrate how the logic and parameters of the proposed model can be applied to provide a tentative account of a complex pattern of socioemotional development.

According to the proposed model, differences in motivation, behavior, and emotion can arise from differences in the strength of the self-guides that children acquire. Differential strength of self-guides, in turn, can arise from differential histories of child–caretaker interactions that provide self-other contingency knowledge. Thus, to begin at the beginning, is there a difference in child–caretaker interactions for girls and boys that produces a sex difference in the strength of self-other contingency knowledge? Unfortunately, the socialization literature has not been explicitly concerned with sex differences in the strength of self-other contingency knowledge. Until more direct evidence is available, then, this basic question must remain open. But the literature does report some differences in child–caretaker interactions that suggest a tentative initial premise.

The socialization literature reports a variety of differences in how girls and boys are treated (see Block, 1983; Fagot, 1978; Huston, 1983; Parke & Slaby, 1983; Radke–Yarrow et al., 1983; Rothbart & Maccoby, 1966; Rothbart & Rothbart, 1976). Mothers, who are typically the primary caretaker, generally apply more pressure on girls than boys to be nurturant, obedient, and socially responsible. Mothers are more restrictive and controlling with girls than boys. They use more individualized appeals to girls than boys. They respond more quickly to mistakes of girls than boys and keep closer track of girls than boys. Parents interrupt, intrude, and attempt to control their daughters' activities more than their son's activities. Girls receive closer adult supervision and more criticism than boys. Parents are more likely to use inductive techniques such as reasoning with daughters than sons. Boys are left to play alone more, to work independently. Girls are "chaperoned" more and spend more time being closely instructed by adults. Even at 12–18 months, difficult boys can cause mothers to back off and discontinue their socialization efforts (see Maccoby & Jacklin, 1984).

This pattern of differences suggests that the types of child–caretaker interactions leading to the acquisition of strong self-guides occur to a greater extent for girls than boys. Indeed, among the socialization variables that might be expected to strengthen self-guide acquisition, the only one reported to be stronger for boys than girls is punishment—in particular, physical punishment (see Huston, 1983; Parke & Slaby, 1983). It is not at all clear, however, that the greater physical punishment received by boys involves the type of child–caretaker interaction associated with acquiring strong self-guides. There are a number of factors to consider. First, physical punishment may be greater for boys than girls, but it may occur only infrequently for both sexes. Second, physical punishment may occur noncontingently or within a general context of rejection. For example, juvenile delinquency is associated with a history of both physical abuse and neglect (see Parke & Slaby, 1983; Rutter & Garmezy, 1983). Third, there may be inconsistency in the administration of physical punishment, both intraparent and interparent inconsistency. Erratic and inconsistent punishment has been found to be associated with antisocial behavior (see Martin & Hetherington, 1971; Parke & Slaby, 1983). Thus, although boys receive more physical punishment than girls, physical punishment itself may not contribute to the acquisition of strong self-guides. Indeed, it may even impair such learning.

In sum, the socialization literature generally supports the premise that females are likely to acquire stronger self-other contingency knowledge and self-guides than males. This premise simply suggests that females may be overrepresented among children acquiring strong self-guides while males may be overrepresented among children acquiring relatively weak self-guides. There could still be substantial overlap in males' and females' acquisition of self-guides. Given the premise that females are likely to acquire stronger self-guides than males, the logic of the present model suggests that females would be likely to have stronger self-guide-related processes of self-regulation and self-evaluation than males. This expectation, in turn, has a number of implications for sex differences in motivation, behavior, and emotion.

Let us begin with the implications for conduct disturbances. Females would be expected to have stronger self-regulatory processes than males. Thus, for the kinds of behaviors in which high motivation is likely to produce matches with self-guides, such as behaviors consistent with social norms (i.e., prosocial rather than antisocial behaviors), females would be expected to show more control. Consistent with this expectation, there is a higher proportion of males than females showing conduct disorders or antisocial disorders throughout childhood and into adolescence (see American Psychiatric Association, DSM–III, 1980; Parke & Slaby, 1983; Rutter & Garmezy, 1983).

Females' stronger self-regulatory processes should make them less vulnerable to other under-control problems as well. Table 4.2 shows those behavioral and emotional disorders for which substantial sex differences have been reported (see American Psychiatric Association, DSM–III, 1980). Consistent with the expectation that males should have more problems of undercontrol than females, Table 4.2 reveals that, for *both* the preadolescent and adolescent/adulthood periods, in every case where there is a clear sex difference in undercontrolled behavior, the behavioral disorder is more common in males than females: (1) Conduct disorder (i.e., persistent pattern of conduct in which either the basic rights of others or major age-appropriate societal norms or rules are violated); (2) Attention deficit disorder (i.e., inattention and impulsivity, failure to follow instructions, inability to stick to activities); (3) Schizoid disorder (i.e., inability to form social relationships, ineptness and awkwardness in social situations, belligerence and aggressiveness); (4) Impulse control disorders (e.g., pathological gambling, pyromania; intermittent explosive disorder [loss of control of aggressive impulses that result in serious assault or destruction of property]); (5) Antisocial personality disorder (i.e., chronic antisocial behavior in which the rights of others are violated; inability to sustain work or to function responsibly); (6) Substance abuse (i.e., inability to cut down or stop use of substance, such as alcohol, despite its harmful effects). It should also be noted that even when impulsivity is defined more broadly to include insufficient control of impulse, the inability to delay gratification, risk taking, and the overreactivity to frustration, males have been found to be more impulsive than females (see Block, 1983).

Consistent with the expectations derived from the model, then, behavioral disorders associated with undercontrol are more common in males than females. The model also suggests that behavioral disorders associated with overcontrol would be more common in females than males. As shown in Table 4.2, there is one type of behavioral disorder associated with overcontrol for which a clear sex

TABLE 4.2
Strong Sex Differences in Behavioral/Emotional Disorders

Developmental Period	*Type of Problem*	*Direction of Difference*
Preadolescence	Attention deficit disorder	M > F
	Conduct disorder	M > F
	Schizoid disorder	M > F
Adolescence and adulthood	Impulse control disorders	M > F
	Antisocial personality disorder	M > F
	Substance abuse	M > F
	Eating disorders	F > M
	Major depressive disorder	F > M
	Panic disorder	F > M
	Histrionic personality disorder	F > M

difference has been reported—eating disorders such as anorexia nervosa and bulimia where individuals attempt to control their weight through dieting and/or vomiting. Consistent with expectations, this type of disorder is much more common in females than in males.

If females are likely to be more controlled than males because their traditional socialization results in acquisition of stronger self-guides, then one might expect that females who were *not* socialized in this traditional manner would be less controlled than females who were. There is some evidence consistent with this expectation as well. Block (1987) reports that undercontrolled adolescent girls were more likely in their preschool years to have parents whose family policy and socialization philosophy were *not* traditional, where manners and propriety were *not* stressed. In addition, Block, Block, and Keyes (1988) report that females whose parents during the preschool years had few expectations for them, were indulgent and permissive (e.g., permitted their daughter to question decisions, make negative remarks, and become dirty while playing), did not pressure them, and placed little emphasis on propriety or conventions were more likely to be hard drug users in adolescence. Hard drug use in adolescence was, in turn, related to children being undercontrolled at an early age (3–4 years).

If females are likely to acquire stronger self-guides than males, then females should have not only stronger self-regulatory processes but also stronger self-evaluative processes than males. When high motivation is likely to produce matches with self-guides, females should experience more positive self-evaluative emotions. But when high motivation is not likely to produce matches, then females should experience more negative self-evaluative emotions. As discussed earlier, there is a shift from the elementary school period in the types of attributes that are valued—from those in which high motivation is likely to produce matches to those in which high motivation is not likely to produce matches. The present model, therefore, suggests that in early elementary school females would be less likely to have self-evaluative emotional problems, but that in high school females would be more likely to have such problems.

The literature is generally consistent with this expectation. Table 4.2 shows two emotional disorders for which clear sex differences have been reported: major depressive disorder and panic disorder. These emotional disorders affect mostly adolescents and adults. Consistent with expectations, these disorders are more common in females than males. More generally, the literature reports that by adolescence there is a higher prevalence of depression, anxiety, and conflict for females than for males (see Block, 1983; Fischer & Lamborn, in press; Nolen–Hoeksema, Girgus, & Seligman, 1987; Rauste–von Wright, 1987; Rutter & Garmezy, 1983; Simmons & Blyth, 1987). There is even a shift between elementary school and high school in how males and females see themselves, with males seeing themselves as more calm while females see themselves as more worrying and later as more emotionally disturbed (Block, 1985). There is less evidence of sex differences in self-evaluative emotional problems during elementary school. What evidence there is suggests that, consistent with expectations, males have more emotional problems than females (see American Psychiatric Association, DSM–III, 1980; Nolen–Hoeksema et al., 1987).

The foregoing analysis suggests that females who acquire strong self-other contingency knowledge in childhood are at risk for emotional problems in adolescence and adulthood. It has been proposed that the traditional socialization of females involves the kinds of child–caretaker interactions that yield strong self-other contingency knowledge. It was also suggested earlier that intellectual capacity plays an important role in the acquisition of self-other contingency knowledge. Given that females are exposed to the kinds of child–caretaker interactions that make self-other contingency information available, one might then expect that females with higher intellectual capacity especially would acquire stronger self-other contingency knowledge. This analysis leads to the nonobvious hypothesis that females' intelligence in childhood would be *positively* correlated with emotional problems in adolescence and adulthood. Consistent with this hypothesis, Block and Gjerde (in press) report a positive correlation for females, but *not* for males, between intelligence measured at 4 years and depression in adolescence.

The premise that females are likely to acquire stronger self-guides than males also has implications for achievement-related behaviors and motivation. Achievement-related behaviors differ from conduct-related behaviors in that there is a developmental shift from elementary school to high school in the likelihood that high motivation will yield achievement-related behaviors that match the self-guides. Adolescents in high school continue to be able to conduct themselves according to prevalent social norms if they are motivated to do so. But even highly motivated adolescents are not always able to meet their achievement-related goals in high school because of the greatly increased difficulty of certain tasks (e.g., doing well in mathematics). Thus, for achievement-related behaviors a developmental shift in sex differences is expected. Consistent with these expectations, females receive higher grades than males in elementary school, but in high school this sex difference disappears or even reverses for difficult courses such as mathematics (see Dweck, 1986; Hoffman, 1972; Minuchin & Shapiro, 1983). In general, one would expect girls with strong self-guides to perform well and one would expect "bright" girls especially to have the capacity to acquire strong self-guides as discussed earlier. It is reasonable, then, to assume that the "brightest" or highest performing girls are those girls with the strongest self-guides (see Dweck, 1986; Dweck & Elliot, 1983). Our analysis suggests that girls with strong self-guides should generally do well when tasks are not too difficult or challenging, which is more likely in elementary school than in high school. The same analysis, however, suggests that when girls with strong self-guides *do* fail on a task, whether in elementary school or in high school, they should experience greater self-evaluative emotional problems and greater loss of intrinsic motivation than others. These self-evaluative emotion problems, in turn, should impair subsequent performance on the task.

There is, in fact, considerable evidence that debilitation from failure on a particular task is especially evident for the brightest or highest performing girls (see Dweck, 1986). Moreover, when boys begin to perform better than girls on the much more difficult math courses they encounter in high school, the sex differences in mathematical achievement are *greatest* among the generally high-achieving boys and girls (see Dweck, 1986). As would be expected, such sex differences are not found in the verbal achievement areas where there is not such an abrupt increase in difficulty after elementary school (see Dweck, 1986), and, therefore, high motivation is still likely to yield success.

This analysis also suggests that high-achieving females would be more likely than males to avoid tasks in which high motivation does not guarantee success, tasks in which performance outcome is uncertain. Consistent with this expectation, the literature reports that high-achieving females prefer tasks in which they know they can succeed, whereas high-achieving males prefer challenging tasks (see Dweck, 1986). More generally, the literature reports that females are more likely than males to avoid challenging courses and careers (see Dweck & Elliot, 1983; Parsons, 1974).

The general premise that females are likely to acquire stronger self-guides than males also suggests that females' achievement motivation is more likely to involve a concern with meeting self-guides than is the achievement motivation of males. Given that strong self-guides develop from strong self-other contingency knowledge, females' achievement motivation should also be tied more to others' evaluations of their performance than should males' achievement motivation. Males' achievement motivation, by being less tied to meeting self-guides, may be more concerned with alternative goals and standards. The literature suggests that these alternatives for males may be instrumental goals and competitive, social comparison standards (see Deci & Ryan, 1985; Kipnis, 1974; Spence & Helmreich, 1983). There is some evidence concerning sex differences in achievement motivation scores that is generally consistent with these suggestions.

The Thematic Apperception Test (McClelland, Atkinson, Clark, & Lowell, 1953) is an excellent measure of the chronic accessibility of procedural knowledge, in particular the chronic orientation to situations in terms of standards of achievement (see Sorrentino & Higgins, 1986). According to the preceding analysis, females' achievement motivation is tied to self-guides as standards, whereas males' achievement motivation is tied either to social comparison, competitive standards or to instrumental concerns that do not involve a standard. To the extent that the TAT measures orientation to situations in terms of achievement *standards,* then, when competitive concerns are *not* aroused, females should obtain higher TAT scores than males. However, this analysis suggests that when competitive concerns are aroused, males should receive higher scores than females. The literature on sex differences in TAT scores is consistent with these expectations (see Sutherland & Veroff, 1985).

The literature generally suggests that the self-concept of females compared with males is tied more to interpersonal relations and conserving societal values and human relationships (Block, 1983). The foregoing analysis also suggests that when social approval or social-evaluative concerns are aroused, then females' achievement motivation should increase. There is, in fact, some evidence that when performance excellence guarantees social approval, females' need achievement scores increase (see Sutherland & Veroff, 1985). Moreover, high achievement-oriented females (compared with males or low achievement-oriented females) have been found to be the most concerned with pleasing others (i.e., high *n*Affiliation) and with having status in the eyes of others (high *n*Power) (see Sutherland & Veroff, 1985).

If females' achievement-related goals are tied to social-evaluative concerns, then achievement situations that highlight social evaluation should activate those concerns. As discussed earlier, activating social-evaluative concerns undermines intrinsic orientations to activities. Therefore, when social-evaluative concerns are activated, intrinsic motivation should be undermined more in females than in males. Consistent with this expectation, Deci and Ryan (1985) report that praise or positive social-evaluative feedback increases intrinsic motivation for males but decreases it for females relative to nonpraised males and females, respectively. There is also evidence that girls' performance is impaired more than boys' performance in achievement situations involving social-evaluative pressure from adults, an effect that has been linked to girls' greater concern with adult evaluation and approval (see Dweck & Elliot, 1983).

Summary

Socialization differences between girls and boys in the frequency, consistency, clarity, and significance of their caretaker–child interactions suggests that females are likely to acquire stronger self-other contingency knowledge, and thus stronger self-guides, than males. Stronger self-guides should lead to better performance and more positive self-evaluative emotions for the kinds of behaviors in which high motivation is likely to yield matches to valued end-states, but should lead to more negative self-evaluations and possibly even worse performance for the kinds of behaviors in which high motivation is not sufficient. By distinguishing these two kinds of behaviors, the achievement-related behaviors and valued self-attributes typical of elementary-school children can be distinguished from those typical of high school children, and conduct-related behaviors can be distinguished from achievement-related behaviors.

When these basic distinctions are combined with the premise that females are likely to acquire stronger self-guides, the model generates a variety of hypotheses concerning sex differences in motivation, emotion, and performance. Although the overall pattern of sex differences expected is rather complex, the available evidence is generally consistent with expectations. What the evidence shows is that there are developmental continuities (e.g., conduct, verbal achievement) and developmental reversals (e.g., self-evaluative emotions, mathematical achievement) between elementary school and high school with respect to which sex is relatively advantaged. Moreover, sex differences can also reverse as a function of momentary situational and task variables. The proposed model can account for both the continuities and the reversals. More generally, these results are consistent with the proposal that there are both costs and benefits, tradeoffs, from modes of socialization that produce strong self-guides and from modes that do not.

CONCLUDING COMMENTS

Self-regulation involves both self-direction to meet some valued end-state and feedback from self-monitoring concerning the amount of discrepancy between one's current state and this valued end-state. Self-system development includes the acquisition of self-guides, which are a person's valued-self end-states representing significant others' standards for him or her. Self-guides, then, are self-regulatory standards. As such, they function both as self-directive standards that motivate and control action and as self-evaluative standards that provide feedback about discrepancies between current and valued states. Because of this dual function of self-guides, stronger self-guides have greater self-directive force *and* greater self-evaluative force. The present chapter proposes that when there are discrepancies between people's self-concepts and self-guides, and motivation alone is not sufficient to reduce the discrepancies, this dual function of self-guides produces *tradeoffs in development*.

The boundary conditions of this proposal are important to emphasize. First, self-directive/self-evaluative tradeoffs are not experienced to the same extent by all individuals in our culture. Indeed, some individuals may be blessed with sufficiently high ability in all the valued regions of their lives that the motivation produced by strong self-guides consistently yields self-concept–self-guide matches and strong positive emotions. Second, the prevalence of self-directive/self-evaluative tradeoffs is likely to vary across cultures. It is possible in some societies for almost all the members to meet the standards set for them.

In most Western cultures, however, many adult tasks are difficult and valued self-attributes tend to be defined in social comparative terms. Although some individuals can match their self-guides, it is *not* possible for all individuals, or even most, to do so. In such cultures, then, there is a built-in tradeoff between the self-directive and self-evaluative functions of self-guides. As self-guides are acquired and strengthened, there is an increase in self-direction that increases the likelihood that valued end-states will be met and maintained, but there is also an increase in self-evaluation that increases the intensity of suffering from any remaining discrepancies. The latter increase in suffering can, in turn, impair subsequent performance. Given the nature of our culture, many people experience at least some discrepancies. From the perspective of the culture as a whole, then, there is a necessary self-evaluative cost that accompanies the self-directive benefit of acquiring strong self-guides.

Is there a solution to this problem? Is there a way to fulfill the "maximization" goal of bringing up children to possess all the person features we value to their utmost? For our culture as a whole, the answer is probably "No." But these may not be the appropriate questions. Perhaps we should not be trying to find a solution for the goal of "maximization." After all, not all goals require the maximization of every valued feature. When cooking a sauce, for example, one does not use all of the available stock, salt, pepper, wine, flour, butter, and cream to the utmost. In order to produce the right "pattern," tradeoffs in the amounts of the different ingredients are necessary. Perhaps, there is also a particular pattern of tradeoffs in self-features that it would be especially nice for children to possess. And, of course, tastes can vary. From this perspective, tradeoffs in socioemotional development would no longer be a problem. They would become the goal!

ACKNOWLEDGMENTS

This chapter was developed while I was a Fellow at the Center for Advanced Study in the Behavioral Sciences. I am grateful for financial support provided by the John D. and Catherine T. MacArthur Foundation and by the Alfred P. Sloan Foundation. Preparation of this paper was also supported by Grant MH 39429 from the National Institute of Mental Health. I would like to thank the members of the "Self and Affect in Society" group at the Center for their many contributions to the ideas contained here—George Bohrnstedt, Robbie Case, Kay Deaux. Dan Olweus, Roberta Simmons, and Shel Stryker. I would also like to thank Robbie Case, Carol Dweck, Diane Ruble, Roberta Simmons, Yaacov Trope, Robin Wells, Stephen West, and Michael Westerman for their highly constructive comments and suggestions on various versions of this article. Correspondence should be directed to E. Tory Higgins, Department of Psychology, Schermerhorn Hall, Columbia University, New York, NY 10027.

REFERENCES

Aboud, F., & Ruble, D. N. (1987). Identity constancy in children: Developmental processes and implications. In T. M. Honess & K. M. Yardley (Eds.), *Self and identity: Individual change and development* (pp. 95–107). New York: Wiley.

Abramson, L. Y., & Martin, D. J. (1981). Depression and the causal inference process. In J. H.

Harvey, W. Ickes, & R. F. Kidd (Eds.), *New directions in attribution research* (Vol. 3). Hillsdale, NJ: Lawrence Erlbaum Associates.

Altshuler, J. L., & Ruble, D. N. (1988). *Developmental changes in children's awareness of strategies for coping with uncontrollable stress.* Manuscript submitted for publication.

Amabile, T. M. (1983). *The social psychology of creativity.* New York: Springer–Verlag.

American Psychiatric Association. (1980). *Diagnostic and statistical manual of mental disorders* (3rd ed.). Washington, DC.

Baldwin, A. L. (1955). *Behavior and development in childhood.* New York: Dryden Press.

Band, E. B., & Weisz, J. R. (1988). How to feel better when it feels bad: Children's perspectives on coping with everyday stress. *Developmental Psychology, 24,* 247–253.

Beck, A. T. (1967). *Depression: Clinical, experimental, and theoretical aspects.* New York: Harper & Row.

Becker, W. C. (1964). Consequences of different kinds of parental discipline. In M. L. Hoffman & L. W. Hoffman (Eds.), *Review of Child Developmental Research* (Vol. 1, pp. 169–208). New York: Sage.

Bemporad, J. (1978). Psychodynamics of depression and suicide in children and adolescents. In S. Arieti, *Severe and mild depression* (pp. 185–207). New York: Basic Books.

Bertenthal, B. I., & Fischer, K. W. (1978). Development of self-recognition in the infant. *Developmental Psychology, 14,* 44–50.

Block, J. H. (1983). Differential premises arising from differential socialization of the sexes: Some conjectures. *Child Development, 54,* 1335–1354.

Block, J. (1985, October). *Some relationships regarding the self emanating from the Block and Block longitudinal study.* Paper presented at S.S.R.C. Conference on Selfhood, Center for Advanced Study in the Behavioral Sciences, Stanford, CA.

Block, J. (1987, April). *Longitudinal antecedents of ego-control and ego-resiliency in late adolescence.* Paper presented at the symposium, "Longitudinal Approaches to Adolescent Adaptation," at a meeting of the Society for Research in Child Development, Baltimore.

Block, J., Block, J. H., & Keyes, S. (1988). Longitudinally foretelling drug usage in adolescence: Early childhood personality and environmental precursors. *Child Development, 59,* 336–355.

Block, J., & Gjerde, P. F. (in press). Depressive symptomatology in late adolescence: A longitudinal perspective on personality antecedents. In J. E. Rolf, A. Mastsen, D. Cicchetti, K. Neuchterlein, & S. Weintraub (Eds.), *Risk and protective factors in the development of psychopathology.* New York: Cambridge University Press.

Blos, P. (1961). *On adolescence.* New York: Free Press.

Bohrnstedt, G. W., & Fisher, G. A. (1986). The effects of recalled childhood and adolescent relationships compared to current role performances on young adults' affective functioning. *Social Psychology Quarterly, 49,* 19–32.

Bruner, J. S. (1964). The course of cognitive growth. *American Psychologist, 19,* 1–15.

Cameron, N. (1963). *Personality development and psychopathology.* Boston: Houghton Mifflin.

Campos, J. J., & Barrett, K. C. (1984). Toward a new understanding of emotions and their development. In C. E. Izard, J. Kagan, & R. B. Zajonc (Eds.), *Emotions, cognition, and behavior* (pp. 229–263). New York: Cambridge University Press.

Carver, C. S., & Scheier, M. F. (1981). *Attention and self-regulation: A control-theory approach to human behavior.* New York: Springer–Verlag.

Case, R. (1985). *Intellectual development: Birth to adulthood.* New York: Academic Press.

Case, R. (1988). The whole child: Toward an integrated view of young children's cognitive, social, and emotional development. In A. D. Pellegrini (Ed.), *Psychological bases for early education* (pp. 155–184). Chichester, England: Wiley.

Case, R., Hayward, S., Lewis, M., & Hurst, P. (1987). Toward a neo-Piagetian theory of cognitive and emotional development. *Developmental Review, 7,* 261–312.

Damon, W., & Hart, D. (1986). Stability and change in children's self-understanding. *Social Cognition, 4,* 102–118.

Deci, E. L., & Ryan, R. M. (1985). *Intrinsic motivation and self-determination in human behavior.* New York: Plenum Press.

Digdon, N., & Gotlib, I. H. (1985). Developmental considerations in the study of childhood depression. *Developmental Review, 5,* 162–199.

Duval, S., & Wicklund, R. A. (1972). *A theory of objective self-awareness.* New York: Academic Press.

Dweck, C. S. (1986). Motivational processes affecting learning. *American Psychologist, 41,* 1040–1048.

Dweck, C. S., & Elliot, E. S. (1983). Achievement motivation. In P. H. Mussen (Ed.), *Handbook of child psychology, Vol. 4: Socialization, personality, and social development* (pp. 643–691). New York: Wiley.

Emde, R. N. (1984). Levels of meaning for infant emotions: A biosocial view. In K. R. Scherer & P. Ekman (Eds.), *Approaches to emotion* (pp. 77–107). Hillsdale, NJ: Lawrence Erlbaum Associates.

Erickson, E. H. (1963). *Childhood and society* (2nd ed.). New York: Norton. (Original publication, 1950)

Fagot, B. I. (1978). The influence of sex of child on parental reactions to toddler children. *Child Development, 49,* 459–465.

Feffer, M. (1970). Developmental analysis of interpersonal behavior. *Psychological Review, 77,* 197–214.

Fischer, K. W. (1980). A theory of cognitive development: The control and construction of hierarchies of skills. *Psychological Review, 87,* 477–531.

Fischer, K. W., & Lamborn, S. (in press). Mechanisms of variation in developmental levels: Cognitive and emotional transitions during adolescence. In A. de Ribaupierre (Ed.), *Transition mechanisms in child development.* New York: Cambridge University Press.

Fischer, K. W., & Watson, M. W. (1981). Explaining the Oedipus conflict. In K. W. Fischer (Ed.), *Cognitive development.* New Directions for Child Development, No. 12. San Francisco: Jossey–Bass.

Flavell, J. H., Botkin, P. T., Fry, C. L., Wright, J. W., & Jarvis, P. E. (1968). *The development of role-taking and communication skills in children.* New York: Wiley.

Freud, A. (1937). *The ego and the mechanisms of defense.* New York: International Universities.

Freud, S. (1952). *A general introduction to psychoanalysis* New York: Washington Square Press. (Original publication, 1920)

Gesell, A., & Ilg, F. (1946). *The child from five to ten.* New York: Harper & Row.

Grusec, J. E. (1983). The internalization of altruistic dispositions: A cognitive analysis. In E. T. Higgins, D. N. Ruble, & W. W. Hartup (Eds.), *Social cognition and social development: A sociocultural perspective* (pp. 275–293). New York: Cambridge University Press.

Harris, P., Olthof, T., & Terwogt, M. M. (1981). Children's knowledge of emotion. *Child Psychology and Psychiatry, 22,* 247–261.

Harter, S. (1983). Developmental perspectives on the self-system. In P. H. Mussen (Ed.), *Handbook of child psychology, Vol. 4: Socialization, personality, and social development* (pp. 275–385). New York: Wiley.

Harter, S. (1986). Cognitive-developmental processes in the integration of concepts about emotions and the self. *Social Cognition, 4,* 119–151.

Hartup, W. W. (1983). Peer relations. In P. H. Mussen (Ed.), *Handbook of child psychology, Vol. 4: Socialization, personality, and social development* (pp. 103–196). New York: Wiley.

Higgins, E. T. (1981). Role-taking and social judgment: Alternative developmental perspectives and processes. In J. H. Flavell & L. Ross (Eds.), *Social cognitive development: Frontiers and possible futures* (pp. 119–153). Cambridge, England: Cambridge University Press.

Higgins, E. T. (1987). Self-discrepancy: A theory relating self and affect. *Psychological Review, 94,* 319–340.

Higgins, E. T. (1989a). Self-discrepancy theory: What patterns of self-beliefs cause people to suffer? In L. Berkowitz (Ed.), *Advances in experimental social psychology* (Vol. 22). New York: Academic Press.

Higgins, E. T. (1989b). Continuities and discontinuities in self-regulatory and self-evaluative processes: A developmental theory relating self and affect. *Journal of Personality, 57,* 407–444.

Higgins, E. T., Bargh, J. A., & Lombardi, W. (1985). The nature of priming effects on categorization. *Journal of Experimental Psychology: Learning, Memory and Cognition, 11,* 59–69.

Higgins, E. T., Bond, R. N., Klein, R., & Strauman, T. (1986). Self-discrepancies and emotional vulnerability: How magnitude, accessibility, and type of discrepancy influence affect. *Journal of Personality and Social Psychology, 51,* 5–15.

Higgins, E. T., King, G. A., & Mavin, G. H. (1982). Individual construct accessibility and subjective impressions and recall. *Journal of Personality and Social Psychology, 43,* 35–47.

Higgins, E. T., Klein, R., & Strauman, T. (1986). Standards and the process of self-evaluation: Multiple affects from multiple stages. In R. M. Sorrentino & E. T. Higgins (Eds.), *Handbook of motivation and cognition: Foundations of social behavior* (Vol. 1, pp. 23–63). New York: Guilford Press.

Higgins, E. T., & Eccles-Parsons, J. E. (1983). Social cognition and the social life of the child: Stages as subcultures. In E. T. Higgins, D. N. Ruble, & W. W. Hartup (Eds.), *Social cognition and social development: A socio-cultural perspective* (pp. 15–62). New York: Cambridge University Press.

Higgins, E. T., Van Hook, E., & Dorfman, D. (1988). Do self attributes form a cognitive structure? *Social Cognition, 6,* 177–207.

Higgins, E. T., & Wells, R. S. (1986). Social construct availability and accessibility as a function of social life phase: Emphasizing the "how" versus the "can" of social cognition. *Social Cognition, 4,* 201–226.

Hoffman, L. (1972). Early childhood experiences and women's achievement motivation. *Journal of Social Issues, 28,* 129–155.

Hoffman, M. L. (1970). Moral development. In P. H. Mussen (Ed.), *Carmichael's manual of child psychology* (Vol. 2, pp. 261–359). New York: Wiley.

Hoffman, M. L. (1983). Affective and cognitive processes in moral internalization. In E. T. Higgins, D. N. Ruble, & W. W. Hartup (Eds.), *Social cognition and social development: A socio-cultural perspective.* (pp. 236–274). New York: Cambridge University Press.

Hoffman, M. L., & Saltzstein, H. D. (1967). Parental Discipline and the child's moral development. *Journal of Personality and Social Psychology, 5,* 45–57.

Horney, K. (1939). *New ways in psychoanalysis.* New York: Norton.

Huston, A. C. (1983). Sex-typing. In P. H. Mussen (Ed.), *Handbook of child psychology, Vol. 4: Socialization, personality, and social development* (pp. 387–467). New York: Wiley.

Huttenlocher, J., & Higgins, E. T. (1978). Issues in the study of symbolic development. In W. A. Collins (Ed.), *Minnesota symposia on child psychology* (Vol. 2, pp. 98–140). Hillsdale, NJ: Lawrence Erlbaum Associates.

Ickes, W., & Layden, M. A., (1978). Attributional styles. In J. H. Harvey, W. Ickes, & R. F. Kidd (Eds.), *New directions in attribution research* (Vol. 2, pp. 119–152). Hillsdale, NJ: Lawrence Erlbaum Associates.

Inhelder, B., & Piaget, J. (1958). *The growth of logical thinking from childhood to adolescence.* New York: Basic Books.

James, W. (1948). *Psychology.* New York: World Publishing Co. (Original publication, 1890)

Kagan, J. (1984). The idea of emotion in human development. In C. E. Izard, J. Kagan, & R. B. Zajonc (Eds.), *Emotions, cognition, and behavior* (pp. 38–72). New York: Cambridge University Press.

Kangas, J., & Bradway, K. (1971). Intelligence at middle age: A thirty-eight year follow-up. *Developmental Psychology, 5,* 333–337.

Kipnis, D. (1974). Inner direction, other direction, and achievement motivations. *Human Development, 17,* 321–343.
Kelman, H. C. (1958). Compliance, identification and internalization: Three processes of opinion change. *Journal of Conflict Resolution, 2,* 51–60.
Kernberg, D. (1976). *Object relations theory and clinical psychoanalysis.* New York: Aronson.
Kohlberg, L. (1976). Moral stages and moralization. In T. Lickona (Ed.), *Moral development and behavior.* New York: Holt, Rinehart, & Winston.
Kruglanski, A. W. (1975). The endogenous–exogeneous partition in attribution theory. *Psychological Review, 82,* 387–406.
Kruglanski, A. W., Friedman, I., & Zeevi, G. (1971). The effects of extrinsic incentive on some qualitative aspects of task performance. *Journal of Personality, 39,* 606–617.
Lepper, M. R. (1983). Social-control processes and the internalization of social values: An attributional perspective. In E. T. Higgins, D. N. Ruble, & W. W. Hartup (Eds.), *Social cognition and social development: A sociocultural perspective* (pp. 294–330). New York: Cambridge University Press.
Lewin, K. (1935). *A dynamic theory of personality.* New York: McGraw–Hill.
Lewin, K., Lippitt, R., & White, R. (1939). Patterns of aggressive behavior in experimentally created social disasters. *Journal of Social Psychology, 10,* 271–299.
Lewis, M., & Brooks–Gunn, J. (1979). *Social cognition and the acquisition of self.* New York: Plenum Press.
Linville, P. W. (1987). Self-complexity as a cognitive buffer against stress-related illness and depression. *Journal of Personality and Social Psychology, 52,* 663–676.
Loevinger, J. (1976). *Ego development: Conceptions and theories.* San Francisco: Jossey–Bass.
Maccoby, E. E., & Jacklin, C. N. (1984). The "person" characteristics of children and the family as environment. In D. Magnusson & V. Allen (Eds.), *Human development: An interactional perspective.* New York: Academic Press.
Maccoby, E. E., & Martin, J. A. (1983). Socialization in the context of the family: Parent–child interaction. In P. H. Mussen (Ed.), *Handbook of child psychology, Vol. 4: Socialization, personality, and social development* (pp. 643–691). New York: Wiley.
McClelland, D., Atkinson, J., Clark, R., & Lowell, E. (1953). *The achievement motive.* New York: Appleton-Century-Crofts.
McConville, B. J., Boag, L. C., & Purohit, A. P. (1973). Three types of childhood depression. *Canadian Psychiatric Association Journal, 18,* 133–138.
Martin, B., & Hetherington, E. M. (1971). *Family interaction and aggression, withdrawal and nondeviancy in children* (Progress Report). University of Wisconsin, National Institute of Mental Health.
Mead, G. H. (1934). *Mind, self, and society.* Chicago: University of Chicago Press.
Miller, S. M., & Green, M. L. (1985). Coping with stress and frustration: Origins, nature, and development. In M. Lewis & C. Saarri (Eds.), *The socialization of emotions* (pp. 263–314). New York: Plenum Press.
Minuchin, P. P., & Shapiro, E. K. (1983). The school as a context for social development. In P. H. Mussen (Ed.), *Handbook of child psychology, Vol. 4: Socialization, personality, and social development* (pp. 197–274). New York: Wiley.
Mischel, W. (1973). Toward a cognitive social learning reconceptualization of personality. *Psychological Review, 80,* 252–283.
Mischel, W., & Patterson, C. J. (1978). Effective plans for self-control in children. In W. A. Collins (Ed.), *Minnesota symposia on child psychology, Volume 11* (pp. 199–230). Hillsdale, NJ: Erlbaum.
Moretti, M. M., & Higgins, E. T. (1989). The development of self-system vulnerabilities: Social and cognitive factors in developmental psychopathology. In R. J. Sternberg & J. Kolligan (Eds.),

Perceptions of competence and incompetence across the lifespan. New Haven, CT: Yale University Press.

Mowrer, O. H. (1960). *Learning theory and behavior.* New York: Wiley.

Nolen–Hoeksema, S., Seligman, M. E. P., & Girgus, J. S. (in press). Sex differences in depression and related factors in children. *Journal of Youth and Adolescence.*

Olweus, D. (1980). Familial and temperamental determinants of aggression behavior in adolescents—A causal analysis. *Developmental Psychology, 16,* 644–660.

Olweus, D. (1984). Aggressors and their victims: Bullying at school. In N. Frude & H. Gault (Eds.), *Disruptive behavior in schools* (pp. 57–76). New York: Wiley.

Parke, R. D., & Slaby, R. G. (1983). The development of aggression. In P. H. Mussen (Ed.), *Handbook of child psychology, Vol. 4: Socialization, personality, and social development* (pp. 547–641). New York: Wiley.

Parsons, J. E. (1974). *Causal attributions and the role of situational cues in the development of children's evaluative judgments.* Unpublished dissertation, University of California at Los Angeles.

Pascual–Leone, J. (1983). Growing into human maturity: Toward a metasubjective theory of adulthood stages. In P. B. Baltes & O. G. Brim, Jr. (Eds.), *Life span development and behavior* (Vol. 5, pp. 117–156). New York: Academic Press.

Piaget, J. (1951). *Play, dreams and imitation in childhood.* New York: Norton.

Piaget, J. (1965). *The moral judgment of the child.* New York: Free Press. (Original trans. published 1932)

Piaget, J. (1970). Piaget's theory. In P. H. Mussen (Ed.), *Carmichael's manual of child psychology* (Vol. 1, 3rd ed., pp. 703–732). New York: Wiley.

Radke–Yarrow, M., Zahn–Waxler, C., & Chapman, M. (1983). Children's prosocial dispositions and behavior. In P. H. Mussen (Ed.), *Handbook of child psychology, Vol. 4: Socialization, personality, and social development* (pp. 643–691). New York: Wiley.

Rauste–von Wright, M. (1987). On the life process among Finnish adolescents. *Commentationes Scientiarum Socialium, 35.*

Rholes, W. S., Blackwell, J., Jordan, C., & Walters, C. (1980). A developmental study of learned helplessness. *Developmental Psychology, 16,* 616–624.

Rholes, W. S., & Ruble, D. N. (1984). Children's understanding of dispositional characteristics of others. *Child Development, 55,* 550–560.

Rosenberg, M. (1979). *Conceiving the self.* Malabar, FL: Robert E. Krieger.

Rothbart, M. K., & Maccoby, E. E. (1966). Parents' differential reactions to sons and daughters. *Journal of Personality and Social Psychology, 4,* 237–243.

Rothbart, M. K., & Rothbart, M. (1976). Birth order, sex of child, and maternal helpgiving. *Sex roles, 2,* 39–46.

Ruble, D. N. (1983). The development of social comparison processes and their role in achievement-related self-socialization. In E. T. Higgins, D. N. Ruble, & W. W. Hartup (Eds.), *Social cognition and social development: A socio-cultural perspective.* (pp. 134–157). New York: Cambridge University Press.

Ruble, D. N., & Frey, K. S. (1987). Social comparison and self-evaluation in the classroom: Developmental changes in knowledge and function. In J. C. Masters & W. P. Smith (Eds.), *Social comparison, social justice, and relative deprivation* (pp. 81–104). Hillsdale, NJ: Lawrence Erlbaum Associates.

Ruble, D. N., & Rholes, W. S. (1981). The development of children's perceptions and attributions about their social world. In J. D. Harvey, W. Ickes, & R. F. Kidd (Eds.), *New directions in attribution research* (Vol. 3, pp. 3–36). Hillsdale, NJ: Lawrence Erlbaum Associates.

Rutter, M., & Garmezy, N. (1983). Developmental psychopathology, In P. H. Mussen (Ed.), *Handbook of child psychology, Vol. 4: Socialization, personality, and social development* (pp. 775–911). New York: Wiley.

Schaefer, E. S. (1959). A circumplex model for maternal behavior. *Journal of Abnormal and Social Psychology, 59,* 226–235.

Seligman, M. E. P., Abramson, L. Y., Semmel, A., & Von Baeyer, C. (1979). Depressive attributional style. *Journal of Abnormal Psychology, 88,* 242–247.

Selman, R. L. (1980). *The growth of interpersonal understanding: Developmental and clinical analyses.* New York: Academic Press.

Selman, R. L., & Byrne, D. F. (1974). A structural-developmental analysis of levels of role-taking in middle childhood. *Child Development, 45,* 803–806.

Shantz, C. U. (1983). Social cognition. In J. H. Flavell & E. M. Markman (Eds.), *Cognitive Development,* Vol. 3, in P. H. Mussen (Ed.), *Carmichael's manual of child psychology,* (4th ed., pp. 495–555.). New York: Wiley.

Simmons, R. G., & Blyth, D. A. (1987). *Moving into adolescence: The impact of pubertal change and school context.* New York: Aldine De Gruyter.

Snyder, M. L., Stephan, W. G., & Rosenfeld, D. (1978). Attributional egotism. In J. H. Harvey, W. Ickes, & R. F. Kidd (Eds.), *New directions in attribution research* (Vol. 2, pp. 91–117). Hillsdale, NJ: Lawrence Erlbaum Associates.

Sorrentino, R. M., & Higgins, E. T. (1986). Motivation and cognition: Warming up to synergism. In R. M. Sorrentino & E. T. Higgins (Eds.), *Handbook of motivation and cognition: Foundations of social behavior* (pp. 3–19). Hillsdale, NJ: Lawrence Erlbaum Associates.

Spence, J. T., & Helmreich, R. L. (1983). Achievement-related motives and behaviors. In J. T. Spence (Eds.), *Achievement and achievement motives,* (pp. 7–74). San Francisco: W. H. Freeman.

Sroufe, L. A. (1984). The organization of emotional development. In K. R. Scherer & P. Ekman (Eds.), *Approaches to emotion* (pp. 109–128). Hillsdale, NJ: Lawrence Erlbaum Associates.

Strauman, T. J. (in press). Self-discrepancies in clinical depression and social phobia: Cognitive structures that underlie affective disorders? *Journal of Abnormal Psychology.*

Strauman, T. J., & Higgins, E. T. (1987). Automatic activation of self-discrepancies and emotional syndromes: When cognitive structures influence affect. *Journal of Personality and Social Psychology, 53,* 1004–1014.

Sullivan, H. S. (1953). In H. S. Perry & M. L. Gawel (Eds.), *The collected works of Harvey Stack Sullivan* (Vol. 1). New York: Norton.

Sutherland, E., & Veroff, J. (1985). Achievement motivation and sex roles. In V. E. O'Leary, R. K. Unger, & B. S. Wallston (Eds.), *Women, gender, and social psychology* (pp. 101–128). Hillsdale, NJ: Lawrence Erlbaum Associates.

Trevarthen, C. (1984). Emotions in infancy: Regulators of contact and relationships with persons. In K. R. Scherer & P. Ekman (Eds.), *Approaches to emotion* (pp. 129–157). Hillsdale, NJ: Lawrence Erlbaum Associates.

Vaillant, G. E. (1977). *Adaptation to life.* Boston: Little, Brown.

Van Hook, E., & Higgins, E. T. (1988). Self-related problems beyond the self-concept: The motivational consequences of discrepant self-guides. *Journal of Personality and Social Psychology.*

Veroff, J. (1969). Social comparison and the development of achievement motivation. In C. P. Smith (Ed.), *Achievement-related motives in children* (pp. 46–101). New York: Sage.

Werner, H. (1957). *Comparative psychology of mental development.* New York: International Universities Press.

Werner, H., & Kaplan, B. (1963). *Symbol formation.* New York: Wiley.

5 Development and Perceived Control: A Dynamic Model of Action in Context

Ellen A. Skinner
Max Planck Institute for Human Development and Education, Berlin

INTRODUCTION

One of the greatest challenges to a developmental discipline is to specify the processes that energize and shape individual trajectories of change. Debates arguing the merits of nature versus nurture, heredity versus environment, or maturation versus experience, have given way to metatheories which focus on the balance between these forces, their interactive contributions, and conflict and disequilibration among them (Baltes, 1987; Harris, 1957; Lerner, 1986; Riegel, 1975).

These emerging orientations, which accept change as a given and assume that individuals are embedded within contexts of multiple levels, call attention to the role of the active and intentional individual amid the dynamic forces of biology and society (Brim & Kagan, 1980; Kimble, 1989; Lerner & Busch–Rossnagel, 1981). Theorists from this perspective assume that, for any given phenomenon, a variety of developmental trajectories are possible. For a particular individual, however, the range and shape of potential available trajectories will be probabilistically constrained by his or her physiology and social address. Psychologists are challenged to discover how individuals guide and manage their developmental pathways within or outside these boundaries.

Developmentalists interested in the self and motivation are among those who have accepted that charge. Motivation represents one avenue by which individuals can influence their own development. More specifically, individuals can use motivational tools, such as goal-directed initiation of behavior, effort, engagement, curiosity, enthusiasm, persistence, and coping in the face of challenge and setbacks, to pave the way for developmental change (cf. Rothbaum, Weisz,

& Snyder, 1982). The investigation of belief systems that underlie and potentially regulate motivation may be a key to understanding how individuals create their own experiences and so shape their development.

This chapter focuses on perceived control, a set of beliefs found to influence individuals' goal-directed transactions with the environment. The study of perceived control occupies a prominent place on the research agendas of social, clinical, personality, and developmental psychologists (Baltes & Baltes, 1986; Brim, 1974; Lefcourt, 1981, 1983). Interest has been sustained by robust findings about the consequences of individual differences in control beliefs. Data accumulated from more than 30 years of research have established that they are an integral link in individual systems of action and emotion regulation, particularly under conditions of challenge.

Initial research, guided by value-expectancy models (Rotter, 1954) and attribution theories (Heider, 1958), indicated that generalized perceptions about the locus of reinforcement predict a variety of achievement behaviors (Crandall, Katkovsky, & Crandall, 1965; Rotter, 1966). Subsequent theoretical refinements guided research which linked individual differences in control beliefs to the intensity, duration, and persistence of actions in the face of difficulties (Bandura, 1977; Heckhausen, 1977; Seligman, 1975). The role of perceived control in the regulation of *emotion* was demonstrated by clinical and social psychologists, who showed that attributions mediate not only subsequent action but also a variety of emotional responses to success and failure (Abramson, Seligman, & Teasdale, 1978; Weiner, 1985). The dual role of perceived control in regulating action and emotion has recently been integrated into the study of the cognitive mediators of stress (Folkman, 1985; Lazarus & Folkman, 1984). Taken together, theory and research from these areas paint a picture of perceived control as critical for understanding how individuals initiate and regulate action, as well as how motivational and emotional reactions to success and failure feed back on expectations of control.

This chapter has as its goal to present a model of how perceived control can influence individual development. Simply stated, the model contends that individuals who believe they have control act in ways that maximize control and individuals who believe that they cannot influence outcomes act in ways that forfeit potential control. Actual successes and failures as well as feedback from the social context serve to confirm initial high perceptions of control or to undermine initial low expectations of control (Seligman, 1975). Throughout this process, the social context is instrumental in the construction, maintenance, and transformation of control-related beliefs. The resulting functional model describes a system of dynamic interrelations among context, beliefs, actions, and outcomes that lead to predictable patterns of developmental change.

The functional model has as its cornerstone a new conceptualization of perceived control. Included under the rubric of perceived control are the causes that people view as responsible for important outcomes in their lives, the roles people perceive themselves to play in influencing events, and the resources people believe they can access in reaching their goals. Taken together these can be thought of as naïve "causal models" about how the world works and about the impact of the self. These naïve models are assumed to be flexibly organized sets of beliefs that change based on disconfirming experiences, but that also create their own stability by generating supportive consistent experiences.[1] With this model as a map for inquiry, the key issues focus on how individuals, through their beliefs and actions, can influence their own development.

At the same time, it will be argued that the structure of control-related beliefs changes with age, resulting in "reorganizations" in the dynamic interrelations among the elements of the functional model. These changes may open or shut windows of opportunity for individual and contextual influence. The basic argument, the specifics of which are speculative, is that the contribution of individuals' perceived control to their development increases with age and at the same time becomes more resistant to influence from the environment.

The presentation of the complete model proceeds in three sections: the conceptualization of perceived control, the model of how beliefs guide development, and a discussion of how developmental change reorganizes these relations. Within each section, the same format will be followed. First, the organizing framework of that section will be explicated; second, empirical evidence for that part of the model will be summarized; and third, it will be placed within the context of existing theories and research. Empirical examples are drawn from research on children's perceived control and action in the domain of academic performance during middle childhood. The conceptual ambitions of the models are considerably broader in scope, but the empirical base of support is currently concentrated in these areas.

A New Conceptualization of Perceived Control

The goal of the current conceptualization was to provide a coordinated map of major categories of perceived control and their interrelations. The attempt was made to distinguish and integrate relevant constructs into a common framework using an action-theoretical perspective. Accordingly, instead of responses, the central units of psychological analysis were viewed as actions, defined as goal-directed intentional behaviors consisting of several components (e.g., Brandtstaedter, 1984). For the present purpose, the action–theoretical distinction between agents, means, and ends is of special interest. Because this conceptualiza-

[1]Hence, this view explicitly rejects two extreme alternative conceptions: Control-related beliefs are not conceived of as fleeting situationally derived perceptions nor as stable personality traits. Within the current framework, the former is not useful because perceived control could not guide or direct action across situations; and the latter is not useful because control-related beliefs could not undergo developmental or contextual transformation.

tion is discussed in detail elsewhere (Skinner & Chapman, 1984; Skinner, Chapman, & Baltes, 1988a), I will only summarize it briefly.

Control, Means–ends, and Agency Beliefs

The present conceptualization was based on the observation that naïve, commonsense accounts of action involve an understanding not only about the *agent*'s effectiveness in producing outcomes in a given context, but also about the role of particular *means* in mediating between agents and their desired ends (Fig. 5.1). Accordingly, three conceptually independent sets of beliefs were distinguished: (1) *Control beliefs,* defined as expectations about the extent to which one can produce desired or prevent undesired outcomes; (2) *Means–ends beliefs,* defined as expectations about the extent to which certain means or causes are effective in producing positive or preventing negative outcomes; and (3) *Agency beliefs,* defined as expectations about the extent to which one possesses or has access to the potential means (Skinner et al. 1988a). It is assumed that all three types of beliefs can be arranged along other possible dimensions. For example, a dimension of specificity–generality (globality), ranging from extremely situation-specific to highly generalized beliefs, may be useful in characterizing the belief sets. In this chapter, relatively generalized yet domain-specific perceived control will be considered.

The empirical viability of the distinction between control, means–ends, and agency beliefs was tested in five studies of children ages 6 to 12, using a questionnaire measure to assess control-related beliefs in the domain of school performance. Four categories of known means, namely, effort, ability, powerful others, and luck, as well as unknown means, were included. (Other categories of means might be used for domains other than school or for other age groups.) Factor analyses of the items, separately for each known cause, revealed the predicted three-factor structure. Likewise, factor analysis of the scale scores indicated that different factors were marked by control, means–ends, and agency

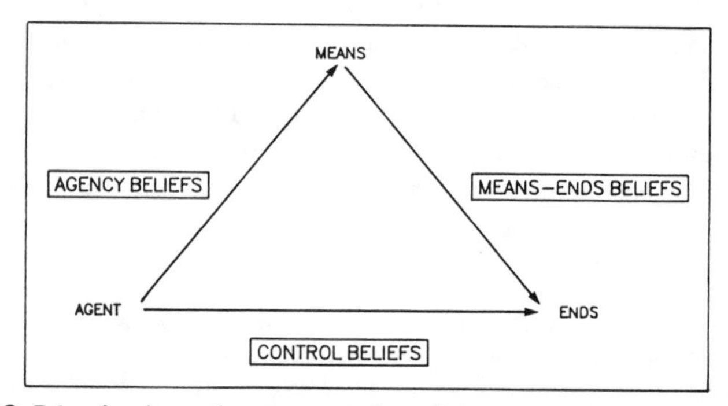

FIG. 5.1. A schematic representation of three sets of control-related beliefs. (From Skinner, Chapman, & Baltes, 1988a. Reprinted by permission of the American Psychological Association.)

subscales, as can be seen in Table 5.1 (Skinner et al., 1988a). In addition, three different means–ends factors were found: One factor was marked by "agent-related" causes (effort and ability), one by "nonagent-related" causes (powerful others and luck), and one by unknown causes. These results provide evidence that children's responses to items tapping their control, means–ends, and agency beliefs, actually do reflect the conceptual distinctions among these beliefs.

TABLE 5.1
Factor Pattern for the Scales of the Control, Means–ends, and Agency Interview

	Control		*Means–ends*		*Agency*
	I	*II*	*III*	*IV*	*V*
Control beliefs					
Positive events	.75				
Negative events	.65				
Means–ends beliefs					
Effort					
Positive events		.51			
Negative events		.78			
Attributes					
Positive events		.37			
Negative events		.57	(.31)		
Powerful others					
Positive events			.61		
Negative events			.71		
Luck					
Positive events			.90		
Negative events			.73		
Unknown					
Positive events				.73	
Negative events				.84	
Agency beliefs					
Effort					.60
Attributes	(.43)				.48
Powerful others					.37
Luck					.81
			Factor Intercorrelations		
Control I	—				
Means–ends II	–.02	—			
Means–ends III	–.23	.38	—		
Means–ends IV	–.05	.10	.45	—	
Agency V	.28	.43	.17	.21	—

Note: $N = 155$ children in grades 2, 4, and 6. Factor analysis was calculated using principal factor analysis with promax/oblique rotation. Factor loadings of less than .30 were omitted for clarity. Factor loadings in parentheses indicate scales that cross-loaded on other factors. (from Skinner, Chapman, & Baltes, 1988a, Table 9, reprinted by permission of the American Psychological Association.)

Theoretical Context

Although the new conceptualization is not the focus of this chapter, a brief overview of its relation to the formulations that it attempts to integrate may be helpful. (A more extended discussion can be found in Skinner et al., 1988a). The tripartite scheme was built on a developmental theory of locus of control (Connell, 1985) that broke with earlier conceptualizations which assumed that internal and external causes were inversely related and thus assessed as a single bipolar dimension (Bialer, 1961; Nowicki & Strickland, 1973; Rotter, 1966). Instead, it was hypothesized that children's beliefs about internal (e.g., effort) and external (e.g., powerful others) factors could be distinguished as different sources of control (Connell, 1985; Lachman, 1986; Levenson, 1973) and it was suggested that a new facet of children's beliefs, namely, unknown source of control, should be included. Unknown source of control taps children's beliefs that they do not know what causes success and failure (Connell, 1985).

The new conceptualization bears similarities to other recent theoretical work which emphasizes the importance of investigating children's beliefs not only about the *causes* of success and failure, but also about whether they themselves can *enact* those causes (Abramson et al., 1978; Bandura, 1977; Gurin & Brim, 1984; Harter & Connell, 1984; Weisz, 1983; Weisz & Stipek, 1982). The new conceptualization can also be contrasted to related constructs on many dimensions (see Skinner et al., 1988a). Table 5.2 provides a summary of prominent related conceptualizations. The most crucial difference between these and the current scheme is the present emphasis on differentiating the three aspects of perceived control. This emphasis has consequences for each set of beliefs.

Control Beliefs. In some conceptualizations, control beliefs are viewed as completely reducible to some combination of means–ends and agency beliefs (e.g., Weisz, 1983). This conclusion is supported by a semantic analysis of the relations among beliefs. However, this argument assumes that the functional relations among beliefs mirror their semantic relations, and there is no a priori basis for this conclusion. Hence, the current conceptualization proceeds from the assumption that each set of beliefs represents a separate cognitive construction. Each can then be assessed separately and the determination of the relations among them becomes an empirical question.

Means–ends Beliefs. In some conceptualizations, beliefs about the connection between causes and outcomes are described retrospectively as causal explanations (Abramson et al., 1978; Weiner, 1985). These are not useful in the present context, however, because retrospective attributions mix means–ends and agency beliefs. That is, attributing an event to a cause (e.g., "I did well on that test because of ability.") implies high means–ends expectations (i.e.,

TABLE 5.2
Comparison of Theoretical Distinctions Similar to Control, Means–ends and Agency Beliefs

Theoretical Framework	*Agent–ends Relation*	*Means–ends Relation*	*Agent–means Relation*
Action theory (Skinner, Chapman, & Baltes, 1987)	Controls beliefs: Generalized expectations about the extent to which an agent can produce desired outcomes	Means–ends beliefs: Generalized expectations about the extent to which certain potential means produce desired outcomes	Agency beliefs: Generalized expectations about the extent to which the self possesses or can access potential means
Self-efficacy (Bandua, 1977, 1986)		Response–outcome expectancy: "A person's estimate that a given behavior will lead to certain outcomes" (1977, p. 193)	Efficacy expectations: "The conviction that one can successfully execute the behavior required to produce the outcome" (1977, p. 193)
Sense of control (Gurin & Brim, 1984)		System responsiveness: "Judgment of the environment's likely response to an individual's action" (p. 285)	Personal efficacy: "Judgment of the self as able to produce acts that should lead to desirable outcomes" (p. 285)
Judgments of contingency and competence (Weisz, 1983; Weisz & Cameron, 1985; Weisz & Stipek, 1982)	Accurate control judgment	Contingency judgment: "The degree to which a target event can be controlled (i.e., causally influenced in the intended direction by variation in people's behavior or attributes (Weisz & Cameron, 1985, p. 101)	Competence judgment: "The individual's capacity to manifest the attributes or behavior on which the event is contingent" (Weisz & Cameron, 1985, p. 102)
Learned helplessness (Abramson, Seligman, & Teasdale, 1978)		Universal helplessness: "Cases in which the individual as well as other individuals do not possess controlling responses" (p. 51)	Personal helplessness: "Cases in which an individual lacks requisite controlling responses that are available to other people" (p. 51)

Note. From Skinner, Chapman, & Baltes, 1988a, Table 1, by permission of the American Psychological Association.

"Doing well on a test is due to ability.") At the same time, when the event is a *success* outcome, the attribution also implies high agency with respect to the cause (i.e., "I'm smart."); conversely, when the attribution is of a *failure* outcome (e.g., "I did badly on that test because of ability."), the attribution implies low agency beliefs (i.e., "I'm not smart.").

The present conceptualization of means–ends beliefs attempts to keep them separate from agency beliefs. This can be accomplished by asking about expectations instead of explanations, either for children in general (e.g., "When kids do well on tests, it's because they're smart.") (Skinner et al., 1988a) or by assessing conditional causal statements for the individual child (e.g., "If I want to do well in school, I have to be smart.") (Wellborn, Connell, & Skinner, 1989). Within this framework, a child can endorse high means–ends beliefs (e.g., either of the preceding statements) without specifying agency beliefs (i.e., whether or not the particular child sees himself or herself as smart). In fact, empirical evidence indicates that means–ends beliefs of these forms load on separate factors from agency beliefs and are not highly intercorrelated with them (Skinner et al., 1987; Skinner, Wellborn, & Connell, in press).

Agency Beliefs. In some conceptualizations, beliefs about the connection between agents and means refer to expectancies about whether the self has access to means effective in producing desired outcomes (Bandura, 1977; Weisz, 1983). The expectation that one can execute *effective* responses, however, also implies something about means–ends beliefs, namely, that outcomes are *contingent* on some effective response.[2] In contrast, in the current conceptualization, agency beliefs are defined for a broad range of *potential* means, and high agency beliefs do not imply anything about means–ends beliefs. An individual can indicate high agency for many potential means and at the same time report that none of these means are effective.

The current tripartite conceptualization may be useful in organizing and integrating diverse aspects of control-related beliefs into a coherent and more inclusive system of causal beliefs. In addition to its theoretical utility, it was also designed to be used in a functional model which describes how perceived control may influence development; as a framework for organizing contextual influences on perceived control; and in a model of structural change in the organization of perceived control during middle childhood. Each of these themes will be discussed in the next sections.

---

[2]This analysis can account for the surprising empirical findings that variations in self-efficacy expectations alone can predict response initiation, effort, and persistence (Bandura, 1986), whereas, according to Bandura (1977), both high efficacy *and* high response-outcome expectations would be required for an individual to initiate action.

A FUNCTIONAL MODEL OF PERCEIVED CONTROL

How do individuals' control-related beliefs influence their development? According to the model, control-related beliefs shape development by means of their impact on action, specifically, on the "motivational" aspects of action. When individuals believe they can influence desired outcomes, they engage in sustained, focused efforts; they cope more actively with challenges; and they are more likely to re-engage following setbacks or failures. Active engagement, of course, is posited by many theories to lead to the development of competence and understanding (e.g., Hartup, 1983; Piaget, 1976).

According to the model, in addition to its cumulative effects on competence, action also has effects on subsequent performance. Sustained effort generally facilitates accomplishments and lack of effort hinders optimal performance. Because actual successes and failures should affect subsequent perceived control, the proposed cycle is complete. By means of their own actions, individuals can create experiences of success and failure which are consistent with their original beliefs about control.

The resulting developmental model can be depicted as a system of perceived control, action, and outcomes (e.g., Chapman, Skinner, & Baltes, 1985). The model was constructed by integrating functional theories of the role of individual differences in perceived control in regulating action and emotion (Abramson et al., 1978; Bandura, 1977; Weiner, 1985) with research on the antecedents of perceived control (Alloy & Tabachnik, 1984; Crandall & Crandall, 1983; Riksen-Walraven, 1983; see Lamb & Easterbrooks, 1981; Skinner, 1985, 1986, for reviews).

Perceived Control and Action

The functional model describes the dynamic interrelations among three elements: perceived control, action, and outcomes. As noted, perceived control is differentiated into beliefs about control, means–ends, and agency. Action encompasses primarily motivational aspects of intentional behavior, including initiation, attempts to reach a goal, amount of effort expended, intensity and duration of behavior, and persistence in the face of obstacles. Outcomes are defined as the occurrence of a positively or negatively valenced event.

The central hypotheses of the theory are: (1) Children's perceptions of control influence the motivational parameters of their actions; (2) The actions children exert in the preparation and execution of tasks have an impact on their performance outcomes; (3) One source of information children use to form judgments of control is the outcomes of their prior performances (success or failure). Before expanding on these propositions, it must be emphasized that the model is not intended as a *comprehensive* account of the determinants of action or performance.

First, the model is not exhaustive with respect to the individual determinants of action. Following other motivational theories (e.g., Connell, in press; Deci & Ryan, 1985; Dweck & Elliott, 1983; Nicholls, 1984), it is assumed that action and emotion are influenced by a number of other factors, in particular what may be collectively referred to as an individual's "goal orientation" (which includes intrinsic task enjoyment, anxiety, and internal pressure).

Second, perceived control is not assumed to be the only determinant of *level* of performance. The effect of perceived control on performance is assumed to be mediated through its effects on active engagement. One primary determinant of level of accomplishment, in addition to engagement, is actual competence (or capacity). Hence, it is hypothesized that (a) in general, sustained effort facilitates accomplishments, and (b) lack of effort hinders performance. Thus, perceived control is expected to explain individual differences in level of performance in the presence of component capabilities, as well as intraindividually, to explain why some children show performances that are near the ceiling of their own capacities and some do not. These two restrictions are common to the three models of motivation considered here (Abramson et al., 1978; Bandura, 1977; Weiner, 1985; but cf. Connell, in press).

From Perceived Control to Action. What are the processes by which control beliefs influence children's action regulation? This question has two parts: (1) *Prior* to performance, what kinds of control-related beliefs lead to maximum effort in preparation and execution of cognitive performances? and (2) *After* performance outcomes, what kinds of control-related beliefs allow children to interpret their performances in a way that leads to continued sustained engagement? In contrast to most researchers, I assume that the answers to these two questions are equally important and may involve two distinct aspects of perceived control.

It is hypothesized that, *prior* to engagement, the beliefs that promote high effort are high *control beliefs*. Hence, control beliefs are hypothesized to have a *regulative* function in relation to action. *After* a performance, there are two possible affectively charged outcomes: success or failure. I would argue that the impact these outcomes have on subsequent action and performance depends crucially on the perceived implications for future control. Following attribution theories (Abramson et al., 1978; Weiner, 1985), it is hypothesized that *means–ends and agency beliefs* are involved in the interpretation of performance outcomes; that is, they have an *interpretative* function. A schematic diagram of the model is presented in Fig. 5.2.

Empirical Study of the Relations Between Control-related Beliefs and Engagement. A study was conducted to examine the connection between teach-

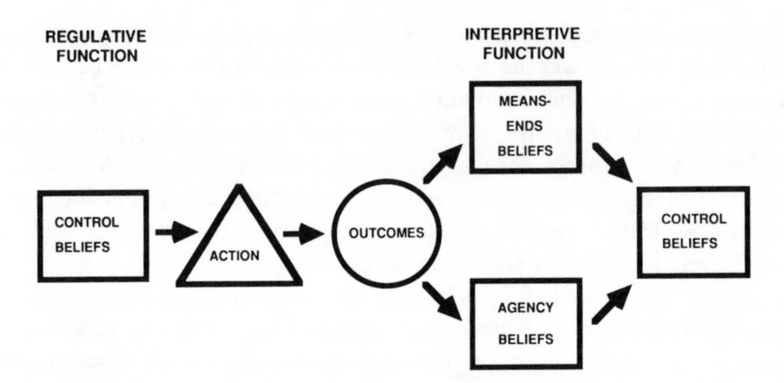

FIG. 5.2. A functional model of the dynamic relations among control beliefs, action, outcomes, and means–ends/agency beliefs.

er's ratings of individual children's engagement and children's reports of their beliefs about control, means–ends, and agency[3] for a sample (N = 220) of middle-school children in grades 3 to 6 (Skinner et al., in press). In predicting from beliefs to action, those control-related beliefs which *undermine* active engagement were distinguished from those which *promote* it.

Engagement would be *undermined* by any beliefs which imply that there is no connection between one's action and desired outcomes. Sufficient for this would be *either* beliefs that outcomes are not contingent on actions (high means–ends beliefs for nonaction causes, such as ability, powerful others, luck, or unknown factors) or beliefs that one is incapable of producing potentially effective actions (low agency beliefs for agent-related causes, such as effort and ability). Predictions about the detrimental effects of nonaction means–ends beliefs are analogous to predictions about the negative effects of an "external" locus of control (Connell, 1985; Lachman, 1986; Levenson, 1973), or low response-outcomes expectations (Bandura, 1977), or of low contingency beliefs (Weisz, 1983). Predictions about undermining effects of low agency for effort and ability are analogous to the hypothesized negative effects of low self-efficacy (Bandura, 1977) and low perceived competence (Weisz, 1983), respectively.

For the nonaction causes, an *interaction* between means–ends and agency was predicted to have the most devastating consequences for engagement. Children who endorse high means–ends beliefs for nonaction causes *and* at the same time possess low agency beliefs for these causes should show the *lowest* levels of engagement (e.g., "School success is due to ability *and* I'm not very smart," or "Good grades are due to luck *and* I'm unlucky."). These predictions are consistent with theories of causal attributions and explanatory style (Abramson et al., 1978; Weiner, 1985).

[3]In this article means–ends beliefs were referred to as strategy beliefs and agency beliefs were referred to as capacity beliefs.

The aspects of control-related beliefs which should *promote* engagement were also specified. First, it was predicted that high control beliefs would be sufficient to promote action. Second, in contrast to predictions about the salutary effects of an "internal" locus of control, effort means–ends beliefs were hypothesized *not* to be sufficient to promote engagement. It was predicted that children must also believe that they *themselves* can produce the required effort (Bandura, 1977; Weisz, 1983). Hence, an interaction was expected between means–ends and agency beliefs for effort in predicting engagement.

As can be seen in Table 5.3, as hypothesized student engagement was related negatively to means–ends beliefs about ability, powerful others, luck, and unknown factors. In addition, it was also related positively to control beliefs and to agency beliefs for all four "known" causes. These findings essentially replicate results from other studies using analogous constructs.

The only constructs for which no "main effects for beliefs" was found in these first analyses were those analogous to means–ends beliefs for effort; these include "internal" locus of control, contingency judgments, and response-outcome expectations. It may be that the power of these constructs comes from the underlying effects of the corresponding negative pole (external locus of control, expected noncontingency, or low response-outcome expectations). If so, then

TABLE 5.3
Correlations between Children's Perceived Control and their Engagement, Grades, and Achievement Test Scores

	Engagement	*Grades*	*Achievement Tests*
Control Beliefs	.33***	.28***	.25***
Means–ends Beliefs[a]			
Effort	.01	.07	.01
Attributes	−.26***	−.18**	−.27***
Powerful others	−.23***	−.11	.15
Luck	−.25***	−.24***	−.31***
Unknown	−.33***	−.30***	−.42***
Agency Beliefs[b]			
Effort	.27***	.28***	.19
Attributes	.34***	.36***	.27***
Powerful others	.23***	.09	.12
Luck	.19**	.08	.01

Note: $N = 220$, grades 3 to 6. Engagement was rated by teachers individually for each student. Grades were the average of arithmetic and verbal (spelling and reading) grades. Achievement tests were the average of the math and reading subscales from the Stanford Achievement Test. From Skinner, Wellborn, & Connell, in press, Table 3, by permission of the American Psychological Association.

[a]In this study, these beliefs were labeled Strategy Beliefs.

[b]In this study, these beliefs were labeled Capacity Beliefs.

$^{**}p < .01$.

$^{***}p < .001$.

correlations between achievement and locus of control (e.g., Findley & Cooper, 1983; Stipek & Weisz, 1981) may actually represent a connection between perceived externality and low achievement. Furthermore, the primary external causes that undermine performance at this age may be centered around powerful others (Crandall et al., 1965) and unknown causes (Connell, 1985).

The second set of questions centered on determining which of the causal categories were unique predictors of engagement. When all five means–ends beliefs were simultaneously entered into a multiple regression equation, unknown factors emerged as the only significant unique (negative) predictor of engagement. When only the four "known" causes were entered, both means–ends for ability and for powerful others were found to be significant unique (also negative) predictors in this elementary school sample. When the four agency beliefs were entered, again both agency for ability and for powerful others (positive) were significant unique predictors. Hence, theories which have emphasized the centrality of beliefs about ability (Weiner, 1985) and about "external" forces like unknown and powerful others (Connell, 1985; Crandall et al. 1965) find support in these analyses of children's school-related beliefs.

The third set of analyses examined the extent to which means–ends and agency beliefs for the same cause were each unique predictors of children's engagement in the classroom. When pairs of means–ends and agency beliefs were entered for each cause, both sets of beliefs were significant unique predictors of engagement. The exception was for the cause effort in which only agency beliefs were significantly related to student engagement. Hence, the unique contribution of both beliefs about causes and about the self's capacities were underscored.

Finally, the *interaction* between the two kinds of beliefs for each cause was also examined. As noted, it was predicted that high means–ends beliefs would enhance the effects of high agency beliefs for the cause effort and that low agency beliefs would exacerbate the effects of high means–ends beliefs for the causes ability, powerful others, and luck. Significant interactions were found for all causes using analyses of variance with extreme groups.[4] The interactions, pictured in Fig. 5.3, indicate that the predictions were supported, and also that the interactions were especially strong for the causes effort and luck. In other words, among children who believed that effort was an effective means, those who also believed that they possessed high agency for effort showed the *highest* levels of engagement whereas those children who reported low agency for effort showed the *lowest* levels of engagement. For the cause luck, children who relied on luck as a strategy *and* who also believed they were unlucky showed the *lowest* levels of engagement in schoolwork.

The results highlight the interactive effects of agency and means–ends beliefs. Consistent with other theories (Bandura, 1977; Weisz, 1983), the main effect of agency for effort was enhanced by beliefs that effort is an effective cause. If these

[4]This was not the pattern found with the entire sample using multiple regression analyses.

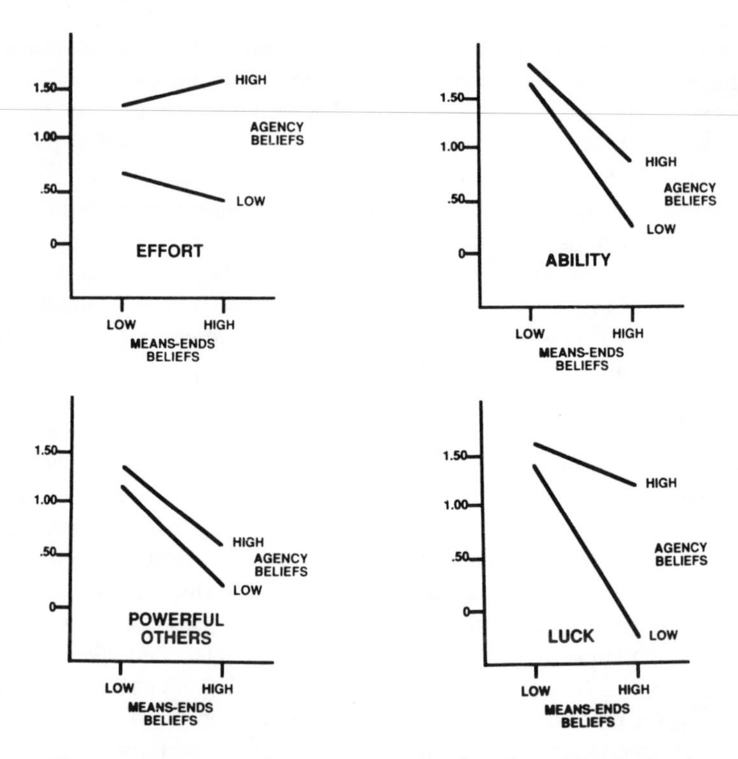

FIG. 5.3. Teacher-rated engagement as a function of the interaction between student's means–ends and agency beliefs (in this study referred to as strategy and capacity beliefs, respectively). Engagement scores were from −3 (disaffected) to +3 (engaged). From Skinner, Wellborn, & Connell, in press, Figure 2, by permission of the American Psychological Association.

interactions can be seen as ways of "unpacking" the effects of causal explanations, then the findings are also consistent with attribution theories (Abramson et al., 1978; Weiner, 1985). In addition to the internal, stable, global causes typically focused on by theories of attributional style, these findings indicate that high means–ends and low agency for external causes such as powerful others and luck may also play an important role in undermining children's engagement in school.

In sum, a framework for the study of the dynamic relations among perceived control, action, and performance outcomes is proposed which has the following features. Control-related beliefs are hypothesized to have both a regulative (prospective) and an interpretative (retrospective) function in relation to performance. On the one hand, control beliefs are expected to facilitate or hinder performance by means of influencing sustained engagement in the preparation and execution of tasks. On the other hand, beliefs about means–ends and agency are expected to act as "filters" for interpreting performance outcomes, and in so doing effect subsequent control beliefs. High means–ends and high agency for effort causes are expected to promote subsequent engagement; whereas the combination of high means–ends and low agency beliefs for nonaction causes is expected to undermine subsequent engagement.

From Action to Perceived Control. One of the processes by which action influences perceived control is through its effects on actual performance outcomes. As noted by many motivational theorists, children who are more engaged usually perform better on challenging tasks and so experience successes more frequently, leading to higher beliefs in control. This action-outcome-control-beliefs link is included in the current model. However, the present discussion will focus on an additional more subtle process by which action may influence control beliefs: the direct effects of action on control judgments.

The basic argument (presented in more detail in Skinner, 1985) is that individuals influence the amount of control they subjectively experience by means of varying the *probability* (frequency) of their own actions. The argument rests on the premise that subjective control experience is partly based on the contingency between actions and outcomes. However, empirical evidence indicates that children's estimates of control, instead of even approximating actual contingencies, are based on information about the co-occurrence of actions and outcomes. This information includes the frequency or probability of confirming cases (e.g., co-occurrence of action and outcome) and disconfirming cases (e.g., action but no outcome; Shaklee & Mims, 1981). Even with objective contingency held constant, the number of confirming and disconfirming cases that individuals experience is directly influenced by how frequently they act compared with how frequently they do not act, or the probability of action. Hence, control beliefs should be directly affected by the probability of action.

Consider the situation in which two children are trying to get help from their mother by means of asking. In this case, asking is the action (A) and getting help is the outcome (O). Assume that the objective contingency is as follows: The mother never gives help unless asked, $p(\text{O} \mid \text{not-A}) = 0$, and will almost always help if asked, $p(\text{O} \mid \text{A}) = .8$; hence, the objective contingency $[p(\text{O} \mid \text{A}) - p(\text{O} \mid \text{not-A})]$ is .8. Let us also assume that these two children differ in probability of action, $p(\text{A})$, such that one child asks frequently, $p(\text{A}) = .8$, and the other very infrequently, $p(\text{A}) = .2$. Finally, let us assume that these children consider as relevant for their judgments of control only those instances in which they ask for help and receive it (positive confirming cases). It is immediately evident that perceived control will differ radically for these two children: The one who acts frequently will experience more control (.64) than the one who is passive (.16). Hence, even with objective contingency held constant, probability of action can influence control beliefs through its effects on action–outcome experience.

The role of action in the experience of control is important for understanding individual differences and developmental changes in the antecedents of perceived control. In terms of interindividual differences, it suggests that one of the important antecedents of control judgments could be an individual's proclivity to be active. It also suggests that social contexts which promote activity in situations of high contingency will maximize a child's experience of control. As will be discussed in subsequent sections, with age children become more sophisticated in their use of strategies to detect covariation. As a result, the effects of action on control will change with age (Skinner, 1985).

Theoretical Background

The integrative model is consistent with other theories of the functions of perceived control in regulating action and emotion. Although each of the major theories focuses primarily on either the regulative or the interpretative function of control-related beliefs, each also gives at least some indication that the other process also operates. None of the theories, however, is centrally concerned with *both* regulation and interpretation, nor with the effects of action on control judgments, nor with the recursive relations between action and perceived control.

Self-Efficacy. Bandura's theory of self-efficacy (1977, 1986) focuses on the *regulative* function of perceived control, positing that perceptions of efficacy "determine whether coping behavior will be initiated, how much effort will be expended, and how long it will be sustained in the face of obstacles or aversive experiences" (1977, p. 191). This theory provides less clear predictions about the relations between performance accomplishments and subsequent self-efficacy expectations, but much of the discussion is consistent with the notion that beliefs about the causes of performance play an important filtering role.

Among the "cognitive processes mediating efficacy information" discussed by Bandura (1977, pp. 200–203), two general categories can be discerned, (1) cognitive processes that facilitate or block the execution of independent performances (such as fear or estimations of task difficulty) and (2) cognitive processes that influence how performance information is interpreted with respect to subsequent efficacy expectations. The latter processes are almost all attributional in character. For example, Bandura notes that

> Successes are more likely to enhance self-efficacy if performances are perceived as resulting from skill than fortuitous or special external aids. Conversely, failures would be expected to produce greater reductions in self-efficacy when attributed to ability rather to unusual situational circumstances (1977, p. 201).

Thus, in my terms, Bandura focuses on the difference between agent-related and nonagent-related means. He continues by emphasizing the effort–ability distinction: "Even under conditions of perceived self-determination of outcomes, the impact of performance attainments on self-efficacy will vary depending on whether one's accomplishments are ascribed mainly to ability or to effort" (1977, p. 201).

In sum, self-efficacy theory focuses on the regulative function of perceived control. At the same time, because the theory is concerned with the (usually therapeutic) process of changing the magnitude and strength of expectations, it also considers procedures for inducing performance accomplishments and factors which ensure that these successes have an impact on efficacy estimations. I would argue that, in large part, the latter factors describe determinants of means–ends and agency beliefs.

Attribution Theory. As its name implies, causal attribution theory (Weiner, 1985) focuses on the interpretative function of control-related beliefs. The model starts with the occurrence of a valenced event (an outcome) and traces the process of causal ascription from specific causes to general dimensions to the psychological consequences for subsequent emotion and action (see Weiner, 1985, Figure 2). Nevertheless, Weiner's concern with the motivational or action consequences of attributions has led him to consider the regulative function of perceived control as well. One of the springboards for action in Weiner's theory seems to be an "expectancy of success," which is depicted as one mediator between attributions and behavior (along with affect or valence, p. 555). Hence, the basic structure of his model is consistent with the position that perceived control has both an interpretative and a regulative function in relation to action and emotion.

Learned Helplessness. The learned helplessness model, in its attributional reformulation, focuses both on the regulative function (expectations of noncontingency) and the interpretative function (attributions of noncontingency) of control-related beliefs (Abramson et al., 1978). However, research following from this perspective has tended to focus on the interpretative function. More specifically, although expectations of noncontingency were originally presumed to be a sufficient condition for the appearance of helplessness, in subsequent endeavors, attributional or explanatory style (the interpretative component) has become the almost exclusive empirical target (e.g., Peterson & Seligman, 1984; Nolen–Hoeksema, Girgus, & Seligman, 1986).

The Current Model. I would argue that the three theories just discussed can be mapped onto the proposed model in the following manner. The regulative function of perceived control, which I ascribe to control beliefs, has parallels in: (1) self-efficacy expectations (self-efficacy theory); (2) expectancies of success (attribution theory); and (3) expectancies of noncontingency (learned helplessness theory).[5] The interpretative function of perceived control, which I ascribe to means–ends and agency beliefs, has parallels in: (1) a subset of cognitive processes relevant to the interpretation of performance outcomes (self-efficacy

---

[5]The learned helplessness proposition reflects the strong prediction of the current model, namely, that low control beliefs lead to low action.

theory); (2) attributions of success and failure (attribution theory); and (3) causal attributions of noncontingency (learned helplessness theory).

The current model differs from these frameworks in three major respects. First, it focuses on the power of control-related beliefs in *both* regulating and interpreting action. The second and most obvious difference concerns the belief constructs that are hypothesized to accomplish this. It is a conceptual task to distinguish the features of control beliefs, self-efficacy, expectancies of success, and expectations of noncontingency from each other. Then it is an empirical question to determine which one(s) regulate action. Likewise, now that attributions have been analyzed for their relations to means–ends and agency beliefs, it is an empirical question to examine which one(s) mediate the effects of action outcomes on subsequent control beliefs.

The third difference between the present model and prior formulations is its concern with the recursive relations between action and perceived control. Extant theories have focused almost exclusively on the effects of perceived control on action, resulting in a relative neglect on the part of self-efficacy theory of the processes mediating between performance and subsequent control beliefs; and to less consideration on the part of attribution theory to the cognitive mediators between attributions and subsequent action. In addition, the current formulation includes the direct effects of action on control beliefs (Skinner, 1985) as well as the interrelations between social context and perceived control (Crandall & Crandall, 1983; Skinner, 1986; Skinner & Connell, 1986). This framework formed the basis for the functional model of development.

A FUNCTIONAL MODEL OF THE DEVELOPMENT OF PERCEIVED CONTROL

The basic contentions of the model are threefold. First, through their own actions individuals produce the kind of control experiences they expect. If this self-regulating system is allowed to continue unabated, the developmental trends expected for *control beliefs* would be: (1) intraindividual decrements or increments within the context of (2) interindividual stability and (3) increasing magnification of interindividual differences over time (Fig. 5.4). In essence, increasingly veridical perceptions would, with development, serve to cement the beliefs that were in part responsible for the structure of that experience.

Second, a developmental by-product of beliefs, through their effects on engagement, could be changes in cumulative *competence*. Active sustained engagement is more likely to lead to the establishment or maintenence of competence in the domains of engagement. Hence, the predicted developmental trends for competence (in the absence of environmental deflection) would parallel those for perceived control.

Third, according to this model, developmental changes in *means–ends and*

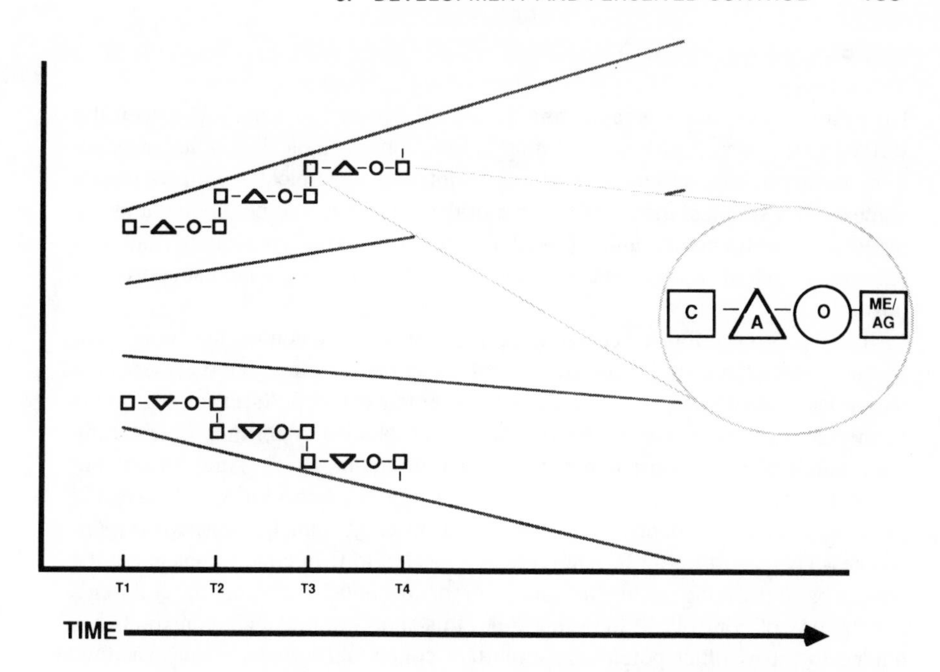

FIG. 5.4. A developmental model of the dynamic relations among control beliefs, action, outcomes, and means–ends /agency beliefs.

agency beliefs would consist of changes in the profiles of beliefs. Empirical evidence shows that children begin the process of understanding the causes of success and failure and their own capabilities from a relatively optimistic standpoint. They see themselves as extremely competent and judge that their efforts will have a powerful influence on performance outcomes (Piaget, 1927/1930; 1926/1975; Skinner & Chapman, 1987; Stipek, 1984; Weisz, 1983).

Some light can be shed on the pattern of means–ends and agency beliefs at the other end of the spectrum by research examining the motivational profiles of children who have been labeled "at-risk" for academic failure or personal maladjustment by their teachers (Vito & Connell, 1988). Using a measurement instrument closely related to the one described previously to assess children's control-related beliefs in the academic domain, Vito and Connell found that relative to random controls, children labeled "at-risk" (1) report that they know less about the causes of school success and failure; (2) endorse ability, powerful others, and luck as playing a bigger role in their school performances; and (3) view themselves as possessing fewer of the corresponding capacities. This is the combination of beliefs most likely to undermine engagement and actual performance in school (Skinner et al., 1989). More research is necessary to document the intermediate profiles of children's means–ends and agency beliefs as they cumulatively succeed or fail in different domains.

The Role of the Context

Up to this point, the self-regulating system of action and beliefs has been described as if it were a process operating in isolation. As indicated in the introduction, however, this system is assumed to interact dynamically with the social context. The simplest model of the role of the context would be to view it as the *origin* of the trajectory and as well as an interlocking *element* of the self-regulating system. Indeed, much evidence has accumulated which supports this position.

It may not be unfair to characterize most of the research on the social contextual antecedents of perceived control as either singling out very specific theoretical constructs or as casting a wide empirical net. As examples of the former, learned helplessness theories have been precise in defining potentiating environmental conditions: noncontingency (Seligman, 1975). And, attachment theorists have specified the dimension of caregiver behavior which lays the groundwork for rudimentary feelings of self-efficacy, namely, sensitive responsiveness (Ainsworth, 1979). Such research has led to firm conclusions about the power of noncontingent versus sensitive social contexts in shaping children's perceptions of control. At the same time, this spotlight on single constructs has tended to throw other potentially important contextual influences into shadow.

At the other end of the continuum are studies which attempt to assess an array of social conditions or parent and teacher behaviors and then to determine their empirical connections to aspects of children's perceived control (Baumrind, 1977; Crandall & Crandall, 1983). These studies have uncovered rich and unexpected linkages between dimensions of actual parent behavior and children's perceptions of competence or locus of control, both concurrently and across time. The challenge has been to provide a coherent theoretical account of these multifaceted findings.

Attempts have been made to construct a bridge between theoretical precision and empirical scope. Researchers in the learned helplessness tradition in their attempts to be more inclusive have begun using indicators of "stressful life events" to encompass a more broad-based set of contextual factors (Nolen–Hoeksma et al., 1986). Likewise, researchers with already more varied data have reached into the conceptual vocabulary of other theorists, attempting to map their dimensions onto constructs such as contingency and responsiveness (Baumrind, 1977). The disadvantages of these strategies include the loss of theoretical precision by embracing broad concepts (such as "stress") and the failure to discover new dimensions by suggesting that current operationalizations fit existing conceptual categories (e.g., rather than analyzing the characteristics of "rational argumentation" for their potential influence on efficacy, simply subsuming it as a form of contingency; Baumrind, 1977). I contend that a few well-defined dimensions of social context can serve as a theoretical base for integration of existing findings as well as for further research on the antecedents of perceived control.

The current process model provides one point of departure (see also, Bandura, 1977).

Influence of the Context on Perceived Control. According to the model, the environment influences perceived control by having an impact on any of the elements of the system or on their relations. Hence, of importance would be contextual factors which have the function of (1) encouraging action, (2) maximizing the contingency between actions and outcomes, (3) increasing the probability of the outcome, and (4) influencing the interpretation of the causal sequence. These suggestions are supported by research on perceived control (e.g., Seligman, 1975), on parent–child interaction (e.g., Baumrind, 1977; Crandall & Crandall, 1983; Lamb & Easterbrooks, 1981), and on intrinsic motivation (especially Connell, in press; Deci & Ryan, 1985; deCharms, 1968; Ryan, Connell, & Deci, 1985) (see Skinner, 1985, for a review).

The working hypothesis is that facilitating any aspect of the process would result in increases in perceived control. However, if any single dimension falls below a certain threshold, then perceived control would be very low. For example, if probability of action or of outcome falls to zero, then perceived control would decline. Examples of each of the four contextual influences will be described, from the educational and the caregiver contexts. The dimensions are summarized in Fig. 5.5.

The summary term for contextual factors that induce action is *expectations*. These can be expressed through verbal means, such as direct orders, instructions, requests, and encouragement. They can also be communicated through systematic nonverbal means, such as previously agreed upon family or classroom rules, responsibilities, and standards of conduct. In addition, their communication can take more idiosyncratic forms, including the extent to which a parent listens to a child's opinion, the length of time a teacher waits for a student's answer, or the number of times a student may attempt answers until the teacher calls on someone else. Expectations can be enforced through explicit sanctions for rule infractions or by more subtle means, such as emotional messages of disappointment or surprise indicating a violation of expectations.

Research has accumulated which indicates that clear, explicit, and consistent parent and teacher expectations for reasonably high performance actually lead children to perform better (Braun, 1976). The proposed dimension of expectations is consistent with this research, but it suggests a specific set of mechanisms which operate to produce the "Pygmalion effect." High expectations would lead to more active engagement, which would result in higher short-term performance, higher perceived control, and cumulatively in improved competence.

The social contextual conditions which maximize the connection between an individual's actions and desired outcomes have been studied under the rubric of *contingency* (Seligman, 1975). Contingency refers to the relation between an individual's actions and the occurrence of an outcome; more specifically, it refers

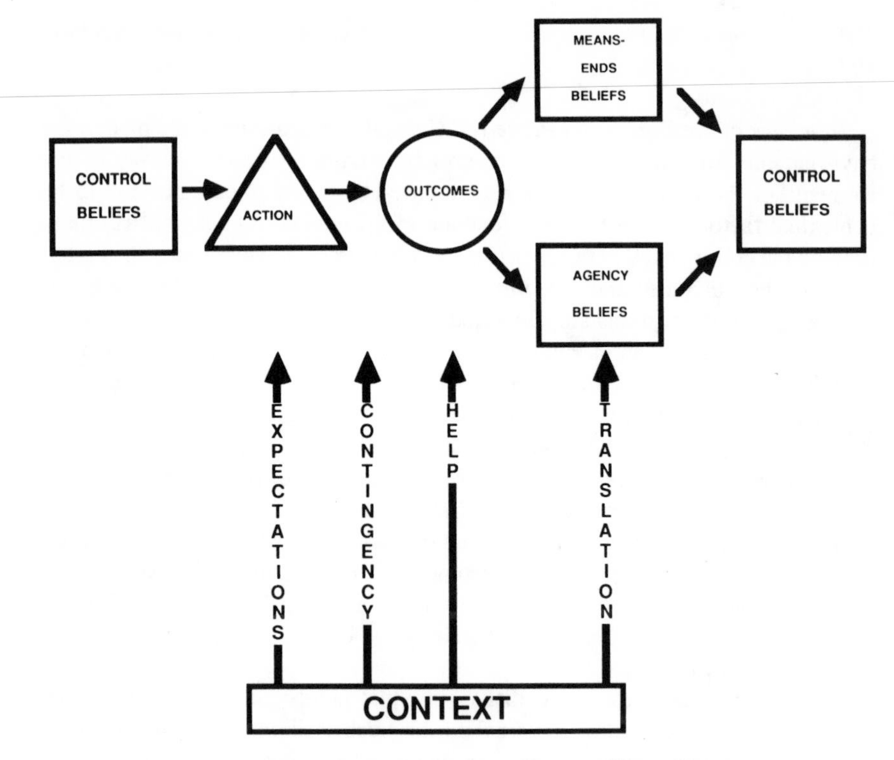

FIG. 5.5. The social contextual factors which influence the elements and relations in the functional model of control beliefs, action, outcomes, and means–ends/agency beliefs.

to the extent to which children's behavior increases the probability of the outcome's occurrence above the probability that that outcome would occur in the absence of their actions (Seligman, 1975; see Alloy & Abramson, 1979, for a review). In social contexts characterized by high contingency, children's behaviors and efforts are consistently and discriminantly followed by outcomes. In contrast, in noncontingent environments, outcomes are just as likely to occur when children act as when they are passive.

It is hypothesized by many theorists that perceived control is the result of an individual's experience with differentially contingent, responsive, and sensitive caregiver environments (Gunnar, 1980; Lamb & Easterbrooks, 1981; Seligman, 1975; Skinner, 1985). For example, experimental and field studies have demonstrated that continued exposure to noncontingency between one's actions and desired outcomes leads to generalized perceptions of noncontingency (Seligman, 1975). Conversely, experimental interventions successful in increasing caregiver contingency and responsiveness have also resulted in increases in infant engagement, presumably based on infants' generalized control beliefs (Ricksen-Walraven, 1978; Watson, 1979).

For caregivers, the contingent outcomes which children desire are often certain behaviors of the caregiver. Hence, caregivers can provide contingency by responding consistently and appropriately to children's actions. In educational contexts, the success and failure children experience with learning tasks become an additional source of contingency. In this context, the level of difficulty of the learning task, or more precisely, the match between the child's current skill level and the difficulty of the task, determines the connection between the child's responses and the task outcome. If the task is too difficult, then the child experiences no contingency between action and outcomes. Conversely, if the task is too easy, then the child will also experience no contingency between his or her *efforts* and task outcomes. The highest contingency will be experienced with tasks of "just manageable difficulty" (Wachs, 1977).

The third social contextual term encompasses factors which increase the probability of outcome, but not through their effects on the child's actions nor on the level of contingency. Direct interventions by which both the caregiver and the teacher can increase the likelihood of a successful outcome will be termed *help*. Help can vary along a dimension ranging from taking over and completing the task for a child at one pole to checking when the task is over at the other. This narrower definition of help excludes "meta-help" in the sense of provision of suggestions or strategies. Such help might increase the likelihood of success, but it would do so through its effects on children's actions.

The fourth, and in many ways most heterogeneous, social contextual factor is labeled *translation* and encompasses the ways in which other people influence interpretation of performance outcomes. Researchers studying the antecedents of attributions have been especially interested in these factors, and it seems likely that different subcategories of translation processes will be identified based on the particular causal attribution or dimension of interest. A wide variety of social influences have been studied, including teacher and caregiver reactions to children's successes and failures; and processes of social comparison, in which peer performance is used to infer ability and task difficulty. For example, research has shown that emotional feedback (anger vs. sympathy) is a particularly potent transmitter of the teacher's view of whether a failure was potentially controllable or not (Barker & Graham, 1987; Graham, 1984). Likewise, both verbal information and the target of evaluation are important in influencing children's interpretations of the contribution of ability to their performances (Dweck & Leggett, 1987).

To complicate matters, attributional researchers have found that earlier elements in the sequence also influence children's causal explanations. For example, high action or effort increases the probability that failure will be attributed to ability (Covington & Omelich, 1985). The nature of outcomes have also shown robust influences on whether children take credit for performances (more likely for success outcomes) or blame others (more likely for failure outcomes; the so-called self-serving attributional bias). Additional research has shown that controlling and constraining environments lead individuals to view their participation and potentially their performance as largely determined by influences outside themselves (Deci & Ryan, 1985).

It may be helpful to think of these influences as hierarchically or sequentially arranged. If the argument is accepted that children enter middle childhood with control-related beliefs that express high potential control and center on effort, then children who experience environments that support action and provide high contingency should remain optimistic. If however, children are exposed to noncontingent environments that discourage action, then it will be impossible for them to maintain high means–ends and agency for effort. In general, prolonged exposure to such environments should escalate children's perceptions that they don't know or understand the strategies for achieving success and avoiding failure in that domain.

The specific alternatives to effort strategies (e.g., ability, powerful others, or luck) would depend on the configuration of other environmental factors. For example, if noncontingency were coupled with consistent failure, then children would tend to focus on ability as the primary explanation. If however, noncontingency were combined with inconsistency then children should attribute performance outcomes to powerful others or luck. Powerful others would be a likely explanation in the presence of controlling or constraining adults. Luck might be a more likely attribution in the presence of a neglectful parent or teacher.

The Correlation Between Perceived Control and Social Context. An exploratory study was conducted to examine the relation between children's beliefs about control, means–ends, and agency and their perceptions of four aspects of teacher behavior: the structure in the classroom (expectations and contingency), the help provided by the teacher, and two aspects of "translation," namely, controlling teacher behavior and neglectful teacher behavior. The correlations between children's beliefs and reports of the context appear in Table 5.4 ($N = 252$, grades 3 through 6); (Skinner, Connell, & Wellborn, in 1989.)[6]

Keeping in mind that the correlations can represent bidirectional effects between perceived context and beliefs, the following links could be determined. (In order to reach a level of conceptual significance and to minimize the effects of common method variance, a criterion of $p < .0001$ was used as a cutoff for interpretation.) All four aspects of perceived teacher context were linked to children's control-related beliefs, although not always in the predicted patterns.

Clear expectations and contingency (structure) was positively related to control beliefs and to means–ends and agency beliefs for effort. In addition, *low* structure was linked to beliefs that powerful others were the cause of school performance. It was surprising that low perceived structure was not more closely related to unknown means–ends beliefs. It may be that perceived teacher non-

[6]In this article, means–ends beliefs were referred to as strategy beliefs and agency beliefs were referred to as capacity beliefs.

TABLE 5.4
Correlations Between Children's Beliefs about Control, Means–ends, and Agency and their Perceptions of Teacher Context

	Teacher Context			
	Contingency	*Help*	*Translation*	
			Neglect	*Constraint*
Control beliefs	.32***	.14	−.24***	−.22***
Means–ends beliefs[a]				
Effort	.23***	.50***	−.31***	−.10
Attributes	−.05	.23***	−.06	.15
Powerful others	−.30***	−.17*	.33***	.42***
Luck	−.18*	.13	.05	.27***
Unknown	−.16*	.13	.05	.27***
Agency Beliefs[b]				
Effort	.37***	.22***	−.44***	−.42***
Attributes	.21***	.11	−.36***	−.26***
Powerful others	.20**	.36***	−.58***	−.49***
Luck	.18**	.22***	−.36***	−.31***

Note: $N = 252$, grades 3 to 6. (From Skinner, Connell, & Wellborn, 1989.)
[a]In this study, these beliefs were labeled Strategy Beliefs.
[b]In this study, these beliefs were labeled Capacity Beliefs.
$p < .05$.
**$p < .01$.
***$p < .001$.

contingency alone would have been more highly related (Skinner et al., 1989).

Teacher provision of help was also related to beliefs in the effectiveness of effort as well as to agency for powerful others. The two aspects of "translation" of performance outcomes (neglect and controlling behaviors), were both *negatively* related to agency beliefs for all four known causes and to overall control beliefs. Both also predicted to beliefs that teachers control school success and failure. Finally, perceived teacher neglect was *negatively* related to effort as a strategy, and controlling teacher behavior was linked to reports of high unknown control.

The results of this study are illustrative rather than conclusive. They indicate that multiple dimensions of the social context may combine to influence or be influenced by children's control-related beliefs. Programmatic research is needed (1) to assess actual teacher and parent behaviors in addition to children's perceptions, (2) to examine the reciprocal relations between social context and children's beliefs and actions, and (3) to determine the causal linkages among context, beliefs, and actions by studying these relations across time. Taken together, a set of theoretically meaningful and empirically robust social contextual factors should emerge which play an instigating and then interlocking role in the cyclical system of children's beliefs, actions, and performance outcomes.

The picture is, however, somewhat more complex. Because the functional model operates in the context of the developing individual, the system itself undergoes change with age. Therefore, the ways in which the context can affect the system, as well as the absolute amount of impact the context can have, is postulated to change with development. These developmental issues are taken up in the final section.

A STRUCTURAL MODEL OF THE DEVELOPMENT OF CONTROL-RELATED BELIEFS

In this section, a speculative model is presented depicting how developmental changes in the elements of the functional model result in changes in the organization of the dynamic system of beliefs, action, and outcomes. The result of these changes is that children successively take over the regulation of their own actions and the interpretation of their performance outcomes. At the same time, the entire system becomes progressively less permeable to the effects of the environment. This can have positive or negative consequences. When a child's actions and beliefs form an incrementing system, the older child is less vulnerable to nonoptimal environments. Conversely, when a child's actions and beliefs form a decrementing system, relatively more powerful environmental interventions would be required to deflect the trajectory.

Development of Perceived Control

The model of structural developmental change was initially empirically driven. A series of studies examining age differences in the mean levels and factor structure of perceived control and in its correlations with engagement and grades converged on a clear but difficult to interpret conclusion: The dimensionalization and functions of perceived control change with age. Because the conceptualization and measure of perceived control were so new, this conclusion necessitated a return to the existing literature. Although only a few studies had examined these questions, it was surprising to discover that their findings supported this conclusion.

Research on other topics, specifically, the development of children's conceptions of causal categories, provided an organizing framework for understanding developmental changes. This, in turn, led to a study which attempted to put together children's changing conceptions of two central causes (effort and ability) with the functions of perceived control. The culmination of these efforts was the construction of a model describing major developmental changes in the structure and functions of perceived control across middle childhood. Before describing its outlines, the developmental findings upon which it is based are summarized.

Developmental Differentiation in Mean Level. The initial goal of this research was to examine whether the three aspects of beliefs, namely, control, means–ends, and agency, manifest different patterns of developmental change in mean level. Robust patterns of age differences were found primarily for means–ends beliefs (Skinner et al., 1988b). Results indicated that children's beliefs about the causes of outcomes become more differentiated across middle childhood. As illustrated in Fig. 5.6, although children's beliefs about effort were the highest at all ages, the mean level differences between the causal categories increased with age. At the same time, the most pronounced decline was in beliefs about the effectiveness of luck: Luck dropped from second place in the youngest ages to last place by age 12.

Additional studies have replicated this pattern in both American and German samples (Connell, 1985; Skinner & Chapman, 1987), and in the domains of school performance and friendship, although the differentiation seems to appear sooner and be more pronounced in the former domain (Skinner, in press). Note that this pattern of differentiation does not contradict studies of the development of locus of control. This may seem surprising since these studies have generally reported increases in perceived internality with age (see Skinner & Connell, 1986, for a review). However, because internal and external locus of control are measured as a single bipolar dimension, these studies have actually found that the *difference* between beliefs about internal and external causes increases with age. This is also the main conclusion here (Skinner & Chapman, 1987).

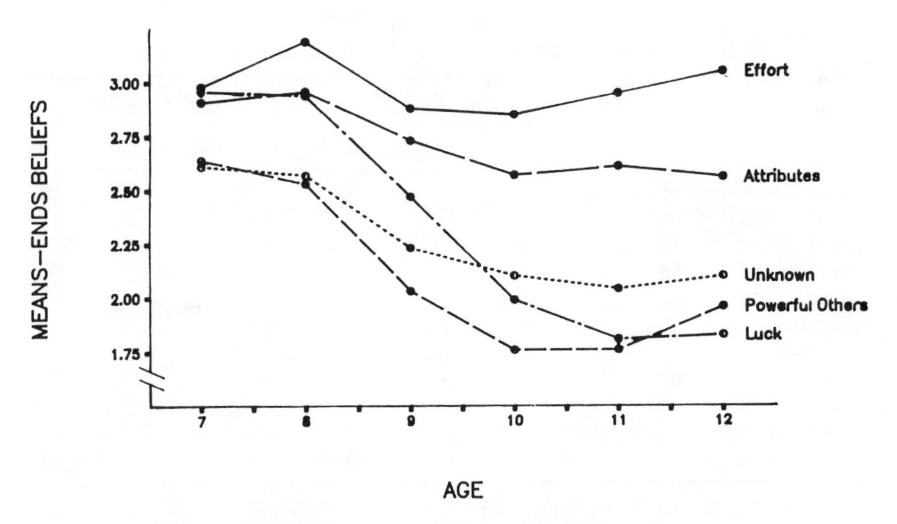

FIG. 5.6. Age differences in means–ends beliefs for five potential causes in the domain of school performance. Effectiveness ratings ranged from 1 (almost never) to four (almost always).

Developmental Differentiation in Structure. An analysis of the factor structure of means–ends beliefs by age revealed that the differentiation of beliefs about causes is also reflected in developmental differences in structure (Skinner, 1989). As can be seen in Table 5.5, between the age of 8 to 12 years, children's means–ends beliefs became more differentiated, increasing from two to four factors, and the causes marking factors changed. For the youngest children, the two factors seemed to represent known vs. unknown causes. At the next age, the known factor was differentiated into means related to agents and those not related to agents. By the oldest ages, the agent-related factor was differentiated into two dimensions marked by effort and ability causes. This patterns has been replicated using a variety of markers of causal categories, such as success and failure, self and other, and even and odd-item subscales (see also Connell, 1985.)

Development of the Functions of Perceived Control. Two studies were conducted to examine age differences in the correlations between perceived control and performance outcomes. The first study (Skinner, 1989) involved a simple follow-up to the factor analyses that have been described in which children's factor scores were calculated individually using the configurations and weights for each child's corresponding age group, and these scores were correlated with children's combined spelling and arithmetic scores on the BTS (*Begabungstest-system*), a standard German intelligence test for children.

For children of the youngest age group, achievement test scores were correlated only with the factor marked by unknown causes ($r = -.36$, $p < .01$) and

TABLE 5.5
Factor Analyses of Means–ends Beliefs for Children of 3 Ages

	Age 7 to 8		*Age 9 to 10*			*Age 11 to 12*			
	I	*II*	*I*	*II*	*III*	*I*	*II*	*III*	*IV*
Means–ends beliefs									
Effort 1	.58		.60			.73			
Effort 2	.55		.56			.33			
Attributes 1	.68		.55				.75		
Attributes 2	.62		.77				.53		
P. Others 1	.61			.68				.44	
P. Others 2	.65			.32				.29	
Luck 1	.68			.90				.63	
Luck 2	.70			.60				.56	
Unknown 1		.71			.80				.70
Unknown 2		.85			.41				.45

Note: n = 80, 93, 121, for grades 1 and 2, 3 and 4, and 5 and 6, respectively. Factor analyses were calculated using principal component factor analysis with promax/oblique rotation. Factor loadings of less than .30 were omitted for clarity. (From Skinner, 1989.)

not by the factor marked by known causes (r = .11, ns, n = 80). For children ages 9 and 10, the factor marked by nonagent-related causes (powerful others and luck) was the primary correlate of achievement scores ($r = -.28, p < .03$); the factor marked by agent-related causes was uncorrelated ($r = -.07$, ns) and the unknown factor was only marginally related $r = -.15, p < .07, n = 93$). Finally, for the older children, only the factor marked by ability causes was significantly correlated with achievement test scores ($r = -.19, p < .018, n =$ 121), although again unknown was also marginally related ($r = .13, p < .08$).

A second study (Chapman, Skinner, & Baltes, in press) focused on age differences in the correlations between agency beliefs (for effort and ability) and intelligence test scores. In general, no relations were found for children in the second grade; significant correlations with agency for effort emerged in grade four and were significantly higher in grade six; correlations with agency for ability emerged first in grade six.

Review of the Literature

The findings on changes in the functions of perceived control opened up the intriguing possibility that the constructs proposed by different theories are central to the regulation and interpretation of performance at different ages. Beliefs principally organized around the known vs. unknown dimension may be the best predictors of engagement and academic performance when children begin school (Connell, 1985). Beliefs about internal (agent-related) vs. external (nonagent-related) causes may predominate when children are about ages 9 or 10 (Crandall et al., 1965; Nowicki & Strickland, 1973), perhaps with beliefs at the external pole accounting for this relationship. Only starting at about age 11 or 12 would children's beliefs about ability begin to play a role in the regulation and interpretation of their performance (Dweck, 1975; Nicholls, 1978).

With this lense, it is possible to return to the existing literature and attempt to identify studies in which relations between aspects of perceived control and motivation or performance were examined for children of different ages. It should be noted that, within the current model, these correlations are interpreted as bidirectional: They represent either effects of beliefs on performance (through action regulation) or effects of performance on beliefs (mediated by the social context) or both.

Unknown source of control has been found to be negatively related to academic performance in children as young as 7 (first grade). It continues to show robust negative relations across age and domain of performance (Connell, 1985; Harter & Connell, 1984; Skinner et al., 1989). Hence, unknown source of control may be the earliest causal dimension which predicts (or is affected by) children's academic performance.

The richest set of empirical studies was found in a meta-analysis of 98 investigations of the correlation between *internal vs. external locus of control* (using typical bipolar measures) and academic achievement (Findley & Cooper, 1983). These researchers found that the magnitude of the correlations showed a curvilinear relation with age from grades one to college. From grades one to three, the relationship between high internality (or low externality) and academic performance was essentially zero (average r = .04, 4 studies); positive relations emerged in grades four to six (average r = .24, 21 studies); remained stable in junior high and high school (average r = .35, and .24, 7 and 8 studies, respectively); and decreased again in college (average r = .14, 32 studies).

If these correlations are based on the external pole of the locus of control scales (which previously described research would suggest), then these beliefs may be thought of as one form of perceived noncontingency, which is the operative construct in classical theories of learned helplessness. Hence, similar results would be expected from developmental studies of learned helplessness. One study of this phenomenon was conducted by Rholes, Blackwell, Jordan, and Walters (1980; cf. Fincham & Cain, 1986) who found a similar developmental trend in the occurance of helplessness. For children in kindergarten, first, and third grade, no decrements in persistence and cognitive performance during failure were found. Decrements emerged first in their fifth-grade subjects. Hence, as with locus of control, for perceived noncontingency, relations with motivation and performance are not found before third grade.

The study of learned helplessness within the reformulated model has emphasized attributions of low performance to *ability vs. effort*. Performance decrements following attributions of failure to ability are hypothesized to be the result of attributing low performance to stable and uncontrollable (Weiner, 1985), or internal, stable, and global causes (Abramson et al., 1978). Two studies reported age differences in performance impairment which can be construed as based on ability attributions. In a longitudinal study by Fincham, Hokoda, and Sanders (1989), children's generalized effort vs. ability attributions were directly assessed when students were in third and fifth grade and then were correlated with concurrent teacher ratings of the children's learned helpless behaviors in the classroom and their grades for math and reading. The connection between children's engagement and their actual performance was found in both grade levels: Learned helplessness behaviors were negatively correlated with math and reading grades at both ages. However, control-related beliefs seemed to regulate actions only at older ages: Effort vs. ability attributions were correlated with classroom behaviors and school grades in fifth grade only.

Finally, Miller (1985) conducted a study of the cognitive basis of performance impairment after failure in which children in grades two and six were presented with unsolvable problems in one of two conditions: instructions implying either moderate or high task difficulty. Because children tried equally hard in both conditions, it was assumed that failure in tasks of reportedly moderate difficulty was more likely to be attributed to ability than failure in high-difficulty tasks (for which task difficulty was a reasonable attribution). Performance decrements were found only for children in grade six and only in the moderate difficulty condition in which ability attributions were more likely. To anticipate the current developmental account of this phenomenon, sixth-grade children were also assessed on the extent to which they possessed mature conceptions of ability (which emerge about age 11 or 12). Performance decrements were found only for sixth graders with mature ability conceptions. Hence, beliefs about ability as a cause seem to emerge as important correlates of motivation and performance around grades five and six.

The summary of existing research does as much to provoke questions as to provide answers. With the exception of research focusing on locus of control, few investigations could be uncovered that examined developmental differences in the relations between control-related beliefs and performance. To some extent this is not too surprising: Researchers in this area have been interested in individual differences in children's beliefs and have focused on specific constructs; from such a perspective age differences in correlations involving single constructs are useful only in that they identify the boundaries of a particular phenomenon. Unless they are combined with the study of other constructs, they do not form a developmental picture (Connell, 1985; Dweck & Elliott, 1983; Weisz, 1983). Taken together, the findings were perceived as tentative yet suggestive. They provoked a developmental explanation and an extrapolation, both of which may serve as guides for future research.

One Explanation of Developmental Change

The explanatory framework was based on the development of children's understanding of causal concepts. Within the current conceptualization of perceived control, these include contingency vs. noncontingency and effort vs. ability and luck. John Nicholls and John Weisz have documented their theories and cumulative supporting evidence at length (Nicholls, 1978, 1984; Nicholls & Miller, 1984, 1985; Weisz, 1980, 1981) and so only key points will be summarized here (see also Chapman & Skinner, in press; Skinner & Chapman, 1987). The basic idea is that children's early conceptions of noncontingency, ability, and luck are undifferentiated from effort. For example, before the age of 8 or so, children report that one can improve one's performance on chance tasks through practice (Weisz, 1980) or that when two children perform equally well on a task, the one who tried harder is smarter (Nicholls, 1978). Only with age and the cognitive developments of concrete operations, do children come to differentiate contingent causes from noncontingent causes and subsequently to differentiate conceptions of effort from those of ability. The former is presumably based on the development of conceptions of chance and the latter on the development of the understanding of inverse compensatory relations.

It should be noted, however, that the theorists who have uncovered these developmental changes do not attribute them to cognitive advances alone. The cognitive changes cited here introduce the possibility that such conceptions can be understood. For children to subscribe to them, they must live in cultures in which, for example, mature adults conceive of ability as a stable, unchangeable, permanent entity (see Dweck & Leggett, 1987 or Nicholls, 1984). If children were exposed to conceptions of ability as changeable through effort or to conceptions of luck as personally modifiable, then no developmental changes in children's conceptions would be observed, despite cognitive advances.

These two developmental changes in conceptions of noncontingency and ability may, in some sense, "activate" individual differences in beliefs about these causes with respect to their power in regulating and interpreting performance. In both cases, new conceptions of noncontingency and of ability would lead children who attribute failure to these causes to "turn off" their actions because subsequent efforts are not expected to be effective in producing desired outcomes. Hence, the decrements on performance following exposure to noncontingency or following ability attributions for failure should occur after mature conceptions are formed. As the literature review indicated, this seems to be the case. It is ironic that developmental "improvements" in the form of more mature conceptions of causes such as ability, luck, and noncontingency should bring with them increased vulnerability to the debilitating effects of failure (Chapman & Skinner, 1985).

A study was conducted to examine the effects of increasingly mature conceptions of ability (successively more differentiated from effort) on the correlations between children's agency beliefs for effort and ability and their academic performance (Chapman & Skinner, 1989). Effort and ability differentiation was measured using open-ended interviews (Nicholls, 1978) in which both children's answers and their rationales are scored on one of four levels. These levels do not reflect anything about how *effective* children reported the two concepts were as causes of performance; they reflect only the extent to which children differentiate between them. The correlations between children's achievement test scores and their agency for effort and for ability as separately assessed by our questionnaire are plotted as a function of level of effort–ability differentiation in Fig. 5.7. As can be seen, the correlations with agency for effort decreased at higher levels of differentiation, whereas the correlations with agency for ability increased; the differences in correlations between Levels I and IV were statistically significant. They provide further evidence suggesting that developmental changes in the conceptions of causes may underlie changes in the functions of perceived control.

The Development of Action–Control Beliefs Systems

Based on the convergence of evidence presented, three possible kinds of systems were hypothesized which may be part of a developmental progression. Each system differs with respect to the extent to which control beliefs are linked to

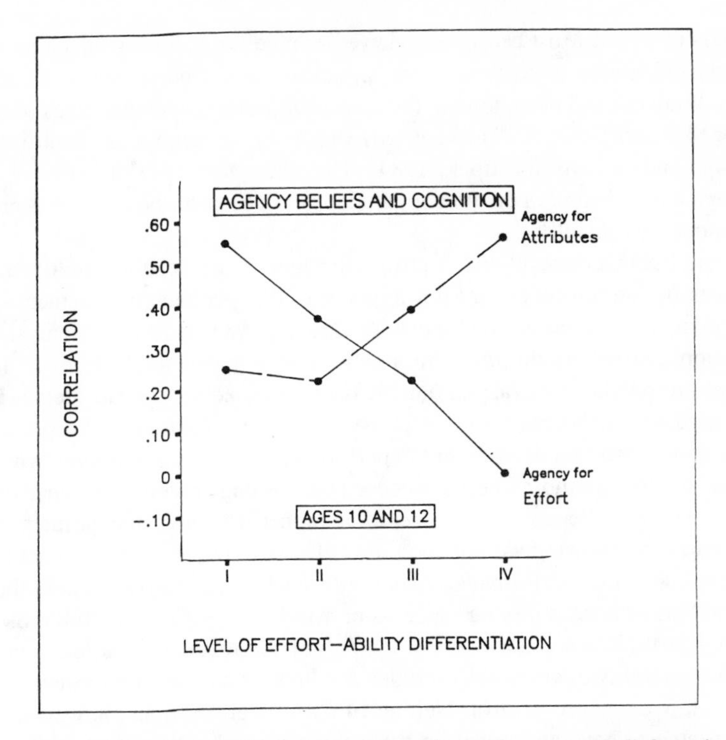

FIG. 5.7. Magnitude of the correlations between agency beliefs and achievement test scores as a function of the level of differentiation of conceptions of effort from those of ability. (Data from Chapman & Skinner, 1989, Table 2, by permission of the University of Chicago Press.) Society for Research in Child Development.

action and the causal categories of means–ends and agency beliefs which interpret performance. Hence, the amount of impact that individuals have on their own development differs as well; in general, it increases with age. Each description ends with a discussion of the effects that these reorganizations can have on the system's openness to influence from outside, and consequently focuses on the changing role of the environment. In general, as development progresses the potential impact of the social context declines. These systems are presented graphically in Figs. 5.8–5.10. Although each is consistent with certain developmental milestones, it is expected that their exact sequence and organizations will be revised as empirical information is brought to bear.

System Organized Around Action and Known/Unknown Means. As described previously, before about age 8 children's conceptions of ability, luck, chance, and noncontingency are not differentiated from conceptions of effort. Hence, their beliefs about strategies and capacities are engulfed by the characteristics of effort. Most causes are viewed as modifiable through personal effort; generalized means–ends beliefs are organized only around the distinction between knowing and not knowing the causes of performance outcomes (Connell, 1985; Skinner, 1989; cf., Heckhausen, 1984). At the same time, control beliefs are high and unrealistic (Stipek, 1984). The consequences of this state of affairs for each dynamic link in the functional model will be described. Fig. 5.8 presents this model graphically.

First, because generalized control expectations are so high, individual differences in control beliefs are not hypothesized to regulate engagement[7] (e.g., Chapman et al., in press; see Findley & Cooper, 1983, for a meta-analysis), and so action and beliefs do *not* form a self-regulating system. Instead, children's actions are regulated by factors outside the beliefs–action system such as intrinsic interest or encouragement from social partners (Skinner, 1986). Second, action is an important determinant in performance outcomes. Children who show sustained effort are more likely to succeed on learning activities (Fincham, et al., 1989). Third, in terms of *interpretation* of performance, the primary causal distinction is "knowing vs. not knowing" effective strategies. With other factors held constant, low performance is likely to lead to generalized beliefs that one does not know how to produce success or avoid failure (Connell, 1985; Skinner, 1989). Fourth, because at this age judgments of control are to a large extent based on the probability of outcomes (Shaklee & Mims, 1981), low performance would lead to low perceived control. Neither of these interpretations, however, would be expected to have an impact on subsequent control expectations.

During this phase, children should appear optimistic and enthusiastic about their potential performance, regardless of their actual successes and failures. They may "give up" if action strategies aren't working, but they do not generalize these experiences; and so they cannot be made helpless through their beliefs. Although relative to children who are doing well, children who are doing poorly report that they know less about strategies for success and failure, this lack of understanding has no concurrent implications for beliefs about the self's capacities (agency beliefs) or about the way the causal world works (means–ends beliefs).

The enthusiasm and optimism of children during this phase may lead adults to underestimate the potential detrimental consequences of high unknown source of control. In the same vein, during this phase, parents and teachers may be un-

[7]Research reported after this chapter was completed (Crandall & Linn, 1989) suggests that children's intellectual achievement expectencies (analogous to control beliefs) may regulate their behavior at very young ages. These researchers found concurrent relations between preschool children's expectencies and their achievement behavior in a free play situation (although these concurrent correlations disappeared in kindergarten and first grade). Longitudinal analyses indicated (for girls only) time-lagged effects of expectancies on behavior from preschool to kindergarten and from kindergarten to grade 1 as well as effects of behavior on expectencies from kindergarten to grade 1.

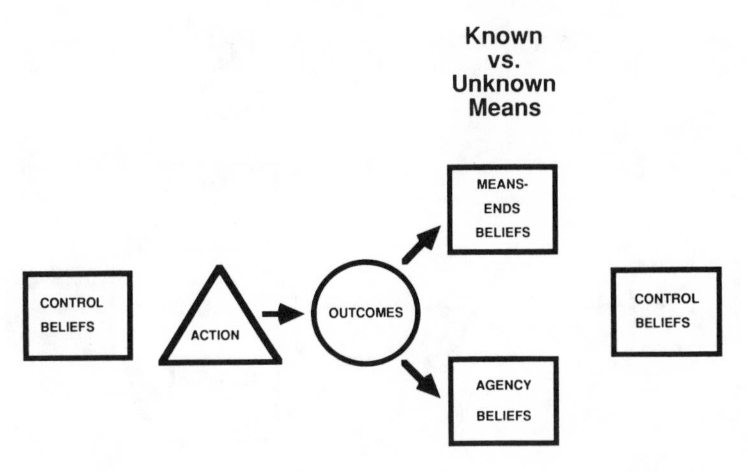

FIG. 5.8. A structural developmental model of changes in the dynamic relations among control beliefs, action, outcomes, and means–ends/agency beliefs: System organized around action and known vs. unknown means.

aware of the long-term effects of their translations of children's successes and failures in terms of effort, ability, powerful others, or luck. The short-term consequences of these beliefs are difficult to detect: First, beliefs have no concurrent consequences for action and, second, action can easily be encouraged and sustained through alternative means, such as social contextual factors. Such beliefs can nevertheless be thought of as developmental traps waiting to be sprung (for better or worse) at subsequent ages.

System Organized Around Action–Outcome Relations and Nonagent-related Causes. The primary developmental change ushering in this phase is the differentiation of conceptions of noncontingency from those of effort (Nicholls & Miller, 1984; Weisz, 1980, 1981). Based on this developmental change, children recognize that luck, chance, and even powerful others may not be able to be influenced by personal means. As a result, children can form generalized perceptions of noncontingency based on uncontrollable causes. Children realize that effort can no longer be counted on to overcome powerful others and luck; for the first time, a child can perceive that there are activities in which no contingency is possible between efforts and desired outcomes (see Weisz, 1986, for a discussion). The suggestion that children begin to understand that powerful others and luck are potentially uncontrollable is consistent with the extreme drop in beliefs about the effectiveness of these causes at this age (especially luck; Skinner & Chapman, 1987; Skinner et al., 1988b). This model is depicted in Fig. 5.9 and its implications for the links in the system are described below.

First, as was the case previously, the system is generally geared toward high

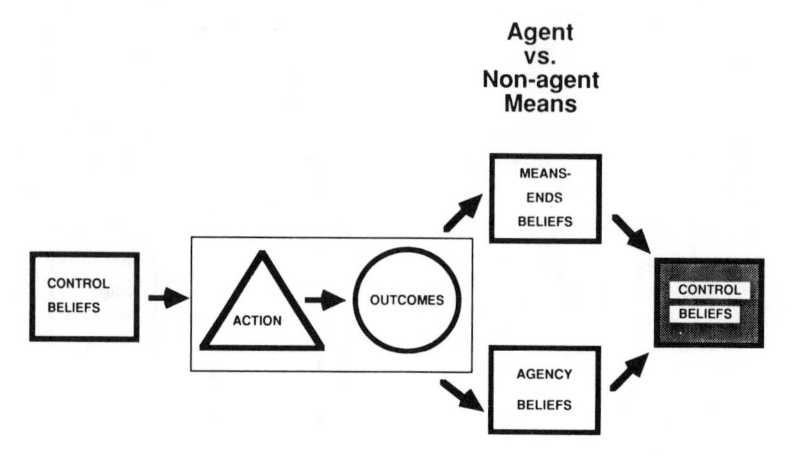

FIG. 5.9. A structural developmental model of changes in the dynamic relations and control beliefs, action, outcomes, and means–ends/agency beliefs. System organized around action-outcome relations and means–ends/agency beliefs that undermine control.

action. At the same time, children's control beliefs begin to *regulate* their actions. Therefore, correlations between control beliefs and subsequent engagement would be expected to emerge at about this age (Chapman et al., in press). Second, during this phase children's means–ends and agency beliefs come to be differentiated into causes which are related to agents and causes which are not related to agents (Skinner, 1989). As a result, low agency for agent-related causes (e.g., effort or ability) and high beliefs in the effectiveness of non-agent related causes (e.g., powerful others or luck) would be sufficient conditions for decreases in subsequent engagement (Skinner et al., in press.) From a locus of control perspective, increasing correlations between external locus of control and children's achievement test scores would be expected at this age (Findley & Cooper, 1983). In the view of the learned helplessness paradigm, noncontingency expectations would begin to undermine subsequent motivation (Rholes et al., 1980).

Third, children's *interpretative* beliefs center not just on the probability of the outcome per se but on the *relations* between actions and outcomes (Shaklee & Mims, 1981). Fourth, for the first time, means–ends and agency beliefs should have direct relevance for children's expectations of their own success. One would expect that during this phase children's control expectancies would become more "realistic" in the sense that their own estimations would begin to allign themselves with their actual performance (e.g., grades) (Stipek, 1984). With the links established between control beliefs and subsequent action, and between means–ends/agency beliefs and subsequent control expectations, the system is potentially capable of influencing the development of beliefs, action, and competencies for the first time.

It is at this phase that "motivational problems" should first be apparent because children are capable of regulating their actions to a standstill, and it is more difficult for the social context to promote engagement than was previously the case. For example, at younger ages, when judgments of control are based on *positive confirming cases,* the probability of outcomes alone has a big influence on perceptions of control. The social context can provide direct help and, by increasing the likelihood of success, increase children's expectations of control. However, when beliefs about control are based on *action-outcome relations,* the positive effects of direct help from the environment are curtailed. In order to perceive that the contingency between one's own actions and outcomes is high, the mediating influence of social help must be eliminated. Help can still be successfully employed to increase perceived control, but its application must take into consideration the constraints of the system: Only by successively fading help and allowing independent mastery, or by redirecting help to induce action (such as by providing suggestions) can the positive impact of help on perceived control be retained (Bandura, 1977).

Just as it does with younger children, the social context may underestimate the long-term impact of its translation messages on children at these ages. Although translations implying the importance of powerful others, luck, and unknown causes may have concurrent impact on children's behavior, both positive and negative information about ability is processed at this age through an undifferentiated "effort/ability filter." Hence, the immediate implications of such messages for behavior are positive. It is especially hard to imagine during this phase that translations which imply ability attributions for *success* may lead to vulnerability at subsequent developmental periods (Dweck & Elliot, 1983).

System Organized Around Ability Causes. The second developmental change which introduces a reorganization of the system is the differentiation of children's conceptions of ability from those of effort (Nicholls, 1978, 1984). Once this occurs, children are capable of understanding adult conceptions of ability, which involve an inverse compensatory relation between ability and effort. At this phase children know that to reach the same performance outcome, smart children have to try less, and that whoever has to try harder possesses less ability. Therefore, it is possible for children to perceive ability as a stable uncontrollable *internal* cause (although empirical evidence indicates that not all children do so; Dweck & Leggett, 1987; Nicholls, 1984). See Fig. 5.10 for a graphic depiction of this new reorganization.

During this phase control beliefs continue to *regulate* action, but they do so by promoting engagement (Skinner et al., in press). The primary predictors of control are children's agency beliefs about effort and ability, even though the

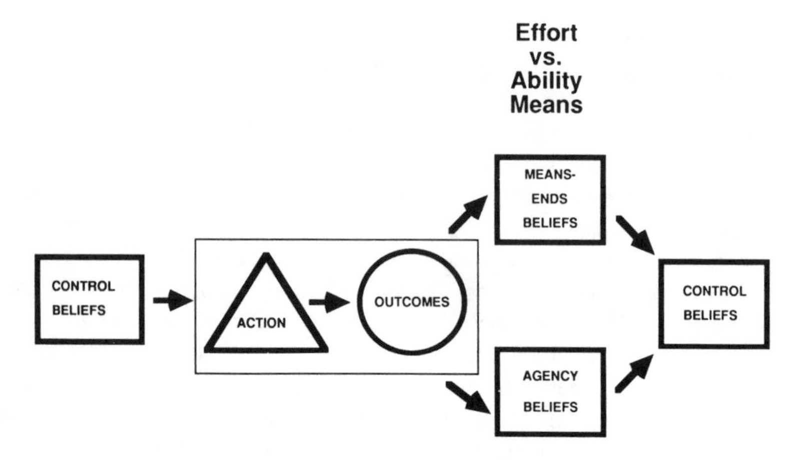

FIG. 5.10. A structural developmental model of changes in the dynamic relations among control beliefs, action, outcomes, and means–ends/agency beliefs. System organized around ability means and means–ends/agency beliefs that promote control.

balance shifts from effort to ability as children's differentiation of these two concepts proceeds (Chapman & Skinner, 1989). At the same time, children who make ability attributions become more vulnerable to the effects of noncontingency, because ability can be interpreted as a stable uncontrollable cause. Hence, one would expect to find the developmental emergence of children's vulnerability to helplessness based on ability attributions (Miller, 1985).

Finally, at this age, individual differences in children's beliefs become most marked and parents and teachers can easily recognize the action and emotion concomitants of beliefs. At the same time, the magnitude of interventions needed to alter belief systems is much greater. Because the potentially most debilitating causes, ability and luck, are inferred, children have a multitude of strategies for interpreting any performance outcome in a way which is consistent with current beliefs. Long and carefully structured interventions may be needed in which actual behavior change is achieved under successively more difficult conditions in order to generate enough irrefutable disconfirming evidence to change beliefs. Although such interventions may be possible in therapeutic situations (see Bandura, 1977, for a detailed description of strategies), they are very difficult to achieve in routine interactions between children and their parents or teachers. Simple retraining of attributions from ability to effort may lead to guilt, self-blame, and self-handicapping (Covington & Omelich, 1979), if they are not accompanied by changes in actual level of performance. Or attempts to increase the probability of success through help or adjustment of task difficulty may serve only to confirm maladaptive patterns of beliefs in which powerful others are believed to be responsible for performance outcomes.

An Empirical Study of Developmental Differences in the Functions of Perceived Control. To close, a longitudinal study has recently been completed which was designed to examine developmental changes in the functions of perceived control across ages 8 to 13, with respect to their effects on both children's engagement in the classroom (as rated by teachers) and their actual school grades (Skinner, et al., 1989). The concurrent bivariate correlations for the sample of 253 children, calculated separately for grades three, four, six, and seven, appear in Table 5.6.

Focusing on the link between beliefs and engagement, the following developmental picture emerges. As predicted, at the youngest ages the primary correlates of engagement were unknown means–ends beliefs. Control beliefs were not related to action, although beliefs about the self's capacity for effort and ability (presumably undifferentiated from each other) were correlated with engagement. At about age 9, children who reported high unknown means–ends beliefs continued to show low engagement, but at the same time beliefs about nonaction causes (high means–ends beliefs for ability, powerful others, and luck) began to undermine action as well. Control beliefs and the two complementary nonagent related beliefs about capacities, namely, luck and powerful others, were also linked to engagement.

At about age 11, children who subscribed to nonaction strategies continued to show lower levels of engagement. At the same time, control beliefs and agency beliefs for action-related means (effort and ability) as well as powerful others were related positively to teacher-rated engagement. The picture which emerged in grade seven (about age 12) was very different. Neither control beliefs nor means–ends beliefs for any causal category were related to engagement. Following the assumed differentiation of effort from ability, agency for effort was no longer a predictor of level of engagement; only agency for ability and for powerful others were related to action.

As can also be seen in Table 5.6, the relations of control-related beliefs to school grades did not show as marked a pattern of developmental change. From grades three to six, school performance was negatively correlated with means–ends beliefs about luck and unknown, and positively related to control beliefs and agency beliefs for effort and ability. Only in grade seven, did a different set of predictors emerge, again focused on perceived ability.

These preliminary results describing the correlates of engagement provide some support for the a priori predictions derived from earlier empirical work and theoretical analyses. The powerful predictors of engagement seem to shift with age from unknown control at the youngest ages, to perceptions of noncontingency at ages 9 to 11, to perceptions of ability at about age 12. More systematic study is needed to assess the longitudinal reciprocal links between control beliefs and behavior and between performance and beliefs (Skinner et al., 1989). It is expected that the model of structural change will undergo revision as it attempts to account for the data from such studies. Already, the differential developmental

TABLE 5.6
Correlations Between Children's Means–ends and Agency Beliefs
and their Engagement in the Classroom and School Grades, Separately by Age

	Engagement				*School Grades*			
Grade:	*3rd*	*4th*	*6th*	*7th*	*3rd*	*4th*	*6th*	*7th*
Means–ends Beliefs[a]								
Effort	.24	−.09	.03	.16	.04	−.02	.17	.15
Ability	−.19	−.29*	−.25*	−.02	−.23	−.23	−.27*	−.04
Powerful others	−.16	−.29*	−.23*	−.12	−.22	−.23	−.06	.19
Luck	−.13	−.41***	−.27*	−.23	−.39**	−.40***	−.21**	−.04
Unknown	−.31**	−.34**	−.34**	−.16	−.57***	−.37**	−.36**	−.02
Agency Beliefs[b]								
Effort	.38**	.21	.29*	.18	.27*	.30*	.34*	.03
Ability	.34**	.21	.50***	.29**	.34**	.37**	.41***	.38**
Powerful others	.19	.29*	.27*	.32**	.23	−.10	.23	−.15
Luck	.13	.31**	.18	.14	−.09	.13	.18	.39**

Note: *n*s for grades 3, 4, 6, and 7 were 59, 65, 72, and 57, respectively. Engagement was rated individually for each child by his or her primary teacher. School grades were the average grades for math and verbal subjects (spelling and reading). (From Skinner, Connell, & Wellborn, 1989).

[a]In this study, these beliefs were labeled Strategy Beliefs.

[b]In this study, these beliefs were labeled Capacity Beliefs.

*$p < .05$.

**$p < .01$.

***$p < .001$.

pattern for engagement as compared with grades poses an interesting problem. Perhaps it will be solved when the full model is examined using longitudinal data and taking social contextual mediators between performance and beliefs into consideration. Perhaps not. At the least, however, the models may sensitize researchers to the possibility of developmental change in mean level, structure, and functions of perceived control with age (Connell & Furman, 1983; Skinner & Connell, 1986).

The model of developmental transformation also implies that different theories of perceived control may be more useful accounts of the connections between control-related beliefs and performance at different ages. Models which emphasize the feedback from performance to beliefs (Heckhausen, 1984) and the importance of unknown source of control (Connell, 1985) may be critical to our understanding of the system at younger ages. Models which focus on action–outcome relations and on the interpretation of noncontingency may be appropriate for studying later phases (Nolen–Hoeksma et al., 1986). And once ability has become an organizing force, models which center on beliefs about stable uncontrollable causes as predictors of performance may be useful (Dweck & Elliot, 1983). Interestingly, research from each of these frameworks has tended to study children within the age range which the structural model would suggest is germane to the respective system.

Taken together, these developments comprise the current rough outlines of a structural developmental model. Its purpose is to explain regular changes in the dynamic interrelations among children's perceived control, their actions, and their performance outcomes. These changes describe a system which is increasingly more differentiated in its understanding of potential means, more veridical, more self-regulating, and which successively operates more independently from environmental input.

CONCLUSION

A new conceptualization of control-related beliefs has been developed which distinguishes among major related constructs and attempts to integrate them into coherent sets of expectations. The new conceptualization was the cornerstone for a functional model of control-related beliefs, action, and performance outcomes. Two functions of beliefs were hypothesized: (1) regulation, in which generalized control beliefs undermine or promote subsequent active engagement in activities; and (2) interpretation, in which generalized means–ends and agency beliefs "filter" the causal information from successes and failure outcomes and so contribute to the calibration of subsequent control beliefs.

Taken together, the regulative and interpretative cycles form a dynamic beliefs–action system. The general notion is that individuals who initially expect high control are more actively engaged, and so experience more control. Conversely, individuals who at first expect low control tend to avoid challenge which in turn undermines subsequent control expectations. Over time this system can magnify initial interindividual differences and so lead to increments or decrements in perceived control, engagement, performance outcomes, and cumulatively, competence. According to this model, the social context plays a critical role in how individuals construct their belief systems and how these are expressed in action and performance. Relevant dimensions of the social environment were organized by considering the factors which influence each element of the system.

A structural model of the developmental reorganization of beliefs–action systems was proposed. This new framework was inspired by empirical evidence that children's control-related beliefs show developmental differentiation and was grounded in theories of developmental changes in children's conceptions of causes. Three sequential systems were suggested which map onto three extant theories of control-related beliefs. Between ages 6 and 8, children's causal beliefs center on action and known vs. unknown causes, which is consistent with a new multidimensional conceptualization of locus of control (Connell, 1985). From ages 9 to 11, causal beliefs about agent-related and nonagent-related causes are differentiated, with the predictive power eminating from causes which undermine motivation (consistent with theories emphasizing external locus of control, Crandall et al., 1965, and judgments of noncontingency, Weisz, 1980, 1981). Finally, at ages 11 to 13, conceptions of ability are differentiated from those of effort, introducing into the system the possibility of uncontrollable *internal* causes for the first time (Nicholls, 1978). This is consistent with attributional theories that focus on ability and other internal, global, and stable factors as explanations for failure (Abramson et al., 1978; Weiner, 1979). Developmental findings consistent with these suggestions were presented and reviewed which indicate that the primary control-related belief correlates of children's engagement and performance change with age.

If different control-related beliefs are central to the regulation of action and the interpretation of performance at different points in development, then the overall amount of impact that the environment can have on control beliefs as well as the specific routes such influences would take may change with age. In general, as the system becomes more self-regulating, the absolute amount of influence available to the environment is expected to decrease.

The limitations of the functional and structural models begin with the fact that their empirical support is restricted to the domain of academic, cognitive, or school performance, and the developmental period of middle childhood. These may be the boundaries of the usefulness of the new conceptualization and the models which build on it. On the other hand, the framework presented here may act as a springboard for research examining developmental changes during other age periods or investigating the motivational basis for engagement in other important domains of functioning.

Implications for Intervention

The distinction among the three sets of control-related expectations may be useful in planning and evaluating intervention efforts. At the most basic level, relative to frameworks which focus on single constructs, they provide a more comprehensive tool for diagnosing the control-related beliefs which may be undermining a particular individual's motivation. More specifically, when engagement is high, most theories would infer that the positive pole of their specific construct is present; and when engagement or motivation is low, each would predict that the negative pole is present. In contrast, within the current system, when engagement is high, a *profile* of beliefs is implied: high control beliefs, high means–ends beliefs for effort, and high agency beliefs for all causes combined with low means–ends beliefs for the nonaction causes. And when motivation is low, multiple profiles are possible and each one would have different implications for intervention. For example, it could be that beliefs about ability, powerful others, luck, or unknown control (or some combination) are the focal problem. Intervention programs which target the specific profile of beliefs from which individuals operate will be more effective in remediating and optimizing those beliefs.

The notion that control-related beliefs and action form a cyclical system may be useful in helping parents and teachers understand the importance of setting initial salutary trajectories. It may also be helpful in explaining the persistence and intractability of individuals' beliefs once they interlock with action systems to generate supportive success or failure experiences. Simple persuasion techniques will not be effective when they contradict a long history of discouraging experiences.

The organization of the dimensions of social contextual influences may also be useful in formulating interventions. First, it sharpens thinking about why particular existing techniques may be effective as well as outlines potential alternative tools for optimizing belief–action systems. Second, it points out the proximal consequences for specific interventions. For example, attribution retraining should have an immediate impact on control expectations, which should in turn promote engagement. In contrast, success experiences, according to the model, are first "interpreted" by means–ends and agency beliefs before they can influence control beliefs and subsequent action. Hence, if increased engagement is the desired outcome, then the effects of the former intervention would appear to be more powerful then those of the latter. And of course, interventions which attend to all the elements of the system simultaneously are more likely to have a strong and lasting effect.

Finally, the proposed developmental changes in the role of the environment have implications for interventions designed to maximize expectations of control. The targets and kinds of interventions as well as specific strategies would vary with age. For example, attribution retraining (Foersterling, 1985) would be most effective after interpretative beliefs have been constructed, but before they are stabilized (between grades three and five). In addition, it is important to note that the factors that were effective in fostering optimal action systems may not be the same factors needed to maintain them. In fact, strategies which promote perceived control at early ages may undermine it later. For example, as mentioned previously, direct help may promote motivation at earlier ages when success, however produced, is enough to increase control expectations, whereas, later it may interfere with attributions of outcomes to one's own efforts. By the same token, translations of performance outcomes which emphasize ability may promote engagement when conceptions of ability are undifferentiated from effort, whereas, after they are differentiated, ability attributions may make a child vulnerable to the implications of failure for his or her perceived ability.

Conversely, social contextual strategies can be identified which have detrimental consequences at earlier developmental periods but none at later ages. For example, an overemphasis on independence may slow motivation at earlier ages when encouragement is needed to fuel engagement; however, at later ages, independence is needed to infer effective effort. Likewise, early translations of negative outcomes which center on luck may undermine engagement when luck is conceived of as a personal capacity, whereas, at later ages, attributions of failure to luck may protect perceived ability.

In any case, interventions would need to be more powerful and more subtle as children reach adolescence. This conclusion underscores the need for early detection and treatment of motivational problems. Most important would be efforts to keep decrementing systems from beginning their downward spiral. Early prevention efforts which maximize both action and perceived control may ensure that children's self-regulating systems are launched into optimal trajectories.

Individuals as Producers of Their Own Development

One pathway toward understanding how individuals guide and shape their own development may be through the study of belief systems which support motivation. Some theorists would argue that from birth, the need for control, competence, or effectance energizes individuals to reach out into the environment and to interact with their physical and social surroundings (White, 1959). If indeed, it is an organismic priority to experience oneself as competent in interacting with one's context, then the desire for competence may be one of the principal organizers of motivation.

A full account of how motivation contributes to individual development will, of course, have to look beyond the limited scope of control-related beliefs. At least three directions for theoretical and empirical elaboration can be identified. First, a closer scrutiny of the proximal regulators of action is needed, especially under conditions of challenge. Coping processes are a likely candidate in this regard. If the functional model can be used as a frame, processes of coping which flow from combinations of means–ends and agency beliefs may be identified, and their short-term effects on re-engagement and their long-term effects on control beliefs may be examined. Many frameworks suggest that the union of coping and control may be fruitful in predicting adaptive outcomes (Band & Weisz, 1988; Compas, 1987; Folkman, 1984).

Second, a full consideration of coping requires one to expand the construct of engagement to include, not just motivated action, but also *emotional* concomitants of behavior. Theorists interested in the functions of coping (Lazarus & Folkman, 1984) as well as motivational theorists focusing on engaged and disaffected patterns of action (see Connell & Wellborn, this volume) highlight the role of emotion.

Finally, a full account of motivation will need to consider basic psychological needs other than control or competence. Motivational theorists have identified the issue of individual autonomy (deCharms, 1968; Deci & Ryan, 1985; Dweck & Elliott, 1983; Harter, 1983; Nicholls, 1984) as well as the issue of relatedness to other people (Ainsworth, 1979; Lynch & Wellborn, 1989). Comprehensive models of the sources of motivation are attempting to integrate these theoretical traditions (see Connell, in press; or Connell & Wellborn, this volume).

As these theoretical models bear empirical fruit, the challenge will be to discover how we can use them to shape social contexts which optimize motivation, and in so doing, maximize active sustained engagement and resilience in the face of setbacks and failures. The task of the social context as children develop is to ensure that their motivational systems maintain their optimism and at the same time gain effectiveness. The structural model indicates that the tools and opportunities available to the social context for engineering optimistic and effective belief–action systems change with development. The successful accomplishment of this task will take on added importance if individuals become increasingly more active in creating their own success and failure experiences through engagement; if the system has long-term effects on the development of understanding and competence; and if the direction of that development is toward successive independence from the environment. Hence, it is critical for the social context to set and then to support adaptive developmental trajectories.

ACKNOWLEDGMENTS

I would like to extend my heartfelt appreciation to my closest collaborators for their participation in our endeavors to understand the phenomena described in this chapter: both those in Berlin, Paul B. Baltes, Michael Chapman, Thomas Kindermann, Rainer Reisenzein, Bernhard Schmitz; and those in Rochester, Michael Belmont, James Connell, Edward Deci, Richard Ryan, and James Wellborn. For their contributions to all phases of the data collection and analyses for the series of studies conducted in Berlin, I thank especially Peter Usinger and also Anita Guenther, Birgit Herback, Ulman Lindenberger, Anita Schindler, Christa Schmidt, and Martin Tschechne.

REFERENCES

Abramson, L. Y., Seligman, M. E. P., & Teasdale, J. D. (1978). Learned helplessness in humans: Critique and reformulation. *Journal of Abnormal Psychology, 87,* 49–74.

Ainsworth, M. D. S. (1979). Infant–mother attachment. *American Psychologist, 34,* 932–937.

Alloy, L. B., & Abramson, L. Y. (1979). Judgment of contingency in depressed and nondepressed students: Sadder but wiser? *Journal of Experimental Psychology: General, 108*(4), 441–485.

Alloy, L. B., & Tabachnik, N. (1984). Assessment of covariation by humans and animals: The joint influence of prior expectations and current situational information. *Psychological Review, 91,* 112–149.

Baltes, M. M., & Baltes, P. B. (1986). *The psychology of control and aging.* Hillsdale, NJ: Lawrence Erlbaum Associates.

Baltes, P. B. (1987). Theoretical propositions of life-span developmental psychology: On the dynamics between growth and decline. *Developmental Psychology, 23,* 611–626.

Band, E. B., & Weisz, J. R. (1988). How to feel better when it feels bad: Children's perspectives on coping with everyday stress. *Developmental Psychology, 24,* 247–253.

Bandura, A. (1977). Self-efficacy: Toward a unified theory of behavioral change. *Psychological Review, 84,* 191–215.

Bandura, A. (1986). *The social foundations of thought and action: A social cognitive theory.* Englewood Cliffs, NJ: Prentice–Hall.

Barker, G. P., & Graham, S. (1987). Developmental study of praise and blame as attributional cues. *Journal of Educational Psychology, 79,* 62–66.

Baumrind, D. (1977). *Socialization determinants of personal agency.* Paper presented at the Meeting of the Society for Research in Child Development, New Orleans.

Bell, R. Q. (1979). Parent, child, and reciprocal influences. *American Psychologist, 34,*(10), 821–826.

Bialer, I. (1961). Conceptualization of success and failure in mentally retarded and normal children. *Journal of Personality, 29,* 303–320.

Brandtstaedter, J. (1984). Personal and social control over development: Some implications of an action perspective in life-span developmental psychology. In P. B. Baltes & O. G. Brim, Jr. (Eds.), *Life-span development and behavior* (Vol. 6, pp. 1–32). New York: Academic Press.

Braun, C. (1976). Teacher expectation: Socio-psychological dynamics. *Review of Educational Research, 46,* 185–212.

Brim, O. G., Jr. (1974, September). *The sense of personal control over one's life.* Paper presented at the meeting of the American Psychological Association, New Orleans.

Brim, O. G., Jr., & Kagan, J. (1980). Constancy and change: A view of the issues. In O. G. Brim, Jr. & J. Kagan (Eds.), *Constancy and change in human development.* Cambridge, MA: Harvard University Press.

Chapman, M., & Skinner, E. A. (1985). Action in development—development in action. In M. Frese & J. Sabini (Eds.), *Goal-directed behavior: The concept of action in psychology* (pp. 199–213). Hillsdale, NJ: Lawrence Erlbaum Associates.

Chapman, M., & Skinner, E. A. (1989). Children's agency beliefs, cognitive performance and conceptions of effort and ability: Interaction of individual and developmental differences. *Child Development, 60,* 1229–1238.

Chapman, M., Skinner, E. A., & Baltes, P. B. (1985, July). Children's current beliefs and cognition as a self-organizing system. In E. A. Skinner & J. P. Connell (Convenors), *Theoretical perspectives on the development of self-regulation.* Symposium presented at the Meetings of the International Society for the Study of Behavioral Development, Tours, France.

Chapman, M., Skinner, E. A., & Baltes, P. B. (in press). Interpreting correlations between children's perceived control and cognitive performance: Control, agency, or means–ends beliefs? *Developmental Psychology.*

Compas, B. E. (1987). Coping with stress during childhood and adolescence. *Psychological Bulletin, 101,* 393–403.

Connell, J. P. (1985). A new multidimensional measure of children's perceptions of control. *Child Development, 56,* 1018–1041.

Connell, J. P. (in press). Context, self and action: A motivational analysis of self-system processes across the life-span. In D. Cicchetti (Ed.), *The self in transition: Infancy to childhood.* Chicago: University of Chicago Press.

Connell, J. P., & Furman, W. (1984). Conceptual and methodological considerations in the study of transition. In R. Emde & R. Harmon (Eds.). *Continuities and discontinuities in development* (pp. 153–173). New York: Plenum Press.

Covington, M., & Omelich, C. (1979). Effort: The double-edged sword in school achievement. *Journal of Educational Psychology, 71,* 169–182.

Covington, M. V., & Omelich, C. L. (1985). Ability and effort valuation among failure-avoiding and failure-accepting students. *Journal of Educational Psychology, 77,* 446–459.

Crandall, V. C., & Crandall, B. W. (1983). Maternal and childhood behaviors as antecedents of internal–external control perceptions in young adulthood. In H. M. Lefcourt (Ed.), *Research with the locus of control construct,* Vol. 2, *Developments and social problems* (pp. 53–103). New York: Academic Press.

Crandall, V. C., Katkovsky, W., & Crandall, V. J. (1965). Children's beliefs in their control of reinforcement in intellectual academic achievement behaviors. *Child Development, 36,* 91–109.

Crandall, V. C., & Linn, P. L. (1989, April). Children's achievement orientation: Sex differences, developmental trends, and emergence of motivational functions. In J. G. Nicholls (chair), *Achievement strivings, expectations, and values in the toddler to first grade years.* Symposium presented at the meetings of the Society for Research in Child Development, Kansas City.

deCharms, R. (1968). *Personal causation: The internal affective determinants of behavior.* New York: Academic Press.

Deci, E. L., & Ryan, R. M. (1985). *Intrinsic motivation and self-determination in human behavior.* New York: Plenum.

Dweck, C. S. (1975). The role of expectations and attributions in the alteration of learned helplessness. *Journal of Personality and Social Psychology, 31,* 674–685.

Dweck, C. S., & Elliot, E. S. (1983). Achievement motivation. In P. H. Mussen (Ed.), *Handbook of child psychology* (4th Ed., Vol. 4., pp. 643–691). New York: Wiley.

Dweck, C. S., & Leggett, E. L. (1987). A social-cognitive approach to motivation and personality. *Psychological Review, 95,* 256–273.

Fincham, F. D., & Cain, K. M. (1986). Learned helplessness in humans: A developmental analysis. *Developmental Review, 6,* 301–333.

Fincham, F., Hokoda, A., & Sanders, R., Jr. (1989). Learned helplessness, test anxiety, and academic achievement: A longitudinal analysis. *Child Development, 60,* 138–145.

Findley, M. J., & Cooper, H. M. (1983). Locus of control and academic achievement: A literature review. *Journal of Personality and Social Psychology, 44,* 419–427.

Folkman, S. (1984). Personal control and stress and coping processes: A theoretical analysis. *Journal of Personality and Social Psychology, 46*(4), 839–852.

Foersterling, F. (1985). Attributional retraining: A review. *Psychological Bulletin, 98,* 495–512.

Graham, S. (1984). Communicating sympathy and anger to Black and White children: The cognitive (attributional) consequences of affective cures. *Journal of Personality and Social Psychology, 47,* 40–54.

Gunnar, M. R. (1980). Contingent stimulation: A review of its role in early development. In S. Levine & H. Ursin (Eds.), *Coping and health* (pp. 101–119). New York: Plenum.

Gurin, P., & Brim, O. G., Jr. (1984). Change in self in adulthood: The example of sense of control. In P. B. Baltes & O. G. Brim, Jr. (Eds.), *Life-span development and behavior* (Vol. 6, pp. 282–334). New York: Academic Press.

Harris, D. B. (Ed.). (1957). *The concept of development: An issue in the study of human behavior.* Minneapolis: University of Minnesota Press.

Harter, S. (1983). Developmental perspectives on the self system. In E. M. Hetherington (Ed.), *Handbook of child psychology.* (Vol. 4): *Socialization, personality, and social development.* New York: Wiley.

Harter, S., & Connell, J. P. (1984). A model of the relationships among children's academic achievement and their self-perceptions of competence, control, and motivational orientation. In J. Nicholls (Ed.), *The development of achievement motivation* (pp. 219–250). Greenwich, CT: JAI Press.

Hartup, W. W. (1983). Peer groups. In M. Hetherington (Ed.), *Handbook of Child Psychology,* (Vol. 4, 4th Ed., pp. 103–196). New York: Wiley.

Heckhausen, H. (1977). Achievement motivation and constructs: A cognitive model. *Motivation and Emotion, 1*(4), 283–329.

Heckhausen, H. (1984). Emergent achievement behavior: Some early developments. In J. G. Nicholls (Ed.), *The development of achievement motivation.* Greenwich, CT: JAI Press.

Heider, F. (1958). *The psychology of interpersonal relations.* New York: Wiley.

Kimble, G. A. (1989). Psychology from the standpoint of a generalist. *American Psychologist, 44,* 491–499.

Lachman, M. E. (1986). Personal control in later life: Stability, change, and cognitive correlates. In M. M. Baltes & P. B. Baltes (Eds.), *The psychology of control and aging* (pp. 207–236). Hillsdale, NJ: Lawrence Erlbaum Associates.

Lamb, M. E., & Easterbrooks, M. A. (1981). Individual differences in parental sensitivity: Some thoughts about origins, components, and consequences. In M. E. Lamb & L. R. Sherrod (Eds.), *Infant social cognition: Empirical and theoretical considerations* (pp. 127–153). Hillsdale, NJ: Lawrence Erlbaum Associates.

Lazarus, R. S., & Folkman, S. (1984). *Stress, appraisal, and coping.* New York: Springer.

Lefcourt, H. (1981). *Research with the locus of control construct.* Vol. 1: *Assessment methods.* New York: Academic Press.

Lefcourt, H. (1983). *Research with the locus of control construct.* Vol. 2: *Developments and social problems.* New York: Academic Press.

Lerner, R. M. (1986). *Concepts and theories of human development* (2nd. ed.). New York: Random House.

Lerner, R. M., & Busch–Rossnagel, N. A. (Eds.). (1981). *Individuals as producers of their development: A life-span perspective.* New York: Academic Press.

Levenson, H. (1973). Perceived parental antecedents of internal, powerful others, and chance locus of control orientations. *Developmental Psychology, 9,* 260–265.

Lynch, M., & Wellborn, J. G. (1989, April). *Patterns of relatedness in maltreated and matched control children: A look at mother–child relationships beyond infancy in high-risk groups.* Meetings of the Society for Research in Child Development, Kansas City, MO.

Miller, A. (1985). A developmental study of the cognitive basis of performance impairment after failure. *Journal of Personality and Social Psychology, 49,* 529–538.

Nicholls, J. G. (1978). The development of the concepts of effort and ability, perception of academic attainment, and the understanding that difficult tasks require more ability. *Child Development, 49,* 800–814.

Nicholls, J. G. (1984). Achievement motivation: Conceptions of ability, subjective experience, task choice, and performance. *Psychological Review, 91,* 328–346.

Nicholls, J. G., & Miller, A. T. (1984). Development and its discontents: The differentiation of the concept of ability. In J. G. Nicholls (Ed.), *The development of achievement motivation.* Greenwich, CT: JAI Press.

Nicholls, J. G., & Miller, A. T. (1985). Differentiation of the concepts of luck and skills. *Developmental Psychology, 21,* 76–82.

Nolen–Hoeksema, S., Girgus, J. S., & Seligman, M. E. P. (1986). Learned helplessness in children: A longitudinal study of depression, achievement, and explanatory style. *Journal of Personality and Social Psychology, 51,* 435–442.

Nowicki, S., & Strickland, B. R. (1973). A locus of control scale for children. *Journal of Consulting and Clinical Psychology, 40,* 148–155.

Peterson, C., & Seligman, M. E. P. (1984). Causal explanations as a risk factor for depression: Theory and evidence. *Psychological Review, 91*(3), 347–374.

Piaget, J. (1930). *The child's conception of physical causality.* London: Routledge & Kegan Paul. Original work published 1927)

Piaget, J. (1975). *The child's conception of the world.* Totowa, NJ: Littlefield-Adams. (Original work published 1926)

Piaget, J. (1976). *The grasp of consciousness: Action and concept in the young child.* Cambridge, MA: Harvard University Press.

Rholes, W. S., Blackwell, J., Jordan, C., & Walters, C. (1980). A developmental study of learned helplessness. *Developmental Psychology, 16,* 616–624.

Riegel, K. F. (1975). Toward a dialectical theory of development. *Human Development, 18,* 50–64.

Riksen-Walraven, J. M. (1978). Effects of caregiver behavior on habituation rate and self-efficacy in infants. *International Journal of Behavioral Development, 1,* 105–130.

Rothbaum, F., Weisz, J. R., & Snyder, S. S. (1982). Changing the world and changing the self: A two-process model of perceived control. *Journal of Personality and Social Psychology, 42,*(1), 5–37.

Rotter, J. B. (1954). *Social learning and clinical psychology.* Englewood Cliffs, NJ: Prentice–Hall.

Rotter, J. B. (1966). Generalized expectancies for internal versus external control of reinforcement. *Psychological Monographs, 80*(Whole No. 609).

Ryan, R. M., Connell, J. P., & Deci, E. L. (1985). A motivational analysis of self-determination and self-regulation in education. In C. Ames & R. E. Ames (Eds.), *Research on motivation in education: The classroom milieu.* New York: Academic Press.

Seligman, M. E. P. (1975). *Helplessness: On depression, development, and death.* San Francisco: Freeman.

Shaklee, H., & Mims, M. (1981). Development of rule use in judgments of covariation between events. *Child Development, 52,* 317–325.

Skinner, E. A. (1985). Action, control judgments, and the structure of control experience. *Psychological Review, 92,* 39–58.

Skinner, E. A. (1986). The origins of young children's perceived control: Caregiver contingent and sensitive behavior. *International Journal of Behavioral Development, 9,* 359–382.

Skinner, E. A. (1989). *Age differences in the structure of perceived control during middle childhood: Implications for developmental conceptualizations and research.* Unpublished manuscript, Max Planck Institute for Human Development and Education, West Berlin.

Skinner, E. A. (in press). What causes success and failure in school and friendship? Developmental differentiation of children's beliefs across middle childhood. *International Journal of Behavioral Development.*

Skinner, E. A., & Chapman, M. (1984). Control beliefs in an action perspective. *Human Development, 27,* 129–132.

Skinner, E. A., & Chapman, M. (1987). One resolution of a developmental paradox: How can perceived internality increase, decrease, and remain the same across middle childhood? *Developmental Psychology, 23,* 44–48.

Skinner, E. A., Chapman, M., & Baltes, P. B. (1988a). Beliefs about control, means–ends, and agency: A new conceptualization and its measurement during childhood. *Journal of Personality and Social Psychology, 54,* 117–133.

Skinner, E. A., Chapman, M., & Baltes, P. B. (1988b). Children's beliefs about control, means–ends, and agency: Development differences during middle childhood. *International Journal of Behavioral Development, 11,* 369–388.

Skinner, E. A., & Connell, J. P. (1986). Control understanding: Suggestions for a developmental framework. In M. M. Baltes & P. B. Baltes (Eds.), *The psychology of control and aging* (pp. 35–69). Hillsdale, NJ: Erlbaum.

Skinner, E. A., Connell, J. P., & Wellborn, J. G. (1989). *A longitudinal study of children's beliefs about strategies and capacities: A model of context, self, and action.* Unpublished manuscript, University of Rochester, Rochester, NY.

Skinner, E. A., Wellborn, J. G., & Connell, J. P. (in press). What it takes to do well in school and whether I've got it: The role of perceived control in children's engagement and school achievement. *Journal of Educational Psychology.*

Stipek, D. J. (1984). Young children's performance expectations: Logical analysis or wishful thinking? In M. Haehr (Ed.), *Advances in motivation and achievement* (Vol. 3, pp. 33–56). Greenwich, CT: JAI Press.

Stipek, D. J., & Weisz, J. R. (1981). Perceived personal control and academic achievement. *Review of Educational Research, 51,* 101–137.

Vito, R. C., & Connell, J. P. (1988). *A longitudinal study of at-risk high school students: A theory based description and intervention.* Unpublished manuscript. University of Rochester, Rochester, NY.

Wachs, T. D. (1977). The optimal stimulation hypothesis and early development: Anybody got a match? In I. C. Uzgiris & F. Weizman (Eds.), *The structuring of experience,* (pp. 153–178). New York: Plenum.

Watson, J. S. (1979). Perception of contingency as a determinant of social responsiveness. In E. B. Thoman (Ed.), *Origins of the infant's social responsiveness* (pp. 33–64). Hillsdale, NJ: Lawrence Erlbaum Associates.

Weiner, B. (1979). A theory of motivation for some classroom experiences. *Journal of Educational Psychology, 71,* 3–25.

Weiner, B. (1985). An attributional theory of achievement motivation and emotion. *Psychological Review, 92,* 548–573.

Weisz, J. R. (1980). Developmental change in perceived control: Recognizing noncontingency in the laboratory and perceiving it in the world. *Developmental Psychology, 16,* 385–390.

Weisz, J. R. (1981). Illusory contingency in children in the state fair. *Developmental Psychology, 17,* 481–489.

Weisz, J. R. (1983). Can I control it? The pursuit of veridical answers across the life-span. In P. B. Baltes & O. G. Brim (Eds.), *Life-span development and behavior* (Vol. 5, pp. 233–300). New York: Academic Press.

Weisz, J. R. (1986). Contingency and control beliefs as predictors of psychotherapy outcomes among children and adolescents. *Journal of Consulting and Clinical Psychology, 54,* 789–795.

Weisz, J. R., & Cameron, A. M. (1985). Individual differences in the student's sense of control. In C. Ames & R. E. Ames (Eds.), *Research on motivation and education: The classroom milieu* (Vol. 2, pp. 93–140). New York: Academic Press.

Weisz, J. R., & Stipek, D. J. (1982). Competence, contingency, and the development of perceived control. *Human Development, 25,* 250–281.

Wellborn, J. G., Connell, J. P., & Skinner, E. A. (1989). The Student Perceptions of Control Questionnaire (SPOCQ). University of Rochester, Rochester, NY.

White, R. W. (1959). Motivation reconsidered: The concept of competence. *Psychological Review, 66,* 297–333.

6 Learning to Love: Mechanisms and Milestones

Everett Waters
Kiyomi Kondo-Ikemura
German Posada
State University of New York at Stony Brook
John E. Richters
National Institute of Mental Health

The central questions in any developmental analysis are "What develops?", "What is the course of development?", and "What are the mechanisms of change?" Highlighting seemingly purposeful and context sensitive secure base behavior that organizes attachment relationships, Bowlby (1958) defined attachment as an emotional bond that ties the child to one or a few figures across time and space. He described its development in terms of emerging preference for one or a few figures, the onset of secure base behavior, and a change in the representation of attachment figures during the childhood transition from sensorimotor to representational thought.

Here we re-examine Bowlby's developmental outline with an eye toward providing finer detail, incorporating traditional mechanisms of learning into attachment theory, and placing greater emphasis on the parent's contribution to the organization of attachment behavior throughout childhood. We also emphasize the role of self awareness, self-observation, and self-consistency in attachment development and in ties between attachment and socialization outcomes. Although most questions regarding attachment and the self are unresolved (e.g. Connell & Wellborn, this volume; Sroufe, in press), the processes of self-observation and "informal inference" implicated here in developing attachment relationships are also central to cognitive theories of the self (e.g. Epstein, 1973, 1980, this volume). This common thread provides important hints about the role of attachment in the development of one's *self theory*.

PARADIGMS AND PERSPECTIVES

Differences among paradigms in personality research are nowhere more evident than in competing perspectives on the development of attachment relationships. Freud (e.g., 1949) viewed the infant's tie to its mother in terms of drive reduction and emerging mental structures that channel and transform instinctual drives. Social learning theorists (e.g., Maccoby & Masters, 1972) and behaviorists (e.g., Gewirtz, 1972) saw only discrete behaviors, displayed differentially toward the mother, and maintained by her attention and responsiveness. To date, neither of these views has produced powerful assessment tools or sustained productive research programs.

John Bowlby's (1958, 1960, 1969) ethological/control systems theory of attachment was founded upon important new insights into what develops. Instead of working to reconcile traditional perspectives, Bowlby offered a new paradigm that comprehended both affective and behavioral facets of attachment. His approach also made sense of previously inexplicable fears in infancy and of attachment behavior's sensitivity to infant state and the state of the environment. The assessment paradigms and research programs that have prospered under the rubric of Bowlby's "ethological theory" attest to the validity of his insights into what develops.

In Bowlby's view, attachment is a tie that binds individuals together over time and space. A person comes to use another as a secure base from which to explore and as a haven of safety. This "secure base phenomenon" is regulated by a behavior control system that emerges during the first year of life and influences the organization of affect, cognition, and behavior in attachment relationships across the lifespan. According to Bowlby, the attachment control system is analogous to control systems that regulate complex adaptive behavior patterns in other species. Both biological biases in human learning abilities and social experience guide its development. Bowlby's emphasis on the secure base phenomenon has led to powerful attachment measures and sustained bountiful research programs. As we shall see, it also suggests a great deal about the role of close social relationships in the origin and development of the self.

Bowlby summarized the developmental course of attachment behavior and the underlying control system in terms of four stages: (1) undiscriminating social responsiveness, (2) focused responsiveness to one or a few figures, (3) the emergence of secure base behavior, and (4) the transformation of secure base behavior into a goal-corrected partnership with the primary caregiver. This description has organized attachment research for over 20 years. Early research concentrated on infant-mother interaction and the development of focussed responsiveness. In the mid-1970s, theory and research concentrated on individual differences in secure base behavior. More recently, attention has turned to attachment beyond the secure base period (e.g., Ricks, 1986; Main & Kaplan, 1989; Parkes & Stevenson-Hinde, 1985).

After 2 decades of theoretical and descriptive work, we know a great deal about what develops and about the developmental course of early attachment relationships. The long deferred question remains "What are the mechanisms of change?" Indeed, the most pressing issue in contemporary attachment theory is to describe complete causal pathways to explain well-replicated correlations between early care and subsequent patterns of secure base behavior, and between secure base behavior in infancy and subsequent behavior with parents and siblings, social competence, self esteem, and behavior problems.

Correlational data played a critical role in the initial phases of attachment research when we were asking how best to define the construct, checking the broad outlines of attachment theory against empirical data, and trying to translate Bowlby's theory into valid and economical measurement procedures. Are patterns of secure base behavior stable? Are they related to socialization or only to behavior in relationships? Does temperament offer an alternative to the control system interpretation of secure base behavior? This is the essence of construct validation. Although definition and description must precede explanation, they do not replace it. Eventually, we have to *explain* the correlations that helped us define the parameters of our construct.

FROM DRIVES TO CONTROL SYSTEMS

Freud's Contribution

We need only review Freud's last work, *Abriss der psychoanalyse* (1949; An outline of psychoanalysis), to realize that developmental psychologists are still working from the agenda he set. In this brief work he touches upon personality, the self, gender roles, social competence, emotion, prosocial and antisocial behavior, social cognition, and moral judgment; and on processes involving reinforcement, punishment, imitation, memory and information processing skills, family interaction, and parenting.

Freud's descriptive insights about human attachment include the following:

1. An individual's attachment to another cannot be equated with the amount of overt behavior toward that person or with the amount or duration of protest that follows separation.
2. Loss of a loved one is always painful and is a major challenge to an individual's adaptive resources.
3. Attachment is never given up voluntarily or completely.
4. Grief and mourning are processes rather than behavior and they serve an adaptive function for the individual who experiences a significant loss.
5. The process of grieving is not concluded when the crying stops.

6. Human infants lead an exceedingly complex cognitive and emotional life.
7. Early attachment relationships are prototypes of later love relationships.

It is important to distinguish Freud's genuine insights about human attachments from the psychodynamic metaphors and models used to express them and knit them together. Although psychodynamic formulations have almost no explanatory role in contemporary theory and research, Freud's descriptive insights remain at the heart of contemporary attachment theory. Having set so much of our current agenda, Freud, like Piaget, will be long remembered for his descriptive insights, even if cognitive and brain sciences eventually replace the motivational theory that tied them together. Genuine descriptive insights remain, even after explanatory devices and methods tied to particular moments in the history of science are replaced by more adequate ones. As in the work of so many grand theorists, there is genius merely in defining what the question should be and in recognizing what the answers might be like.

Bowlby's Contributions

If we were to organize John Bowlby's many contributions to psychiatry, psychoanalysis, and the behavioral sciences into just a few categories, we might include (1) his role in preserving Freud's insights about attachment, (2) his own contributions to attachment theory, (3) the role he has played in translating attachment theory into practice, and (4) the role he, working in tandem with Mary Ainsworth, played in the training and development of scholars who have advanced attachment theory and research during the last 20 years. For our present purposes, Bowlby's role in preserving Freud's insights about attachment and his own contributions to attachment theory are of primary importance.

Beginning in the early 1960s, the mainstream in developmental psychology shifted from grand theory toward methodological rigor and empiricism. Bowlby recognized that a genuine paradigm clash was in progress and that psychoanalytic insights might be discarded wholesale. In a series of early papers (Bowlby 1958, 1960, 1962) he identified key attachment-related insights in psychoanalytic theory, noted that they were not inextricably tied to Freud's mental energy and drive reduction models, and preserved them by providing an alternative motivational model based on ethological and control systems theories of the day. Were it not for Bowlby's timely intercession, the past 20 years might have been spent rediscovering rather than building upon Freud's insights.

In addition to preserving important psychoanalytic insights about attachment, Bowlby contributed insights of his own. First, he emphasized that the infant-mother relationship is a genuine attachment not merely an infantile precursor. He also emphasized that infants' reactions to separation and loss are more than mere cries. They reflect the same grief and mourning process experienced by adults.

The similarity of infant separation responses to phases of adult grief and mourning was subsequently documented in several striking films by Bowlby's colleagues, Joyce and James Robertson.

An Ethological Control-systems Analysis of Attachment Motivation. Bowlby's goal in developing an ethological/control systems view of attachment was to replace Freud's drive reduction model of motivation with one that was better grounded in contemporary biological theory and research. Many telling criticisms leveled at psychoanalytic theory focussed on Freud's motivational models. Bowlby recognized that only an alternative motivational model could preserve Freud's genuine insights about emotional bonds in infancy and adulthood. Control-systems theory allowed Bowlby to emphasize the seemingly motivated and purposeful organization of infant attachment behavior without attributing to the infant sophisticated cognitive abilities or intentions.

In brief, Bowlby proposed that human infants' behavior toward their primary caregivers is under the control of an attachment behavior control system. He described this control system as a neurally based feedback system that integrated several functions:

1. *defining a set goal* that the system uses as a criterion for activation of adaptive behaviors. In the case of attachment, Bowlby defined the goal as a degree of proximity or access to the caregiver. This set goal can be modified in the short term in response to contextual factors and, in the long term, in response to experience with a particular caregiver.
2. *collating information* about the infant's previous experience with the caregiver, the infant's state, the caregiver's location and activities, interesting objects and events in the environment, special cues to danger (e.g., looming objects, darkness, novelty.)
3. *comparing information* about the current state of the infant, caregiver, and environment with the criterion defined by the set goal.
4. *activating behavior patterns* that correct deviations from the set goal and maintain the infant within the bounds defined by the set goal. Critical behaviors here include crying, approach, following, clinging, and exploration.

Descriptively, the control system is said to maintain a balance between attachment behavior (proximity seeking) and exploratory behavior. As with any control system, the key parameter of individual differences is not the quantity of any particular behavioral output but the efficiency and success with which the behavioral system maintains the infant within the parameters defined by the set goal.

Bowlby cited a wide range of examples from ethology to establish that control system models were respectable and powerful concepts in behavioral biology. He also discussed at length evidence that natural selection could account for the presence of such control systems in animal nervous systems. The following postulates outline the logic of Bowlby's analysis:

1. Humans and their ancestors were under considerable pressure from predators in the environment in which key characteristics of our species evolved.
2. Maintaining a degree of proximity or access to adults reduces the likelihood of depredation.
3. Species specific behavior patterns and learning abilities have genetic substrates whose representation in a population is influenced by the effects of the behavior pattern or learning ability on reproductive success.
4. As a result of the selective advantages conferred by certain behavior patterns and learning abilities, an attachment control system is part of our primate evolutionary endowment.
5. The organization of the attachment behavioral system is encoded in the underlying plan of the human nervous system and becomes readily available when perceptual and motor systems mature, if the infant experiences patterns of care and living circumstances that are not entirely foreign to our species. Bowlby used the term "average expectable environment."
6. The attachment behavioral system is sensitive to a variety of prepotent environmental and infant state variables that would have been associated with increased risk of depredation in the environment in which key human characteristics evolved ("the environment of evolutionary adaptedness"). These include darkness, separation from adults, and unfamiliar settings or individuals, as well as illness, hunger, or exhaustion. In this respect, many aspects of contemporary infant behavior can only be understood in terms of the environment to which they are adapted.
7. Because the attachment control system requires experience in order to become operational, differences in early experience can lead to different operating characteristics in different individuals. These tend to be stable over time and are important contributors to individual differences in adjustment and personality. They may change in response to experience in significant relationships or experience in psychotherapy.

Bowlby's Developmental Model

Bowlby (1969, ch. 14) described four phases in the development of infant-mother attachment and mentioned mechanisms that might underlie developments within and across phases. The model is summarized in Fig. 6.1.

Phase 1. The first phase in Bowlby's model is a brief period of undiscriminating responsiveness. His analysis is much like Piaget's in that he describes

The Development of Attachment:
Bowlby's Four Phase Model

Phase	Age (months)
1. Non-focussed orienting and signaling	(0-3)
2. Focus on one or more figure(s)	(3-6)
3. Secure base behavior	(6-24)
4. Goal-corrected partnership	(24-30 ->)

Bowlby (1969), pp. 266-267.

FIG. 6.1. The development of attachment: Bowlby's four phase model.

innate behavior patterns as the foundations upon which later organized behavior develops and proposes that interaction with the environment is critical. The notion that attachment arises from interaction rather than emerging fully formed is important both in demystifying the processes involved and in accounting for the adaptedness of attachment behavior.

The mechanisms Bowlby mentions include reflex patterns of grasping, crying, sucking, and other neonatal adaptations that clearly serve a variety of non-attachment related functions. The common element they share is in increasing the time the mother spends with the infant. Woodson, Shepherd, and Chamberline (1981; see also, Woodson 1983) demonstrated a remarkable relationship between infant crying, maternal holding, infant body temperature, and bilirubin metabolism that clearly illustrates the multiple functions of these behaviors as well as the interplay between behavior and physiology that must have played a role in their evolution. Mechanisms that might be more narrowly adapted to serve the development of attachment have received less attention.

In brief, Bowlby's view is that attachment arises from *interaction,* but not from interaction alone. From the beginning, attachment involves the interplay of *experience* and *species specific biases in learning abilities.* Surprisingly, very little has been said about what these biases might be.

Phase 2. The second phase in Bowlby's model describes a period of differential responsiveness and focusing on one or a few figures. Bowlby mentions an in-built bias to orient toward certain classes of stimuli, exposure learning, and an in-built bias to approach that which is familiar as potentially relevant mechanisms underlying this process. Interaction with a parent providing species typical patterns of care is also critical.

On the face of it, it would seem difficult to disentangle the contributions of biases in infant learning abilities, the structure of parental behavior, and infant cognitive processes to the infant's focusing on one or a few figures. Bowlby does stipulate, for example, that the emergence of attachment depends on the infant's encountering patterns of care that are coadapted to the attachment behavioral system. He refers to this as the "*average expectable environment,*" the caretaking environment that is taken for granted in the design of the attachment behavioral system. Underlying processes and limits on an infant's ability to establish concurrent focal relationships with more than one figure have not been examined in detail.

Phase 3. The centerpiece in Bowlby's model is, of course, his description of the infant's tendency to maintain proximity to a focal figure through locomotion and signaling, which Ainsworth subsequently designated the *secure base phenomenon.* This brilliant descriptive insight concerning the nature of the child's tie to its parent allowed Bowlby to highlight the apparently purposeful organization of infant attachment behavior without invoking drive concepts and without attributing goals or other cognitive guidance that might simply have replaced one bit of magic with another. Or was it simply one bit of magic replacing another?

This is the only point at which evolutionary theory plays a critical role in Bowlby's theory. The argument is this: Attachment arises from interaction between an infant with certain biases in its learning abilities and an average expectable environment (i.e., responsive mother). The biases in infant learning abilities, taken with the expectable environment, essentially guarantee that the attachment behavioral system will be put together according to the species specific pattern.

Bowlby proposed that these biases evolved by natural selection. This was a perfectly reasonable hypothesis, if it could be supported by evidence that specific biases in learning abilities can indeed evolve. Research on imprinting in precocial birds offered clear and well-studied examples of species specific biases in socially significant learning abilities that can plausibly be attributed to evolution. The point here is not that imprinting is a mechanism involved in human infant attachment. Imprinting is cited merely as an example of socially significant learning that had been shaped by evolution. Any example of biases in socially significant learning abilities would have done as well. In retrospect, it is unfortunate that, in addition to illustrating biases in a species learning abilities, locomotor imprinting also resembles following in human infant attachment. This had led to misinterpretations of Bowlby's argument and to misinterpretations of the role ethology plays in his work.

The reference to evolution at this point in Bowlby's theory serves a very specific role—that is, to tie the biases in learning abilities that underlie the development of a behavioral control system to a specific mechanism. Citing a well understood mechanism that is neither drive related nor tied to prevailing contingencies of reinforcement sets Bowlby's theory apart from those that preceded it. Beyond this, there is nothing inherently evolutionary, ethological, or biological about Bowlby's view of attachment. While the designation "ethological attachment theory" commemorates the influence of ethological theory and research on Bowlby's early thinking, it also leads to misapprehensions.

Note also that the theory does not depend on identifying predation or any other specific factor as *the* selective pressure that led to the biases in our learning abilities. The key is that attachment behavior is expected to enhance an individual's reproductive success and the success of its offspring. Predation is but one factor influencing this. Attachment behavior may also have helped maintain supervision and thus reduce the likelihood of accidents and injuries unrelated to predation. Moreover, its contributions to reproductive success may have changed during the course of primate evolution, ultimately contributing more as a precursor to the capacity for adult bonds and parental care than as an anti-predator strategy in infancy. This has been a source of naive and fruitless speculation that is more likely to discredit attachment theory than to add depth or clarity. There is every reason to be interested in the evolution of attachment behavior, but the issue is not central to Bowlby's analysis of relationships between early attachment and either later personality or later relationships.

As the theory stands today, it seems more appropriate to refer to it as the *control systems,* or even the *affective/cognitive control systems* perspective. If this were more widely appreciated, there might be fewer misapprehensions regarding the "biological" orientation of attachment theory; moreover, attachment theorists might feel more comfortable demurring when asked about the "adaptive significance" of specific attachment patterns.

Bowlby's analysis of the attachment control system clearly offers much more than one bit of magic to replace another. Indeed, if Bowlby finessed anything at all, it is not the role of biases in learning abilities, but rather the relationship between maternal care and the emergence of secure base behavior. Both Bowlby and Ainsworth initially worked toward a normative theory of attachment—that is, the emphasis was on the typical infant rather than on individual differences among infants. The individual differences orientation, which would have been a long term goal in any event, entered the work not as a substantive interest but, rather, as a methodological strategy. Ainsworth was interested in identifying patterns of maternal behavior that explained the emergence of secure base behavior. The obvious strategy would have been to identify maternal behaviors that distinguish between infants who do and do not become attached. However, virtually all home-reared infants become attached.

Because attachment arises from interaction, different histories of interaction should account in part for different outcomes among attached infants. That is, the maternal behaviors that best predict differences in attachment outcomes were viewed as more likely than others to play critical causal roles in the normative development of attachment. In effect, this correlational strategy assumes that information about differences among individuals can support (causal/developmental) inferences about changes within individuals over time. This assumption also underlies many popular designs in causal analysis and structural equation modeling.

In retrospect, we might criticize this strategy on several counts. Evidence that a particular maternal behavior is correlated with attachment outcomes is necessary but not sufficient evidence that it plays a causal role as attachment develops. We must also show that the maternal behavior precedes the attachment behavior and specify a plausible causal mechanism. Research designs that measure maternal behavior early and outcome variables later, assessing neither the outcome variable in the first phase nor the influence of maternal behavior at the final phase of the study, are not decisive on this point.

From an evolutionary perspective, we should note that traits critical to survival tend to be relatively uniform within a species and not particularly amenable to analysis in terms of individual differences. Insofar as attachment behavior evolved to reduce depredation, we could argue that its development would be highly canalized and primarily dependant upon maternal behaviors in which there is little diversity. In this light, the correlates of diversity would remain interesting but might not prove critical to the onset of attachment behavior.

More importantly, Ainsworth's longitudinal/correlational strategy reflects what might be called "the developmental bias," that is the tendency to look for the causes of behavior in the relatively remote past rather than in contemporaneous influences. Ainsworth's descriptions of maternal sensitivity, cooperation vs. interference are descriptive insights of the first order. Sensitive and responsive care are clearly the most consistent and significant interactive behavior correlates of later attachment outcomes. That the correlations between maternal sensitivity and secure base behavior are rarely greater than .40 is easily accounted for in terms of methodological and measurement issues. What is missing is a detailed explanation of how these particular patterns of maternal behavior would lead to the emergence of secure base behavior. Even a descriptive analysis, something similar to Piaget's descriptions of stage transitions in sensorimotor development, would be extremely useful. As it is, there seems to be a bit of magic here. Once recognized, however, the need to identify plausible causal mechanisms relating maternal behavior to secure base behavior is quite manageable.

Phase 4. Bowlby describes the fourth phase in attachment, which begins sometime after the second year, as the phase of "goal-corrected partnership." Very little is said about this phase, except that the infant is increasingly able and willing to take the mother's immediate goals and activities into account when the attachment behavioral system is active. In a word, attachment behavior becomes somewhat less peremptory under ordinary circumstances. Bowlby's description of this phase is clearly influenced by Piaget's description of changes at the end of the sensorimotor period of cognitive development. The only descriptive data we have on this stage are Marvin's (1977) dissertation, which shows relationships between attachment security, cooperation/self-control tasks when the mother is too busy to respond, and tolerance of separation.

In principle, this should be a critical part of Bowlby's developmental model: As the last phase in the sequence, it is the one that must interface with "mature" attachment patterns. Developing this interface is one of the critical tasks of attachment theory. Until it is accomplished, the Bowlby/Ainsworth perspective will remain vulnerable to the criticism that it is a theory of infant attachment, a theory of adult attachment, and a great deal in between left to the imagination.

Advantages and Limitations

In the early years, Bowlby's outline of development from interaction to goal-corrected partnership played an important definitional role in attachment theory. It clearly expressed his view that having biological underpinnings does not imply that attachment springs fully formed into the infant's behavioral repertoire or operates without environmental input. His view remains that attachment arises from interaction—biology conditions but does not determine the outcome.

Bowlby's four-phase model also serves as a framework within which to present his key descriptive insight—the control system analysis of infant attachment behavior. It also formalizes important insights about changes in attachment at the end of infancy. First, attachment does not decline along with separation protest. Second, the trend from sensorimotor to representational thought, detailed so eloquently in Piaget's work, has a parallel in the development of attachment and establishes early attachment as similar to, and even a prototype of, later love relationships.

Clearly, the four-phase model has served attachment theory very well. Important insights have been preserved. The view that attachment arises from interaction is well understood and empirical evidence has favored the secure base phenomenon as the better of several competing descriptions of attachment behavior. It should be noted, however, that we have not yet demanded a great deal of the theory. As we move from the descriptive phase of research into a more formal mode of hypothesis testing, weaknesses in the four-phase model become increasingly apparent.

First of all, Bowlby's developmental description abstracts attachment from the context of related behavioral and cognitive developments. This was useful when the attachment construct was less familiar; today we gain more by placing the secure base phenomenon in a broader context. Second, although control systems theorists have mentioned a number of mechanisms relevant to the development of attachment, they have not systematically followed the influence of specific mechanisms across the full course of attachment development. Moreover, they have overlooked some mechanisms, placed too much emphasis on very early influences, and placed relatively little emphasis on concurrent influences and traditional learning mechanisms.

Perhaps most importantly, attachment theorists in the Bowlby/Ainsworth tradition have placed little emphasis on the secure base figure's role in organizing and providing coherence and consistency to early secure base behavior. The observational/ethological underpinnings of the outline have not been updated since Ainsworth's early home studies in Baltimore. It is our impression that the current description underestimates how long it takes for secure base behavior to become consolidated and efficient and suggests a more discrete onset than actually occurs.

While highlighting that onset of secure base is not the final stage in attachment development, the goal-corrected partnership concept doesn't capture later development of attachment very well. Among other things, it seems easier to describe how the child's interests and goals diverge from the parents' than to identify common goals that are attachment-related and could serve as the basis for such a partnership. Thus, Triver's (1972, 1974, 1985) analyses of competing parent and child interests and the biology of parent-offspring conflict seem to provide a more powerful evolutionary perspective on developmental changes after infancy. Problems inherent in the goal-corrected partnership concept may, in part, account for the fact that it receives less attention in the second and third volumes of Bowlby's attachment series and has not been the starting point for recent advances in attachment theory and assessment. Main and Kaplan (1989), for example, develop their theory of adult working models from the secure base concept rather than the goal-corrected partnership.

Fortunately, the genuine insight at the core of attachment theory can be preserved in the context of alternative developmental descriptions. The undertaking here is clearly evolutionary rather than revolutionary, but it is directly relevant to the theme of this year's Minnesota Symposium. As we will see, an alternative view of developmental changes in attachment brings with it the prospect of closer coordination with self-related constructs.

It is in the nature of developmental research that the question "What develops?" recurs at different levels of analysis. At each turn, the course of development is described in more detail and questions about mechanisms of change come into sharper focus. Thus, research inspired by Bowlby's four-stage model has brought us to the threshold of new, finer-grained descriptions, better understanding of ties between attachment and developmental change in other domains, and a more comprehensive view of mechanisms underlying developmental changes in attachment behavior.

We propose recasting Bowlby's four-stage model in terms of the following developmental phases: (1) early dyadic interaction, (2) emergence of the self-other distinction, (3) self as object, (4) onset of secure base behavior in infancy, (5) declining separation protest, (6) consolidation of secure base behavior in early childhood, (7) emergence of a positive orientation toward parental socialization goals and internalization of family values in early childhood, and (8) a period in which a partnership of sorts develops around the task of maintaining communication and supervision once the child begins to be independent. The last of these phases reconceptualizes Bowlby's notion of the goal-corrected partnership, which in this analysis is placed in middle childhood and tied to socialization practices in specific cultures and social strata.

This description is more detailed than Bowlby's. It casts a broader descriptive net and emphasizes that attachment related development continues throughout childhood and beyond. It also suggests that secure base behavior (and thus any underlying control system) takes much longer to become organized and is much more dependent on supportive parental behavior than Bowlby suggested. Although these departures from Bowlby's original outline complicate the picture somewhat, they pave the way toward incorporating traditional learning mechanisms into attachment theory. This is a critical integration, one that psychoanalytic theory never achieved. Our presentation also highlights the role of cognitive/reflective processes in developmental change. Particular note is paid to processes of self-observation and to a process we term "informal inference." As a step toward understanding relationships between attachment and the self, we also consider the extent to which early attachment relationships provide important information during the formative stages of what Epstein (1973) has called one's theory of one's self.

A REVISED DEVELOPMENTAL ANALYSIS

Phase 1: From Interaction to Familiarity and Preference. The initial phase in our revised developmental analysis corresponds to the first phase in Bowlby's analysis. In the course of interaction and routine care, the infant acquires at least sensorimotor familiarity with one or a few primary caregivers. The first sensorimotor anticipations can be described as "islands of predictability" organized around interaction and caregiving routines. In the first weeks, these "islands of predictability" are too closely tied to behavior to be described as "expectations," but they are the foundations on which the infant builds expectations and expands its temporal horizons. From predictability grows preference.

One of Bowlby's most important insights was placing the origins of attachment this early in infancy, long before secure base behavior emerges. Correlations between early care and later secure base behavior (e.g., Ainsworth, Blehar, Waters, & Wall, 1978) provide evidence for this insight. Nonetheless, they do not allow us to choose between alternative causal models. Attachment theorists have often interpreted these correlations as evidence that early care has a direct causal influence on later behavior. Such influences are not unimaginable: Direct effects of early experience on later behavior are well documented in ethological literature. In many instances, the critical environmental input is available only for a brief time and the effects may not be evident until maturation.

Although compelling, in several respects ethological data do not parallel early maternal care and secure base behavior in human infants. First, although the examples Bowlby cited are often complex, the behaviors are typically more stereotyped than secure base behavior in human infants. In addition, human infants interact with primary caregivers almost continuously throughout infancy and early childhood. Consequently, the correlational data are equally consistent with the hypothesis that early interaction predicts later interaction, and only the later having direct effects on secure base behavior. To decide this matter, we must first specify *in detail* what develops and then test hypotheses about proposed mechanisms of change. Figure 6.2 presents the first three phases of our revised developmental outline. Mechanisms are presented on the left and products on the right.

Mechanisms relevant to the development of familiarity, predictability, and preference in early infancy might include traditional mechanisms of learning, the type of contiguity learning often mentioned by Robert Cairns (e.g., 1972), less well known mechanisms that underlie species identification and preferences in mammals and birds (e.g. Roy, 1980), and perhaps species-specific biases in the infant's learning abilities. The last of these is central to Bowlby's theory as currently formulated. Among these biases affective response to contingency seems to be a biologically prepared response in human infants. However, it is not necessarily adapted specifically to the development of attachment relationships.

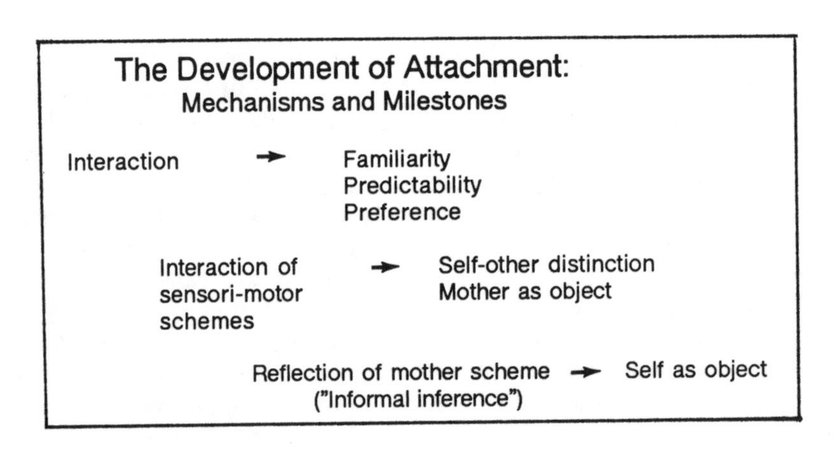

FIG. 6.2. Precursors of attachment: Mechanisms and milestones in early infancy.

Other biases in our learning abilities, such as the fact that affective contrast does not interfere with bonding at this age, may have evolved specifically to accommodate attachment formation. Unfortunately, the range of learning biases in play during attachment formation has never been catalogued or even examined in detail.

Far from being the general purpose learning machines envisioned in traditional learning theories, humans are peculiar learners indeed. Consider how easily we learn about sounds at the beginnings and ends of words, that we remember both the beginning and the end of a word list better than the middle, that we learn better if practice is spaced rather than concentrated in time, that we learn musical patterns so easily and have strong and memorable affective responses to them. Consider too how readily we learn to enjoy throwing things in the air. These and a host of other biases in our learning abilities are so distinctive that in the aggregate they distinguish our species from any other as well as any suite of physical of physiological traits.

With strong assertions about our learning abilities at the core of Bowlby's attachment theory, it is somewhat of a mystery that the task of uncovering and cataloguing attachment-related biases in human infant learning abilities has received so little attention. Here, for Bowlby's admirers and critics alike, is the prospect of a strong and dangerous test that goes to the foundations of the theory. What could be plainer than predicting that human infants are endowed with an array of learning biases that map so completely and so redundantly into the predictable caregiving environment as to guarantee the emergence of preference and eventually attachment *in virtually every case?*

Phase 2: Mother as the Intersection of Sensorimotor Schemes. The second phase in our proposed analysis begins with the coordination of sensorimotor schemes. In *The Origins of Intelligence,* Piaget described how an infant comes to recognize particular objects as occasions for practicing particular action patterns. As these action patterns become increasingly intercoordinated, objects become more discriminable and eventually become identified as objects distinct from the actions the infant can perform on them.

An attentive adult is, of course, the opportunity *par excellence* for sensorimotor expression, and none is encountered more often, at closer range, and in more modes than the primary caregiver. According to Piaget, objects are recognized first as suckables, lookables, and graspables, and then as suckable-lookables, lookable-graspables, etc. How much more vivid then must be the infant's view of a caregiver who is at once nutritively and nonnutritively suckable, graspable, lookable, listenable, and all of this in every combination? Suppose the caregiver is good at identifying infant signals, selecting responses, and delivering them in a timely manner (i.e., she is, in Ainsworth's terms, "sensitive"). Suppose further that she coordinates her behavior with the infant's ongoing behavior in a way that supports sensorimotor coordinations and establishes bridging ties from one moments activities to the next (i.e., again in Ainsworth's terms, she is "cooperative" rather than interfering). In all likelihood, such a partner will be more uniquely defined than inanimate objects and sooner recognized as existing independent of the infant's behavior (e.g., Bell 1970, Kaye, 1982; Winnicott, 1965). Here, in the context of early interaction, previously acquired familiarity, and preference, is the first true external object.

Perhaps there is nothing specific to attachment in all this. Our point is not that we should mark the onset of attachment here at 3–5 months-of-age. We should not; nonetheless, there are compelling reasons to present developing attachment relationships and emergence of the self-other distinction in a common developmental outline. First, each of the learning biases mentioned in the previous section is in full play here. Second, the infant has to recognize the caregiver as an object existing in its own right before the concept of attachment can make any sense at all. Third, and more importantly, we can see here the first example of a process that is influential throughout infancy and early childhood. The *caregiver* modifies the environment in order to serve as a *matrix* upon which the organization of the infant's behavior can play out. She does this both incidentally, as a consequence of entailing so many behavioral possibilities for the infant, and intentionally, by arranging objects and her own behavior in coordination with or anticipation of the infant's ongoing behavior. The caregiver provides much of the organization that is eventually consolidated in the infant's sensorimotor schemata and in the first conceptual catagories. This is the sense in which Winnicott (1965) observed that, without the mother's contribution, "there is no such thing as an infant."

Note especially that, from the infant's point of view, the experience is the same as if he had arranged it all himself—that is, attributing a major organizing role to the caregiver does not diminish in the child's eyes the significance of ongoing interactions. This is not to concede that the development of attachment is trivially under stimulus control, as proposed by traditional learning theorists. As we see shortly, the primary caregiver provides important elements of structure throughout the development of the first attachment relationship; indeed, she probably structures the infant's secure base behavior to a far greater degree and for a much longer time than attachment theory currently envisions.

Phase 3: Reflection of the Mother Scheme: Self as Object. As outlined earlier, the mother is the *aliment* to an entire suite of sensori-affective schemata. As these schemata become well practiced and intercoordinated, she becomes better and better defined, until she is recognized as an object in her own right. This is a significant step beyond the ability to recognize and discriminate that developed in Phase 2. Of course, to the sensorimotor infant there are no differences among objects upon which the same acts can be performed. The mother, however, is virtually unique in the range and complexity of intersections between her caretaking and play behavior and the infant's schemata.

Thus, just as the primary caregiver is defined as the intersection of the things she does toward the infant, there comes a moment in which the infant recognizes itself as the intersection of the schemes she directs at him—that is, "*She* is the common element in a vast array of sensori-affective contexts and experiences." Then by a process of "informal inference," for the first time, "*I* am the common element that ties her behavior together across these contexts and behaviors." Through a process perhaps akin to perceptual learning, the infant notices *itself* in the reflection of the experiences that define its mother as an independent object. In subsequent months, this *I* is mapped into a physical self-representation and eventually becomes evident in mirror self-recognition tests.

Piaget might have described this as a process of cognitive reorganization. Such explanations leavened his theory with an element of magic—about which it was just a trifle rude to ask. In contrast, we propose that the tendency to *observe one's own behavior* is a biological given, easily verified by empirical research. Thus, reference to informal inference has considerably more explanatory potential than Piaget's appeals to cognitive reorganization.

If such mechanisms are critical to developing attachment relationships, why are they left to cognitive/perceptual psychologists? Why haven't they attracted attention as key issues for attachment research? They are obviously relevant to the task of cataloguing species-specific learning abilities that support developing attachment relationships. A variety of factors seem to have contributed to this. It is at least partly an unintended consequence of elegant simplifications employed when Bowlby introduced his theory. Foremost among these devices is the four-phase model outlined earlier. The model clarifies a new paradigm by abstracting milestones in attachment behavior from the complex developmental context in which they are embedded.

Attention to mechanisms was also delayed by desire to complete basic descriptive research before analyzing processes and mechanisms of change in detail. The proper relationship between description and explanation is, of course, a matter of strategy, one that sharply divides research programs into construct- vs. operationist-oriented approaches. One limitation of traditional learning approaches has been the tendency to define attachment in certain terms in order that could be explained by a standard litany of mechanisms. In contrast, Bowlby and his construct-oriented colleagues view attachment as a biological phenomenon that had to be discovered and described on its own terms before we can know what needs to be explained.

Phase 4: Initiation of Secure Base Behavior. As indicated in Bowlby's model and confirmed in research employing the Ainsworth Strange Situation, secure base behavior is evident in most infants by 12 months. In the proposed analysis, however, the boundaries of the secure base phase are considerably wider than in the traditional model and the emergence and consolidation of secure base behavior are placed in separate phases.

Informal observations suggest that the rudiments of secure base behavior emerge within a few days or weeks of the first free crawling. It seems likely, therefore, that important cognitive substrates of secure base behavior are *available* and in some preliminary way even *organized,* before the onset of locomotion. These substrates might include, among other things, knowledge of the spatial layout of the home, expectations about mother's typical behavior and her responsiveness to infant signals, and at least some ideas about using her as a resource when interacting with interesting toys and objects.

Granting this, a problem remains. In a word, the notion that attachment arises from interaction doesn't explain exactly *how* sensitive care early in infancy could affect secure base behavior 6 months to 1 year later. Pressed to account for the relationship between maternal sensitivity and the behavioral details of secure base behavior, attachment theorists traditionally cite biases in the infant's learning abilities. Given certain biases in the infant's learning abilities, sensitive early care is said to initiate or catalyze the process by which components of the attachment control system fall into place. This is an interesting hypothesis with implications for behavioral development in general, and in view of the ethological literature it is not altogether implausible. It will not become compelling, however, until we have detailed research on biases in infant learning abilities and an empirically based catalogue of control system components.

The search for mechanisms that can have direct effects from early infancy into later infancy and toddlerhood should not be left to specialists in learning theory or to comparative psychologists. It should be placed at the top of the attachment agenda. We should not, however, construe this search as a critical test of Bowlby's attachment theory. Correlations between early care and later behavior are clearly replicable, as are relationships between attachment status in infancy and later adaptive behavior in many domains. The critical issue is to explain them. In this context, it matters not whether early care affects later behavior directly or merely predicts later care, which then proves to be the proximal cause. Although theorists in the Bowlby/Ainsworth tradition (e.g., Sroufe, Egeland, & Kreutzer, in press) have favored the former, any explanation combining biases in infant learning abilities, structure provided by the primary caregiver, and traditional learning mechanisms could be equally consistent with Bowlby's control systems model. The significance of these mechanisms is highlighted in Fig. 6.3, which continues our revised model through Bowlby's secure base stage.

Just as play and caregiving interactions can help organize sensorimotor schemes and provide information relevant to secure base behavior prior to the onset of locomotion, care and interaction with a sensitive caregiver continue to *provide* and *organize* information related to secure base behavior throughout infancy. In a sense then, early secure base behavior is closely tied to spatial and temporal patterns seen in early care. The infant knows the general outline of the "secure base strategy (or game)" before the onset of locomotion. Distance, accessibility, and caregiver responsiveness provide information that modifies affective state. Interaction, proximity, and contact can reestablish hedonic equilibrium. The infant learns that the key to the puzzle is to use the mother.

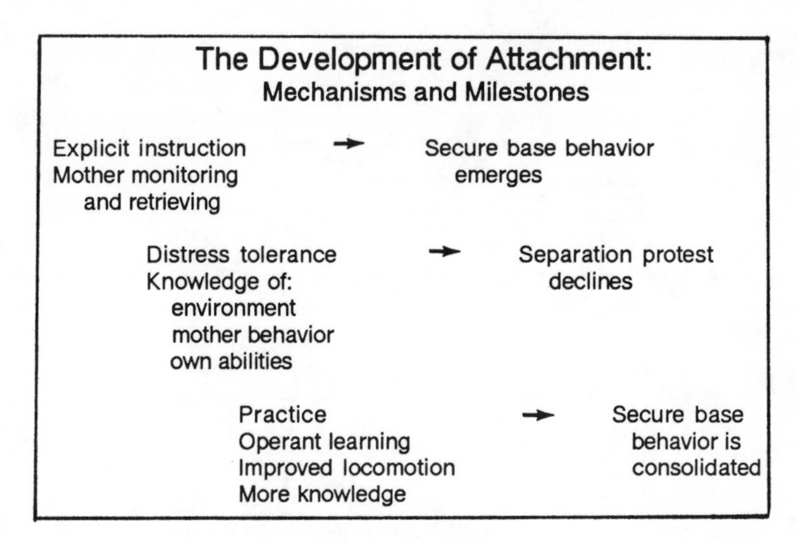

FIG. 6.3. Attachment and secure base behavior: Mechanisms and milestones in infancy and early childhood.

It matters little whether the distance between infant and caregiver is managed by coordinating infant communication with maternal locomotion or by the infant's own locomotion. This being the case, the rapid onset of secure base behavior is not surprising, nor is it strong evidence of biological priming; indeed, it requires little explanation at all. As in other domains, new skills are applied to familiar problems as soon as they are learned (i.e., without explicit instruction related to each potential application). When locomotion enters the infant's repertoire, it is promptly applied to the already familiar problem of balancing exploration and hedonic state. Biases in the infant's learning abilities may have to be invoked to explain (1) the speed and complexity of prelocomotor learning, (2) the infant's ability to monitor mother's access and responsiveness consistently, and (3) the selection and coordination of exploratory, proximity seeking, and contact related behaviors. These biases may account for the fact that eliciting and terminating conditions of attachment and exploratory behavior are so similar across cultures. The important task for attachment theorists is to detail these biases rather than merely alluding to them.

Although extensive pre-locomotor experience with organized patterns of maternal care may facilitate the onset of secure base behavior, some of our recent work suggests that *explicit instruction* plays a critical role in perfecting it—that is, secure base behavior is not merely learned, it is taught. Once we expect this, it is easy to confirm both in humans and nonhuman primates. Figure 6.4 shows a mother macaque teaching her infant to return to her. Our home observations of human infants suggests that similar behavior is common in our species as well. This should be recognized in attachment theory, and the learning mechanisms involved should be examined in detail.

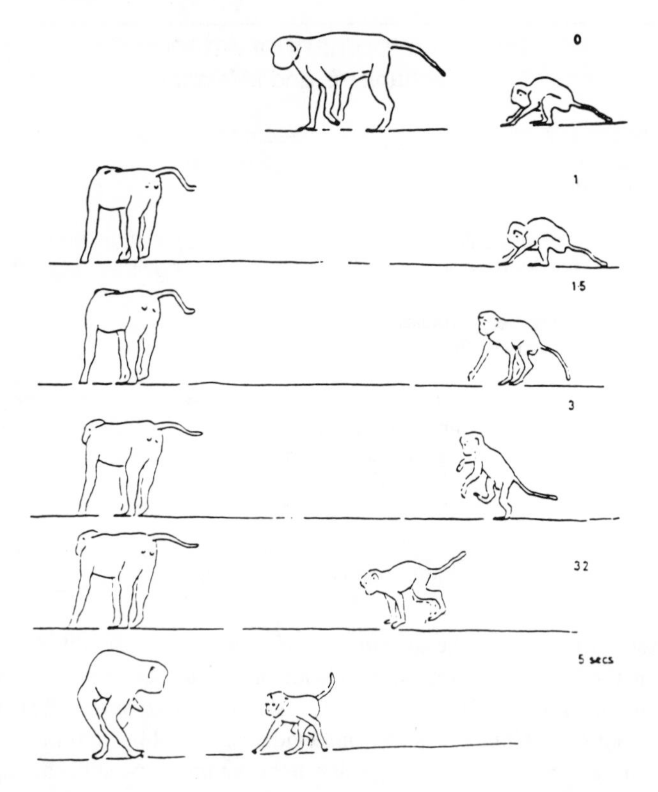

FIG. 6.4. The leaving game. Mother leaves, then pauses and calls or makes a partial return. Infant goes to mother. Mother repeats leaving sequence. Five second sequence drawn from film. From Hinde and Simpson (1975, p. 52).

Maternal influences on the organization of infant secure base behavior are not limited to explicit instruction and prompting. In a recent study of 24 female Japanese macaques and their infants at the South Texas Primate Observatory, Waters and Kondo-Ikemura (submitted for publication) examined the maternal behavior correlates of individual differences in infants' ability to use the mother as a secure base. Our goal was to determine whether there are strong links between infant attachment behavior and concurrent maternal behavior in free-ranging animals and to identify the domains in which these are most evident. To assess infant attachment security, we developed a 90-item Q-set similar to the Attachment Q-set used in our research on human infants. A Q-sort definition of the hypothetical infant macaque "most able to use its mother as a secure base" was used to assign each infant a score on attachment security. Each infant was observed for approximately 2 hours and then described by sorting the Q-sort items in terms of how characteristic they were of the infant in question. Items that described the infant well received higher score (maximum = 9). Items that were less characteristic or the opposite of the infant in question were assigned lower scores (minimum = 1). The correlation between the array of scores describing the infant and the array of scores describing the hypothetical most secure infant served as the infant's score on attachment security.

Maternal behavior was observed using a 90-item maternal behavior Q-set that focused on social interaction with other adults, caregiving, protection, interaction, supervision, communication, and other behaviors that mapped onto the items in the infant secure base Q-set. Two-hour observations of maternal behavior were obtained on a schedule insuring that maternal and infant Q-sorts were not obtained during the same time interval for any dyad.

As summarized in Table 6.1, there are indeed very strong correlations between infant security and concurrent maternal behavior in support of secure base behavior. Interestingly, the strongest concurrent correlates of infant secure base

TABLE 6.1
Correlations Between Maternal Behavior and Infant Security Scores Among Japanese Macaques[a]

Q-Set Item	*Pearson Correlation*
Does not allow other monkeys to hold infant (R)[b]	.64
Occupied in caretaking, to the exclusion of other activities	.64
Keeps infant closer for some time after unusual event has ceased	.55
Carries infant when moving from place to place (i.e., Doesn't just walk off)	.54
Devotes more time to infant than to older siblings	.53
Does not quickly become bored with caretaking (R)	.52
Accepts or tolerates infant using mother's tail or body during play	.50
Alert to subtle changes in the environment	.50
Does not hesitate to punish infant in appropriate circumstances	.47
Rarely changes attitude toward infant (R)	.46
Continues caretaking behavior even if infant (R) wiggles or gets annoyed	.45
Monitors infant's location and activities consistently	.44
Retrieves infant or drives adults away if infant approaches them (Esp. adult males or dominant females)	.44
Allows infant to leave in unfamiliar settings	.42
Recognizes infant signals of fear, etc.	.41
Allows infant to play with novel objects (R)	.40

Note. All values significant at $p < .05$ or less.

[a]For additional items related to maternal rank see Waters & Kondo-Ikemura (submitted).

[b](R) = Wording of original Q-set item is reversed in this table (as is the sign of the correlation coefficient) for clearer presentation.

behavior are related to the quality of maternal supervision. Infants who were most able to use their mothers as a secure base had mothers who supervised them closely and consistently, were persistent in caregiving, and were willing and powerful enough to defend them if they came into conflict with juveniles or other adults. Face-to-face interaction is not a primary mode of infant-mother interaction in this species, and there was little evidence that this or other behavior analogous to "sensitivity" in humans was related to the infants' secure base behavior. Indeed, by standards applied to human mothers, the mothers of even the more secure infant macaques could be remarkably insensitive and intrusive.

The salience of supervision and consistency in these data is attributable in part to the fact that these infant macaques were constantly at risk of serious injury from other macaques; nonetheless, the data clearly illustrate the fact that an infant's use of its mother as a secure base depends on her behaving as one. If she is predictable, consistent, powerful, and available, she provides a matrix or template around which the infant can organize exploration and effective attachment behavior. It is unnecessary to attribute all the structure of the secure base phenomenon to the attachment behavior control system; indeed it is most reasonable to imagine that the components of such a behavioral control system depend on a matrix of maternal behavior in order to become intercoordinated and begin to act as a system (Waters, 1981). Although mechanisms that might tie early care to later secure base behavior deserve attention in theory and research, mechanisms that relate infant behavior to concurrent maternal behavior deserve special attention, if only because they have been overlooked for so long.

Early competition between attachment theory and learning theory was as much over the description of the basic phenomenon as it was over mechanisms. The control systems model has clearly proved to be the better description. The task now is to explicate the roles of traditional learning mechanisms in the development of secure base behavior. The understandable concern among attachment theorists is that admitting a role for traditional learning mechanisms may reopen old debates with learning theorists. This should not deter us. Although every operational definition of attachment proposed by traditional learning theorists has proven utterly sterile, the *mechanisms* detailed in traditional learning theory may play important roles that learning theorists never anticipated. In a word, learning may yet prove more interesting and useful than Learning Theory.

The notion that mother's behavior plays a significant role in organizing and maintaining attachment behavior has an important implication for longitudinal research. We need to pay more attention to the possibility that consistency in parental behavior and supervision can explain predictive/correlational results in attachment research. This is why we developed a measure of mother monkey's behavior and why we are developing a parallel one for human mother's behavior. In brief, the fact that Infant Behavior A predicts Child Behavior B is likely to reflect the fact that parenting is consistent. As discussed earlier, this could be the case for early security and later socialization, where mechanisms that would give direct effects of security on socialization are hard to imagine.

Phase 5: The Decline of Separation Protest. The fifth phase in the proposed model covers the period during which separation protest declines. Most research places this between 12 and 30 months-of-age, though for this presentation the timing is not critical and we are not implying that any phase begins and ends discretely. Several factors contribute to the decline of separation protest. Specifically, the infant becomes:

1. More able to tolerate distress without becoming disorganized;
2. More able to predict caregiver behavior and to monitor caregiver location and behavior;
3. More able to regulate and re-establish contact on his own (i.e., gains a degree of control that makes situations less novel and thus less threatening);
4. More experienced with various types of environments and can devote less effort and attention to the features of the situation per se and more attention to monitoring and forethought in a wider range of circumstances;
5. More experienced with coping in various environments and thus has a better estimate of his ability to cope under various circumstances (a degree of "self-knowledge") and is less likely to initiate retreat to mother early in encounters with novel situations.

Note that the infant's reflecting on past behavior does not have to be explained. As above, self-observation is a fundamental fact of adaptation in humans. Note also that the tendency to observe, represent, and reflect on one's own behavior is central to Epstein's self theory (1972, and this volume).

This phase is included in our outline to consolidate the important observation that decline in separation protest does not imply decline in the infant-caregiver attachment. On the contrary, as cognitive development and experience are causing separation protest to decline, the same mechanisms are contributing to the consolidation of secure base behavior, as described in the next phase. Changing perceptions of separation have obvious implications for attachment behavior, but they reflect little about changes in the underlying control system.

Phase 6: Consolidating Secure Base Behavior. In Bowlby's model, secure base behavior emerges by age 1-year, begins to decline along with separation protest at around age 2, and gives way to what he calls the "goal-corrected partnership," around the beginning of the 3rd year. This is a point at which our own naturalistic observations begin to diverge somewhat from Bowlby's description. Despite early signs of secure base behavior along with the onset of locomotion and the rather reliable separation related responses that can be elicited in the laboratory, secure base behavior in naturalistic settings does not seem very well organized or very consistent in 12-month-olds. Traditional descriptions underestimate the time it takes to consolidate this complex behavior; moreover, our observations do not point strongly to the emergence of a meaningful goal-corrected partnership at either the end of infancy or during early childhood.

The secure base phenomenon has received surprisingly little attention in naturalistic research on human infants. Ainsworth's (Ainsworth et al. 1978) descriptions of secure base behavior in the fourth quarter of the first year in her Baltimore study and Anderson's (1972) observations in public parks stand almost alone and are rarely cited. This is more than a curiosity or an oversight; it reflects several difficulties associated with control system models. Patterns of behavior are inherently more difficult to define and describe than are discrete behaviors. In addition, the performance of a control system cannot be equated with the quantity of behavioral output. For proper assessment, we must focus instead on the success and efficiency with which the control system maintains itself within specified set goals (see, Waters, 1981; Waters & Deane, 1985). A behavioral control system's performance is not inherently beyond quantitative analysis, but it presents measurement problems much more difficult than those associated with rates and frequencies of specific behaviors. Thus, Ainsworth et al. (1978) summarized infants' ability to use the mother as a secure base in terms of highly subjective ratings, and in Anderson et al. the phenomenon seems rather elusive when they moved beyond discrete frequency counts and timing intervals. Our efforts to address these measurement problems warrant a brief description.

During the past few years, we have tried to resolve some of the difficult methodological problems that arise from the control systems conceptualization of infant attachment relationships. Among these are the following:

1. Researchers from other methodological traditions have found it difficult to understand the control systems view of the attachment construct and to fully appreciate all it implies about the range of relevant behavior and the responsiveness of secure base behavior to context.
2. It is very expensive to collect detailed behavioral data on a phenomenon as complex as the secure base phenomenon by conventional time sampling methods, with the consequence that we use small samples, rarely replicate studies, and often under-design projects to keep down the number of subjects.
3. It is difficult to evaluate the attachment behavioral system if the starting point is rate or frequency data obtained through conventional observational methods. This problem arises in part from the fact that conventional methods have only a very limited ability to take contextual information into account within manageable observational coding systems.
4. Definitions of constructs such as attachment security have been difficult to formalize, which makes them difficult to communicate, evaluate, and improve.
5. It has been difficult to establish discriminant validity of attachment con-

structs and to address alternative interpretations proposed at the end of longitudinal studies.

Much of our work has involved developing and validating an economical, behaviorally specific Q-sort methodology for assessing secure base behavior. For the most part, these problems are proving much more manageable with the Attachment Q sort methodology we have developed. The method has proved quite easy to learn; moreover, students, parents, and even researchers from other theoretical perspectives have consistently reported strong "ah-ha" experiences and a sense of what attachment theory is all about as soon as they have spent some time with the Q-set items.

Both observer and mother reports are reliable with only a few hours of observation. Q-sort data on 1- and 2-year-olds map quite well into Strange Situation data on attachment security (e.g., Vaughn & Waters, 1990). Table 6.2 summarizes some of the Q-set items that distinguish significantly between secure and anxiously attached 1-year-olds.

We encountered one of our most important results almost as soon as we began using the Attachment Q-set. In the first informal comparison of Q-sort security scores between small samples of 1- and 3-year olds, it was evident that the mean score was much higher in the older group. This struck us as more of a nuisance than anything else. After all, unless it entailed some sort of problem for the methodology we were trying to develop, it could probably be ignored, put off until later, or scaled away. Soon, however, the same result appeared in a larger set of parent reports we were collecting on different children, and later in other parent report data and in Q-sort data from other laboratories. Across laboratories and studies, the mean security score for 12-month-olds has ranged from .2–.3. The mean score in typical samples of 3–4 year-olds ranges from .4–.7!

Rather than interpret these results as evidence that older children are more attached, we take them literally: Correspondence between children's behavior and the pattern of behavior that defines the secure base phenomenon increases with age. That is, they become much better at using the mother as a base from which to explore as they get older. This is a very striking result, yet it is quite understandable in light of the preceding discussion.

Relevant mechanisms are likely to include practice, operant learning, and improved locomotion. The infant also becomes increasingly familiar with and confident about its abilities and limitations, caregiver behavior, and facets of increasingly diverse environments. There is nothing mysterious in this. Every element can be examined in detail. The more fully we appreciate that attachment behavior is learned, even taught, the more evident it becomes that *it must take time*. Accordingly, the 12-month Ainsworth Strange Situation probably assesses nascent rather than mature secure base behavior. Viewed in this light, it is amazing that 12-month Strange Security Situation data are at all correlated with patterns of care in early infancy; yet the pattern of results is clear and replicable.

TABLE 6.2
Attachment Q-Set Home Observations of One-Year-Olds:
Differences Between Infants Classified Secure and Insecure
in the Strange Situation

Q-Sort Item-title[a] *(Item number)*	*Item Means*		
	Secure	*Insecure*	*t (56)*
Enjoys playful physical contact with mother (64R)[b]	8.09 (.90)[c]	7.27 (2.11)	1.86+
Does NOT expect mother to be unresponsive (54R)	7.78 (1.12)	6.40 (1.92)	3.24***
Affectively responsive and expressive (25)	7.70 (1.51)	6.58 (2.40)	2.08*
Prefers to be comforted by mother (35)	7.55 (1.21)	6.67 (1.76)	2.15*
Looks to mother for reassurance when wary (31)	7.54 (1.00)	6.75 (1.56)	1.99+
Person oriented rather than object oriented. (65R)	7.08 (1.07)	6.02 (1.60)	2.93**
Easily comforted by mother (4)	7.03 (1.51)	6.10 (2.02)	2.02*
Laughs easily with mother (87R)	6.98 (1.37)	6.12 (2.17)	1.78+
Affective sharing occurs during play (77)	6.83 (1.84)	5.73 (1.89)	2.23*
Predominant mood is happy (3)	6.67 (2.24)	5.35 (2.60)	2.09*
Acts to maintain social interaction (40)	6.64 (1.94)	5.17 (2.06)	2.79**
Imitates mother's behavior (88)	6.61 (1.53)	5.67 (1.59)	2.28*
Easily distracted from distress (22)	6.52 (1.93)	5.52 (1.90)	1.93+
Transition from exploration to proximity is smooth (52)	6.36 (1.34)	5.23 (1.63)	2.89***
Gross motor control is smooth and coordinated (46R)	6.33 (1.65)	5.46 (2.02)	1.76+
Does NOT Lack self-confidence (48R)	6.20 (1.41)	5.42 (1.43)	2.09*
Done NOT become angry with mother easily. (82R)	6.03 (1.72)	5.06 (2.05)	1.93+
Stays closer to mother in unfamiliar settings (72)	5.77 (1.44)	5.15 (1.29)	1.69+
Transition from proximity to exploration is smooth (68R)	5.66 (1.73)	4.85 (1.74)	1.77+
Prefers tasks that are difficult (6R)	5.20 (1.30)	4.58 (1.19)	1.89+

(*Continued*)

TABLE 6.2
(*continued*)

Q-Sort Item-title[a] *(Item number)*	*Item Means*		*t (56)*
	Secure	*Insecure*	
NOT Demanding when initiating activities with mother (74R)	5.03 (1.69)	3.71 (2.18)	2.52*
Explores objects thoroughly (19)	5.00 (1.75)	4.17 (1.69)	1.82+
Adapts active play to avoid hurting mother (84R)	4.83 (.91)	4.23 (1.25)	2.04*
Careful with toys (27)	4.78 (1.15)	3.83 (1.83)	2.31*
Cries to prevent separation (29)	4.27 (2.10)	3.25 (1.47)	2.16*
Remains fearful of moving toys or animals (1)	3.87 (.84)	3.19 (.93)	2.93***

Note. *** = $p < .005$, ** = $p < .01$, * = $p < .05$, + = $p < .10$.

[a]Item numbers from the 100-item Q-set are in parentheses.

[b]"R" beside an item number indicates that the item wording from the 100-item Q-set has been reversed to clarify tabular presentation and the raw scores have been reflected (i.e. value in table is 10 − mean score.) Signs of the *t*-values are correspondingly reversed.

[c]Values in parentheses are standard deviations.

Of course, correlations between early maternal sensitivity and later attachment security do not *explain* attachment security. They are new facts *in search of an explanation,* as are correlations between secure base behavior and later developmental outcomes. Our Q-sort research highlights the need for additional descriptive/observational data on secure base behavior at various ages. The Attachment Q-sort is an economical method of surveying a wide range of behavior in advance of surgically precise time sampling and sequential analysis of specific behavior patterns.

Phase 7: Identification. If our goal were to cover only the time period spanned by Bowlby's four-phase model, we could conclude our presentation with the consolidation of secure base behavior in the second or third year, leaving out the goal corrected partnership concept altogether. In doing so, however, we would overlook the important transition from sensorimotor to cognitive representation of attachment relationships that Bowlby tried unsuccessfully to capture in terms of the goal corrected partnership. As Main and Kaplan (1989) have recently demonstrated, this move to this level of representation is the key to linking developmental theories of attachment with perspectives on attachment among adults.

Concluding our analysis with consolidation of secure base behavior would also leave open the task of explaining widely cited empirical relationships between patterns of secure base behavior and later developmental outcomes. As earlier, correlations are not explanations; rather, they are facts in search of explanations. Detailing mechanisms that account for the predictive validity of attachment data broadens the foundations of attachment theory and clarifies the place of attachment in development. Accordingly, let us at least briefly turn to sequelae of secure base behavior that carry attachment relationships from sensorimotor to representational thought and from preference to values.

Correlations between infant attachment security and later socialization outcomes are among the most widely cited findings in the attachment literature. At the same time, they present attachment theory with one of its most difficult challenges. Specifically, it is not obvious a child's confidence in its mother's availability and responsiveness (i.e., secure attachment) could keep it from putting a rock through the schoolhouse window. (Were it not contrary to the empirical data, one could just as easily imagine that confidence in Mom or Dad saving him would *increase* the likelihood of the child throwing the rock.)

Obviously, few parents would approve of their children vandalizing the neighborhood school; nonetheless, given opportunity and ammunition, some children would transgress and others would not. Given comparable socialization pressure against vandalism, why the diverse outcomes? Part of the explanation turns on the fact that socialization pressures on children are not entirely comparable across families. Individual differences in temperament, IQ, and other traits might contribute as well. Most importantly, literature on behavior problems and delinquency suggests that children exposed to entirely appropriate socialization practices and conventional norms of good behavior differ in their orientation toward these norms. In short, some children don't care as much as others. Some don't care at all. They take their lumps and do what they want.

Hypotheses relating early attachment relationships to later orientation toward socialization were central to Freud's theory of psychosocial development and were extensively investigated in early social learning research. Unfortunately, empirical confirmation was beyond the concepts and methodologies of the day, and these hypotheses have received little attention in recent theory or research. They deserve renewed attention in light of Bowlby's attachment theory and new methods of assessing attachment related constructs. To this end, Richters and Waters (in press) redefined the traditional concept of identification in terms consistent with current views of cognitive-social learning and empirical research on development in infancy and early childhood. Although their formulation is neither psychodynamic nor focused on gender and explicit imitation, the term *identification* was retained to acknowledge the origins of the attachment-socialization hypothesis in psychoanalytic and social learning theory.

Preliminary empirical support for a link between attachment and a child's orientation toward socialization is emerging in an ongoing longitudinal study of attachment, identification, and socialization in 3.5–7-year-old boys at SUNY Stony Brook. In brief, maternal reports of attachment security were obtained at age 3.5 years, using our Attachment Q-set. We scored identification from parent reports regarding the child's orientation toward socialization practices at age 5, using an 81 item Likert format survey. Typical correlations between attachment security and subsequent scores on identification items are presented in Table 6.3.

In brief, we described two facets of identification: encapsulation during infancy and commitment during early and middle childhood. During infancy the child is typically enmeshed in secure base relationships with both parents. As already described, the parents provide much of the matrix upon which the child organizes its behavior. In a sense, the family is a behavioral/affective economy from which the child derives considerable benefits in the form of nurturance and support for exploration and cognitive development. Figure 6.5 extends our developmental outline through middle childhood. It captures the transition to representational thought emphasized in Bowlby's goal corrected partnership stage and also emphasizes the foundations of socialization and later supervision that are established at this age.

TABLE 6.3
Attachment Security at 3.5 Years-Old and Identification Q-Set Items at 4–5 Years-Old (N = 81 males)

Identification Q-Set Item	*Pearson Correlation*
When he realizes he is doing something wrong, he tries to undo it.	.47
Readily accepts (parent's) suggestions or advice.	.42
Does not persist in begging for things after (parent) tells him "No!" (R)	.42
Stops doing things (parent) has punished him for. (R)	.41
Tells (parent) what family rules are (as if checking to see if he has them right.	.41
Points (to parent) out ways he and (parent) are alike.	.40
Does not refuse to obey (parent) by saying "No!" (R)	.38
Does not become angry when (parent) has to interrupt something he likes to do.	.37
Doesn't hit, throw toys, or yell at (parent) when he is angry. (R)	.37
Learns family rules quickly; doesn't have to be told twice.	.37
Becomes sad rather than angry when (parent) has to punish him.	.36
Embarrassed when (parent) catches or punishes him for misbehaving; offers to make amends.	.35
Asks before doing something that might be unsafe or not allowed.	.35

Note. (R) = Wording of original Q-set item is reversed in this table (as is the sign of the correlation coefficient) for clearer presentation.

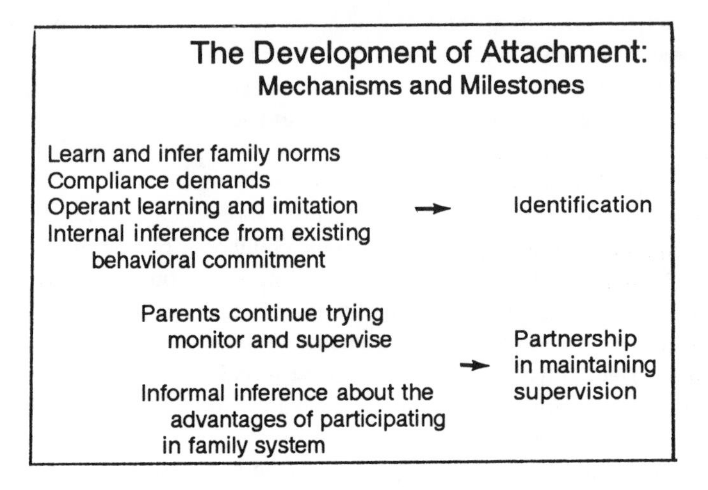

FIG. 6.5. Attachment, identification, and the supervision partnership: Mechanisms and milestones beyond early childhood.

During infancy and toddlerhood, the home-reared child is largely insulated from rule systems that differ dramatically from or offer alternatives to the family's. Parents are in a position to state the rules of the game and to shape the child's initial conceptualization of itself, of them, and of the world beyond the family. When sensitive, consistent, facilitative caretakers make the most of this situation, a predictable outcome is the development of secure attachment, self-confidence, and their concurrent correlates.

Although the child does not yet make an intentional commitment to the family's norms of good behavior, he or she is *behaviorally* committed to the family system long before these norms are even explained or imposed as rules. Participating in attachment relationships allows the child to maintain organized behavior and to maximize a wide range of benefits over time. Accordingly, the child enmeshes itself in the family system to whatever extent parental behavior supports. Herein lie the seeds of prosocial motivation.

During middle childhood, the rules of the game become increasingly complex. Parents begin to expect more consistent conformity to family rules, and the range of rules and contingencies expands at whatever rate parents estimate cognitive development allows. If, up to this point, conformity had simply been a matter of contingency management, we might expect it to extinguish rapidly as the child moves out from under the parents' constant direct supervision; however this is not the typical outcome. In most respects, children retain significant elements of the family's behavioral norms and values in the face of novel alternatives, competing input, and opportunities to observe other children operating under different sets of contingencies.

This is not to suggest that contingency management is irrelevant to socialization or that early socialization inoculates a child against every untoward influence encountered in the peer culture; rather, a variety of factors related to the economics of family living, the encapsulated context of early socialization, and the behavioral commitment entailed in early attachments have the predictable outcome of rendering a child receptive to parental socialization practices. Of course, even if the child's behavior is not integrated with that of one or a few caregivers as described in the preceding phases, he or she can be controlled by contingency management, until independence renders this impractical. Control, however, will remain extrinsic and the child's orientation toward norms will remain one of conformity rather than commitment.

We employ the term identification to summarize (though not to explain) the child's investment in the family system and readiness to accept newly articulated demands. As long as the child's social world is mainly within the family, identification can be explained as an informal inference from participation in parental attachments and the behavioral affective economy of the family. When parents first "reveal" that a particular behavior or attitude is part of the family's system, the child can reasonably (if informally) infer that "If that's the system, then that's for me." Insofar as the child is already behaviorally committed to parental attachments and to the family, he or she is biased toward accepting the new behavior or attitude without explicit training or persuasion. As Epstein suggests, anything less would challenge postulates of the child's self definition or self theory and engender negative emotion. Indeed, the child should find that conformity and advocacy of newly defined norms confirms central self-theory postulates and, thus, engenders positive emotion.

This is a positive alternative to views of socialization as an inherently coercive process. It assigns reinforcement and punishment important roles in shaping the behavioral commitment upon which such informal inferences are predicated. But beyond this, contingency management is simply another source of information available from the environment and from self-observation. These are the cognitive and motivational mechanisms underlying social and observational learning in early childhood.

Our conceptualization differs considerably from the traditional view of identification. It does not specifically involve gender or focus on the same sex parent. The focus is on identification with family norms rather than with one parent or the other. Our concept is also much less focused on literal imitation than is traditional social learning theory. It most closely approximates Rotter's notion of individual differences in the reinforcement value of stimuli. Secure attachment makes the child value the parent more, want to avoid parental censure, and overlook models that are discordant with family norms. As summarized in Fig. 6.6, identification provides a missing mechanism necessary to explain the correlations between attachment and specific socialization outcomes. Attachment is correlated with socialization outcomes because of its influence on the child's

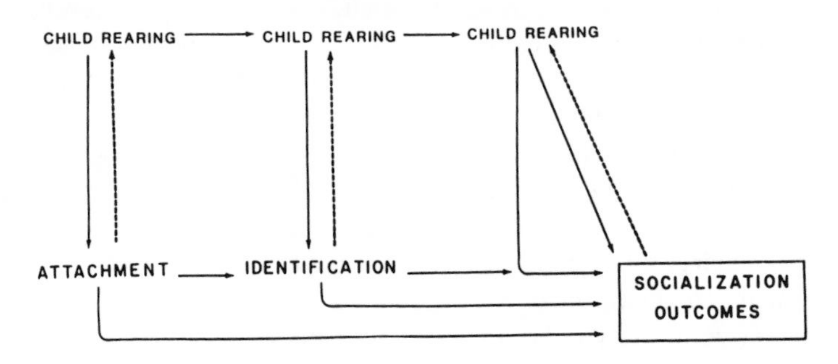

FIG. 6.6. Links between attachment and socialization outcomes: Identification and the consistency of parental behavior as mediating mechanisms.

orientation toward socialization. This, in turn, interacts with childrearing practices to yield differential socialization outcomes.

If a child cares about parental socialization goals and if the parents' socialization practices are sound, then effective and enduring outcomes are expected. If, on the other hand, attachment problems have resulted in an indifferent attitude toward socialization pressures, then even appropriate practices will only be effective in the short term. In addition, even secure attachment and a positive orientation toward parental socialization goals can be followed by significant socialization failures if parents' socialization practices are inconsistent, unclear, or in other respects inappropriate. That is, attachment does not explain socialization outcomes; it moderates them through the interaction of identification with child rearing practices.

Viewed in this light, it is ironic that attachment theory and social learning theory continue to be viewed (and practiced) as competing perspectives. After all, the paradigm clash between the control system view and learning theory was precipitated by disagreements about the level of complexity and organization at which attachment should be defined. No one disputed the importance of the causal mechanisms detailed in the literature on human learning, and the definitional issue has been resolved in favor of the control system/secure base conceptualization. Although traditional learning theorists never defined attachment in very useful terms, the well studied mechanisms of operant and social learning are not the exclusive property of one theoretical perspective. They are obviously relevant to a comprehensive explanation of the development and developmental significance of attachment relationships. In fact, a sophisticated theory of social learning and social- (including self-) cognition is essential to the success of Bowlby's effort to demystify and preserve Freud's insights about human attachment.

Phase 8: A Supervision Partnership. A key function of attachment in infancy and early childhood is to foster the development of independence. The transition from sensorimotor to representational thought brings major changes in proximity seeking, contact maintaining, and the communication between parent and offspring. The secure base acquires a cognitive representation and, as it becomes portable, exploratory and social excursions can become increasingly extended and extensive. Peremptory proximity and contact seeking in response to moderate uncertainty, discomfort, or stress is replaced by communication and direct coping.

Rather than competing with emerging behavioral systems such as peer affiliation, adult bonding, and parenthood, the attachment behavioral system operates in coordination with them; only when direct coping fails, or in the face of extreme threats, does it reassert the priority among behavioral systems that it enjoyed in infancy and early childhood.

These changes occasion difficult transitions. With the goal-corrected partnership, Bowlby emphasized that age-related changes in overt proximity seeking represent reorganization within and among behavioral systems, not attenuation of the infant-mother relationship. This is a crucial insight. Without it, we might overlook the organizing role that parent behavior serves throughout childhood, adolescence, and early adulthood in many cultures and families. We would also find ourselves puzzled by grief and mourning at the loss of a parent. Thus, although we questioned the view that secure base behavior in the sensorimotor period develops into a goal corrected partnership in early childhood, we conclude our developmental outline by returning to the partnership concept, not as a species' characteristic way to manage attachment relationships in childhood and adolesence, but, rather, as a strategy employed in some families, in some cultures.

Beginning in middle childhood, a child can enter into a wide range of contracts with adults. These arise within and across families. Within families, many key socialization practices entail exchange agreements between parent and child (e.g., rewards for good behavior.) Often, the need to care for younger children, share transportation, and divide household duties lead to agreements about division of labor and reciprocity. Across families, an adult may agree to extend privileges contingent upon a child's good behavior, offer instruction or pay in exchange for the child's assistance, or supervise and assist the child on the expectation that the child's parents will reciprocate.

Unlike early attachment relationships, in which infant and adult share common goals such as maintaining proximity, advancing the infant's cognitive competence, and affect regulating, these relationships are optional and essentially economic; they allow child and adult to meet their differing needs and goals by exchanging material or behavioral assets of comparable worth. They assume neither attachment between the parties nor skills specifically derived from early attachments. Most social arrangements between parents and children at this age are probably of this nature. One exception, however, is a supervision partnership designed to span the transition from family socialization to independence in a particular family, community, or culture.

During infancy and early childhood, parents largely control the level of supervision over the child's behavior. At least, the balance of responsibility falls to the parent. In cultures such as our own, however, 6–16 year-old children spend a considerable amount of time away from the parents' immediate supervision; yet many parents (and children) undertake to maintain some level of consistent supervision. The child's time with the peer group or in other activities is viewed as continuous with *exploration* and *training* begun earlier, not as *detachment* or *independence*. This entails a common goal not found in the commercial relationships described earlier. Specifically, within this arrangement child and parent share the goal of maintaining a degree of supervision and contact when the child is away from direct parental supervision for long periods.

In a sense, a supervision partnership is an extension of the parent's role as a matrix for the child's behavior and as a secure base, but now the balance of responsibility between child and parent is more evenly balanced than in infancy. The parent must want to maintain supervision and availability during this transitional period and insure that the child cooperates. Desire to do this may differ markedly across cultures and communities, and from family to family. Unlike the task of serving an infant as a secure base, however, the parent's intention to supervise an older child is not sufficient. The parent can only supervise and serve as a secure base if he or she is kept aware of the child's excursions and plans, both when the plan is first formulated and later when plans and play sites change significantly during the day. This is a responsibility that only the child can fulfill. Parents, of course, have a similar responsibility to keep the child up to date if they venture forth while the child is away at play. The supervision partnership has to include arrangements for a mode of communication, a set of contingency plans, or alternative supervision when the parent is away. Parents may also want to limit the child's activities to places where supervision by other adults is close at hand. It becomes the child's responsibility to operate within these limits or to negotiate exceptions in advance.

The items listed in Table 6.4 suggest the types of child behavior that might be used to assess the child's participation in such a partnership.

Obviously both the parent's initiative and consistency and the child's willingness to participate are critical to this kind of partnership. It is unlikely that such a partnership could arise solely as a result of early sensitive care or a secure attachment in infancy. Yet the parent's role in the partnership is analogous to sensitive care early, and the quality of early attachment may influence the child's willingness and desire to participate. Early secure base experience may also provide an enduring understanding of what it is to relate to a person over space

TABLE 6.4
Supervision Parnership from 6–12 Years: Preliminary Q-set Items

1. Returns home at a predictable time.
2. Starts playing somewhere or with some group and ends up elsewhere in other activities or with other children without returning home. (–)
3. Comforts parent when upset.
4. Seeks parent when injured.
5. Informs parent of injuries.
6. Screams at parent in anger. (–)
7. Can help parent supervise younger siblings.
8. Helps parent by keeping certain areas of the home or certain sets of toys or clothes tidy.
9. Open with parent about social worries when they occur.
10. Asks parent for information about physical maturation.
11. Reports brushes with danger and near accidents to parent.
12. Accepts restrictions related to safety.
13. Willing to stay within reach of parent's supervision. (informs parent, agrees to report change of activities, follows time restrictions, etc.)
14. Enjoys having parent scratch back or talk before going to bed.
15. Seems confident at home with babysitters at night.
16. Stays angry at parent for a long time. (–)
18. Is cold and indifferent to parent. (–)
19. Shows an interest in parent's work/chores.
20. Uses home as a main base for play activities.
21. Feels like parents are always in the way. (–)
22. Likes to go places with the parent. (Prefers to go off on own activities)
23. Wants to be left alone when in a bad mood. (–)
24. Cuddly when tired.
25. Proud of parent.
26. Interested in parent approval when achieving something new.
27. Confides in parent when upset with or put upon by others.
28. Gets angry when disciplined. (–)
29. Rarely spends as much as an hour at a time helping parent. (–)
30. Glad to get something for parent even if parent could get it just as easily.
31. Thinks that childcare is parent's absolute top priority.
32. Pulls away if parent is affectionate. (–)
33. Says things to hurt parent. (–)
34. Coercive: Bribes (–)
35. Coercive: Threatens to misbehave. (–)
36. Coercive: Threatens to hurt self / get hurt doing risky things. (–)
37. Often goes off for over two hours without telling parent. (–)
38. Vague or evasive about where or with whom he is playing. (–)
39. Requires close supervision. (–)

(Continued)

TABLE 6.4
(continued)

40. Comes to parent for help when in trouble.
41. Accepts that parent is right when disciplined.
42. Fear of doing something is reduced if parent says it is safe or ok.
43. Lies to parent. (−)
44. Takes whatever parent offers—but not really appreciative. (−)
45. Accepts that cooperation or service to parent is reasonable pay back for help parent has provided in the past.
46. Expects parent knows answers to most questions.
47. Willing to profit from parent's experience in matters of risk and safely.
48. Willing to profit from parent's experience in other areas.
49. Resents restrictions imposed so that parent can get own work done. (−)
50. Tells parent about funny experiences or observations.
51. Jokes with parent.
52. Hides bad experiences from parent for fear of being blamed. (−)
53. Hides mistakes and accidents from parent for fear of being blamed. (−)
54. Is clinging and immature with parent. (−)
55. Reminds parent or retells stories of good times had with parent.

and time. In view of the limits that egocentrism poses on social cognition and cooperation at this age, this could be an important asset.

Where supervision partnerships are seen, they validate the insight that Bowlby conveyed in his references to the goal-corrected partnership; attachment does not simply decline as the child's horizons expand. Other attachment-related behavioral strategies that become necessary or possible only beyond early childhood may make this point as well. Our capacity for abstraction, prediction, and communication enables the attachment behavioral system to continue serving as an important resource as other behavioral systems mature, even into adulthood. For example, in our society, even adult children are expected to maintain implicitly agreed upon modes and schedules for "keeping in touch" with parents, who have been known to view lapses with alarm or anger. Moreover, as parents come to depend more and more on their adult children, the children often adopt a similar view of their parents' habits of "keeping in touch."

Research on the secure base analogues in childhood, adolescence, and adulthood has hardly begun. We mention the supervisory partnership to see what can be done with Bowlby's partnership notion and to emphasize that the secure base concept is powerful enough to support a comprehensive perspective on attachment relationships. A complete description of mechanisms and developmental milestones in attachment has to reach well beyond infancy and early childhood.

Although most adolescents and young adults may already have learned *to* love, most still have a great deal to learn about *how* to love. Thus Bowlby's emphasis on attachment in infancy and early childhood is entirely consistent with the view that relationship experience and commitment in adolesence and adulthood can influence cognitive models bearing on the conduct of adult attachment relationships and parenting. There may even be modes of attachment that are encountered only in some cultures or only in the fullness of relationships late in life.

CONCLUSION

Our discussion of milestones and mechanisms in attachment, identity, and identification is firmly rooted in Bowlby's theory and in his efforts to preserve the best conceptual and descriptive insights from the psychoanalytic tradition. Our analysis is evolutionary rather than revolutionary and suggests that a major integration of perspectives is at hand.

Attachment theory and research have a great deal to gain from detailing the roles that active parent behavior and traditional learning mechanisms play in developing attachment relationships. Cognition and inference are also important mechanisms overlooked by traditional learning paradigms. We have described the self-other distinction as a developmental milestone that emerges from sensori-motor understanding of the mother as an object. The mechanism is "informal inference," a process that probably plays a role in a wide range of developmental changes. The sense of security that arises within a well-functioning pattern of secure base behavior also arises initially as an "informal inference" about parental availability and responsiveness. Cognitive/emotional commitment and identification arise from behavioral commitment and meshing by the same process of "informal inference." Such effects on identification and socialization implicate attachment relationships in a wide range of socialization outcomes. As a consequence of self-observation and informal inference, the child takes its own behavior and attitudes as empirical evidence about itself and formalizes these as postulates of a self theory.

Although we have discussed specific mechanisms in association with specific developmental milestones, it should be understood that most of them operate throughout development. The same must be said of parental influence on attachment behavior. Secure base behavior is not simply elicited by early care, parental behavior provides a matrix that continues to help organize it far beyond infancy. The combination of multiple mechanisms acting concurrently and continuing parental support provide an element of redundancy and consistency that accounts in part for the virtual inevitability of attachment within what Bowlby called our environment of evolutionary adaptedness.

Neither the evolution of the self theory nor the ability to establish and maintain love relationships reaches a decisive conclusion in childhood or even in adolescence. Even if early experience proves critical for learning *to* love, learning *how* to love takes a very long time. Some of the mechanisms involved are specific to attachment processes; others are nonspecific and contribute to development in other domains as well. Thus, describing either attachment or the self theory as antecedent to the other oversimplifies a complex sequence of developmental interactions. Throughout development, attachment relationships directly and indirectly generate a vast array of self-relevant data. Even if attachment relationships within the family prove to be the royal road to supportive adult-adult relationships and caring parental bonds, this is only one of the many roads that must be traveled on the way to a well-defined, well-functioning self theory. What we can say for sure is that along this road we find many important clues.

REFERENCES

Ainsworth, M. (1967). *Infancy in Uganda: Infant care and the growth of love*. Baltimore: Johns Hopkins University Press.

Ainsworth, M. (1972). The development of infant-mother attachment. In B. Caldwell & H. Ricciutti (Eds.), *Review of child development research* (Vol. 3). Chicago: University of Chicago Press.

Ainsworth, M., Bell, S., & Stayton, D. (1971). Individual differences in strange situation behavior of one-year-olds. In H. R. Schaffer (Ed.), *The origins of human social relations*. London: Academic Press.

Ainsworth, M., Blehar, M., Waters, E., & Wall, S. (1978). *Patterns of attachment*. Hillsdale, NJ: Lawrence Erlbaum Associates.

Anderson, J. W. (1972). Attachment behaviour out of doors. In N. Blurton-Jones (Ed.), *Ethological studies of child behavior* (pp. 199–215). Cambridge: Cambridge University Press.

Bell, S. (1970). The development of the concept of the object as related to infant-mother attachment. *Child Development, 41*, 291–311.

Bowlby, J. (1958). The nature of the child's tie to its mother. *International Journal of Psycho-Analysis, 39*, 350–373.

Bowlby, J. (1960). Grief and mourning in infancy and early childhood. *Psychoanalytic Study of the Child, 15*, 9–52.

Bowlby, J. (1969). *Attachment and loss:* (Vol. 1), *Attachment*. New York: Basic Books.

Cairns, R. (1972). Attachment and dependency: A psychobiological and social learning synthesis. In J. Gewirtz (Ed.), *Attachment and dependency*. Washington D.C.: Winston.

Cairns, R. (1979). *The origins and plasticity of interchanges*. San Francisco: Freeman.

Epstein, S. (1973). The self-concept revisited: A theory of a theory. *American Psychologist, 28*, 404–416.

Epstein, S. (1980). Self-concept: A review and the proposal of an integrated theory of personality. In E. Staub (Ed.), *Personality: Basic issues and current research*. Englewood Cliffs, NJ: Prentice-Hall.

Freud, S. (1949/1953). *Abriss der psychoanalyse (An outline of psychoanalysis)*. Frankfurt am Main: Fischer Bucherei.

Gewirtz, J. (1972). Attachment and dependence and a distinction in terms of stimulus control. In J. Gewirtz (Ed.), *Attachment and dependency*. Washington D.C.: Winston.

Hinde, R. A. & Simpson, M. (1975). Qualities of infant-mother relationships in rhesus monkeys. In *Parent-Infant Interaction*. CIBA Foundation Symposium, No. 33.

Kaye, K. (1982). *The mental and social life of babies*. Chicago: University of Chicago Press.

Maccoby, E., & Masters, J. (1970). Attachment and dependency. In P. Mussen (Ed.) *Carmichael's manual of child psychology*. New York: Wiley.
Main, M., & Goldwyn, R. (in press). Adult attachment classification system.
Marvin, R. (1977). An ethological-cognitive model for the attenuation of mother-child attachment behavior. In T. Alloway, L. Krames, & P. Pliner (Eds.), *Advances in the study of communication and affect* (Vol. 3). *The development of social attachment*. New York: Plenum.
Parkes, C., & Stevenson-Hinde, J. (Eds.). (1982). *The place of attachment in human behavior*. New York: Basic Books.
Piaget, J. (1936/1952). *The origins of intelligence in children*. New York: Norton.
Piaget, J. (1937/1962). *Play, dreams and imitation in childhood*. New York: Norton.
Richters, J., & Waters, E. (in press). Attachment and socialization: The positive side of social influence. In S. Feinman & M. Lewis (Eds.), *Social influences and behavior*. New York: Plenum.
Ricks, M. (1985). The social transmission of parental behavior: Attachment across generations. In I. Bretherton & E. Waters (Eds.), *Growing points in attachment theory and research. Monographs of the Society for Research in Child Development, 50* (Serial No. 209), 211–227.
Robertson, J. (1952). Film: *A two-year-old goes to hospital*. (16mm). New York: New York University Film Library.
Robertson, J., & Robertson, J. (1967). Film: *Young children in brief separation*. No. 1: Kate aged 2 years 5 months, in foster care for 27 days. (16mm). New York: New York University Film Library.
Rotter, J. (1954). *Social learning and clinical psychology*. Englewood-Cliffs, NJ: Prentice-Hall.
Roy, M. A. (Ed.). (1982). *Species identity and attachment: A phylogenetic evaluation*. New York: Garland STPM Press.
Sroufe, L. A. (in press). An organizational perspective on the self. In D. Cicchetti & M. Beeghly (Eds.), *The self in transition: Infancy to childhood*. Chicago: University of Chicago Press.
Sroufe, L. A., Egeland, B., & Kreutzer, T. (in press). The fate of early experience following developmental change: Longitudinal approaches to individual adaptation in childhood.
Trivers, R. (1972). Parental investment and sexual selection. In B. Campbell (Ed.), *Sexual selection and the descent of man 1871–1971* (pp. 136–179). Chicago: Aldine.
Trivers, R. (1974). Parent-offspring conflict. *American Zoologist, 14*, 249–264.
Trivers, R. (1985). *Social evolution*. Menlo Park, CA: Benjamin/Cummings.
Valenzuela, M. & Waters, E. (in preparation, 1989). Use of the attachment Q-set to validate the Strange Situation in a low SES Chilean population.
Vaughn, B. & Waters, E. (1990). The relationship between observer Q-sort data and attachment classification of one-year-olds. *Child Development*.
Waters, E. (1981). Traits, behavioral systems, and relationships: Three models of infant-mother attachment. In K. Immelman, G. Barlow, L. Petrinovitch, & M. Main, (Eds.), *Behavioral Development: The Bielefeld Interdisciplinary Project* (pp. 621–650). Cambridge, England: Cambridge University Press.
Waters, E., & Deane, K. (1985). Defining and assessing individual differences in attachment relationships: Q-methodology and the organization of behavior in infancy and early childhood. In I. Bretherton & E. Waters (Eds.), *Growing points in attachment theory and research. Monographs of the Society for Research in Child Development, 50* (Serial No. 209), 41–65.
Waters, E., & Kondo-Ikemura, K. (submitted, 1989). Maternal behavior and infant security in Old World monkeys: Conceptual issues and a methodological bridge between human and non-human primate research.
Winnicott, D. (1965). *The maturational processes and the facilitating environment*. London: Hogarth Press.
Woodson, R. (1983). Newborn behavior and the transition to extrauterine life. *Infant Behavior and Development, 6*, 139–144.
Woodson, R., Reader, J. S., & Chamberline G. (1981). Blood pH and crying in the newborn infant. *Infant Behavior and Development, 4*, 41–45.

Author Index

Italics indicate reference pages.

A

Abelson , R. P., 17, *40*
Aboud, F., 149, *159*
Abramson, L. Y., 43, 49, *74*, *77*, 111, 134, 136, *159*, *165*, 168, 172, 173, 175, 176, 177, 180, 183, 188, 196, 208, *212*
Adorno, T. W., 104, *121*
Agnew, J., 21, *34*
Ainsworth, M. D. S., 12, 13, *34*, 45, 48, 52, *74*, 186, 211, *212*, 229, 240, *254*
Alloy, L. B., 175, 188, *212*
Alloy, C. B., 49, *77*
Allport, G. W., 80, 83, *121*
Altshuler, J. L. , 26, 27, *41*, 140, 141, *160*
Amabile, T. M., 150, *160*
Anders, T. F., 13, *41*
Anderson, J. W., 240, *254*
Astington, J. W., 29, *36*
Atkinson, J., 156, *163*

B

Bailer, I., 172, *212*
Baldwin, A. L., 144, *160*
Baldwin, J. M., 1, 2, 3, 4, 5, *34*, 43, *74*
Baltes, P. B., 48, 50, *74*, 168, 170, 171, 173, 175, 177, 195, 200, *212*, *213*, *216*
Baltes, M. M., 167, 168, *212*
Band, E. B., 139, 160, 211, *212*
Bandura, A., 43, 45 *74*, 168, 173, 174, 176, 177, 178, 179, 182, 187, 203, 204, *212*
Bannister, D., 21, *34*
Bartlett, F. C., 16, 27, *34*
Barclay, C. R., 48, 49, *74*
Bargh, J. A., 140, *162*
Barker, G. P., 189, *212*
Barrett, K. C., 129, 131, 133, *160*
Bates, E., 20, 24, 26, *34*, 35, 36, *40*
Baumrind, D., 64, *74*, 186, 187, *212*
Beck, A. T., 91, *121*, 136, *160*
Becker, W. C., 147, *160*
Beegley, M., 26, 27, *36*
Beegley-Smith, M., 23, *36*
Bell, S., 232, *254*
Bell, S. M., 12, *34*
Belsky, J., 65, *74*
Bemporad, J., 136, 138, *160*
Benigni, L., 24, *34*
Bergman, A., 23, *38*, 45, *76*
Bergenthal, B. I., 129, *160*
Biringen, Z., 12, *36*
Blackwell, J., 134, 164, 196, *215*
Blehar, M. C., 12, *34*, 45, *74*, 229, *254*
Block, J., 154, 155, *160*
Block, J. H., 151, 153, 154, *157*, *160*
Bloom, L., 26, 27, *34*, *37*
Blos, P., 137, *160*
Blyth, D. A., 136, 149, 154, *165*
Boag, L. C., 136, *163*
Bohan, J. B., 21, *37*
Bohrnstedt, G. W., 147, *160*
Bond. R. N., 128, *162*
Botkin, P. T., 131, *161*
Bowlby, J., 1, 8, 9, 10, 11, 13, 16, 18, 22, 26, 32, *34*, *35*, *36*, 45, 47, *74*,

83, 121, 217, 218, 220, 222, 254
Boyes, M., 28, *35*
Brandtstaedter, J., 168, *212*
Braun, C., 187, *212*
Bretherton, I., 12, 20, 23, 24, 25, 26, 27, 28, 29, 30, *34, 35, 36*, 45, 47, 52, *74*
Bridges, L., 53, *74*
Brim, O. G., Jr., 44, *76,* 167, 168, 170, 172, 173, *212, 214*
Bronfenbrenner, U., *1, 36,* 72, *74*
Bromley, D. B., 22, *38*
Brooks-Gunn, J., 26, *38,* 129, *163*
Brophy, J., 64, *74*
Brown, J. D., 83, *123*
Bruner, J. S., *23, 39,* 129, *160*
Buchsbaum, H. K., 69, *75*
Bulman, R. J., 108, *121*
Busch-Rossnagel, N. A., 48, 72, *76,* 167, *214*
Byrne, D. F., 131, 136, *165*

C

Cain, K. M., 196, *213*
Cain, A. C., 11, *36*
Cairns, R., 230, *254*
Camaioni, L., 24, *34*
Cameron, N., 139, 141, 142, *160*
Cameron, A. M., 172, *216*
Campos, J. J., 23, *36, 37,* 129, 131, 133, *160*
Carver, C. S., 44, 49, *74,* 127, *160*
Case, R., 126, 128, 129, 131, 133, 136, 140, 141, *160*
Cashdan, S., 83, *121*
Cassidy, J.,12, 13, *36, 38,* 45, *76*
Catlin, G., 110, *122*
Chamberline, G., 223, *255*
Chandler, C. L., 55, *74*
Chandler, M. J., 28, *36*
Chapin, S. L., 52, 53, *74*
Chapman, M., 125, 145, *164,* 170, 171, 173, 175, 177, 185, 193, 195, 197, 198, 200, 201, 204, *212, 213, 215, 216*
Charlesworth, W. R., 23, *36*
Cicchetti, D., 49, 66, 67, *75, 76*
Clark, R., 156, *163*
Coelho, G. V., 12, *38*
Combs, A. W., 83, *123*
Compas, B. E., 211, *213*
Connell, J. P. 48, 51, 52, 53, 54, 55, 56, 57, 58, 60, 62, 66, 67, 69, 70, *74, 75, 76, 77,* 170, 172, 176, 177, 178, 179, 180, 184, 185, 187, 189, 190, 191, 193, 194, 195, 197, 200, 206, 207, 208, 211, *213, 214, 215, 216*
Cooley, C., 43, 45, 49, *75*
Cooley, C. H., 1, 2, 3, *35,* 95, *122*
Cooper, H. M., 52, 60, *75,* 179, 196, 200, 202, *213*
Coopersmith, S., 45, 64, *75*
Covington, M.V., 46, *75,* 189, 204, *213*
Craik, K., 8, 16, 29, *36*
Crandall, B. W., 168, 184, 186, 187, 195, *213*
Crandall, V. C., 168, 175, 179, 184, 186, 187, 200, 208, *213*
Crandall, V. J., 179, 208, *213*
Crichlow, W., 58, 59, 60, 62, 72, *75*

D

Damon, W., 21, *36,* 44, *75,* 128, *160*
Dannefer, D., 48, 72, *75*
Deane, K., 240, *255*
deCharms, R., 187, 211, *213*
Deci, E. L., 46, 47, 50, 51, 53, 55, 64, *75, 77,* 150, 156, 157, *161,* 176, 187, 189, 190, 211, *213, 215*
Digdon, N., 136, *161*
Dorfman, D., 136, *162*
Dunkel-Schetter, C., 109, *123*
Dunn, J., 26, *36*
Duval, S., 127, *161*
Dvir, R., 14, *39*
Dweck, C. S., 64, *75,* 125, 134, 139, 149, 150, 155, 156, 157, *161,* 176,

189, 195, 197, 198, 203, 207, 211, *213*

E

Easterbrooks, M. A., 175, 187, 188, *214*
Eccles-Parsons, J. E., 149, *162*
Egeland, B., 31, *40*, 234, *255*
Eichberg, D., 12, *36*
Elder, G. H., Jr., 48, *75*
Elliot, E. S., 64, *75*, 134, 139, 149, 155, 156, 157, *161*, 176, 197, 203, 207, 211, *213*
Ellis, A., 91, *122*
Emde, R. N., 23, *36*, *37*, 69, *75*, 129, *161*
Epstein, S., 18, 21, *36*, 44, *75*, 79, 81, 83, 84, 93, 95, 98, 102, 103, 106, 108, 110, 114, 117, 119, *122*, 217, 229, 239, *254*
Erdelyi, H. M., 19, 32, *36*
Erickson, E. H., 137, 138, *161*
Erikson, E., 43, 46, *75*
Erskine, N., 79, 93, 98, *122*
Escher-Graeub, D., 25, *36*
Estes, D., 28, 31, *39*, *40*

F

Fagan, C. W., 19, *39*
Fagot, B. I., 150, *161*
Fairbairn, W. R. D., 5, 9, *36*
Farber, E. A., 28, *36*
Fast, I., 11, *36*
Feffer, M., 131, *161*
Feinman, S., 23, 24, *36*
Fincham, F. D., 196, 200, *213*
Findley, M. J., 52, 60, *75*, 179, 196, 200, 202, *213*
Fischer, K. W., 48, *75*, 126, 128, 129, 131, 132, 133, 136, 137, 154, *160*, *161*
Fisher, G. A., 147, *160*
Fivush, R., 20, *36*
Flavell, E. R., 29, *36*
Flavell, J. H., 29, *36*, *38*, 131, *161*
Fletcher, K. E., 116, 119, *122*
Foersterling, F., 209, *213*
Folkman, S., 103, *122*, 168, 211, *213*, *214*
Fremmer-Bombik, E., 12, *36*
Frenkel-Brunswik, E., 104, *121*
Frese, M., 44, *76*, *77*
Freud, A., 43, *76*, 131, 133, 135, 140, 141, 142, *161*
Freud, S., 43, 46, 47, 48, 49, *76*, *161*, 218, 219, *254*
Friedman, I., 150, *163*
Fritz, J., 27, *36*
Fry, C. L., 131, 149, *161*
Furman, W., 207, *213*

G

Gallup, G. G., 95, *122*
Garmesy, N., 125, 152, 154, *164*
Gergen, K. J., 44, 47, *76*
Gesell, A., 132, *161*
Gewirtz, J., 48, *76*, 218, *254*
Girgus, J. S., 125, 154, 155, *164*, 183, *215*
Gjerde, P. F., 155, *160*
Gnepp, J., 29, *36*
Goldwyn, R., 12, 13, *38*
Goodman, G. S., 20, *39*
Gopnik, A., 29, *36*
Gotlib, I. H., 136, *161*
Gove, F. L., 29, *36*
Graham, S., 30, *41*, 189, 212, *213*
Green, F. L., 29, *36*
Green, M. L., 129, 140, *163*
Greenberg, I., 6, 12, *38*
Greenfield, P. M., 20, 25, *36*
Grolnick, W. S., 53, 56, 62, 64, 66, 67, *75*, *76*, *77*
Grossman, K., 12, 14, 25, 30, 31, *36*, *37*, *40*
Grossman, K. E., 12, 14, 25, 30, *36*, *37*
Gruendel, J., 17, 19, 20, *29*

Grusec, J. E., 134, 135, *161*
Guardo, C. J., 21, *36*
Guidano, V. F., 10, *37*
Gunnar, M. R., 188, *214*
Guntrip, J. S., 5, *37*
Gurin, P. 170, 171, 172, *214*
Gustafson, J. P., 31, *37*

H

Hamburg, D. A., 12, *38*
Hand, H., 22, *37*
Harris, D. B., 167, *214*
Harris, P., 140, *161*
Harris, P. L., 29, *37*
Hart, D., 44, 75, 128, *160*
Harter, S., 22, *37*, 45, 46, 50, 52, 64, *76*, 126, 129, 134, 136, 137, 149, *161*, 172, 195, 211, *214*
Hartmann, H., 9, 32, *37*
Hartup, W. W., 141, *161*, 175, *214*
Havinghurst, R. J., 12, *39*
Hayward, S., 126, 140, 141, *160*
Heckhausen, H., 168, 200, 207, *214*
Heider, F., 168, *214*
Helmreich, R. L., 156, *165*
Hendrix, 16, 29, *37*
Hesse, E., 13, *38*
Hetherington, E. M., 152, *163*
Higgins, E. T., 126, 127, 128, 129, 131, 133, 136, 137, 138, 140, 141, 142, 143, 144, 145, 147, 149, 150, 156, *162*, *163*, *165*
Hinde, R. A., 236, *254*
Hodges, R. M., 48, 49, *74*
Hoffman, M. L., 133, 135, 144, *162*
Hoffman, L., 155, *162*
Hofgrefe, J., 29, *40*
Hokoka, A., 196, *213*
Hood, L., 27, *37*
Horney, K., 96, 122
Huber, F., 14, *36*
Hubley, P., 23, 24, *40*
Hudson, J., 20, *37*
Hurst, P., 126, 140, 141, *160*
Huston, A. C., 125, 151, 152, *162*
Huttenlocher, J., 129, *162*

I

Ickes, W., 134, *162*
Ilg, F., 132, *161*
Inhelder, B., 136, *162*
Izard, C. E., 19, *37*

J

Jacklin, C. N., 152, *163*
Jacobson, E., 32, *37*
James, W., 1, 2, 13, 32, *37*, *43*, 45, 46, 52, *76*, 79, 80, *122*, *162*
Janoff-Bulman, R., 109, *122*
Jarvis, P. E., 131, *161*
Johnson, L. R., 28, *40*
Johnson-Laird, P. N., 16, 18, 29, 32, *37*, *40*
Jordan, C., 134, *164*, 196, *215*

K

Kagan, J., 26, 129, 131, *162*, 167, *212*
Kaplan, B., 129, *165*, 218, 228, 243
Kaplan, K., 12, *38*
Kaplan, N., 45, *76*
Kaslow, N. J., 49, *77*
Katkovsky, W., 168, 179, 195, 208, *213*
Kay, D. A., 24, *39*
Kaye, K., 232, *254*
Keating, D., 29, *36*
Keener, M. A., 13, *41*
Kelley, G. A., 18, *37*
Kelly, G. A., 83, 93, *122*
Kelman, H. C., 133, 135, *163*
Kernberg, D., 141, *163*
Kernberg, O., 5, 9, *37*
Kessel, F., 1, 29, *36*, *38*
Kessen, W., 1, *36*
Keyes, S., 154, *160*
Kimble, G. A., 167, *214*

Kindermann, T. A., 66, 67, *77*
King, G. A., 141, 143, *162*
King. R., 26, *41*
Kipnis, D., 156, *162*
Klein, R., 128, 150, *162*
Klinnert, M. D., 23, *37*
Kobak, R. R., 12, *38*
Kohlberg, L., 134, 137, *163*
Kohut, H., 45, 48, *76*
Kohut, O., 5, *38*
Kondo-Ikemura, K., 236, 237, *255*
Kreutzer, M. A., 23, *36*
Kreutzer, T., 234, *255*
Kruglanski, A. W., 150, *163*
Kuczaj, S. A., 26, *39*
Kuhl, J., 49, *76*
Kuhn, T. S., 90, *122*

L

Lachman, M. E., 172, 177, *214*
Lamb, M. E., 13, 31, *38, 39, 40,* 175, 187, 188, *214*
Lamborn, S., 137, 154, *161*
Larson, M. E., 30, *40*
Layden, M. A., 134, *162*
Lazarus, R. S., 103, *122,* 168, 211, *214*
Lecky, P., 83, *122*
Lefcourt, H., 168, *214*
Leggett, E. L., 189, 198, 203, *213*
Legrenzi, M. S., 16, *37*
Legrenzi, P., 16, *37*
Lepper, M. R., 134, 135, *163*
Lerner, R. M., 48, 72, *76,* 167, *214*
Leslie, A. M., 16, 18, 29, *38*
Lewis, M., 26, *38,* 126, 129, 140, 141, *160*
Lewkowicz, K. S., 14, *39*
Levenson, H., 170, 177, *214*
Levinson, D. J., 104, *121*
Lewin, K., 128, 138, 144, *163*
Lewis, M., 126, 129, 140, 141, *160*
Lichtman, R. R., 109, *123*
Lieberman, A. F., 12, *34*
Liotti, G., 10, *37*
Linn, P. L., 200, *213*
Linville, P. W., 136, *163*
Lippitt, R., 144, *163*
Lipsitt, L. P., 19, *39*
Livesley, W. J., 22, *38*
Loevinger, J., 135, 136, 137, *163*
Lombardi, W., 140, *162*
Lowell, E., 156, *163*
Lynch, J. H., 69, *77*
Lynch, M., 211, *214*
Lynch, M. D., 53, 65, 66, *75, 76, 77,* 211, *214*
Lynch, M. L., 211, *214*

M

Maccoby, E., 218, *255*
Maccoby, E. E., 125, 145, 147, 151, 152, *163, 164*
McNew, S. 23, *36*
Mahler, M. S., 23, *38,* 45, 52, 69, *76*
Main, M., 12, 13, 14, 30, 31, *38,* 45, *76,* 218, 228, 243, *255*
Mandler, G., 16, *38*
Mandler, J. H., 17, *38*
Markus, H.,5, 18, *38,* 44, 49, *76*
Martin, B., 152, *163*
Martin, D. J., 134, *159*
Martin, J. A., 125, 145, 147, *163*
Marvin, R., 227, *255*
Maslin, 12, *35*
Maslow, A. H., 46, 47, *76*
Masters, J., 218, *255*
Mavin, G. H., 141, 143, *162*
McClelland, D., 156, *163*
McClelland, D. C., 46, *76*
McConville, B. J., 136, *163*
McGuire, W., 44, *76*
Mead, G. H., 1, 2, 3, 13, 32, *38,* 43, *76,* 95, *122,* 128, *163*
Meier, P., 102, 103, 106, *122*
Messer, D. J., 23, *38*
Miller, A., 204, *214*
Miller, A. T., 196, 197, 201, *215*
Miller, P. H., 29, *38*

Miller, S. M., 131, 140, *163*
Mims, M., 181, 200, 202, *215*
Minuchin, P. P., 149, 155, *163*
Mischel, W., 129, 140, *163*
Mitchell, J. R., 6, *36*
Moely, B. F., 28, *37*
Moretti, M. M., 143, *163*
Morris, D., 31, *38*
Mowrer, O. H., 133, *163*
Munn, P., 26, *36*
Murphey, E. B., 12, *38*
Murphy, D. J., 23, *38*

N

Nelson, K., 17, 20, 37, 38, *39*
Nicholls, J. G., 176, 195, 197, 198, 201, 203, 208, 211, *214, 215*
Nolen-Hoeksema, S., 125, 154, 155, *164*, 183, 186, 207, *215*
Nowicki, S., 172, 195, *215*

O

O'Brien, E. J., 95, 122
O'Connell, B., 20, 26, 36, *40*
Offer, D., 12, *39*
Olthof, T., 29, *37*, 140, *161*
Olweus, D., 145, 148, *164*
Omelich, C. L., 189, 204, *213*

P

Parke, R. D., 125, 145, 151, 152, *164*
Parkes, C., 218, *255*
Parsons, J. E., 156, *164*
Pascual-Leone, J. E., 126, *164*
Patterson, C. J., 131, *163*
Patterson, G. R., 69, 72, *76*
Peck, R. F., 12, *39*
Perner, J., 16, 18, 28, 29, *39, 41*
Peterson, C., 49, *77*, 183, *215*
Piaget, J., 9, 15, 20, 23, *39*, 95, *122*, 128, 129, 131, 133, 136, *162, 164*, 175, 185, *215*
Pierson, L. H., 70, *75*
Pine, F., 23, *38*, 45, *76*
Premack, D., 24, *39*
Price, D., 20, *39*
Purohit, A. P., 136, *163*

R

Radke-Yarrow, M., 26, 27, *39, 41*, 125, 145, 151, *164*
Rauste-von Wright, M., 154, *164*
Reigle, K. F., 47, *76*
Rholes, W. S., 133, 134, *164*, 196, 202, *215*
Richters, J., 244, *255*
Ricks, M., 218, *255*
Ricks, M.H., 14, 18, 31, *39*
Ridgeway, D., 12, 26, 27, *36, 39*
Riegel, K. F., 167, *215*
Riksen-Walraven, J. M., 175, 188, *215*
Rogers, C. R., 46, 48, 83, *123*
Rohner, R. P., 10, *39*
Rosenberg, M., 22, *39*, 64, *76*, 134, 149, *164*
Rosenfeld, D., 134, *165*
Ross, G., 17, 24, *39*
Ross, H. S., 24, *39*
Rothbart, M. K., 151, *164*
Rothbaum, F., 167, *215*
Rotter, J. B., 43, 45, *76*, 168, 170, *215*
Rovee-Collier, C. K., 19, *39*
Roy, M. A., 230, *255*
Ruble, D. N., 133, 134, 139, 140, 141, 149, *159, 160, 164*
Rudolph, J., 12, *36*
Rutter, M., 125, 152, 154, *164*
Ryan, R. M., 48, 50, 51, 53, 55, 56, 62, 64, 66, 67, 69, 70, *75, 76*, 150, 156, 157, *161*, 176, 187, 189, 190, 211, *213, 215*
Rygh, J., 26, 27, *41*

S

Sabini, J., 44, *77*
Sagi, A., 14, *39*
Saltzstein, H. D., 133, *162*
Sanders, R., Jr., 196, *213*
Sandler, A., 9, *39*
Sandler, J., 9, *39*
Sanford, R. N. 104, *121*
Scaife, M., 23, *39*
Sceery, A., 12, *38*
Schaefer, E. S., 147, *164*
Schank, R. C., 17, 18, 19, 21, 39, *40*
Scheier, M. F., 44, 48, 49, *74, 77,* 127, *160*
Schneider, W., 10, *40*
Scheinman, L., 64, *75*
Schwan, A., 25, *36*
Schwartz, A. J., 64, *75*
Scollon, R., 25, 36, *40*
Seligman, M. E. P., 43, 49, 125, 136, 154, 155, *165,* 168, 173, 175, 183, 186, 187, 188, *212, 215*
Selman, R. F., 22, *40*
Selman, R. L., 29, *40,* 128, 131, 136, *165*
Semmel, A., 136, *165*
Shaklee, H., 181, 200, 202, *215*
Shantz, C. U., 131, 132, 134, *165*
Shatz, M., 26, 27, *40*
Shapiro, E. K., 149, 155, *163*
Shepherd, J., 223
Shiffrin, R. M., 10, *40*
Shore, C., 20, 26, *40*
Shoham, R., 14, *39*
Shultz, T. R., 28, 29, *40*
Simmons, R. G., 136, 137, 149, 154, *165*
Simpson, M., 236, *254*
Skinner, B. F., 45, *77*
Skinner, E. A., 53, 56, 59, 60, 62, 63, 66-70, *77,* 170, 171, 173-175, 177-185, 187-189, 190, 191, 193-195, 197-205, 207, *212, 213, 215, 216*
Slaby, R. G., 125, 145, 151, 152, *164*
Slackman, E., 20, *36*
Smith, J. H., 20, 25, *36*
Smith, M. B., 48, *77*
Smith, 149
Snyder, M. L., 134, *165*
Snyder, S. S., 167, 168, *215*
Snygg, D., 83, *123*
Sorce, J. F., 23, *37*
Sorrentino, R. M., 156, *165*
Spence, J. R., 156, *165*
Sroufe, L. A., 20, 22, 31, *40, 46*, 52, *77,* 129, 131, *165,* 217, 234, *255*
Stayton, D., 12, *34*
Stephan, W. G., 134, *165*
Stein, N. L., 28, *40*
Stern, D. N., 19, 23, 24, 25, 26, *40,* 48, *77*
Stern, P., 30, *41*
Sternberg, C. R., 23, *36*
Stevenson-Hinde, J., 218, *255*
Stewart, J., 44, *76*
Stewart, L., 13, *41*
Stipek, D. J., 172, 179, 185, 200, 202, *216*
Strauman, T. J., 128, 150, *162, 165*
Strickland, B. R., 172, 195, *215*
Sullivan, H. S., 5, 6, 9, 32, *40,* 77
Sutherland, E., 157, *165*
Svejda, M., 23, *37*
Swann, W. B., Jr., 98, *123*

T

Tabachnik, N., 175, *212*
Tanenbaum, R. L. 49, *77*
Taylor, S. E., 83, 109, *123*
Teasdale, J. D., 43, 49, *74,* 168, 171, 175, *212*
Tero, P. F., 57, *77*
Terwogt, M. M., 29, *37,* 140, *161*
Thompson, R. A., 26, 31, 40, 48, *74*
Trabasso, T., 28, *40*

Trevarthen, C., 23, 24, *40,* 129, *165*
Trivers, T., 228, *255*
Tulving, E., 17, *40*

V

Vaillant, G. E., 141, 142, *165*
VanHook, E., 136, 137, *162, 165*
Vaughn, B., 31, *40,* 241, *255*
Veroff, J., 149, 157, *165*
Vito, R. C., 58, 59, 60-62, *75,* 185, *216*
Volterra, V., 24, *34*
Von Baeyer, C., 136, *165*
Vygotsky, L. S., 47, *77*

W

Wachs, T. D., 189, *216*
Wall, S., 45, *74,* 229, *254*
Walters, C., 134, *164,* 196, *215*
Wartner, U. G., 14, 31, *36, 40*
Wason, P. C., 16, *40*
Waters, E., 26, 31, *39, 40, 41,* 45, 46, 52, *74, 77,* 229, 236, 237, 238, 240, 241, 244, *254, 255*
Watson, J. B., 45, 47, *77*
Watson, M. W., 126, 132, *161*
Watson, J. S., 188, *216*
Weiner, B., 30, 40, 168, 172, 175-177, 179, 180, 183, 196, 208, *216*
Weisz, J. R., 139, *160,* 167, 170, 173, 174, 177, 178, 179, 185, 197, 201, 208, 211, *212, 215, 216*
Wellborn, J. G., 52, 53, 56, 58, 60, 66, 70, *75, 76, 77,* 172, 178, 180, 185, 189, 190, 191, 193, 206, 211, *214, 216*
Wellman, H. M., 26, 27, 28, *40, 41*
Wells, R. S., 142, *162*
Werner, H., 129, 131, 138, *165*
Weston, D., 13, 14, 31, *38*
White, R., 144, *163*
White, R. W., 46, 47, 50, *77,* 95, 123, 210, *216*
White, S., 1, *36*
Wicklund, R. A., 127, *161*
Wimmer, H., 29, *39*
Winnicott, D., 232, *255*
Winnicott, D. W., 5, 7, 32, *41,* 45, 48, *77*
Wood, J. V., 109, *123*
Woodson, R., 223, *255*
Wolf, D. P., 26, 27, *41*
Woodruff, G., 24, 27, *39*
Wooley, J. D., 28, *36*
Wortman, C. B., 108, 109, 121, *123*
Wunsch, J. P., 20, *40*
Wright, J. W., 131, *161*

Z

Zahn-Waxler, C., 26, 27, 36, 39, *41,* 125, 145, *164*
Zeanah, C. H., 13, *41*
Zeevi, G., 150, *163*

Subject Index

A

Action-control belief system, 198-204
agency beliefs and achievement test scores, 199(f)
agent vs. nonagent means,202(f)
effort vs. ability means, 204(f)
known vs. unknown beliefs, 201(f)
Attachment
developmental model of(Waters'), 229
early infancy, 230(f)-232, 234
infancy and early childhood, 234(f)
middle childhood, 246(f)-252
beyond childhood, 252-254
Freud and, 219
identification and, 243-245(t), 248(f)
socialization outcomes, 248(f)
methodology in the study of problems, 240-241
Q-sort (Waters'), 241-243(t)
self as object, 232-233
separation protest, decline in, and, 239
supervision and, 246-251(t)
see also: Caretaker-child interactions; Modes of Secure base behavior
Attachment theory, 1-2, 8-15
unresolved issues and, 13-15
see also: Internal working models
Autonomy, 51
see also: Self-system processes, assessment methods; Self-system processes, model of, empirical evidence

B

Bowlby, 217-229
developmental model of attachment relationships, 222, 223(f)-227
advantages/limitations, 227-229
see also: Attachment theory

C

Caretaker-child interactions, modes of child's situational response, 145
classification scheme for, 146-147(t), 148
see also: Attachment
Secure base behavior
Cognitive experiential self theory (CEST)
and developmental psychology, implications for, 119-121
Competence, 51
see also: Self-system processes, assessment methods;
Self-system processes, model of, empirical evidence
Constructive thinking, 101-108
defined, 101
coping ability and, 106(t), 107(t), 108
research (methodology), 102-106(t) 107(t), 108
Constructive Thinking Inventory (CTI), and Mother-Father-Peer-Inventory (MFP), 105(t)
and Primary Emotions and Traits

Scales (PETS), 104(t)
Control-related beliefs, 170(f)-174
age differences in means-end beliefs, 193
engagement and, study of, 176, 177(t), 180
factor analysis of means-end beliefs, 194(t)
measure of, 171(t)
school performance and, 170, 176-182
structural model of development and, 192-207
see also: Perceived control
Action-control belief system
Control systems theory, 221-225
attachment, 240-241
and methodological problems in the study of
Coping
constructive thinking and, 106(t), 107(t), 108

E

Event representation in internal working models, 15-19
see also: Personal theories of reality, maladaptive schemata, 96-100

F

Freud and attachment, 219

I

I
see: Self, definition of
Internal working models ego and, 32-34
event representation and, 15-19
development of, 19-20
hierarchical structure of, 21-22
individual differences in, 6, 11-13, 29-32
see also: Attachment theory

J

James
see: Self, definition of

L

Locus of control, 172-173(t)-175

M

Macaques, secure base behavior in, 235, 236(f), 237(f)
Me
see: Self, definition of

O

Object relations theory (psychoanalysis), 5-8
Sullivan, 5-7
Winnicott, 7-8

P

Perceived control
developmental differences in the functions of, 205, 206(f), 207
developmental model of, 175-177(f)-178(t)-180(t)-184
and action, 175-182
discussion of, 167-169
functional model of, 184, 185(t)
context and, 187-188(f)
implications for intervention and, 209
performance outcomes and, 194
research, 195-197
causal concepts in, 197-199(f)
social context and, 190, 191(t)-192
structural model of, 192-207
theories of, 182-184
self-efficacy (Bandura), 182

attribution, 183
learned helplessness, 183
see also: Control-related beliefs
Personal theories of reality,
basic beliefs and, 108-113(t)-115(f) -118(f), 119
conceptual systems of, 84
experiential vs. rational, 85-87(t) -90
emotions and moods in, 91-92
development of, 92-96
precursors to, 93-94
functions of, 82, 83
beliefs associated with, 83-84
maladaptive schemata within, 96-100
sensitivities and compulsions in, 98-100
posttraumatic stress disorder in Vietnam Vets, 116-118(f), 119
see also: Self, theories of
Post traumatic stress disorder in Vietnam Vets, 116-118(f)-119

R

RAPS
see: Rochester Assessment Package for Schools
Relatedness, 51
see also: Self-system processes, model of, empirical evidence
Self-system processes, assesment methods
Rochester Assessment Package for Schools, 53

S

Schemata (maladaptive) and personal theories of reality, 96-100
see also: Event representation
School
agency beliefs and achievement test scores, 199(f)
performance and control related beliefs, 170, 176-182
self-system processes and, 53
assessment package (RAPS), 53
Secure base behavior, 224-228
consolidation of, 239-242(t) 243(t)
initiation of, 233-238
instruction and, 235
in macaques, 236(f), 237(f)
Self, theories of, 43-53(f)
cognitive, 44-50
motivational, 45-50
social, 45-50
Self system processes
context, self and action in, 51(f) - 53, 68-73(f)
assessment methods (RAPS), 53
competence, 54
autonomy, 55
relatedness, 55
school context variables 56
action variables, 56-57
and school, 54(f)
Self, definition of, 79-81
I/Me, 46, 79-81
James, 46, 79
Self concept
see Internal working models
Self discrepancy theory, 126-157
coping and intellectual development in, 138-142
self-guides (strong), 143
acquisition of, 143-145
socialization and, 144-145
cost/benefit for the development of, 148-151
sex differences and, 151-153(t)-158
behavioral/emotional disorders, 152, 153(t)-156
stage of development and, 128-130(f), 138
early sensorimotor, 128-129
late sensorimotor/early interrelational, 129-131
late interrelational/early dimensional, 131-133

late vectorial, 136-138
representational capacities in, 138-142
Self-system processes, model of
applications for, 70-73
empirical evidence for, 58-68
competence, 59, 60-61(f), 62
"at risk" students, 61-62
autonomy, 62- 63(f)
relatedness, 64-65(f), 66
social context, 66-68
interrelation of needs, 68-70
patterns of action in, 52-53, 56-58
engaged vs. disaffected, 52, 53(f)
in school, 51(f), 54(f), 57(f), 60(f), 61(f), 63(f), 65(f)
transactional model of relationships, 71(f)
Sex differences
behavioral/emotional disorders and, 152, 153(t)-156
development of self-guides and, 151-157
Social self, classic developmental theories, of, 1-5
Baldwin, 3-5
Cooley, 3
James, 2
Mead, 3

T

Theory of mind, development of, 22-30
early verbal, 25-26
preschool, 28
preverbal stage, 23-25
school age, 29
Traumatic life events
and personal theories of reality, 108-113(t), 119